AF334489

A SYSTEM-WIDE ANALYSIS OF INTERNATIONAL CONSUMPTION PATTERNS

Advanced Studies in Theoretical and Applied Econometrics

Volume 29

Managing Editors:
A.J. Hughes Hallet, *University of Strathclyde, Glasgow, United Kingdom*
J. Marquez, *The Federal Reserve System, Washington, D.C., U.S.A.*

Editorial Board:
F.G. Adams, *University of Pennsylvania, Philadelphia, U.S.A.*
P. Balestra, *University of Geneva, Switzerland*
M.G. Dagenais, *University of Montreal, Canada*
D. Kendrick, *University of Texas, Austin, U.S.A.*
J.H.P. Paelinck, *Netherlands Economic Institute, Rotterdam, The Netherlands*
R.S. Pindyck, *Sloane School of Management, M.I.T., U.S.A.*
H. Theil, *University of Florida, Gainesville, U.S.A.*
W. Welfe, *University of Lodz, Poland*

The titles published in this series are listed at the end of this volume.

A System-Wide Analysis of International Consumption Patterns

by

Saroja Selvanathan

Griffith University, Queensland, Australia
and
Economic Research Centre, The University of Western Australia

KLUWER ACADEMIC PUBLISHERS
DORDRECHT / BOSTON / LONDON

Library of Congress Cataloging-in-Publication Data

```
Selvanathan, Saroja.
   A system-wide analysis of international consumption patterns / by
Saroja Selvanathan.
      p.   cm. -- (Advanced studies in theoretical and applied
econometrics ; v. 29)
   Includes bibliographical references (p.           ) and index.
   ISBN 0-7923-2344-0 (hb : acid-free paper)
   1. Consumption (Economics)--Econometric models.  2. Demand
functions (Economic theory)  3. International trade--Econometric
models.   I. Title.  II. Series.
HB801.S387  1993
339.4'7--dc20                                          93-10998
```

ISBN 0-7923-2344-0

Published by Kluwer Academic Publishers,
P.O. Box 17, 3300 AA Dordrecht, The Netherlands.

Kluwer Academic Publishers incorporates
the publishing programmes of
D. Reidel, Martinus Nijhoff, Dr W. Junk and MTP Press.

Sold and distributed in the U.S.A. and Canada
by Kluwer Academic Publishers,
101 Philip Drive, Norwell, MA 02061, U.S.A.

In all other countries, sold and distributed
by Kluwer Academic Publishers Group,
P.O. Box 322, 3300 AH Dordrecht, The Netherlands.

Printed on acid-free paper

Printed in the Netherlands

(vii)

(viii)

(ix)

PREFACE

The modern system-wide approach to applied demand analysis emphasizes a unity between theory and applications. Its firm foundations in economic theory make it one of the most impressive areas of applied econometrics. This book presents a large number of applications of recent innovations in the area. The database used consist of about 18 annual observations for 10 commodities in 18 OECD countries (more than 3,100 data points). Such a large body of data should provide convincing evidence, one way or the other, about the validity of consumption theory.

A PREVIEW OF THE BOOK

The overall importance of the analysis presented in the book can be seen from the following table which shows the significant contribution of the OECD to the world economy. As can be seen, the 24 member countries account for about 50 percent of world GDP in 1975. In this book we present an extensive analysis of the consumption patterns of the OECD countries.

Chapter 1 of the book reviews the previous literature and places the book in the context of that literature. A brief introduction to the system-wide

Table

GDP AND POPULATION IN OECD COUNTRIES IN 1975

| Country | Per capita GDP in 1975 | | Population in 1975 (millions) | Total GDP in international dollars (billions) | (5) as a percentage of world GDP |
| | International dollars | (2) with U.S.=100 | | | |
(1)	(2)	(3)	(4)	(5)	(6)
1. U.S.	7132	100	213.5	1523.0	18.9
2. Canada	6788	95	22.7	154.3	1.9
3. Sweden	6749	95	8.2	55.3	.7
4. Switzerland	6082	85	6.4	38.9	.5
5. Denmark	5969	84	5.1	30.2	.4
6. Australia	5919	83	13.6	80.7	1.0
7. Luxembourg	5915	83	.4	2.1	.0
8. France	5864	82	52.7	309.1	3.8
9. Germany	5758	81	61.8	356.0	4.4
10. Belgium	5554	78	9.8	54.4	.7
11. Norway	5419	76	4.0	21.7	.3
12. Netherlands	5321	75	13.7	72.7	.9
13. Iceland	5201	73	.2	1.1	.0
14. Finland	5192	73	4.7	24.5	.3
15. Austria	4994	70	7.5	37.6	.5
16. Japan	4905	69	111.5	547.0	6.8
17. NewZealand	4769	67	3.1	14.7	.2
18. U.K.	4601	65	56.0	257.8	3.2
19. Spain	4032	57	35.6	143.5	1.8
20. Italy	3870	54	55.8	216.1	2.7
21. Greece	3360	47	9.1	30.4	.4
22. Ireland	3067	43	3.1	9.6	.1
23. Portugal	2397	34	9.4	22.6	.3
24. Turkey	1738	24	40.1	69.6	.9
OECD total			748.1	4072.9	49.5

Source: Summers, R. and A. Heston (1984). Column 5 is obtained by multiplying per capita GDP presented in column 2 by the corresponding population in column 4. Column 6 is obtained by dividing GDP in column 5 by 8062 billion, world GDP in 1975, and then multiplying by 100.

approach and some of its recent innovations and a review of international consumption comparisons are presented in this chapter.

Chapter 2 describes the database pertaining to 10 commodities in 18 OECD countries over a 18-year period. It presents summary measures and a preliminary analysis of the data. The findings take the form of following empirical regularities: (i) Consumers tend to move away from those goods having above-average price increases. (ii) The variability of prices is less than the variability of quantities. (iii) Food and housing are necessities; durables are a luxury. (iv) Price elasticities tend to be less than one in absolute value. (v) Those commodities which are more price elastic also tend to be more luxurious and vice versa. We also introduce a new nonparametric approach for describing the dependence of consumption on prices.

Chapter 3 deals with hypothesis testing. We first present the results of the conventional asymptotic test of homogeneity (the absence of money illusion). The results support the claim that the asymptotic test almost universally rejects homogeneity. Using Laitinen's (1978) exact test, however, the results become substantially more positive. Then we introduce Theil's (1987) recently-developed testing procedures for homogeneity and Slutsky symmetry (the symmetry of the substitution effects). These are distribution-free and hence do not require any asymptotic theory. We present an extensive application of this methodology and find that the hypotheses are reasonably acceptable in all OECD countries. We also introduce a new distribution-free procedure to test the hypothesis of preference independence (i.e., the utility function is additive in the individual goods). In contrast to previous findings reported in the literature, our results indicate that preference independence is also generally acceptable.

The OECD countries are all high-income, industrialized countries and thus share a number of common features. At the same time, however, there are obvious differences in language, culture and geography. Are these differences of economic importance? In Chapter 4 we use consumption data to analyse this issue. After adjusting for differences in income and prices across countries, we ask, are consumption patterns different internationally? This amounts to hypothesizing that tastes are the same. The hypothesis of identical tastes across consumers is advocated by Stigler and Becker (1977). Remarkably, the data do seem to indicate that there are more similarities than differences in tastes across countries.

Maximum likelihood (ML) is the standard approach to estimating demand systems, especially those nonlinear in parameters. Recently, however, researchers have become aware of the inadequacies of this approach, particularly for large systems. In Chapter 5, we use Monte Carlo simulation experiments to analyse the reliability of the ML-estimators of the OECD demand systems. We find that the estimators do not perform well when the standard ML approach is used. The source of the inadequacies of ML is the use of the residual moment matrix as the estimator of the error covariance matrix. The difficulty is with estimating the large number of unknown elements of this matrix in an unrestricted fashion. To deal with the problem we propose an alternative estimator which has far less unknowns. Re-doing the simulation experiments, we find that there is a spectacular improvement in the results when this new approach is employed.

Chapter 5 introduces four-dimensional (4-D) demand analysis. Traditionally, consumption economics is 2-D in that the analysis proceeds over time and commodities. When countries are added as a third dimension and all this is embedded in the Monte Carlo simulation framework, we have the 4-D approach.

In a widely quoted passage, Frisch (1959) conjectures that the income flexibility (the reciprocal of the income elasticity of the marginal utility of income) is dependent upon real income. In Chapter 6 we present 322 estimates of the income flexibility for the OECD countries to test this hypothesis. We find that the flexibility seems to be more or less unrelated to differences in income.

A SUMMARY OF MAJOR FINDINGS

The main empirical results contained in the book are:

(i)   Consumers satisfy the hypotheses of demand theory of homogeneity and Slutsky symmetry. These results, which are obtained using recently-developed Monte Carlo testing procedures, are in stark contrast to most previous findings based on the conventional asymptotic tests.

(ii)   The economic theory of the consumer (i.e., demand equations derived from utility maximization) accounts for a large part of the variation in consumption patterns.

(iii)   Consumers behave as if their utility functions are of the simplest possible form, viz. additive in the individual goods.

(iv)   Remarkably, demand equations exhibit quite a deal of similarity across countries. This implies that it is differences in economic variables (prices and incomes in particular) that account for observed differences in consumption patterns internationally; differences in tastes seem to play a much smaller role. In other words, a simple, common story can be told about all consumers in all countries.

(v)   Own-price elasticities of demand are approximately proportional to the corresponding income elasticities. This finding, which supports what is known as Pigou's law, is also in contrast to previous results.

(vi)   The income elasticity of the marginal utility of income does not seem to depend on income. This result does not support Frisch's famous conjecture.

(xv)

These findings come from 18 countries, rather than just a single country. Consequently, we have more than the usual degree of confidence that the results are of general applicability and not specific to a particular period or country.

METHODOLOGICAL INNOVATIONS

The book also introduces four methodological innovations:

(i)   A new nonparametric analysis of the dependence of quantities on prices. This involves the frequency distributions of the joint signs of price and quantity changes.

(ii)   A new test of the hypothesis of preference independence. Under preference independence, goods exhibit no interaction in the consumer's utility function; that is, the utility function is additive. In contrast to previous tests, ours is distribution-free and does not rely on asymptotic theory.

(iii)   A new approach to pooling consumption data across countries. Since data for individual countries are expressed in terms of national currencies, they are not directly comparable. The usual procedure is to convert the data to a common currency using prevailing exchange rates or purchasing power parities. In our approach, prices, quantities and incomes are all expressed in logarithmic-change form. As these changes are unit-free, they can be pooled internationally.

(iv)   The four-dimensional (4-D) approach to demand analysis -- time $\times$ commodities $\times$ countries $\times$ simulations. This approach is used to evaluate the performance of econometric procedures under ideal conditions when everything is known.

THE USE OF THE BOOK

This book will be of interest and useful to economists who require reliable estimates of income and price elasticities of demand for broad commodity groups. It will also be useful to applied econometricians interested in applications of recently-developed econometric and simulation techniques and their applications to consumption economics. Finally, general economists should be encouraged by the extensive results and applications which show the great power and usefulness of the utility-maximizing theory of the consumer.

The book can also be used for teaching purposes in microeconomics and econometrics courses at the graduate and advanced undergraduate levels.

REFERENCES

Frisch, R. (1959). 'A Complete Scheme for Computing All Direct and Cross Demand Elasticities in a Model with Many Sectors,' _Econometrica_ 27: 177-96.

Laitinen, K. (1978). 'Why is Demand Homogeneity So Often Rejected?' _Economics Letters_ 1: 187-91.

Stigler, G.J. and G.S. Becker (1977). 'De Gustibus Non Est Disputandum,' _American Economic Review_ 67: 76-90.

Summers, R. and A. Heston (1984). 'Improved International Comparisons of Real Product and its Composition: 1950-1980,' _Review of Income and Wealth_ 30: 207-62.

Theil, H. (1987). 'The Econometrics of Demand Systems,' Chapter 3 in H. Theil and K.W. Clements, _Applied Demand Analysis: Results from System-Wide Approaches_. Cambridge, Mass.: Ballinger Publishing Company, pp.101-162.

TECHNICAL NOTES

This book contains six chapters. To aid the reader, each chapter has been written so that it is more or less self-contained.

Each chapter contains a number of sections, subsections, appendices (in some cases) and a list of references. The sections in each chapter are numbered at two levels. The first level refers to the chapter and the second to the order of occurrence of the section within the chapter. For example, Section 2.4 is the fourth section in Chapter 2. Subsections are unnumbered.

Equations are indicated by two numbers, the first refers to the section and the second to the order of occurrence within that section. For example, 'equation (9.3)' of Chapter 3 denotes the third equation in Section 9 of that chapter. This equation is referred to in Chapter 3 as 'equation (9.3)'. If this equation is referred to in another chapter, then we use the terminology 'equation (9.3) of Chapter 3'.

If there is more than one appendix to a chapter, then appendices are numbered at three levels. For example, 'Appendix A4.3' refers to the third appendix of Chapter 4. If there is more than one appendix to a chapter, then the equations of the appendices are numbered at three levels. For example, 'equation (A3.10)' refers to equation 10 of the third appendix of that chapter. If there is only one appendix to a chapter, it is unnumbered. The equations in a single appendix are numbered at two levels, so that equation (A3), for example, refers to the third equation of the appendix.

Tables and figures are indicated by two numbers, the first refers to the chapter and the second to the order of occurrence. For example, 'Table 4.5' refers to the fifth table of Chapter 4 and 'Figure 1.2' refers to the second figure of Chapter 1.

Matrices are indicated by a boldface uppercase symbol (e.g., $\mathbf{A}$). Vectors are indicated by a boldface lowercase symbol (e.g., $\mathbf{a}$). The notation $[a_{ij}]$ refers to a matrix whose $(i,j)^{th}$ element is a_{ij}, while $[a_i]$ refers to a column vector whose i^{th} element is a_i. Thus, combining this notation, $\mathbf{A} = [a_{ij}]$ and $\mathbf{a} = [a_i]$.

ACKNOWLEDGEMENTS

This book is based on my Ph.D. project which was carried out under the supervision of Professor Ken Clements of The University of Western Australia (UWA). I am indebted to Professor Clements for his suggestions and valuable comments in the writing of this book. I would also like to thank Professor Kym Anderson, Professor Erwin Diewert, Professor David Giles, Dr. E.A. Selvanathan, Professor Henri Theil, Mr. David Treloar and Professor Ross Williams and the two anonymous reviewers of the book whose comments and suggestions improved the quality of the presentation of the book.

The research project on which this book is based on was supported by a University Western Australia Research Studentship, the UWA Department of Economics, the Economic Research Centre at UWA, Professor Clements' Computational Economics Project and the Faculty of Commerce and Administration, Griffith University. I gratefully acknowledge this support. I also acknowledge the support of the Western Australian Regional Computing Centre and the Prentice Computing Centre at the University of Queensland in providing the necessary assistance and low-cost computing facilities.

I would also like to thank the staff at Kluwer Academic Publishers, especially the Senior Editor Ms. Marie Stratta, for their support during this project.

CHAPTER 1:   INTRODUCTION

The study of consumption patterns is important for a number of reasons. First, as total consumption absorbs more than 70 percent of GDP in most countries, it is the largest of the macroeconomic aggregates, thus having great significance for the state of the economy as a whole and business conditions. Second, the pattern of consumption contains a wealth of useful information regarding economic welfare and living standards. Closely allied to this is that as consumption (both current and future) is the ultimate objective of all economic activity and economic systems (mercantilists notwithstanding), in a fundamental sense consumption patterns are an objective way of measuring and assessing economic performance. Finally, an understanding of the price-responsiveness of consumption is of crucial importance for a host of microeconomic policy issues including public-utility pricing, the measurement of distortions, optimal taxation and the treatment of externalities.

It is partly for these reasons that the analysis of consumption has attracted the attention of some of the best minds in economics and econometrics. Additional reasons which account for the extent of sophisticated econometric analysis of consumption patterns include advances in econometric methodology and computing technology, as well as the availability of large-scale databases, both time series and cross sectional (Theil, 1980). But perhaps the most important is the near perfect marriage of theory and econometrics offered by consumer demand, a situation almost unparalleled in any other field of economics. The utility-maximising theory of the consumer gives rise to demand equations which can be aggregated over individuals to yield market demand curves which, under certain conditions (much weaker than usually believed), have more or less the same properties, enabling them to be applied to aggregate data. The hypotheses derived from utility theory such as homogeneity and symmetry can then be tested econometrically, so that there is a smooth transition from theory to application. This book uses the economic theory of the consumer to analyse a huge and diverse OECD database.

This chapter reviews the previous literature and places the book in the context of that literature. Sections 1.1-1.4 present a brief introduction to the system-wide approach and some of its recent innovations. In Sections 1.5-1.8 we introduce international consumption comparisons and illustrate some of the attractions and principles of this body of research. Later sections deal with Working's (1943) model, a model which is used extensively in subsequent chapters. Using a variety of arguments, we present a strong case for this model. Finally, we briefly outline some of the policy implications of the results presented in the book.

1.1   THE SYSTEM-WIDE APPROACH TO CONSUMPTION ECONOMICS

This and the next three sections deal with the system-wide approach. We give a brief account of the general principles of the approach, present two specific examples of systems of demand equations and discuss recent developments. For surveys of this material, see Barten (1977), Brown and Deaton (1972), Clements (1987), Phlips (1974), Powell (1974), E.A. Selvanathan (1987), Theil (1975/76,1980) and Thomas (1987).

Let q_i be the quantity consumed of good i; p_i be the corresponding price; and $M = \sum_{i=1}^{n} p_i q_i$ be total expenditure, where n is the number of goods. For short, we shall refer to M as 'income'. The demand equation for good i is

$$q_i = q_i(M, p_1, ..., p_n). \qquad (1.1)$$

It is to be noted that (1.1) refers to the demand for only one of the n goods. Early work in applied demand analysis, such as the pioneering studies of Schultz (1938) and Stone (1954a), focused on a single demand equation like (1.1). The more modern systems approach does not take this single-equation perspective; rather, it considers simultaneously all n demand equations, i.e., the system of equations given by (1.1) for i=1,...,n.

There are at least three reasons for pursuing this multivariate approach. First, the consumer's budget constraint, $M = \sum_{i=1}^{n} p_i q_i$, implies that an increase in expenditure on one good must come from reduced expenditure on at least one other. Thus there is an inherent interrelationship between the consumption of the n goods. This interrelatedness can only be exploited when the n demand equations are considered simultaneously.

Second, the economic theory of the consumer implies that demand equations have a number of properties which translate into testable restrictions. This theory states that demand equations are homogeneous of degree zero in income and prices so that an equiproportional increase in M and the p_i's has no effect on the quantities consumed. In other words, the consumer is not subject to money illusion. This property is known as *demand homogeneity*.

Consumption theory also predicts that the substitution effects are symmetric. That is, the effect on consumption of good i brought about by a one-dollar increase in the price of a different good j is exactly the same as the effect on q_j of a one-dollar increase in p_i under the condition that the consumer's real income is held constant. Algebraically,

$$\frac{\partial q_i}{\partial p_j} = \frac{\partial q_j}{\partial p_i}, \qquad\qquad i \neq j, \qquad\qquad (1.2)$$

where it is understood that the derivatives hold real income constant. This property is known as *Slutsky symmetry*. As equation (1.2) refers to the demand equations for two different goods i and j, it is a cross-equation constraint. Similar constraints hold for all pairs of goods i,j=1,...,n for i≠j.

Obviously, it is only when we use a system of demand equations that the constraints of Slutsky symmetry are usable in applied work. Homogeneity and symmetry are called 'general restrictions' by Phlips (1974).

Third, considerations of generality of economic theory point against taking one good in isolation from the rest. For a genuinely general theory, we should be able to tell a common story for all n goods rather than having to rely on commodity-specific demand equations for individual goods. Consequently, the systems approach is a guard against ad hocery.

1.2 TWO EXAMPLES

In Section 1.1 we discussed the advantages of using a system-wide approach rather than the traditional single-equation approach. In this section we give two examples of systems of demand equations, namely, the linear expenditure system (LES) and the Rotterdam demand system.

Our starting point for the LES is the well-known Klein-Rubin (1948) utility function,

$$u = \sum_{i=1}^{n} \mu_i \log (q_i - \gamma_i), \tag{2.1}$$

where μ_i and γ_i are constants satisfying $\mu_i > 0$, $\sum_{i=1}^{n} \mu_i = 1$ and $q_i > \gamma_i$ for each i. (Here and elsewhere log denotes natural logarithm.) Maximizing (2.1)

subject to the budget constraint gives the corresponding demand equations. It is

convenient to express these in expenditure form,

$$p_i q_i = p_i \gamma_i + \mu_i \left[M - \sum_{j=1}^{n} p_j \gamma_j \right], \qquad i=1,\dots,n. \qquad (2.2)$$

These are known as the LES. This is our first example of a system of demand

equations.

The linearity of LES is attractive in its simplicity. When the γ_i's are all

positive, the model has the following intuitive interpretation: The consumer

first purchases the 'subsistence' quantities $\gamma_1,\dots,\gamma_n$ at a cost of $\sum_{j=1}^{n} p_j \gamma_j$. This

leaves $M - \sum_{j=1}^{n} p_j \gamma_j$ of unspent income which can be called 'supernumerary'

income. Then a fraction μ_i of this supernumerary income is spent on good i.

(Note that μ_i is indeed a positive fraction as $\mu_i > 0$ and $\sum_{i=1}^{n} \mu_i = 1$.)

Moreover, as LES is founded on the economic theory of the consumer,

it satisfies the general restrictions of homogeneity and symmetry. Since it was

first used by Stone (1954b), LES has probably been the most popular demand

system. Notable studies using LES include Deaton (1975), Goldberger and

Gamaletsos (1970), Kravis et al. (1982), Lluch and Powell (1975), Parks (1969),

Pollak and Wales (1969) and Yoshihara (1969). We shall discuss LES further

in the next section.

The differential demand system, due to Theil (1980), is our second example.   Like LES, these demand equations are derived from the budget-constrained maximization of a utility function; unlike LES, the algebraic form of the utility function is unspecified. The demand system is

$$w_i d(\log q_i) \; = \; \theta_i d(\log Q) + \sum_{j=1}^{n} \pi_{ij} d(\log p_j), \qquad i=1,\dots,n, \qquad (2.3)$$

where $w_i = p_i q_i / M$ is the budget share of commodity i; $\theta_i = \partial(p_i q_i)/\partial M$ is the ith marginal share; $d(\log Q) = \sum_{i=1}^{n} w_i d(\log q_i)$ is a volume index of the change in real income; and π_{ij} is the $(i,j)^{th}$ Slutsky coefficient.

The marginal share θ_i measures the change in expenditure on good i resulting from a one-dollar increase in income. The Slutsky coefficient π_{ij} gives the effect of a change in the price of good j on the demand for i when real income is held constant. As the 'coefficients' of (2.3) need not be constants, these demand equations are completely general. However, when the coefficients are assumed to be constants and the infinitesimal changes in the variables are replaced with finite-changes, one obtains the Rotterdam model due to Barten (1964) and Theil (1965). We shall return to this model in Section 1.9.

The above demand equations pertain to a single consumer. Usually, however, data are available only in some aggregate form, for example, per capita. Therefore, the question arises whether the micro demand equations continue to hold at the macro level. Under certain conditions, this question can be answered in the affirmative; see Barnett (1979), E.A. Selvanathan (1991) and Theil (1975/76) for details.

1.3 MORE ON THE LINEAR EXPENDITURE SYSTEM

Notwithstanding its popularity, LES has its drawbacks. The first problem is that the model cannot be used to test the homogeneity and symmetry hypotheses. In LES, these are built in or maintained hypotheses. This is not the case with the Rotterdam model.

The second problem is that LES imposes restrictions in addition to homogeneity and symmetry. It is derived from the Klein-Rubin utility function which is a sum of n sub-utility functions, one for each good. Thus the marginal utility of each good is independent of the consumption of all other goods. This type of utility structure is known as *preference independence*. Preference independence implies certain additional restrictions on the demand equations such as ruling out specific substitutes or complements (see, e.g., Clements, 1987, for details). Phlips (1974) calls these 'particular restrictions' as opposed to the general restrictions of homogeneity and symmetry.

A third difficulty relates to the particular parameterization of LES. In general, the marginal share of commodity i is defined as $\theta_i = \partial(p_i q_i)/\partial M$. It follows from (2.2) that the marginal share in LES is equal to the constant coefficient μ_i. The income elasticity of good i is the ratio of the marginal share to the corresponding budget share, $\eta_i = \theta_i/w_i$. Thus, under LES, $\eta_i = \mu_i/w_i$. This shows that the income elasticity is inversely proportional to the corresponding budget share.

Consider the case of food, which, by Engel's (1857) law, is a necessity (i.e., $\eta_i < 1$). If prices remain constant, a rise in income causes consumption of food to increase less than proportionately so that the food budget share falls. It then follows from $\eta_i = \mu_i/w_i$ that as the consumer becomes more affluent, the income elasticity rises. That is, food becomes less of a necessity or more of a luxury with increasing income. This behaviour of the elasticity under LES is clearly implausible. This criticism was made by Theil (1983).

1.4   RECENT INNOVATIONS IN THE SYSTEM-WIDE APPROACH

In this section we briefly discuss four prominent developments in the area dealing with functional form, testing, estimation and data.

Flexible Functional Forms

As discussed in the previous section, LES cannot be used to test hypotheses of homogeneity and symmetry. Nor can it be used to test the assumption of preference independence as this also is built into the model. This has given rise to flexible functional forms which are more general and can be used for hypothesis testing. Flexible functional forms give a second-order approximation to an arbitrary utility (or cost) function. Examples include the Rotterdam model which was mentioned in Section 1.2 (see Mountain, 1988, for a proof that this model is a second-order approximation); the translog model (Christensen et al., 1975); and the almost ideal demand system (Deaton and Muellbauer, 1980). For a survey, see Diewert (1974).

Hypotheses Testing

Section 1.1 noted that consumption theory has two major predictions, homogeneity and symmetry. Until recently, most empirical applications found that these two basic hypotheses were rejected by the data; see Barten (1977) for a review. Barten concludes that the negative results could be due to the inadequacy of the large-sample tests of these hypotheses. That is, with the small sample sizes typically used, the asymptotic basis for the tests could be misleading and lead to wrong inferences.

Using simulation experiments, Laitinen (1978) and Meisner (1979) confirmed Barten's conjecture by showing that the conventional asymptotic Wald tests of homogeneity and symmetry are biased towards rejection, particularly for large systems. (See also Bera et al., 1981; Bewley, 1983; and Theil, 1987b for related results.) To overcome the problems associated with the asymptotic tests, Theil (1987b) developed alternative procedures which are distribution-free and hence do not require any asymptotics. These tests are based on Barnard's (1963) Monte Carlo simulation procedure.

The Reliability of the Estimators

In large systems, there are problems not only with testing, but also with the reliability of the conventionally-computed estimators. Using Monte Carlo simulations, Theil (1987b) demonstrates that, for large systems, when the unknown error covariance matrix is approximated by its usual estimator (the matrix of mean-squares and cross products of the residuals), the estimates suffer from two problems. First, the asymptotic standard errors severely understate the true sampling variability of the estimates. Second, the efficiency of the estimates is greatly impaired. This simulation approach is now becoming a popular method to evaluate the performance of the econometric procedures under ideal conditions when everything is known.

New Databases

The data used in applied demand analysis are usually time-series or cross-sectional. Recently, however, a third type of database is being used, viz. cross-country. A leading example of a cross-country application is by Theil (1987a) who uses data compiled by Kravis et al. (1982). These data, which are part of the International Comparisons Project sponsored by the United Nations and the World Bank, cover 34 countries and provide comparable price and volume indexes for more than 100 detailed categories of consumption.

1.5 INTERNATIONAL CONSUMPTION COMPARISONS

The attraction of using cross-country data in demand analysis is that there is usually much more variation in consumption, income and prices internationally than within a country. (Note that in a cross-sectional application within a given country there may be large variations in consumption and income, but there is usually little, if any, variation in prices over consumers.) It is a challenge to explain consumption patterns which exhibit such diversity. Also, of course, it may be possible to obtain better estimates of demand parameters when the data are more variable.

The modern literature on international consumption comparisons probably started with Houthakker (1957) who estimates double-log Engel curves from cross-sectional data for a large number of countries. As Houthakker uses cross-sectional data with no variation in prices, he does not estimate price elasticities. Subsequently, others have used time-series data for a number of countries to provide estimates of both income and price elasticities. Table 1.1 provides a tabulation of the major studies.

TABLE 1.1

MAJOR STUDIES IN INTERNATIONAL CONSUMPTION COMPARISONS

Author(s) (1)	Countries (2)	Type of data (3)	Number of goods (4)	Model (5)	Major finding regarding the similarity of tastes internationally (6)
Clements and Theil (1979)	16 countries	Cross-country	4	Working's	Similarity of tastes is taken as a maintained hypothesis.
Camaletsos (1973)	11 OECD countries	Time series, 1950-65	5	LES, GLES & IAES	
Goldberger and Camaletsos (1970)	13 OECD countries	Time series, 1950-61	5	LES & DL	
Houthakker (1957)	30 countries	Cross-sectional	4	DL	Elasticities are similar across the 30 countries.
Houthakker (1965)	13 OECD countries	Time series, ≈ 1948-59	5	DL	Elasticities show considerable variation across countries.
Kravis, Heston and Summers (1982)	34 countries	Cross-country	103 & 25	DL & LES	Tastes are similar internationally.
Lluch and Powell (1975)	19 countries	Time series ≈ 1946-68	8	LES	
Lluch, Powell and Williams (1977)	17 countries	Time series ≈ 1953-69	8	ELES	
Lluch and Williams (1975)	14 countries	Time series ≈ 1955-69	8	ELES	
Parks and Barten (1973)	14 OECD countries	Time series 1950-67	5	Variant of LES	Population composition has a significant influence on consumption patterns.
Pollak and Wales (1987)	Belgium, U.K. & U.S.	Time series/ cross-country 1961-78	3	QES	Caution is appropriate in pooling international consumption data.
Theil (1987a)	30 countries	Cross-country	10	Working's	Similarity of tastes is taken as a maintained hypothesis.
Theil and Suhm (1981)	15 countries	Cross-country	8	Working's	Similarity of tastes is taken as a maintained hypothesis.

Working's = Working's model; LES = linear expenditure system; GLES = generalized linear expenditure system; IAES = indirect addilog expenditure system; DL = double-log model; ELES = extended linear expenditure system; and QES = quadratic expenditure system.

A new approach to international consumption comparisons was adopted by Clements and Theil (1979) who used data from Kravis et al. (1978) on 16 countries to estimate a common system of demand equations for all countries. In comparison with the usual time-series application for a given country, here countries play the role of time periods. This idea has been built on by Theil (1987a) and Theil and Suhm (1981). Under this approach, tastes are taken to be the same internationally. Although this is obviously a rather bold assumption, it is one forcely advocated by Stigler and Becker (1977) who argue that tastes neither change capriciously nor differ importantly between people. Pollak and Wales (1987), who use time-series/cross-country data, provide a test of this hypothesis and reject it.

1.6 SOME INTERNATIONAL CONSUMPTION DATA

In this and the next two sections we illustrate some aspects of international consumption comparisons. For this purpose we quote extensively from the highly influential study by Lluch, Powell and Williams (1977), hereafter LPW.

The basic LPW data consist of current- and constant-price expenditures for 8 commodity groups and income in 17 countries. Table 1.2 presents the sample period and GNP per capita for 13 of the 17 countries; note that

TABLE 1.2

CHARACTERISTICS OF THE LPW DATABASE

Country	Sample period	Per capita GNP at sample midpoint	
		In 1970 U.S. dollars	(3) with U.S. = 100
(1)	(2)	(3)	(4)
1. U.S.	1955-68	3669	100
2. Sweden	1955-68	2962	81
3. Australia	1955-66	2192	60
4. U.K.	1955-68	1900	52
5. Israel	1959-68	1468	40
6. Italy	1955-68	1207	33
7. Puerto Rico	1955-67	1023	28
8. Ireland	1955-68	1014	28
9. Greece	1958-68	676	18
10. South Africa	1955-68	596	16
11. Panama	1960-68	564	15
12. Thailand	1960-69	148	4
13. Korea	1955-68	142	4

Source: Lluch et al. (1977, Table 3.2).

countries are ordered in terms of declining per capita GNP. (See the appendix
to this chapter for the reasons for not considering 4 of the LPW countries.) As
can be seen, the data cover both developed and less developed countries. The
U.S. has the highest per capita GNP, while Korea has the lowest with only
4 percent of the U.S. value.

Let $\overline{w}_{ic}$ be the sample mean of the budget share of commodity i (=1,...,8) in country c (=1,...,13). Table 1.3 presents the mean budget shares for the 8 commodities in each of the 13 countries. Note the strong tendency for the food budget share to decline with increasing GNP which is in accordance with Engel's law. The last row presents the mean budget shares averaged over the 13 countries. On average in these countries, a consumer spends 42 percent of his income on food, 10 percent on clothing, 16 percent on housing and so on.

Let Dp_{ic} be the average annual log-change in the price of commodity i in country c and Dq_{ic} be the corresponding per capita quantity log-change. When multiplied by 100, log-changes are approximately percentage changes. The upper-half of Table 1.4 presents the price log-changes, while the lower-half presents the quantity log-changes. As can be seen from rows 14 and 28, on average, food prices increase by 4 percent per annum, while per capita food consumption grows by 2 percent. Among all prices, personal care has the highest annual growth rate of 4 percent. The consumption of transport grows the fastest, while food is the slowest.

1.7   INDEXES OF INTERNATIONAL CONSUMPTION DATA

A convenient way of summarizing consumption data is by means, variances and correlations. We use weighted versions which take into account

TABLE 1.3

SAMPLE MEANS OF BUDGET SHARES FOR 8 COMMODITIES
IN 13 COUNTRIES

Country (1)	Food (2)	Clothing (3)	Housing (4)	Durables (5)	Personal care (6)	Transport (7)	Recreation (8)	Other services (9)
1. U.S.	26.7	9.5	22.7	7.3	8.1	15.2	5.5	4.9
2. Sweden	36.6	11.5	15.9	7.0	3.7	14.2	8.9	2.4
3. Australia	33.3	11.0	12.7	7.8	5.7	13.1	4.3	12.1
4. U.K.	39.7	10.7	18.3	6.6	2.3	10.9	7.5	4.0
5. Israel	31.9	9.4	19.2	7.4	6.6	7.3	8.1	10.0
6. Italy	46.3	10.1	16.6	3.2	6.3	8.1	7.5	1.8
7. Puerto Rico	35.6	10.6	15.3	6.9	6.9	12.3	8.8	3.7
8. Ireland	49.2	10.0	12.8	5.7	1.3	8.8	6.3	5.9
9. Greece	46.8	12.2	18.3	3.9	3.6	6.9	6.1	2.3
10. South Africa	36.8	11.8	16.7	7.8	4.8	13.2	4.7	4.1
11. Panama	45.5	7.4	16.7	6.4	4.7	9.4	7.5	2.3
12. Thailand	57.6	8.4	8.0	3.2	5.6	7.9	7.5	1.8
13. Korea	59.9	10.4	11.4	2.8	4.2	4.7	4.4	2.2
14. Mean	42.0	10.2	15.7	5.8	4.9	10.2	6.7	4.4

All entries are to be divided by 100. Source: Lluch et al. (1977, Table 3.3).

of the relative importance of each commodity. Our approach is to use Divisia index numbers as descriptive statistics: these indexes use budget shares as weights. The Divisia first-order moments measure the overall growth rates in prices and quantities, while the second-order moments measure the variability in prices and quantities and their co-movement.

TABLE 1.4

AVERAGE ANNUAL PRICE AND QUANTITY LOG-CHANGES
FOR 8 COMMODITIES IN 13 COUNTRIES

Country	Food	Clothing	Housing	Durables	Personal care	Transport	Recreation	Other services
(1)	(2)	(3)	(4)	(5)	(6)	(7)	(8)	(9)
Prices								
1. U.S.	1.85	1.62	1.70	.55	3.04	1.52	2.35	4.31
2. Sweden	4.00	2.25	3.85	1.79	2.85	3.46	4.22	3.70
3. Australia	2.32	1.39	4.87	.48	3.15	1.96	2.92	3.02
4. U.K.	2.11	1.70	4.68	1.69	3.09	2.93	4.62	3.80
5. Israel	4.85	4.65	7.81	1.94	6.46	8.06	5.97	7.22
6. Italy	2.52	2.17	3.65	-.16	4.24	2.27	4.07	4.19
7. Puerto Rico	2.62	1.44	1.27	.83	5.76	2.38	3.20	2.46
8. Ireland	3.18	.89	3.98	3.15	1.33	3.13	3.63	4.24
9. Greece	2.57	1.20	1.59	.67	2.48	1.87	.55	.69
10. South Africa	2.27	.20	3.50	.32	3.90	2.40	2.49	3.40
11. Panama	1.95	.59	.54	.11	2.24	.04	.97	.00
12. Thailand	3.24	.19	-2.63	-1.64	1.33	.06	2.43	2.02
13. Korea	13.28	14.75	11.27	12.54	16.70	12.69	13.91	14.80
14. Mean	3.60	2.54	3.55	1.71	4.35	3.29	3.95	4.14
Quantities								
15. U.S.	.99	2.42	2.79	3.70	3.90	2.78	2.86	3.63
16. Sweden	1.51	1.76	2.77	5.25	5.62	5.32	2.28	4.03
17. Australia	.78	.66	2.34	3.14	4.09	3.12	.10	1.89
18. U.K.	1.62	2.44	1.98	3.08	3.75	5.53	1.37	6.48
19. Israel	4.62	6.87	5.41	11.67	5.96	9.24	8.58	5.17
20. Italy	4.09	4.62	4.62	8.51	5.96	9.46	4.28	4.47
21. Puerto Rico	-.28	3.91	3.25	4.45	1.40	5.13	4.89	5.89
22. Ireland	1.91	4.88	2.51	5.85	2.71	5.32	3.72	2.47
23. Greece	4.14	7.92	5.99	6.41	5.67	8.94	8.08	6.48
24. South Africa	1.04	2.20	.57	3.21	1.81	3.32	1.22	2.48
25. Panama	2.59	3.23	1.92	5.06	2.55	2.01	4.36	2.84
26. Thailand	2.15	5.30	1.06	10.16	3.70	6.55	5.59	7.16
27. Korea	1.94	2.35	2.27	6.88	4.95	11.55	5.69	3.31
28. Mean	2.08	3.74	2.88	5.95	4.01	6.02	4.08	4.33

All entries are to be divided by 100. Source: Derived from Lluch et
al. (1977, Tables 3.4 and 3.5); see the appendix to this chapter for
details.

In this section we introduce the Divisia indexes for two reasons. The first is to present summary information about the LPW data and the second is that the demand equations used throughout the book involve the Divisia indexes. For full details of these indexes, see Theil (1967).

The Divisia price and volume indexes for country c are

$$DP_c = \sum_{i=1}^{8} \overline{w}_{ic} Dp_{ic}, \qquad DQ_c = \sum_{i=1}^{8} \overline{w}_{ic} Dq_{ic}.$$

These are budget-share-weighted means of the price and quantity log-changes and measure the overall growth in prices and per capita consumption. Columns 2 and 3 of Table 1.5 present these indexes for the 13 LPW countries. As can be seen from the last row of the table, on average, prices in these countries increase by 4 percent per annum while per capita consumption grows by 3 percent.

The Divisia price and quantity variances for country c are

$$\Pi_c = \sum_{i=1}^{8} \overline{w}_{ic} (Dp_{ic} - DP_c)^2, \qquad K_c = \sum_{i=1}^{8} \overline{w}_{ic} (Dq_{ic} - DQ_c)^2.$$

When all prices and quantities change proportionately, these two variances vanish. Columns 4 and 5 of Table 1.5 present these variances. Comparing these two columns, we see that the quantity variance systematically exceeds the

TABLE 1.5

DIVISIA MOMENTS FOR 13 COUNTRIES

Country	Price index	Volume index	Price variance	Quantity variance	Price-quantity covariance	Price-quantity correlation
	DP_c	DQ_c	Π_c	K_c	Γ_c	ρ_c
(1)	(2)	(3)	(4)	(5)	(6)	(7)
1. U.S.	1.89	2.47	.57	.98	.15	.19
2. Sweden	3.52	2.83	.56	2.41	-.49	-.42
3. Australia	2.51	1.75	1.28	1.32	.12	.09
4. U.K.	2.88	2.52	1.34	2.15	.08	.05
5. Israel	5.85	6.30	2.90	4.40	-1.09	-.30
6. Italy	2.82	4.94	.78	2.53	-.43	-.30
7. Puerto Rico	2.40	2.49	1.31	5.17	-.79	-.30
8. Ireland	3.11	2.97	.73	1.95	-.50	-.42
9. Greece	1.93	5.71	.50	2.86	-.96	-.80
10. South Africa	2.23	1.67	1.24	.96	-.52	-.48
11. Panama	1.21	2.76	.65	.73	-.10	-.15
12. Thailand	1.91	3.36	3.63	4.51	-1.53	-.38
13. Korea	13.36	2.93	1.27	5.11	.13	.05
14. Mean	3.51	3.29	1.29	2.70	-.46	-.24

All entries in columns 2 and 3 are to be divided by 100 and in columns 4-6 are to be divided by 10000.

corresponding price variance, a result which has been found in other applications (see, e.g., Theil and Suhm, 1981).

The Divisia price-quantity covariance is

$$\Gamma_c = \sum_{i=1}^{8} \overline{w}_{ic}(Dp_{ic} - DP_c)(Dq_{ic} - DQ_c).$$

This measures the co-movement of the prices and quantities. Column 6 of Table 1.5 presents this covariance. The corresponding correlation is

$$\rho_c = \frac{\Gamma_c}{\sqrt{\Pi_c K_c}},$$

which is given in column 7. As one would expect, the correlations are mainly negative, reflecting the tendency of the consumer to move away from those commodities having above-average price increases.

1.8 SOME RESULTS FROM THE LPW STUDY

LPW use mainly Lluch's (1973) extended linear expenditure system (ELES), where total consumption expenditure is endogenous. This model takes the form

$$p_i q_i = p_i \gamma_i + \mu_i^* \left[y - \sum_{j=1}^{n} p_j \gamma_j \right], \qquad i=1,...,n, \qquad (8.1)$$

where γ_i and μ_i^* are constants; and y is now truly income, defined as total expenditure M plus savings. LPW estimate ELES for 11 countries. Since income data are not available for Panama and Puerto Rico, LES is used for these two countries.

Model (8.1) (or LES) is estimated with time-series data for $n=8$ commodities for each of the 13 countries. The model is estimated for each country independently of the other 12. In other words, all parameters (and variables) in (8.1) are endowed with a country subscript. For simplicity, we shall continue to suppress the country subscript whenever there is no ambiguity. The marginal share for good i implied by (8.1) is μ_i^*/μ, where $\mu = \Sigma_{i=1}^{n} \mu_i^*$. The upper-part of Table 1.6 presents the estimates of the marginal shares for the 8 commodities in the 13 countries.

Let θ_{ic} be the LPW estimate of the marginal share of i in c. The lower-part of Table 1.6 presents the implied income elasticities,

$$\eta_{ic} = \frac{\theta_{ic}}{\bar{w}_{ic}}, \qquad\qquad \begin{array}{l} i=1,...,8, \\ c=1,...,13. \end{array} \qquad (8.2)$$

As can be seen from the last row, on average, food and housing are necessities, clothing is borderline case, while the other five goods are luxuries. Later in the chapter we return to LPW.

TABLE 1.6

FIRST SET OF MARGINAL SHARES AND INCOME ELASTICITIES

FOR 8 COMMODITIES IN 13 COUNTRIES

Country	Food	Clothing	Housing	Durables	Personal care	Transport	Recreation	Other services
(1)	(2)	(3)	(4)	(5)	(6)	(7)	(8)	(9)
Marginal shares								
1. U.S.	.090	.108	.206	.106	.137	.174	.065	.113
2. Sweden	.278	.071	.145	.079	.052	.253	.097	.024
3. Australia	.143	.050	.220	.082	.133	.224	.009	.138
4. U.K.	.120	.067	.258	.076	.030	.277	.066	.106
5. Israel	.210	.103	.172	.119	.066	.116	.117	.097
6. Italy	.401	.087	.171	.069	.066	.117	.070	.019
7. Puerto Rico	.177	.112	.144	.068	.114	.176	.137	.072
8. Ireland	.315	.134	.108	.114	.014	.170	.075	.070
9. Greece	.341	.168	.175	.050	.048	.107	.083	.028
10. South Africa	.295	.164	.066	.115	.049	.206	.046	.059
11. Panama	.418	.081	.113	.113	.044	.085	.127	.019
12. Thailand	.482	.101	.013	.052	.052	.123	.150	.028
13. Korea	.434	.069	.085	.077	.074	.146	.078	.038
14. Mean	.285	.101	.144	.086	.068	.167	.086	.062
Income elasticities								
15. U.S.	.337	1.137	.907	1.452	1.691	1.145	1.182	2.306
16. Sweden	.760	.617	.912	1.129	1.405	1.782	1.090	1.000
17. Australia	.429	.455	1.732	1.051	2.333	1.710	.209	1.140
18. U.K.	.302	.626	1.410	1.152	1.304	2.541	.880	2.650
19. Israel	.658	1.096	.896	1.608	1.000	1.589	1.444	.970
20. Italy	.866	.861	1.030	2.156	1.048	1.444	.933	1.056
21. Puerto Rico	.497	1.057	.941	.986	1.652	1.431	1.557	1.946
22. Ireland	.640	1.340	.844	2.000	1.077	1.932	1.190	1.186
23. Greece	.729	1.377	.956	1.282	1.333	1.551	1.361	1.217
24. South Africa	.802	1.390	.395	1.474	1.021	1.561	.979	1.439
25. Panama	.919	1.095	.677	1.766	.936	.904	1.693	.826
26. Thailand	.837	1.202	.163	1.625	.929	1.557	2.000	1.556
27. Korea	.725	.663	.746	2.750	1.762	3.106	1.773	1.727
28. Mean	.654	.994	.893	1.572	1.346	1.712	1.253	1.463

Source: The marginal shares are from Lluch et al. (1977, Table 3.6).
The income elasticities are derived using (8.2).

1.9 THE ROTTERDAM MODEL

In this and the next two sections we discuss some further demand systems. This material is based mainly on Clements (1987).

The differential demand system (2.3) is formulated in terms of infinitesimal changes. As noted in Section 1.2, when the infinitesimal changes are replaced by first differences and the 'coefficients' are taken to be constants, we have the Rotterdam model, due to Barten (1964) and Theil (1965). Let $Dx_{it} = \log x_{it} - \log x_{i,t-1}$ be the log-change from period t-1 to t in any positive variable x_{it} and $\overline{w}_{it} = \frac{1}{2}(w_{it} + w_{i,t-1})$ be the arithmetic average of w_{it}. The ith equation of the Rotterdam model is then

$$\overline{w}_{it}Dq_{it} = \theta_i DQ_t + \sum_{j=1}^{n} \pi_{ij}Dp_{jt},\qquad(9.1)$$

where $DQ_t = \sum_{i=1}^{n} \overline{w}_{it}Dq_{it}$ is a finite-change version of the Divisia volume index; and θ_i and π_{ij} are constant parameters. This is known as the absolute price version of the Rotterdam model.

Unlike LES, the Rotterdam model can be used to test the validity of the general restrictions of demand theory. Also, as the model is linear in the parameters, it is straightforward to estimate. However, the model has some disadvantages. The first is that the number of π_{ij}'s to be estimated in (9.1) increases rapidly with n, the number of commodities. Consequently, this version of the model is not suitable for large systems. (The so-called relative price version is, however, suitable for such systems.)

The second problem with (9.1) is the constancy of the marginal shares. As discussed in Section 1.3 in the context of LES, this leads to implausible behaviour of the income elasticities. Thus, both the Rotterdam model and LES suffer from this difficulty. In the following section we discuss an alternative model which alleviates this problem.

1.10 WORKING'S MODEL

Working (1943) analysed family expenditure data and observed that the budget share for food seemed to be a linear function of the logarithm of income. This observation was generalized by Leser (1963) to a complete set of commodities to yield

$$w_i = \alpha_i + \beta_i \log M, \qquad i=1,\dots,n, \qquad (10.1)$$

where α_i and β_i are constants. As $\Sigma_{i=1}^n w_i = 1$, it follows that $\Sigma_{i=1}^n \alpha_i = 1$ and $\Sigma_{i=1}^n \beta_i = 0$. If we choose the income unit such that $M = 1$ for the poorest consumer, then α_i is interpreted as the budget share of i for such a consumer. Taking the differential of (10.1), we have $dw_i = \beta_i d(\log M)$. Thus, the income coefficient β_i is 100 times the change in w_i resulting from a 1 percent increase in income. We shall refer to (10.1) as Working's model.

Theil (1987a), using data from Kravis et al. (1982) for 34 countries, plots the budget share of food against the log of total real per capita consumption.   Figure 1.1 gives such a plot (with consumption scaled such that M=1 for Malawi, the poorest country).   The solid line is the least-squares (LS) regression line.   As can be seen, the points are all scattered around a downward sloping line which gives strong visual support for the Working's model (at least for food).

The intercept of the LS line is an estimate of α_i, the food budget share for Malawi (as M=1 for that country). This estimate is .57 (with standard error .03) which is to be compared with the observed budget share for that country of .53.   The slope of the LS line is -.15 (standard error .01), which is an estimate of β_i for food.   To analyse the implications of this estimate, consider moving from one country to another; assume that the first country's per capita income is M, while that of the second is twice as large, 2M.   For this move, $\Delta(\log M) = \log 2M - \log M = \log 2 = .69$.   It then follows from $\Delta w_i = \beta_i \Delta(\log M)$ that the effect of doubling income on the food budget share is $\Delta w_i = -.15 \times .69 = -.10$.   That is, when income doubles, the budget share declines by 10 percentage points.   This is known as the strong version of Engel's law (Theil et al., 1989).

Budget Share of Food Against Scaled Total Consumption Expenditure

Per Capita in 1975 for 34 Countries

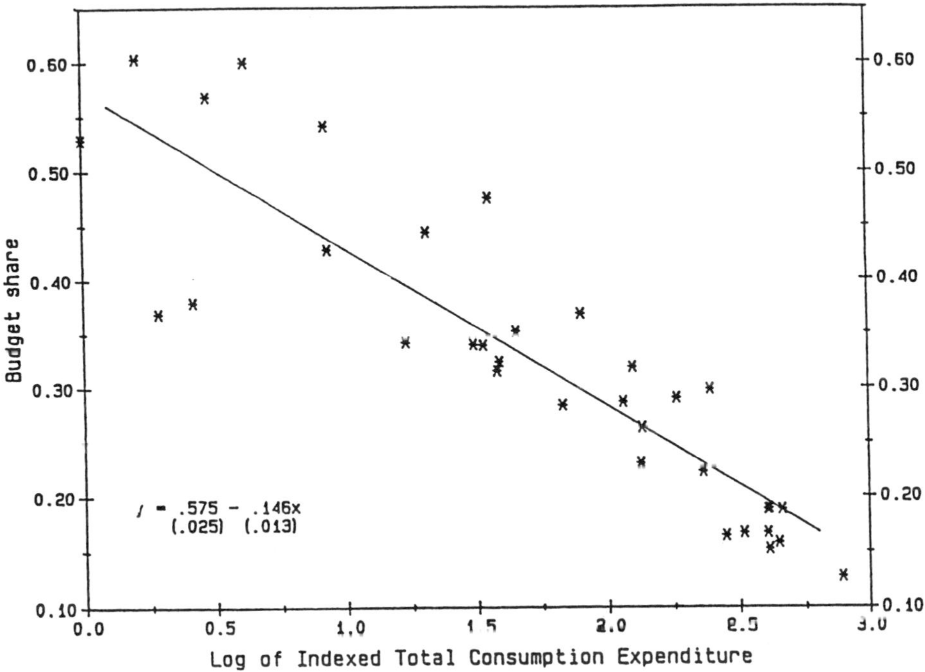

Figure 1.1

Using $w_i = p_i q_i / M$ in (10.1) and multiplying both sides by M, we get

$$p_i q_i = \alpha_i M + \beta_i M \log M.$$

Differentiating both sides of this equation with respect to M and using (10.1), we get the marginal share implied by Working's model,

$$\theta_i = w_i + \beta_i \tag{10.2}$$

Thus under Working's model the marginal share and the budget share for commodity i differ by the constant coefficient β_i. Since the budget share w_i is not a constant, neither is the marginal share.

The income elasticity is the ratio of the marginal share to the corresponding budget share, $\eta_i = \theta_i/w_i$. It then follows from (10.2) that the income elasticity of i implied by Working's model is

$$\eta_i = 1 + \frac{\beta_i}{w_i}. \tag{10.3}$$

This shows that a commodity is a necessity (luxury) if β_i is negative (positive). As the budget share of a necessity falls with increasing income, this expression implies that the income elasticity of such a good falls when income increases. By a similar argument, the income elasticity of a luxury also falls. That is, as the consumer becomes more affluent, all goods become less luxurious under Working's model, which is plausible. This result is in contrast to the behaviour of the income elasticities from LES and the Rotterdam model in which the marginal shares are constants; see Sections 1.3 and 1.9. Therefore, Working's model is a plausible alternative to taking the marginal shares as constants.

Table 1.7 presents previous estimates of Working's income coefficient for food. As can be seen, the estimates are quite stable over countries and fall in the range of -.13 to -.18. It is to be noted that the estimate of this coefficient given in Figure 1.1 of -.15 is almost exactly in the middle of this range.

TABLE 1.7

PREVIOUS ESTIMATES OF WORKING'S INCOME COEFFICIENT

FOR FOOD

Author(s) (1)	Country (2)	Estimate (3)
Aasness and Rodseth (1983)	Norway	-.17
Blanciforti and Green (1983)	U.S.	-.13
Chung and Lopez (1988)	Spain	-.18 & -.16
Deaton and Muellbauer (1980)	Britain	-.16
Finke et al. (1984)	Japan	-.15
Musgrove (1985)	Dominican Republic	-.14
Theil (1987a)	Cross country	-.14 to -.16
Theil et al. (1987)	China	-.13
Theil and Finke (1984)	Netherlands	-.13

Source: Chung and Lopez (1988, Table 1).

1.11 WORKING'S MODEL AND DIFFERENTIAL DEMAND EQUATIONS

Working's model (10.1) represents an incomplete specification of demand functions since it contains no price substitution term, although it can be applied to the analysis of household budget data where all participating families pay the same price for each commodity. In this section we add a price term by incorporating Working's model into the framework of differential demand equations.

We return to the differential demand system (2.3) and note again that the coefficients are not necessarily constants. To use Working's model, we substitute the right-hand side of (10.2) for θ_i in (2.3) to give

$$w_i d(\log q_i) \; = \; (w_i + \beta_i) d(\log Q) + \sum_{j=1}^{n} \pi_{ij} d(\log p_j).$$

Therefore,

$$w_i [d(\log q_i) - d(\log Q)] \; = \; \beta_i d(\log Q) + \sum_{j=1}^{n} \pi_{ij} d(\log p_j).$$

A finite-change form of this is

$$\overline{w}_{it}(Dq_{it} - DQ_t) \; = \; \beta_i DQ_t + \sum_{j=1}^{n} \pi_{ij} Dp_{jt}. \tag{11.1}$$

This is the ith equation of Working's model with a substitution term added. Note that the only difference between (11.1) and the Rotterdam model (9.1) is the variable on the left. Although we previously referred to (10.1) as Working's model, there will be no confusion if, from now on, we refer to (11.1) for $i=1,...,n$ as Working's model. For further details of (11.1), see, e.g., Clements (1987) and Keller and van Driel (1985).

Recall that in Section 1.3 we noted that the assumption of preference independence is built into LES. Working's model is more flexible as preference independence is only a special case, as shall now be shown. Under preference independence, the Slutsky coefficients take the form (see, e.g., Clements, 1987)

$$\pi_{ij} = \phi\theta_i(\delta_{ij} - \theta_j), \tag{11.2}$$

where ϕ is the income flexibility (the reciprocal of the income elasticity of the marginal utility of income); and δ_{ij} is the Kronecker delta ($\delta_{ij} = 1$ if $i=j$, 0 otherwise).

To obtain the demand equation under preference independence, we proceed in three steps: We (i) substitute the right-hand side of (11.2) for π_{ij} in (11.1); (ii) substitute the right-hand side of (10.2) for θ_i; and (iii) replace w_i with $\overline{w}_{it}$, the arithmetic average of the budget share. This yields

$$\overline{w}_{it}(Dq_{it} - DQ_t) = \beta_i DQ_t + \phi(\overline{w}_{it} + \beta_i)Dp'_{it}, \tag{11.3}$$

where

$$Dp'_{it} = Dp_{it} - \sum_{j=1}^{n} (\overline{w}_{jt} + \beta_j)Dp_{jt}$$

is the change in the relative (or deflated) price of good i. We shall refer to (11.3) for i=1,...,n as Working's model under preference independence.

Note that (11.3) contains only the own relative price. Note also the dramatic reduction in the number of unknown parameters in the substitution term as a result of the preference independence assumption: Model (11.1) contains π_{ij} for i,j=1,...,n, while (11.3) contains only ϕ (the β_i's are not additional unknown parameters in the substitution term as these are the income coefficients). Whether or not such an assumption is legitimate is, of course, an empirical question. This question is pursued in Chapter 3.

1.12 FURTHER EVIDENCE ON WORKING'S MODEL

Thus far we have seen three attractions of Working's model, (i) the behaviour of the income elasticities is plausible; (ii) it seems to do quite well with the Kravis et al. food data; and (iii) the estimates of the β_i for food appear to be fairly stable across countries. In this and the next section, we provide a fourth attraction, viz. it provides a reasonable model of consumer behaviour for the world as a whole, the world being defined by the LPW countries.

From equation (10.2), in Working's model the marginal share differs from the corresponding budget share by a constant (β_i); that is,

$$\beta_i = \theta_i - w_i.$$

Thus, if we have a number of estimates of the marginal share for commodity i, θ_{ic}, c=1,...,N, as well as w_{ic}, c=1,...,N, we can obtain a simple estimate of β_i by averaging,

$$\hat{\beta}_i = \frac{1}{N} \sum_{c=1}^{N} (\theta_{ic} - w_{ic}). \tag{12.1}$$

Note that as $\Sigma_{i=1}^{n} \theta_{ic} = \Sigma_{i=1}^{n} w_{ic} = 1$, the estimates defined by (12.1) for i=1,...,n satisfy $\Sigma_{i=1}^{n} \hat{\beta}_i = 0$.

To implement (12.1), we use the N=13 countries from LPW, the estimates of the θ_i's given in Table 1.6 and the corresponding budget shares from Table 1.3. Note that these estimates of the marginal shares are obtained country-by-country by LPW, so that each value is independent of the other. Column 2 of Table 1.8 gives the results. The estimates for food and housing are negative; that for clothing is close to zero; and the remaining ones are positive. This shows that food and housing are necessities, clothing is a

TABLE 1.8

TWO SETS OF ESTIMATES OF WORKING'S MODEL

Parameter	First set of estimates	Second set of estimates
(1)	(2)	(3)
Income coefficients, β_i		
Food	-.135 (.018)	-.128 (.014)
Clothing	-.001 (.009)	.010 (.009)
Housing	-.013 (.014)	-.013 (.010)
Durables	.028 (.005)	.031 (.007)
Personal care	.019 (.007)	.010 (.007)
Transport	.066 (.012)	.062 (.009)
Recreation	.019 (.008)	.021 (.007)
Other services	.018 (.006)	.005 (.006)
Income flexibility, ϕ	-	-.222 (.097)

The figures in parentheses in column 2 are standard errors; and those in column 3 are asymptotic standard errors.

borderline case, while the other five goods are luxuries. This is in agreement with the average income elasticities from LPW given in Table 1.6. The food income coefficient is -.14 (with standard error .02). This is to be compared with the previous estimates in Table 1.7 (-.13 to -.18) and that from Figure 1.1 (-.15); clearly, the three sets of estimates are in satisfactory agreement with each other. Column 3 of Table 1.8 will be discussed in the next section.

Whilst the above estimates of the income coefficients are reasonable and consistent with previous evidence, are the cross-country data really consistent with Working's model? To answer this, we use (10.2), the specification for the marginal share under Working's model, as a regression equation. That is, for each good we regress the 13 values of the marginal share θ_{ic} presented in Table 1.6 on the budget share w_{ic} of Table 1.3,

$$\theta_{ic} = \lambda_i + \gamma_i w_{ic} + \xi_{ic}, \qquad\qquad c=1,\dots,13, \qquad\qquad (12.2)$$

where λ_i and γ_i are coefficients to be estimated; and ξ_{ic} is a disturbance term. Under Working's model γ_i in (12.2) equals 1, while under LES, $\gamma_i = 0$.

Figure 1.2 gives the scatter associated with (12.2) for food, together with the LS line. As can be seen, the points are all scattered around an upward-sloping line with slope 1.12 (standard error .20), which is not significantly different from 1. We conclude that the evidence for food is not inconsistent with Working's model.

Table 1.9 presents the results for all 8 commodities obtained by estimating (12.2) by single-equation LS. As can be seen from column 3, all the estimates of γ_i are not significantly different from 1; and all except one (for clothing) are significantly different from zero. Looking at the coefficients of determination presented in column 4, we see that the fit of the model is not unsatisfactory for all commodities except clothing. Note that as the marginal share is independent of the budget share in LES, all R^2s would be zero if that

Marginal Shares Against Budget Shares for Food

in 13 Countries

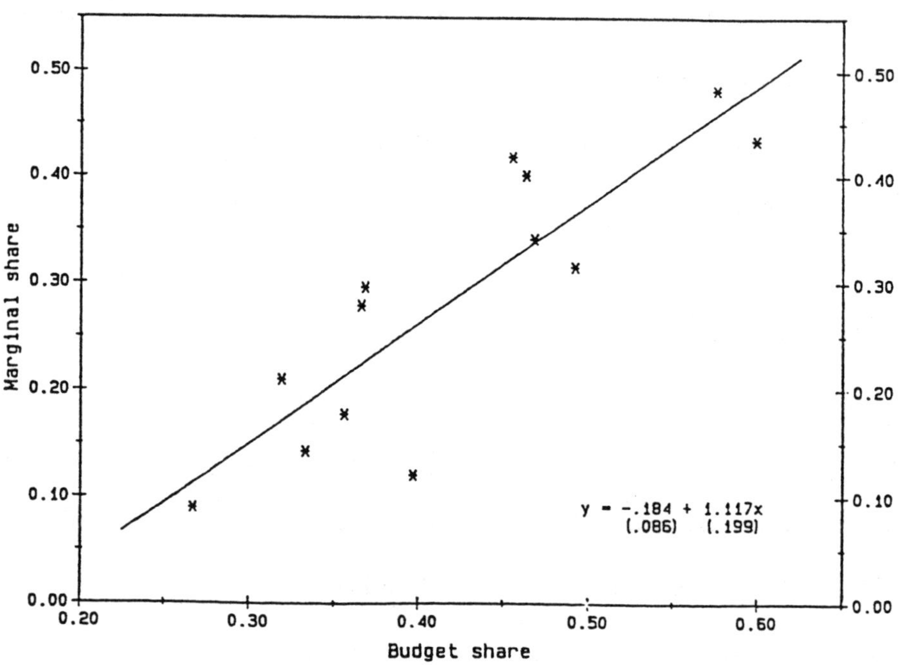

Figure 1.2

model were true.   This evidence unambiguously supports Working's model
rather than LES for these cross-country data.

1.13   A DEMAND SYSTEM FOR THE WORLD

As the above results are encouraging, we now proceed more formally.
In the previous section we estimated the income coefficients only of Working's

TABLE 1.9

CROSS-COUNTRY REGRESSION RESULTS

$$\theta_{ic} = \lambda_i + \gamma_i w_{ic}$$

(Standard errors are in parentheses)

Commodity (1)	Intercept λ_i (2)	Slope γ_i (3)	R^2 (4)
1. Food	-.184 (.086)	1.117 (.199)	.74
2. Clothing	.016 (.081)	.835 (.781)	.09
3. Housing	-.034 (.066)	1.135 (.409)	.41
4. Durables	.040 (.019)	.794 (.309)	.37
5. Personal care	-.010 (.019)	1.578 (.368)	.63
6. Transport	.047 (.045)	1.188 (.422)	.42
7. Recreation	-.032 (.035)	1.769 (.505)	.53
8. Other services	.017 (.012)	1.028 (.218)	.67

model. Now we estimate these coefficients simultaneously with the price substitution term. Following LPW, preference independence will be assumed.

We use Working's model under preference independence, equation (11.3) with the time subscripts (t) replaced with country subscripts (c),

$$\overline{w}_{ic}(Dq_{ic} - DQ_c) = \beta_i DQ_c + \phi(\overline{w}_{ic} + \beta_i)Dp'_{ic} + \varepsilon_{ic}. \qquad (13.1)$$

Here ε_{ic} is a zero-mean disturbance term which is assumed to be uncorrelated over countries but correlated across commodities. We use the LPW data given in Tables 1.3-1.5 to estimate (13.1) for $i=1,...,8$ and $c=1,...,13$. That is, $\bar{w}_{ic}$ is now interpreted as the sample mean of the budget share of i in c; Dq_{ic} and Dp_{ic} as the average annual log-changes in per capita consumption and the price of i in c; and $DQ_c = \Sigma_{i=1}^{8} \bar{w}_{ic} Dq_{ic}$ as the Divisia volume index of the change in real income in c. Note that the coefficients of (13.1), β_i ($i=1,...,8$) and ϕ, are taken to be constants across countries. Consequently, this model can be described as a cross-country demand system. This is in contrast to LPW who estimate ELES/LES country-by-country whereby the parameters vary internationally (see Section 1.8).

We estimate (13.1) by maximum likelihood under the assumption that the ε_{ic}'s are multivariate normal. (The details of the estimation procedure are set out in the appendix to Chapter 3 with the time subscripts interpreted as country subscripts.) The results are presented in column 3 of Table 1.8. The β_i-estimates are mainly very close to the previous set given in column 2. The estimate of ϕ is significantly negative, but lower (in absolute value) than most previous values (Theil, 1980). These estimates of (13.1), together with the results of the previous section, provide no prima facie evidence against the pooling of consumption data across countries.

To explore the implications of the cross-country demand system, we compute the implied marginal shares and income elasticities. Table 1.10 contains the results. These are to be compared with the LPW values given in

TABLE 1.10

SECOND SET OF MARGINAL SHARES AND INCOME ELASTICITIES

FOR 8 COMMODITIES IN 13 COUNTRIES

Country	Food	Clothing	Housing	Durables	Personal care	Transport	Recreation	Other services
(1)	(2)	(3)	(4)	(5)	(6)	(7)	(8)	(9)
				Marginal shares				
1. U.S.	.139	.105	.214	.104	.091	.214	.076	.054
2. Sweden	.238	.125	.146	.101	.047	.204	.110	.029
3. Australia	.205	.120	.114	.109	.067	.193	.064	.126
4. U.K.	.269	.117	.170	.097	.033	.171	.096	.045
5. Israel	.191	.104	.179	.105	.076	.135	.102	.105
6. Italy	.335	.111	.153	.063	.073	.143	.096	.023
7. Puerto Rico	.228	.116	.140	.100	.079	.185	.109	.042
8. Ireland	.364	.110	.115	.088	.023	.150	.084	.064
9. Greece	.340	.132	.170	.070	.046	.131	.082	.028
10. South Africa	.240	.128	.154	.109	.058	.194	.068	.046
11. Panama	.327	.084	.154	.095	.057	.156	.096	.028
12. Thailand	.448	.094	.067	.063	.066	.141	.096	.023
13. Korea	.471	.114	.101	.059	.052	.109	.065	.027
14. Mean	.292	.112	.144	.089	.059	.164	.088	.049
				Income elasticities				
15. U.S.	.521	1.105	.943	1.425	1.123	1.408	1.382	1.102
16. Sweden	.650	1.087	.918	1.443	1.270	1.437	1.236	1.208
17. Australia	.616	1.091	.898	1.397	1.175	1.473	1.488	1.041
18. U.K.	.678	1.093	.929	1.470	1.435	1.569	1.280	1.125
19. Israel	.599	1.106	.932	1.419	1.152	1.849	1.259	1.050
20. Italy	.724	1.099	.922	1.969	1.159	1.765	1.280	1.278
21. Puerto Rico	.640	1.094	.915	1.449	1.145	1.504	1.239	1.135
22. Ireland	.740	1.100	.898	1.544	1.769	1.705	1.333	1.085
23. Greece	.726	1.082	.929	1.795	1.278	1.899	1.344	1.217
24. South Africa	.652	1.085	.922	1.397	1.208	1.470	1.447	1.122
25. Panama	.719	1.135	.922	1.484	1.213	1.660	1.280	1.217
26. Thailand	.778	1.119	.838	1.969	1.179	1.785	1.280	1.278
27. Korea	.786	1.096	.886	2.107	1.238	2.319	1.477	1.227
28. Mean	.679	1.099	.912	1.605	1.257	1.680	1.333	1.160

The marginal shares are computed from equation (10.2) with the β_i-estimates given in column 3 of Table 1.8 and the observed budget shares given in Table 1.3. The income elasticities are computed from (10.3) using the the same approach.

Table 1.6. We can regard the values in Table 1.10 as "fitted" and those in Table 1.6 as "observed". The correlation coefficients between the two sets of marginal shares are:

Food	.86
Clothing	.31
Housing	.64
Durables	.61
Personal care	.79
Transport	.65
Recreation	.73
Other services	.82

As can be seen, except for clothing, the two sets of marginal shares agree well.

The conclusion of this section is that the cross-country demand system (13.1) can be used to analyse the consumption patterns of all countries with common demand model parameters. Consequently, world consumption patterns can be adequately described with just 9 parameters, $\beta_1,...,\beta_8$ and ϕ. Some policy implications of the use of these parameters are discussed in Section 1.15.

1.14   THE COMPARABILITY OF INTERNATIONAL DATA

A major problem with international consumption comparisons is that the data are not directly comparable across countries as they are expressed in terms of the national currencies of the individual countries. Until now, there have been two approaches to this problem.

The first is to use prevailing exchange rates to convert the data into a common currency, U.S. dollars for example. However, this approach has two disadvantages. (i) As most services do not enter into international trade, exchange rates do not reflect international differences in their prices. Added to this is the fact that services tend to be cheaper in poorer countries. Consequently, the use of prevailing exchange rates has the effect of amplifying the differences between rich and poor countries (see Balassa, 1964; Kravis et al., 1982). (ii) In the past fifteen years, exchange rates have been very unstable and thus do not provide a reliable basis for currency conversions for cross-country consumption comparisons.

The second approach to the problem uses purchasing power parities (PPPs) which involve different transformation factors for each good. This approach is applied extensively by Kravis et al. (1982). They use the country-product-dummy (CPD) method to estimate PPPs. Suppose that the ith commodity group comprises n_i individual goods. Let p_{jc} be the price of good j $(=1,...,n_i)$ in country c $(=1,...,N)$, expressed in terms of the national currency of that country. Then the CPD method expresses the log of the price as the sum of a commodity-specific term (μ_j), a country-specific term (v_c) and an error term (ζ_{jc}),

$$\log p_{jc} = \mu_j + v_c + \zeta_{jc}, \qquad \begin{aligned} j&=1,...,n_i, \\ c&=1,...,N . \end{aligned} \qquad (14.1)$$

The country effect v_c is set at zero for the base country, the U.S. Let $\hat{v}_c$ be the LS estimate of v_c in (14.1). This $\hat{v}_c$ is the mean over all j of log p_{jc}. Thus the antilog of $\hat{v}_c$ equals the geometric mean of p_{jc} over $j=1,...,n_i$; this antilog is the PPP of commodity group i in country c relative to the U.S. This PPP is then used as the factor which transforms expenditure on i in country c into a common currency. Given the problems associated with using prevailing exchange rates, the PPP approach has become the most widely used (see, e.g., Pollak and Wales, 1987; and Theil, 1987b).

The approach we used in Section 1.13 to pool data internationally is an alternative to employing exchange rates or PPPs. We formulated all variables in terms of log-changes rather than in level form. As these changes are unit-free, they can be directly pooled internationally. Our approach is attractive as the data are fundamentally untouched. It also avoids having to make the assumptions implicit in the PPP approach, the assumptions revolving around model (14.1) and the properties of the error term ζ_{ic}.

1.15 POLICY IMPLICATIONS

The estimates of the demand systems to be presented in later chapters of this book are useful for purposes of forecasting consumption patterns and policy evaluation associated with changes in income and prices. Examples of such applications are: (i) predicting food expenditures of OECD consumers for a future period; (ii) deriving optimal tax rates; (iii) measuring the level of substitutability between food and beverages; (iv) measuring how changes in income will affect the consumption of different products; (v) calculating cost-of-living indices for measuring changes in consumer welfare; etc.

One of the most common policy uses of demand parameters involves estimating the revenue to be collected from the imposition of consumption taxes and the measurement of the resulting change in social welfare. The revenue and welfare cost are directly dependent on the tax rates and the expenditure on the commodities concerned. As the demand system simultaneously measures the effects of changes in the consumption of all commodities due to changes in prices, the estimated parameters of the system play an important role in measuring the tax-related effects. One such application is the alcohol and tobacco taxes. From time to time governments increase alcohol and tobacco taxes as a way of increasing their revenue. On the one hand, the alcohol and tobacco industries argue that tax increases would cost jobs in their industries. At the same time, the medical profession lobby governments to allocate a major proportion of the tax revenue for the prevention of alcohol misuse and smoking, for the rehabilitation of those affected and for the improvement of medical facilities. Thus the calculation of social welfare due to tax changes is crucial. See Harberger (1964) and Clements and Johnson (1983) for further details.

The income and price elasticities presented in this book are also key parameters used in computable general equilibrium models which are now commonly used for simulating the micro and macroeconomic effects of policy changes.   The estimation results have further policy implications at the cross-country level with the formation of economic blocks such as the European Economic Community (EEC), the North American Free Trade Agreement, the possible Asian trading block etc. Such mergers, especially the EEC, may have now become possible due to the similarity of the consumers - a question which is extensively analysed in Chapter 4 of the book.

APPENDIX TO CHAPTER 1

THE LPW DATA

LPW present data for 17 countries. There are 8 commodity groups for all countries except Taiwan and West Germany. For comparability, we omit these two countries. We also omit Jamaica as it has a negative marginal share for one commodity, other services; and the Philippines for which all prices move approximately proportionately. Thus we are left with $17 - 4 = 13$ countries.

Let p_{ict} and q_{ict} be the price and per capita consumption of good i $(=1,...,8)$ in country c $(=1,...,13)$ in year t $(=1,...,T^c)$. Then the corresponding budget share is

$$w_{ict} = \frac{p_{ict} \, q_{ict}}{M_{ct}}, \tag{A1}$$

where $M_{ct} - \Sigma_{i=1}^{8} p_{ict} q_{ict}$ is income. LPW use time-series data on consumption, prices and income to estimate demand equations. However, they present in their monograph only summaries of these data in two forms. First, for each good and country, the ratio of the budget share in the last year of the sample to that in the first, $w_{icT}c/w_{ic1}$. Table A1.1 gives these ratios. Second,

TABLE A1.1

RATIOS OF BUDGET SHARES FOR 8 COMMODITIES
IN 13 COUNTRIES

Country (1)	Food (2)	Clothing (3)	Housing (4)	Durables (5)	Personal care (6)	Transport (7)	Recreation (8)	Other services (9)
1. U.S.	.821	.960	1.019	.987	1.400	.994	1.118	1.594
2. Sweden	.900	.740	1.039	1.097	1.322	1.377	1.022	1.200
3. Australia	.883	.786	1.388	.935	1.392	1.097	.875	1.077
4. U.K.	.807	.852	1.182	.925	1.210	1.494	1.084	1.893
5. Israel	.791	.951	1.109	1.148	1.031	1.600	1.250	1.029
6. Italy	.863	.883	1.070	1.081	1.377	1.680	1.082	1.126
7. Puerto Rico	.745	1.070	.968	1.061	1.328	1.385	1.485	1.533
8. Ireland	.882	.963	1.058	1.466	.769	1.366	1.182	1.089
9. Greece	.912	1.160	.995	.947	1.054	1.375	1.106	.955
10. South Africa	.929	.825	1.025	.955	1.269	1.270	.978	1.295
11. Panama	1.046	.987	.885	1.100	1.067	.857	1.114	.913
12. Thailand	1.015	1.025	.543	1.347	.983	1.133	1.288	1.428
13. Korea	.883	1.128	.710	1.524	2.040	2.857	1.560	1.287
14. Mean	.883	.948	.999	1.121	1.249	1.422	1.165	1.263

Source: Lluch et al. (1977, Table 3.4).

similar ratios for the prices, p_{icT}^{c}/p_{ic1}, and income, M_{cT}^{c}/M_{c1}. These are given in Table A1.2.

We now convert the above data to log-change form. We define the average annual log-change in the budget share of i as

$$Dw_{ic} = \frac{1}{T^{c}-1} \log \frac{w_{icT}^{c}}{w_{ic1}} = \frac{1}{T^{c}-1} \left[\log w_{icT}^{c} - \log w_{ic1} \right]. \qquad (A2)$$

TABLE A1.2

RATIOS OF PRICES OF 8 COMMODITIES AND INCOME
IN 13 COUNTRIES

Country	Food	Clothing	Housing	Durables	Personal care	Transport	Recreation	Other services	Income
(1)	(2)	(3)	(4)	(5)	(6)	(7)	(8)	(9)	(10)
1. U.S.	1.272	1.234	1.248	1.074	1.485	1.219	1.358	1.751	1.761
2. Sweden	1.683	1.340	1.650	1.262	1.449	1.569	1.730	1.618	2.276
3. Australia	1.291	1.165	1.709	1.054	1.414	1.240	1.379	1.394	1.593
4. U.K.	1.315	1.248	1.838	1.246	1.494	1.464	1.824	1.639	2.011
5. Israel	1.547	1.519	2.020	1.191	1.788	2.066	1.712	1.915	2.965
6. Italy	1.388	1.326	1.607	.979	1.736	1.344	1.697	1.724	2.737
7. Puerto Rico	1.369	1.189	1.165	1.105	1.995	1.330	1.468	1.343	1.777
8. Ireland	1.512	1.122	1.677	1.506	1.189	1.503	1.602	1.736	2.198
9. Greece	1.293	1.127	1.172	1.069	1.282	1.206	1.057	1.071	2.144
10. South Africa	1.344	1.027	1.577	1.042	1.661	1.366	1.383	1.555	1.657
11. Panama	1.169	1.048	1.044	1.009	1.196	1.003	1.081	1.000	1.375
12. Thailand	1.338	1.017	.789	.863	1.127	1.005	1.245	1.199	1.599
13. Korea	5.617	6.802	4.329	5.102	8.771	5.208	6.097	6.849	8.187
14. Mean	1.703	1.628	1.679	1.423	2.045	1.656	1.818	1.907	2.483

Source: Lluch et al. (1977, Table 3.5).

Note that the divisor is $T^c - 1$ and not T^c as one year is lost in going from levels to changes. Similarly, the average annual log-changes in the ith price and income are

$$Dp_{ic} = \frac{1}{T^c - 1} \log \frac{p_{icT^c}}{p_{ic1}} , \qquad DM_c = \frac{1}{T^c - 1} \log \frac{M_{cT^c}}{M_{c1}} . \qquad (A3)$$

Although (A2)-(A3) involve only the beginning and ending years, they are genuine average growth rates over the whole period since the intermediate values drop out. That is, the average of $Dx_2,...,Dx_T$ is

$$\frac{1}{T-1} \sum_{t=2}^{T} Dx_t$$

$$= \frac{1}{T-1} \left[(\log x_2 - \log x_1) + (\log x_3 - \log x_2) + ... + (\log x_T - \log x_{T-1}) \right]$$

$$= \frac{1}{T-1} \left[\log x_T - \log x_1 \right].$$

From (A1)-(A3) it can be easily shown that

$$Dw_{ic} = Dp_{ic} + Dq_{ic} - DM_c.$$

Thus

$$Dq_{ic} = Dw_{ic} - Dp_{ic} + DM_c. \tag{A4}$$

As LPW give no explicit information on quantities, we use (A4) to derive the average annual quantity log-changes presented in Table 1.4 of the text. Table 1.4 also contains the corresponding price log-changes.

REFERENCES

Aasness, J. and A. Rodseth (1983). 'Engel Curves and Systems of Demand Functions,' European Economic Review 20: 95-121.

Balassa, B. (1964). 'The Purchasing Power Parity: A Reappraisal,' Journal of Political Economy 72: 584-96.

Barnard, G.A. (1963). In discussion, Journal of the Royal Statistical Society, Series B, 25: 294.

Barnett, W.A. (1979). 'Theoretical Foundations for the Rotterdam Model,' Review of Economic Studies 46: 109-30.

Barten, A.P. (1964). 'Consumer Demand Functions Under Conditions of Almost Additive Preferences,' Econometrica 32: 1-38.

——————— (1977). 'The Systems of Consumer Demand Functions Approach: A Review,' Econometrica 45: 23-51.

Bera, A.K., R.P. Byron and C.M. Jarque (1981). 'Further Evidence on Asymptotic Tests for Homogeneity and Symmetry in Large Demand Systems,' Economics Letters 8: 101-5.

Bewley, R.A. (1983). 'Tests of Restrictions in Large Demand Systems,' European Economic Review 20: 257-69.

Blanciforti, L. and R. Green (1983). 'An Almost Ideal Demand System

Incorporating Habits: An Analysis of Expenditures on Food and Aggregate Commodity Groups,' Review of Economics and Statistics 65: 511-5.

Brown, A. and A.S. Deaton (1972). 'Surveys in Applied Economics: Models of Consumer Behaviour,' Economic Journal 82: 1145-236.

Chung,C.-F. and E. Lopez (1988). 'A Regional Analysis of Food Consumption in Spain,' Economics Letters 26: 209-13.

Clements, K.W. (1987). 'Alternative Approaches to Consumption Theory,' Chapter 1 in H. Theil and K.W. Clements, Applied Demand Analysis: Results from System-Wide Approaches. Cambridge, Mass.: Ballinger Publishing Company, 1-35.

Clements, K.W. and L.W. Johnson (1983). 'The Demand for Beer, Wine and Spirits: A System-Wide Analysis,' Journal of Business 56: 273-304.

Clements, K.W. and H. Theil (1979). 'A Cross-country Analysis of Consumption Patterns,' Report 7924 of the Center for Mathematical Studies in Business and Economics, University of Chicago.

Christensen, L.R., D.W. Jorgenson and L.J. Lau (1975). 'Transcendental Logarithmic Utility Functions,' American Economic Review 65: 367-83.

Deaton, A. (1975). Models and Projections of Demand in Post-War Britain. London: Chapman and Hall.

Deaton, A. and J. Muellbauer (1980a). 'An Almost Ideal Demand System,' American Economic Review 70: 312-26.

Diewert, W.E. (1974). 'The Applications of Duality Theory,' in M.D. Intriligator and D.A. Kendrick, <u>Frontiers of Quantitative Economics</u>, Vol.2, Amsterdam: North Holland.

Engel, E. (1857). 'Die Productions - Und Consumtionsverhältnisse des Könichreichs Sachsen,' <u>Zeitschrift des Statistischen Büreaus des Königlich Sächsischen Ministeriums des Innern</u> 8-9: 1-54. Reprinted in the <u>Bulletin de l'Institut International de Statistique</u> 9, 1895.

Finke, R., L.R. Flood and H. Theil (1984). 'Maximum Likelihood and Instrumental Variable Estimation of a Consumer Demand System for Japan and Sweden,' <u>Economics Letters</u> 15: 13-9.

Frisch, R. (1959). 'A Complete Scheme for Computing All Direct and Cross Demand Elasticities in a Model with Many Sectors,' <u>Econometrica</u> 27: 177-96.

Gamaletsos, T. (1973). 'Further Analysis of Cross-Country Comparison of Consumer Expenditure Patterns,' <u>European Economic Review</u> 4: 1-20.

Goldberger, A.S. and T. Gamaletsos (1970). 'A Cross-Country Comparison of Consumer Expenditure Patterns,' <u>European Economic Review</u> 1: 357-400.

Harberger, A.C. (1964). 'Taxation, Resource Allocation and Welfare,' in <u>The Role of Direct and Indirect Taxes in the Federal Revenue System</u>, J.Due (ed.), Princeton: Princeton University Press.

Houthakker, H.S. (1957). 'An International Comparison of Household Expenditure Patterns, Commemorating the Centenary of Engel's Law,' <u>Econometrica</u> 25: 532-51.

__________ (1965). 'New Evidence in Demand Elasticities,' Econometrica 33: 277-88.

Keller, W.J. and J. van Driel (1985). 'Differential Consumer Demand Systems,' European Economic Review 27: 375-90.

Klein, L.R. and H. Rubin (1948). 'A Constant-Utility Index of the Cost of Living,' Review of Economic Studies 15: 84-7.

Kravis, I.B., A.W. Heston and R. Summers (1978). International Comparisons of Real Product and Purchasing Power. Baltimore, Md.: The John Hopkins University Press.

__________ (1982). World Product and Income: International Comparisons of Real Gross Product. Baltimore, Md.: The John Hopkins University Press.

Laitinen, K. (1978). 'Why is Demand Homogeneity So Often Rejected?' Economics Letters 1: 187-91.

Leser, C.E.V. (1963). 'Forms of Engel Functions,' Econometrica 31: 694-703.

Lluch, C. (1973). 'The Extended Linear Expenditure System,' European Economic Review 4: 21-32.

Lluch, C. and A.A. Powell (1975). 'International Comparisons of Expenditure Patterns,' European Economic Review 5: 275-303.

Lluch, C., A.A. Powell and R.A. Williams (1977). Patterns in Household Demand and Saving. Oxford: Oxford University Press.

Lluch, C. and R.A. Williams (1975). 'Cross Country Demand and Savings Patterns: An Application of the Extended Linear Expenditure System,' <u>Review of Economics and Statistics</u> 57: 320-8.

Meisner, J.F. (1979). 'The Sad Fate of the Asymptotic Slutsky Symmetry Test for Large Systems,' <u>Economics Letters</u> 2: 231-33.

Mountain, D.C. (1988). 'The Rotterdam Model: An Approximation in Variable Space,' <u>Econometrics</u> 56: 477-84.

Musgrove, P. (1985). 'Household Food Consumption in the Dominican Republic: Effects of Income, Price and Family Size,' <u>Economic Development and Cultural Change</u> 34: 83-101.

Parks, R.W. (1969). 'Systems of Demand Equations: An Empirical Comparison of Alternative Functional Forms,' <u>Econometrica</u> 37: 629-50.

Parks, R.W. and A.P Barten (1973). 'Cross-Country Comparison of the Effects of Prices, Income and Population Composition on Consumption Patterns,' <u>Economic Journal</u> 83: 834-52.

Phlips, L. (1974). <u>Applied Consumption Analysis</u>. Amsterdam: North Holland Publishing Company.

Pollak, R.A. and T.J. Wales (1969). 'Estimation of the Linear Expenditure System,' <u>Econometrica</u> 37: 611-28.

——————————— (1987). 'Pooling International Consumption Data,' <u>Review of Economics and Statistics</u> 69: 90-9.

Powell, A.A. (1974). Empirical Analytics of Demand Systems. Lexington, Mass.: D.C. Health.

Selvanathan, E.A. (1987). Explorations in Consumer Demand. Ph.D. Thesis, Murdoch University, Western Australia.

————————— (1991). 'Further Results on Aggregation of Differential Demand Equations,' The Review of Economic Studies 58: 799-805.

Schultz, H., (1938). The Theory and Measurement of Demand. Chicago University Press.

Stigler, G.J. and G.S. Becker (1977). 'De Gustibus Non Est Disputandum,' American Economic Review 67: 76-90.

Stone, R. (1954a). The Measurement of Consumers' Expenditure and Behaviour in the United Kingdom, 1920-1938. Vol.1, Cambridge: Cambridge University Press.

————————— (1954b). 'Linear Expenditure Systems and Demand Analysis: An Application to the Pattern of British Demand,' Economic Journal 64: 511-27.

Summers, R. and A. Heston (1984). 'Improved International Comparisons of Real Product and its Composition: 1950-1980,' Review of Income and Wealth 30: 207-62.

Theil, H. (1965). 'The Information Approach to Demand Analysis,' Econometrica 33: 67-87.

——————— (1967). <u>Economics and Information Theory</u>. New York: American Elsevier Publishing Company.

——————— (1975/76). <u>Theory and Measurement of Consumer Demand</u>. 2 vols., Amsterdam: North Holland Publishing Company.

——————— (1980). <u>The System-wide Approach to Microeconomics</u>. Chicago: The University of Chicago Press.

——————— (1983). 'World Product and Income: A Review Article,' <u>Journal of Political Economy</u> 91: 505-17.

——————— (1987a). 'Evidence from International Consumption Comparisons,' Chapter 2 in H. Theil and K.W. Clements, <u>Applied Demand Analysis: Results from System-Wide Approaches</u>. Cambridge, Mass.: Ballinger Publishing Company, pp.37-100.

——————— (1987b). 'The Econometrics of Demand Systems,' Chapter 3 in H. Theil and K.W. Clements, <u>Applied Demand Analysis: Results from System-Wide Approaches</u>. Cambridge, Mass.: Ballinger Publishing Company, pp.101-162.

Theil, H. and R. Finke (1984). 'A Time-Series Analysis of a Demand System Based on Cross-Country Coefficient Estimates,' <u>Economics Letters</u> 15: 245-50.

Theil, H., J.L Seale and C.-F. Chung (1987). 'A Regional Analysis of Food Consumption in China,' <u>Empirical Economics</u>, forthcoming.

——————————————— (1989). International Evidence on Consumption Patterns in Advances in Econometrics, Supplement 1, London: JAI Press Inc.

Theil, H. and F.E. Suhm (1981). International Consumption Comparisons: A System-Wide Approach. Amsterdam: North-Holland Publishing Company.

Thomas, R.L. (1987). Applied Demand Analysis. London: Longman Group.

Working, H. (1943). 'Statistical Laws of Family Expenditure,' Journal of the American Statistical Association 38: 43-56.

Yoshihara, K. (1969). 'Demand Functions: An Application to the Japanese Expenditure Pattern,' Econometrica 37: 257-74.

CHAPTER 2

EMPIRICAL REGULARITIES IN OECD CONSUMPTION

2.1. INTRODUCTION

The textbook exposition of the theory of consumer demand typically emphasises two major results. First, that the demand curve slopes down so that a rise in the relative price of a good causes its consumption to fall, other factors remaining unchanged. Second, when discussing income elasticities and the luxury/necessity distinction, almost invariably food is mentioned as the leading example of a necessity. At the risk of oversimplification, these are the only two aspects highlighted.

One of the primary objectives of this chapter is to present evidence on these two 'stylized facts'. We do this by estimating demand equations for 10 broad commodity groups, not just for a single country but for 18 countries individually and combined. Such a large body of data should provide convincing evidence (one way or the other) about the validity of the two stylized facts of textbook consumption economics. In addition, we present summary measures of the data in each country in the form of Divisia index numbers.

In this chapter we also present new evidence regarding the interrelationship between income and price elasticities. In particular, we find that, on average, luxuries tend to be more price elastic than necessities. In addition, we introduce new nonparametric methods for describing the dependence of quantities on prices.

Our overall findings from the 18 countries can be summarized in the form of the following five empirical regularities:

(i)   Consumers tend to move away from those goods having above-average price increases. In other words, demand curves do indeed slope down.

(ii)   The variability of prices is less than the variability of quantities.

(iii)   Food and housing are necessities; durables are a luxury.

(iv)   Price elasticities tend to be less than one in absolute value.

(v)   Those commodities which are more price elastic also tend to be more luxurious and vice versa.

The structure of this chapter is as follows. In Section 2.2 we describe the database pertaining to 10 commodities in 18 OECD countries. Sections 2.3-2.5 present summary measures of the data in the form of budget shares, price and quantity log-changes, Divisia moments (Theil, 1967) and a graphical representation of the relative price and quantity log-changes. In Sections 2.6 and 2.7 we present a preliminary analysis of the data by estimating double-log demand equations for each country and for all countries combined, and by providing an analysis of the elasticity estimates. Sections 2.8 and 2.9 explore the interrelationships between the elasticities. Finally, in Sections 2.10 and 2.11 we present a nonparametric picture of the pattern of prices and quantities. This methodology allows the dependence of quantities on prices to be analysed from a new perspective.

2.2 THE OECD DATABASE

The basic data, consisting of annual consumption expenditures (in current and constant prices) and mid-year population for 18 OECD countries are from Stening (1985). These data are compiled mainly from the <u>Yearbook of National Accounts Statistics 1981</u> (United Nations: New York, 1983), Vol.1; <u>National Accounts of OECD Countries 1960-1977</u> (OECD: Paris, 1979), Vol.II; <u>National Accounts 1964-1981</u> (Department of Economics and Statistics, OECD: Paris, 1983), Vol II; and various issues of <u>Demographic Yearbook</u> (United Nations: New York). There are 25 OECD countries of which we omit 7 due to the unavailability of data. For most countries, goods and services are classified into 10 commodity groups, which we give in Table 2.1. For further details of the commodity classification, see   A System of National Accounts and Supporting Tables (Series F, No.2, New York: United Nations, 1964).

Table 2.2 summarizes the general characteristics of the database. Column 2 presents the sample period for each country and column 3 gives the sample size. In column 4 we present per capita gross domestic product (GDP) expressed in 1975 international dollars (from Summers and Heston, 1984). Column 5 gives per capita GDP in index form with U.S.= 100.   The 18 countries are listed in the order of declining per capita GDP.   As can be seen, the U.S. has the highest GDP per capita while Italy has the lowest, it being 54 percent of the U.S. value. Column 6 gives the number of commodity groups considered in each country.   All except three of the countries have 10 commodity groups. Germany and Japan have 8, as beverages are included in food and education is included in recreation.   Switzerland has 9 groups as education is included in recreation.

2.3 BUDGET SHARES AND PRICE AND QUANTITY LOG-CHANGES

Let p_{it} be the price and q_{it} the per capita quantity consumed of good i during year t ($t=1,...,T$, the sample size). Let there be n goods. Total expenditure is then $M_t = \Sigma_{i=1}^{n} p_{it}q_{it}$ and the proportion of total expenditure

TABLE 2.1

DETAILS OF THE COMMODITY GROUPS

Commodity	Details
1. Food	Food
2. Beverages	Non-alcoholic and alcoholic beverages and tobacco
3. Clothing	Clothing, footwear and other personal effects
4. Housing	Actual and imputed gross rents on owner occupied houses, rates and water charges, fuel and power
5. Durables	Furniture, furnishings and household equipment
6. Medical care	Personal care and health expenses
7. Transport	Transport and communication
8. Recreation	Recreation, entertainment and cultural services
9. Education	Education and research
10. Miscellaneous	Miscellaneous goods and services

devoted to commodity i is $w_{it} = p_{it}q_{it}/M_t$. This w_{it} is called the budget share

of good i.

Table 2.3 presents the budget shares at sample means,

$$\bar{w}_i = \frac{1}{T} \sum_{t=1}^{T} w_{it}$$

for each commodity in the 18 countries. For example, looking at the sixth row

of the table we see that, on average, Australians spend 19 percent of their total

TABLE 2.2

CHARACTERISTICS OF THE DATABASE

Country	Sample period	Sample size	Per capita GDP in 1975		Number of commodity groups	Comments
			International dollars	(4) with U.S.=100		
(1)	(2)	(3)	(4)	(5)	(6)	(7)
1. U.S.	1960–1981	21	7132	100	10	
2. Canada	1960–1981	21	6788	95	10	
3. Sweden	1964–1981	17	6749	95	10	
4. Switzerland	1960–1981	21	6082	85	9	Education is included in recreation
5. Denmark	1966–1981	15	5969	84	10	
6. Australia	1960–1981	21	5919	83	10	
7. France	1964–1981	17	5864	82	10	
8. Germany	1960–1981	21	5758	81	8	Beverages are included in food, and education is included in recreation
9. Belgium	1960–1981	21	5554	78	10	
10. Norway	1964–1981	17	5419	76	10	
11. Netherlands	1952–1977	25	5321	75	10	
12. Iceland	1960–1973	13	5201	73	10	
13. Finland	1960–1977	17	5192	73	10	
14. Austria	1964–1981	17	4994	70	10	
15. Japan	1970–1981	11	4905	69	8	Beverages are included in food, and education is included in recreation
16. U.K.	1964–1981	17	4601	65	10	
17. Spain	1964–1977	13	4032	57	10	
18. Italy	1964–1981	17	3870	54	10	

Note: Sample size is after lagging.

expenditure on food, 9 percent on beverages, 9 percent on clothing, 16 percent on housing and so on. The last row of the table presents the budget share of each commodity averaged over the 18 countries. As can be seen, an average OECD consumer spends 24 percent of his total expenditure on food. Food,

TABLE 2.3

BUDGET SHARES OF 10 COMMODITIES IN 18 COUNTRIES

(Means × 100)

Country	Food	Beverages	Clothing	Housing	Durables	Medical care	Transport	Recreation	Education	Miscellaneous
(1)	(2)	(3)	(4)	(5)	(6)	(7)	(8)	(9)	(10)	(11)
1. U.S.	14.38	4.24	8.03	19.29	7.28	9.46	15.93	6.25	1.81	13.33
2. Canada	16.42	6.21	8.41	18.85	8.73	3.84	15.02	5.96	2.33	14.22
3. Sweden	20.72	7.96	8.41	22.79	7.66	2.27	13.65	9.18	.18	7.18
4. Switzerland	22.73	9.42	6.77	18.06	7.80	6.52	10.99	9.36		8.35
5. Denmark	19.18	9.09	6.97	20.92	8.98	1.92	15.04	7.88	.83	9.19
6. Australia	19.48	8.96	9.13	15.77	8.19	6.04	15.13	5.71	.69	10.89
7. France	21.20	4.69	8.22	14.41	10.23	10.50	11.99	6.05	.29	12.42
8. Germany	30.38		10.36	15.79	12.04	2.68	13.06	7.44		8.55
9. Belgium	23.11	6.95	7.53	15.72	14.14	6.74	10.67	3.98	.23	10.93
10. Norway	23.45	7.56	9.97	14.54	8.86	4.20	13.31	7.68	.54	9.89
11. Netherlands	26.20	6.38	14.78	10.81	12.48	6.67	6.67	3.41	3.10	9.50
12. Iceland	23.50	7.86	10.66	19.06	10.00	6.07	12.13	5.24	.44	5.05
13. Finland	28.24	8.62	8.26	14.36	7.51	2.54	13.60	5.92	1.44	9.49
14. Austria	22.06	7.29	11.37	11.99	8.89	3.49	13.36	5.67	.35	15.54
15. Japan	27.45		7.76	16.78	6.76	8.92	8.97	0.05		14.32
16. U.K.	18.92	6.26	8.40	18.20	7.78	.85	13.13	7.88	1.98	16.50
17. Spain	38.53	3.51	10.58	13.99	8.55	4.62	9.50	4.28	2.02	0.07
18. Italy	30.85	5.69	9.41	12.94	6.79	3.73	10.48	7.05	.43	12.62
Mean	23.71	6.92	9.16	16.35	9.04	5.05	12.37	6.56	1.11	10.94

housing and transport in total occupy about 50 percent of the total in most countries.

The log-change in the price of i is defined as $Dp_{it} = \log p_{it} - \log p_{i,t-1}$. Similarly, $Dq_{it} = \log q_{it} - \log q_{i,t-1}$ is the quantity log-change. When multiplied by 100, these can be interpreted as percentage changes or percentage growth rates from year t-1 to t. Here and elsewhere, log refers to the natural logarithm. The Divisia price index is a budget-share-weighted average of the price log-changes,

$$DP_t = \sum_{i=1}^{n} \bar{w}_{it} Dp_{it},$$ (3.1)

where $\bar{w}_{it} = \frac{1}{2}(w_{it} + w_{i,t-1})$ is the arithmetic average of the budget share of commodity i in years t-1 and t. The arithmetic average is the obvious choice for the weight as it is the budget share mid-way between t-1 and t. The index (3.1) measures the overall growth in prices. The analogous Divisia volume index is defined as

$$DQ_t = \sum_{i=1}^{n} \bar{w}_{it} Dq_{it}.$$ (3.2)

This measures the overall growth in per capita consumption or the growth in real income. [It should be noted that Divisia (1925) originally defined indexes as line integrals. In (3.1) and (3.2) we use the widely-used discrete approximation of the continuous time Divisia indexes.]

Table 2.4 contains the mean price log-changes of each commodity,

$$D\bar{p}_i = \frac{1}{T} \sum_{t=1}^{T} Dp_{it}$$

TABLE 2.4

PRICES OF 10 COMMODITIES AND DIVISIA PRICE INDEX IN 18 COUNTRIES

(Mean Log-Changes × 100)

Country	Food	Beverages	Clothing	Housing	Durables	Medical care	Transport	Recreation	Education	Miscellaneous	Divisia price index
(1)	(2)	(3)	(4)	(5)	(6)	(7)	(8)	(9)	(10)	(11)	(12)
1. U.S.	5.00	4.85	3.29	4.67	4.25	5.81	4.87	3.56	5.91	5.37	4.78
2. Canada	6.15	4.71	3.87	5.18	4.49	4.96	4.72	3.89	8.43	6.73	5.27
3. Sweden	7.17	7.27	4.82	8.50	7.30	6.14	7.66	6.57	9.13	9.10	7.43
4. Switzerland	4.00	4.06	3.39	5.43	3.86	6.49	4.55	4.10		5.47	4.55
5. Denmark	8.69	6.68	6.57	11.43	8.55	8.91	8.79	7.62	9.54	9.30	8.90
6. Australia	6.05	6.58	6.12	7.43	4.33	8.42	6.31	6.97	8.38	7.53	6.58
7. France	7.30	6.47	6.74	8.80	6.76	6.99	8.13	6.13	9.02	8.28	7.48
8. Germany	3.23		3.67	5.57	3.04	5.58	4.13	3.74		4.61	3.96
9. Belgium	4.56	4.61	3.89	5.76	4.36	6.02	5.28	5.00	4.54	6.88	5.13
10. Norway	6.96	6.99	6.74	7.20	7.02	8.25	7.32	5.36	7.85	7.91	7.05
11. Netherlands	3.71	2.91	3.48	5.08	2.29	7.73	3.38	5.51	5.91	4.80	4.07
12. Iceland	13.74	11.25	9.69	11.66	10.13	14.10	11.25	12.66	12.78	11.48	11.79
13. Finland	7.75	6.87	6.09	5.90	6.25	6.22	7.16	6.32	9.44	8.17	7.02
14. Austria	4.57	2.93	3.67	7.49	3.59	8.94	6.12	4.21	4.20	6.53	5.28
15. Japan	7.61		7.99	7.58	6.71	7.36	8.70	7.35		8.00	7.85
16. U.K.	9.00	8.49	6.88	11.28	8.68	9.36	10.25	8.85	10.73	9.99	9.56
17. Spain	9.79	7.57	11.24	8.58	11.07	11.09	7.00	13.54	12.92	10.87	10.06
18. Italy	9.67	7.07	10.37	10.89	10.37	8.72	10.83	9.25	10.03	11.65	10.13
Mean	6.94	6.21	6.03	7.69	6.28	7.87	7.08	6.64	8.58	7.98	7.05

for all countries. The last column of that table presents the mean of the Divisia

price index for each country,

$$\mathrm{D\overline{P}} \; = \; \frac{1}{T} \sum_{t=1}^{T} \mathrm{DP}_{t}.$$

The last row of the table presents the mean price changes averaged over all countries. On average, the annual growth rates in prices lie between 6 and 9 percent and their weighted average is 7 percent.

Columns 2-11 of Table 2.5 present the mean log-changes in per capita consumption of each commodity,

$$D\bar{q}_i = \frac{1}{T} \sum_{t=1}^{T} Dq_{it}$$

for each of the 18 countries. Column 12 of that table presents the mean of the Divisia volume index,

$$D\bar{Q} = \frac{1}{T} \sum_{t=1}^{T} DQ_t$$

for each country. Looking at column 2 of Table 2.5 we see that per capita food consumption grows by .15 percent per annum in the UK while in Spain its growth rate is almost 20 times larger (2.8 percent per annum). The last row of the table presents the mean quantity log-changes and Divisia volume indexes averaged over all countries. As can be seen, transport and recreation have the highest average growth rates of 4.9 and 4.5 percent per annum, respectively, while food has the lowest growth rate of 1.4 percent per annum. Per capita consumption as a whole, as measured by the Divisia volume index, on average increases by 3.0 percent per annum.

TABLE 2.5

PER CAPITA QUANTITIES CONSUMED OF 10 COMMODITIES

AND DIVISIA VOLUME INDEX IN 18 COUNTRIES

(Mean Log-Changes × 100)

Country	Food	Beverages	Clothing	Housing	Durables	Medical care	Transport	Recreation	Education	Miscellaneous	Divisia volume index
(1)	(2)	(3)	(4)	(5)	(6)	(7)	(8)	(9)	(10)	(11)	(12)
1. U.S.	.60	1.41	2.33	2.97	1.64	4.49	2.80	4.10	3.33	1.77	2.43
2. Canada	.91	2.57	3.12	3.17	3.02	.22	4.17	6.27	4.20	2.79	2.87
3. Sweden	.50	.80	2.66	2.35	1.18	3.02	2.06	4.53	3.17	-.95	1.71
4. Switzerland	1.72	1.57	.75	2.08	.62	2.85	3.63	2.98		2.79	2.13
5. Denmark	.17	1.43	.59	3.23	-1.01	1.50	1.49	3.34	8.53	.75	1.42
6. Australia	1.35	1.03	.71	3.54	4.45	1.23	3.49	4.33	-2.40	1.95	2.37
7. France	1.62	1.37	1.71	4.89	3.31	6.68	4.65	5.37	2.43	3.20	3.57
8. Germany	2.02		2.36	3.24	3.51	1.45	5.69	3.90		3.77	3.15
9. Belgium	1.53	2.58	2.76	2.80	4.20	5.13	4.52	4.04	1.98	2.98	3.11
10. Norway	1.35	2.08	1.40	3.43	3.21	2.14	4.06	5.56	1.26	2.17	2.68
11. Netherlands	2.22	4.39	3.19	3.93	6.91	5.53	7.52	4.07	5.15	5.20	4.34
12. Iceland	1.64	5.11	5.65	2.54	8.12	7.20	8.58	5.92	4.54	8.56	5.07
13. Finland	1.77	4.89	1.62	3.60	5.41	6.43	6.48	6.18	-1.60	5.58	3.86
14. Austria	1.90	2.34	4.26	4.29	3.61	2.62	5.58	4.35	1.94	1.98	3.27
15. Japan	1.50		1.47	4.93	1.58	6.07	4.10	3.26		3.40	3.13
16. U.K.	.15	1.48	2.52	1.87	1.58	.90	2.81	3.65	2.10	1.70	1.76
17. Spain	2.82	4.01	3.00	3.79	3.44	9.24	10.66	5.31	4.24	5.72	4.40
18. Italy	2.20	3.15	2.81	2.80	3.50	6.82	5.71	3.98	1.61	3.65	3.33
Mean	1.44	2.51	2.39	3.30	3.26	4.08	4.89	4.51	2.70	3.17	3.04

2.4 DIVISIA MOMENTS

Tables 2.6 and 2.7 present the Divisia price and volume indexes for each year for the 18 countries. The means of these indexes given in the last rows of the tables are identical to those presented in column 12 of Tables 2.4 and 2.5.

The Divisia variances of the price and quantity log-changes are

$$\Pi_t = \sum_{i=1}^{n} \overline{w}_{it}(Dp_{it} - DP_t)^2$$

and

$$K_t = \sum_{i=1}^{n} \overline{w}_{it}(Dq_{it} - DQ_t)^2.$$

These variances measure the degree to which the prices and quantities of the individual goods change disproportionately. When all the prices and quantities change proportionately, these two variances vanish. For brevity, we shall refer to Π_t and K_t as the Divisia price and quantity variances. Tables 2.8 and 2.9 present these variances. Comparing these two tables, we see that the Divisia quantity variances systematically exceed the corresponding price variances. This pattern agrees with the results of Clements (1982,1983), Meisner (1979), Selvanathan (1987) and Theil and Suhm (1981).

TABLE 2.6

DIVISIA PRICE INDEXES IN 18 COUNTRIES

Year	U.S.	Canada	Sweden	Switzerland	Denmark	Australia	France	Germany	Belgium	Norway	Netherlands	Iceland	Finland	Austria	Japan	U.K.	Spain	Italy
(1)	(2)	(3)	(4)	(5)	(6)	(7)	(8)	(9)	(10)	(11)	(12)	(13)	(14)	(15)	(16)	(17)	(18)	(19)
1953	–	–	–	–	–	–	–	–	–	–	-.62	–	–	–	–	–	–	–
1954	–	–	–	–	–	–	–	–	–	–	3.43	–	–	–	–	–	–	–
1955	–	–	–	–	–	–	–	–	–	–	1.10	–	–	–	–	–	–	–
1956	–	–	–	–	–	–	–	–	–	–	.88	–	–	–	–	–	–	–
1957	–	–	–	–	–	–	–	–	–	–	5.54	–	–	–	–	–	–	–
1958	–	–	–	–	–	–	–	–	–	–	1.28	–	–	–	–	–	–	–
1959	–	–	–	–	–	–	–	–	–	–	.61	–	–	–	–	–	–	–
1960	–	–	–	–	–	–	–	–	–	–	1.24	–	–	–	–	–	–	–
1961	1.19	.55	–	2.69	–	.39	–	3.32	2.77	–	1.40	8.99	1.66	–	–	–	–	–
1962	1.48	1.21	–	4.92	–	1.77	–	3.14	1.03	–	1.52	10.25	3.07	–	–	–	–	–
1963	1.47	1.52	–	3.51	–	.50	–	2.92	3.61	–	2.07	9.22	5.24	–	–	–	–	–
1964	1.45	1.27	–	4.04	–	3.13	–	2.37	3.99	–	6.10	14.98	7.94	–	–	–	–	–
1965	1.67	1.96	5.38	3.91	–	3.29	2.64	3.12	4.44	4.13	3.31	9.32	3.48	4.37	–	4.82	9.18	3.51
1966	2.70	3.32	6.31	4.65	–	2.96	3.17	3.58	4.12	3.33	5.57	10.28	2.75	2.44	–	3.92	6.97	2.82
1967	2.41	3.48	5.11	4.36	6.55	3.48	3.10	1.62	2.45	4.44	3.21	4.10	4.80	3.88	–	2.61	5.61	3.00
1968	3.95	4.00	1.51	2.57	7.54	3.19	4.94	1.62	2.70	3.01	3.02	11.93	9.68	2.48	–	4.39	5.03	1.42
1969	4.38	3.77	3.21	2.69	4.60	3.13	6.85	2.09	2.97	3.43	6.43	18.89	2.04	3.33	–	5.43	3.34	2.82
1970	4.45	3.44	4.91	3.86	6.93	5.80	4.85	3.73	2.48	9.50	2.92	10.86	2.19	3.71	6.17	5.79	6.37	4.88
1971	4.34	2.47	7.77	6.84	7.74	6.57	5.37	5.46	4.93	6.23	7.22	8.32	5.65	4.98	6.28	8.26	7.71	5.33
1972	3.51	4.08	6.48	7.43	7.89	6.12	5.71	5.40	5.27	6.49	6.86	13.28	6.69	6.28	5.28	6.42	7.99	6.21
1973	5.47	7.12	7.05	8.96	10.32	11.75	6.61	7.15	5.91	7.43	7.74	22.82	9.72	7.03	10.00	8.33	10.87	11.77
1974	9.55	10.86	8.71	9.65	13.65	15.95	12.44	6.69	11.54	8.86	8.72	–	14.91	9.88	19.60	15.94	16.11	19.05
1975	7.36	10.13	10.29	6.37	9.57	14.01	10.83	5.65	11.97	11.26	8.66	–	15.48	7.82	10.98	21.11	14.52	16.32
1976	5.36	7.79	10.17	2.40	9.39	10.97	9.38	4.27	7.60	8.48	8.13	–	12.69	6.56	8.47	14.45	15.51	16.60
1977	5.82	7.56	9.92	1.11	9.23	9.01	8.65	3.56	6.76	8.28	5.47	–	11.41	5.60	6.91	14.18	21.55	16.75
1978	6.73	7.14	10.31	1.16	8.72	8.50	8.46	2.59	4.06	7.68	–	–	–	4.08	4.73	8.68	–	12.07
1979	8.62	8.89	7.07	4.18	9.69	9.72	9.90	4.06	3.66	4.59	–	–	–	4.19	3.32	12.39	–	13.91
1980	9.99	10.12	11.08	4.09	10.55	9.10	12.37	5.21	6.74	9.50	–	–	–	6.46	6.36	15.32	–	18.36
1981	8.57	10.84	10.97	6.13	11.19	8.88	11.83	5.56	8.77	13.18	–	–	–	6.71	4.47	10.51	–	17.47
Mean	4.78	5.27	7.43	4.55	8.90	6.58	7.48	3.96	6.13	7.05	4.07	11.79	7.02	5.28	7.85	9.56	10.06	10.13

All entries are to be divided by 100.

TABLE 2.7

DIVISIA VOLUME INDEXES IN 18 COUNTRIES

Year	U.S.	Canada	Sweden	Switzerland	Denmark	Australia	France	Germany	Belgium	Norway	Netherlands	Iceland	Finland	Austria	Japan	U.K.	Spain	Italy
(1)	(2)	(3)	(4)	(5)	(6)	(7)	(8)	(9)	(10)	(11)	(12)	(13)	(14)	(15)	(16)	(17)	(18)	(19)
1953	–	–	–	–	–	–	–	–	–	–	6.46	–	–	–	–	–	–	–
1954	–	–	–	–	–	–	–	–	–	–	7.11	–	–	–	–	–	–	–
1955	–	–	–	–	–	–	–	–	–	–	5.00	–	–	–	–	–	–	–
1956	–	–	–	–	–	–	–	–	–	–	7.62	–	–	–	–	–	–	–
1957	–	–	–	–	–	–	–	–	–	–	-1.27	–	–	–	–	–	–	–
1958	–	–	–	–	–	–	–	–	–	–	-2.14	–	–	–	–	–	–	–
1959	–	–	–	–	–	–	–	–	–	–	4.54	–	–	–	–	–	–	–
1960	–	–	–	–	–	–	–	–	–	–	5.98	–	–	–	–	–	–	–
1961	.37	-.71	–	5.22	–	.66	–	4.03	1.24	–	5.09	-1.60	6.93	–	–	–	–	–
1962	2.96	3.08	–	3.47	–	2.99	–	3.59	3.37	–	5.26	7.10	5.19	–	–	–	–	–
1963	2.36	3.11	–	2.52	–	5.22	–	1.35	3.48	–	7.77	7.78	2.86	–	–	–	–	–
1964	3.97	3.77	–	2.93	–	2.79	–	4.33	1.67	–	3.74	4.63	4.38	–	–	–	–	–
1965	4.27	4.05	2.92	2.15	–	.95	3.12	5.22	3.23	1.54	6.11	3.50	4.69	4.06	–	.79	5.73	2.95
1966	3.91	3.10	.87	1.84	–	2.97	3.92	1.94	2.52	2.96	1.29	10.06	2.33	2.77	–	1.40	5.72	6.42
1967	1.77	3.92	1.41	1.68	2.35	4.18	3.69	.96	2.28	2.64	2.92	.59	1.85	1.82	–	1.83	4.80	6.16
1968	4.43	2.06	3.47	2.52	.75	4.18	2.79	4.12	5.07	2.69	4.66	-4.24	.41	3.59	–	2.95	4.72	4.28
1969	2.65	2.83	3.64	4.10	5.56	4.35	5.84	6.17	4.69	6.88	5.88	-4.45	9.77	2.86	–	.26	5.64	5.71
1970	1.14	1.00	1.99	2.95	2.05	2.32	3.65	6.93	4.39	-.50	6.86	14.16	7.43	5.79	–	2.95	3.05	6.39
1971	2.74	6.36	-.86	3.43	-.61	.43	5.14	3.72	4.19	3.80	3.08	14.00	3.00	6.89	4.46	2.81	3.80	2.24
1972	4.91	5.97	2.80	4.29	1.16	3.35	5.02	3.73	5.60	2.03	3.81	7.43	7.97	5.86	7.64	5.36	6.83	2.60
1973	2.89	5.36	2.89	1.70	4.47	2.43	4.58	1.15	7.05	2.05	4.21	6.96	5.67	3.75	7.58	4.49	6.62	4.63
1974	-1.48	3.52	4.52	-.68	-2.77	1.55	2.43	.51	2.95	2.80	2.54	–	3.10	.31	-1.91	-1.55	4.07	1.60
1975	1.18	2.99	2.57	-2.29	2.91	2.39	2.73	3.73	.10	3.85	3.64	–	2.82	3.41	2.86	-.44	1.31	-2.20
1976	4.49	4.59	3.48	1.72	7.03	1.58	5.01	4.27	4.78	5.13	4.56	–	-.26	3.49	2.26	.69	3.50	2.83
1977	3.64	1.47	-1.37	3.15	1.52	.27	2.73	3.66	2.31	5.73	3.75	–	-2.48	4.05	2.59	.19	1.43	1.73
1978	3.11	1.78	-.93	1.16	.21	2.11	4.21	3.73	2.30	-2.10	–	–	–	-.38	3.43	4.97	–	2.56
1979	1.54	1.77	2.46	.80	.76	.89	3.02	2.66	4.37	3.64	–	–	–	4.41	4.87	4.24	–	4.87
1980	-.81	.04	-.10	2.00	-3.55	2.06	1.20	1.25	1.02	1.96	–	–	–	1.89	.69	-1.00	–	4.03
1981	.94	.28	-.77	.12	-.50	2.08	1.70	-.93	-1.34	.42	–	–	–	1.06	-.03	.04	–	-.11
Mean	2.43	2.87	1.71	2.13	1.42	2.37	3.57	3.15	3.11	2.68	4.34	5.07	3.86	3.27	3.13	1.76	4.40	3.33

All entries are to be divided by 100.

TABLE 2.8

DIVISIA PRICE VARIANCES IN 18 COUNTRIES

Year	U.S.	Canada	Sweden	Switzerland	Denmark	Australia	France	Germany	Belgium	Norway	Netherlands	Iceland	Finland	Austria	Japan	U.K.	Spain	Italy
(1)	(2)	(3)	(4)	(5)	(6)	(7)	(8)	(9)	(10)	(11)	(12)	(13)	(14)	(15)	(16)	(17)	(18)	(19)
1953	–	–	–	–	–	–	–	–	–	–	.34	–	–	–	–	–	–	–
1954	–	–	–	–	–	–	–	–	–	–	1.18	–	–	–	–	–	–	–
1955	–	–	–	–	–	–	–	–	–	–	.21	–	–	–	–	–	–	–
1956	–	–	–	–	–	–	–	–	–	–	.93	–	–	–	–	–	–	–
1957	–	–	–	–	–	–	–	–	–	–	.49	–	–	–	–	–	–	–
1958	–	–	–	–	–	–	–	–	–	–	.84	–	–	–	–	–	–	–
1959	–	–	–	–	–	–	–	–	–	–	.09	–	–	–	–	–	–	–
1960	–	–	–	–	–	–	–	–	–	–	.86	–	–	–	–	–	–	–
1961	.03	.08	–	.25	–	.72	–	.45	1.82	–	.10	1.39	.28	–	–	–	–	–
1962	.07	.07	–	.12	–	.95	–	.17	.59	–	.08	3.56	.38	–	–	–	–	–
1963	.03	.15	–	.24	–	.89	–	.18	.96	–	.18	3.18	.47	–	–	–	–	–
1964	.82	.17	–	.26	–	.27	–	.21	.18	–	.67	2.29	1.39	–	–	–	–	–
1965	.04	.19	.17	.32	–	.47	.17	.18	.53	.19	.37	1.00	.87	.35	–	.38	.97	.15
1966	.22	.35	.32	.15	–	.13	.18	.23	.65	.20	.64	2.03	.39	.24	–	.13	.20	.08
1967	.26	.34	.32	.50	1.15	.19	.32	.41	.22	.37	.95	.26	.56	.50	–	.11	.72	.18
1968	.11	.31	.15	.46	.64	.22	.38	.90	.15	.12	.45	.92	3.36	.58	–	.20	.91	.19
1969	.12	.22	.51	.29	.38	.63	.15	.29	.14	.16	.57	6.08	.05	.19	–	.08	.72	.05
1970	.07	.40	.19	.25	.62	.52	.11	.09	.49	.32	.79	2.45	.22	3.16	–	.17	.88	.13
1971	.16	.34	.21	.22	.68	.56	.10	.19	.36	.22	.97	2.16	.17	.51	.39	.29	.37	.23
1972	.15	.35	.42	.41	.50	.16	.14	.08	.45	.08	.67	3.79	.33	.34	.41	.47	.84	.34
1973	1.48	1.71	.39	.59	1.25	.96	.28	.04	.51	.09	.49	2.69	.25	.69	1.68	.99	.59	.52
1974	.62	1.07	2.19	.23	1.09	1.54	.74	.43	.76	.45	1.02	–	1.84	1.04	2.82	.46	.88	1.77
1975	.33	.47	.34	.25	.24	1.65	.20	.05	.88	.90	.90	–	1.87	.37	.75	1.01	.54	.91
1976	.44	.95	.27	.72	.79	.66	.25	.06	.54	.07	55	–	.91	.52	.47	.36	1.11	1.13
1977	.30	.83	.42	.02	.34	.44	.28	.11	.51	.07	64	–	1.45	.35	.40	.18	1.56	.67
1978	.40	.98	.62	.41	.30	.77	.06	.08	.27	.32	–	–	–	.45	.81	.40	–	.43
1979	.47	.27	.64	.85	1.83	.42	.24	.43	.76	.25	–	–	–	.40	.24	.54	–	.46
1980	.96	.13	.47	.25	.79	.35	1.01	.16	1.76	.55	–	–	–	.51	.42	1.17	–	1.00
1981	.40	.53	.42	.28	.43	.29	.20	.23	3.45	1.10	–	–	–	.69	.03	2.20	–	.16
Mean	.36	.47	.47	.34	.73	.61	.28	.24	.81	.32	.60	2.45	.87	.64	.77	.54	.79	.49

All entries are to be divided by 1000.

INTERNATIONAL CONSUMPTION PATTERNS

TABLE 2.9

DIVISIA QUANTITY VARIANCES IN 18 COUNTRIES

Year	U.S.	Canada	Sweden	Switzerland	Denmark	Australia	France	Germany	Belgium	Norway	Netherlands	Iceland	Finland	Austria	Japan	U.K.	Spain	Italy
(1)	(2)	(3)	(4)	(5)	(6)	(7)	(8)	(9)	(10)	(11)	(12)	(13)	(14)	(15)	(16)	(17)	(18)	(19)
1953	–	–	–	–	–	–	–	–	–	–	2.10	–	–	–	–	–	–	–
1954	–	–	–	–	–	–	–	–	–	–	1.94	–	–	–	–	–	–	–
1955	–	–	–	–	–	–	–	–	–	–	2.21	–	–	–	–	–	–	–
1956	–	–	–	–	–	–	–	–	–	–	1.86	–	–	–	–	–	–	–
1957	–	–	–	–	–	–	–	–	–	–	1.16	–	–	–	–	–	–	–
1958	–	–	–	–	–	–	–	–	–	–	2.35	–	–	–	–	–	–	–
1959	–	–	–	–	–	–	–	–	–	–	1.42	–	–	–	–	–	–	–
1960	–	–	–	–	–	–	–	–	–	–	.60	–	–	–	–	–	–	–
1961	.63	8.64	–	.89	–	.55	–	.62	1.45	–	.60	2.69	2.07	–	–	–	–	–
1962	.72	.57	–	.65	–	2.35	–	.81	.25	–	.68	7.51	1.29	–	–	–	–	–
1963	.44	.63	–	.28	–	3.22	–	.51	.52	–	.48	11.38	1.74	–	–	–	–	–
1964	.34	.47	–	.66	–	.48	–	.56	1.23	–	3.35	5.52	3.86	–	–	–	–	–
1965	.30	.63	.83	.30	–	.19	.52	.81	.50	.54	2.18	1.41	4.49	.84	–	.66	1.72	.50
1966	.46	.87	.71	.30	–	.57	.41	.18	.31	.28	1.98	4.23	.76	.90	–	.16	4.23	.52
1967	.15	.50	.49	.21	.42	.65	.33	.34	.42	.52	1.71	2.69	.93	.30	–	.32	.70	1.06
1968	.59	.61	1.31	.15	.54	.85	.29	.64	.78	.52	1.33	8.39	.75	.31	–	.30	1.75	.10
1969	.55	.35	.76	.21	1.19	1.10	.50	1.91	.52	2.32	2.41	3.33	3.80	.56	–	.24	.97	.73
1970	.69	1.82	.53	.11	.94	.28	.57	1.10	.24	2.61	1.88	19.19	.95	1.60	–	.43	.40	.59
1971	.92	2.51	1.38	.22	1.09	.37	.63	.28	.74	1.02	1.06	8.40	1.06	2.36	.66	.98	.88	.40
1972	.65	1.51	.83	.17	.86	.38	.55	.26	.99	.94	2.86	4.32	1.79	2.39	.49	1.94	2.67	.60
1973	1.31	2.35	1.06	.73	1.17	2.52	.75	.95	2.10	.43	1.61	1.80	2.43	.60	1.29	1.02	1.11	1.03
1974	1.55	1.96	1.45	.93	3.82	1.49	1.19	.62	1.81	.51	1.74	–	2.52	1.16	3.31	1.11	.89	.77
1975	.68	.23	.32	1.78	2.08	1.54	.75	1.21	2.04	.73	4.38	–	2.95	.45	1.59	.21	.48	.97
1976	.54	.35	.40	.47	1.64	.58	.99	.69	.75	1.39	.52	–	3.15	.61	1.06	.16	.28	.32
1977	.31	.67	.73	.35	.55	.56	.44	.88	1.07	1.30	1.49	–	2.04	2.32	.63	.44	.39	.56
1978	.54	.61	.58	.46	.88	.99	.69	.18	.57	2.85	–	–	–	2.21	.97	.71	–	.15
1979	.36	.27	.13	.21	.33	.25	.32	.16	.88	.72	–	–	–	.82	.87	.32	–	.66
1980	1.21	.38	.46	.13	1.96	.44	.55	.26	1.75	.68	–	–	–	.50	1.41	.41	–	.31
1981	.26	.23	.61	.34	.44	.16	.41	.43	.75	1.21	–	–	–	.45	1.07	.52	–	.69
Mean	.63	1.25	.74	.45	1.19	.93	.58	.64	.94	1.09	1.78	6.22	2.15	1.08	1.21	.58	1.27	.59

All entries are to be divided by 1000.

The associated Divisia price-quantity covariance is

$$\Gamma_t = \sum_{i=1}^{n} \bar{w}_{it}(Dp_{it} - DP_t)(Dq_{it} - DQ_t).$$

This measures the co-movement of the prices and quantities. The corresponding correlation is defined as

$$\rho_t = \frac{\Gamma_t}{\sqrt{\Pi_t K_t}}.$$

This is known as the Divisia price-quantity correlation.

Table 2.10 presents the Divisia price-quantity correlations. As can be seen, 241 of the 322 correlations are negative which is about 75 percent. The last row of the table shows that, on average, the correlations are all negative for each country. This reflects the tendency of the consumer to move away from those commodities having above-average price increases.

2.5 RELATIVE PRICES AND CONSUMPTION

The log-change in the relative price of commodity i from year t-1 to t is defined as $D(p_{it}/P_t) = Dp_{it} - DP_t$. The corresponding relative quantity

TABLE 2.10

DIVISIA PRICE–QUANTITY CORRELATIONS IN 18 COUNTRIES

Year	U.S.	Canada	Sweden	Switzerland	Denmark	Australia	France	Germany	Belgium	Norway	Netherlands	Iceland	Finland	Austria	Japan	U.K.	Spain	Italy
(1)	(2)	(3)	(4)	(5)	(6)	(7)	(8)	(9)	(10)	(11)	(12)	(13)	(14)	(15)	(16)	(17)	(18)	(19)
1953	—	—	—	—	—	—	—	—	—	—	-.45	—	—	—	—	—	—	—
1954	—	—	—	—	—	—	—	—	—	—	-.88	—	—	—	—	—	—	—
1955	—	—	—	—	—	—	—	—	—	—	.21	—	—	—	—	—	—	—
1956	—	—	—	—	—	—	—	—	—	—	-.95	—	—	—	—	—	—	—
1957	—	—	—	—	—	—	—	—	—	—	.33	—	—	—	—	—	—	—
1958	—	—	—	—	—	—	—	—	—	—	.13	—	—	—	—	—	—	—
1959	—	—	—	—	—	—	—	—	—	—	-.64	—	—	—	—	—	—	—
1960	—	—	—	—	—	—	—	—	—	—	-.33	—	—	—	—	—	—	—
1961	.45	.01	—	-.32	—	-.11	—	-.40	-.97	—	-.67	-.27	-.57	—	—	—	—	—
1962	.33	-.69	—	-.61	—	.06	—	-.69	-.38	—	-.01	-.65	-.06	—	—	—	—	—
1963	.10	-.69	—	-.55	—	-.22	—	.74	.59	—	-.82	-.70	.30	—	—	—	—	—
1964	-.08	-.45	—	-.39	—	-.87	—	-.71	.31	—	-.57	-.49	-.72	—	—	—	—	—
1965	.10	-.31	-.38	-.59	—	-.01	.42	-.73	-.04	.05	-.38	-.35	-.57	-.78	—	-.21	-.58	.08
1966	-.30	-.57	.15	.13	—	.61	.15	.10	-.31	-.16	-.43	-.62	.22	.54	—	.15	-.58	-.15
1967	-.06	.22	-.23	.19	-.12	-.29	.63	.12	-.21	-.36	-.14	.17	.50	.11	—	.27	-.08	-.13
1968	-.18	-.37	-.19	.61	.69	.05	.20	.11	.29	-.87	-.25	-.46	-.53	.15	—	.41	-.78	.01
1969	-.22	.07	-.47	-.07	-.52	-.74	.44	-.62	-.58	-.67	-.02	-.80	-.25	-.20	—	-.01	.34	-.66
1970	.45	-.06	-.36	-.47	-.10	-.26	.43	-.10	-.25	-.26	-.51	-.16	-.07	-.36	—	-.02	-.30	-.36
1971	.67	.17	-.66	-.06	.19	-.48	-.09	-.07	.27	-.23	-.44	.30	.05	-.42	-.04	.23	.24	.34
1972	-.82	-.65	-.70	-.08	-.71	-.50	-.87	-.89	-.48	-.28	.16	-.61	-.25	-.39	-.27	-.60	-.61	-.60
1973	-.97	-.78	-.64	.37	-.75	-.65	-.77	-.57	-.56	-.45	-.66	-.55	-.43	-.34	-.34	-.90	-.69	-.58
1974	-.59	-.77	-.20	-.26	-.35	-.53	-.62	-.20	-.46	-.08	-.37	—	-.46	-.10	-.75	-.76	-.54	-.63
1975	-.59	-.62	-.56	-.09	-.13	-.67	.04	-.06	.02	-.87	-.49	—	-.32	.38	.34	-.05	-.19	-.52
1976	.08	-.55	-.43	.29	-.59	-.31	-.11	.14	-.38	-.32	-.21	—	-.65	.27	-.74	-.28	.57	.23
1977	.04	-.76	-.61	-.41	-.46	.34	-.58	-.77	.65	.45	-.80	—	-.37	-.55	.29	-.29	-.01	-.31
1978	-.88	-.88	-.16	-.72	-.53	-.58	-.05	-.22	-.11	-.23	—	—	—	.03	-.19	-.36	—	-.30
1979	-.70	-.69	-.44	-.59	.28	.00	-.22	-.10	-.31	-.04	—	—	—	.25	.07	.06	—	-.04
1980	-.70	-.46	-.56	-.42	-.07	-.77	-.48	-.69	-.82	-.49	—	—	—	.00	-.67	-.26	—	.42
1981	-.19	-.67	-.14	-.77	-.28	.04	-.60	-.35	-.70	-.85	—	—	—	-.83	.22	-.26	—	-.03
Mean	-.19	-.45	-.39	-.23	-.23	-.28	-.12	-.28	-.21	-.33	-.37	-.40	-.25	-.13	-.19	-.17	-.25	-.19

log-change is $D(q_{it}/Q_t) = Dq_{it} - DQ_t$. In this section we present the distributions of the relative price and quantity log-changes.

Figures 2.1 and 2.2 present the relative price and quantity log-changes for all commodities in all years in 18 countries. The total number of observations plotted in each figure is $\sum_{c=1}^{18} n^c T^c = 3135$; where n^c is the number of commodities in country c and T^c is the sample size of country c. Figures 2.3-2.22 present the frequency distributions of the relative price and quantity log-changes for each of the 10 commodities individually in all years in 18 countries. Here there are 322 observations in each figure except for beverages and education; beverages has 290 observations while education has 269. We also present their means and standard deviations. These means differ from those which can be derived from the entries in the last rows of Tables 2.4 and 2.5 since for a certain commodity, the former is averaged over time and countries concurrently while the latter is first averaged over time in each country and then averaged over countries. These values are not equal since the sample size T^c of country c varies for each country, so that

$$\frac{1}{\sum_{c=1}^{18} T^c} \sum_{c=1}^{18} \sum_{t=1}^{T^c} (Dq_{it}^c - DQ_t^c) \neq \frac{1}{18} \sum_{c=1}^{18} \frac{1}{T^c} \sum_{t=1}^{T^c} (Dq_{it}^c - DQ_t^c),$$

where the superscript c denotes country c.

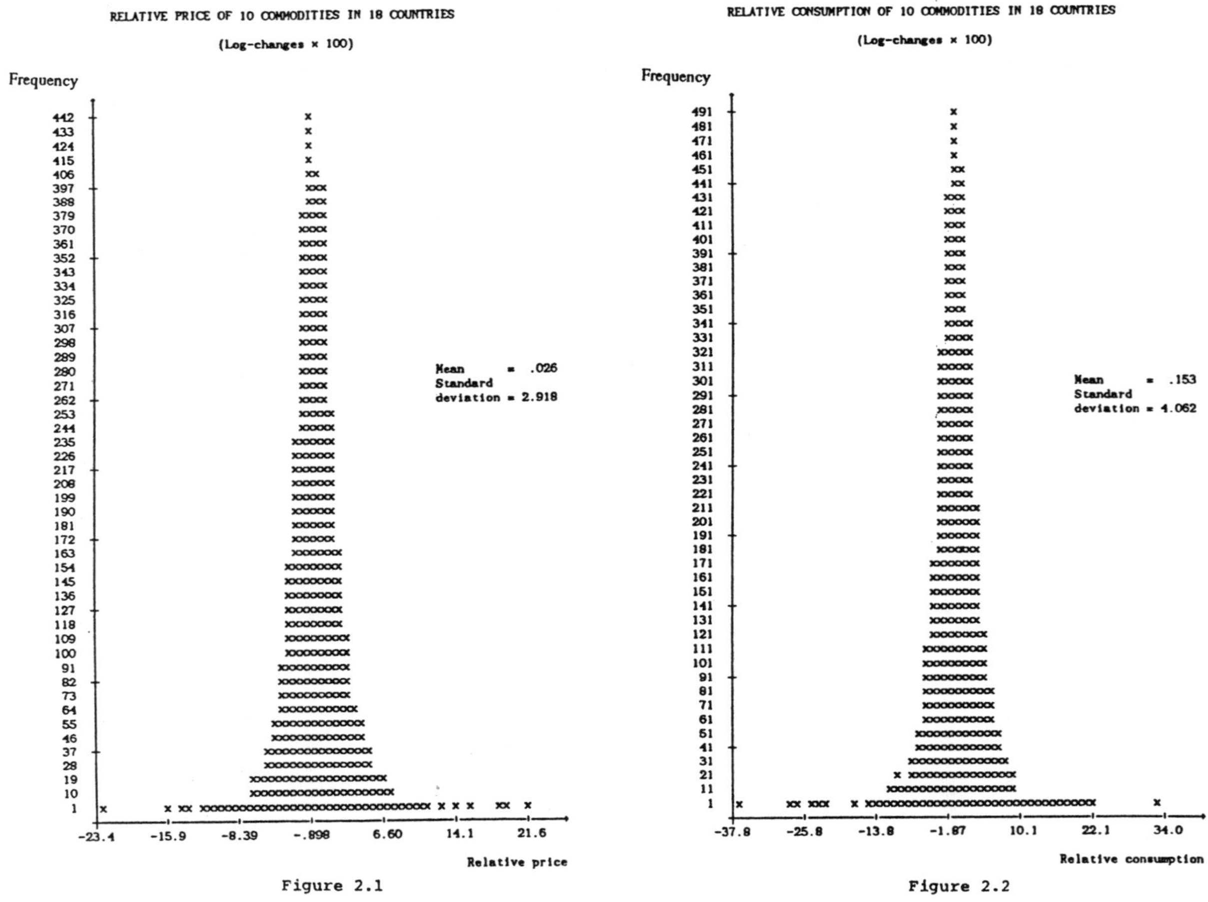

Figure 2.1   Figure 2.2

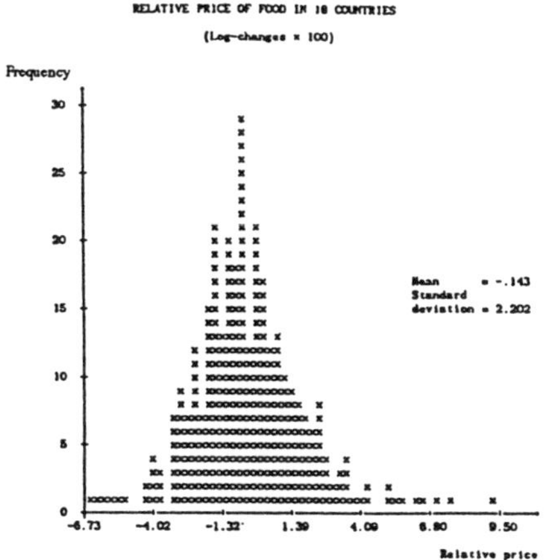

Figure 2.3

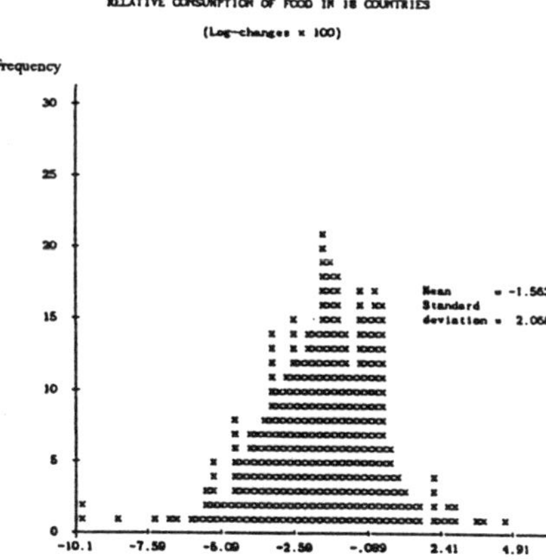

Figure 2.4

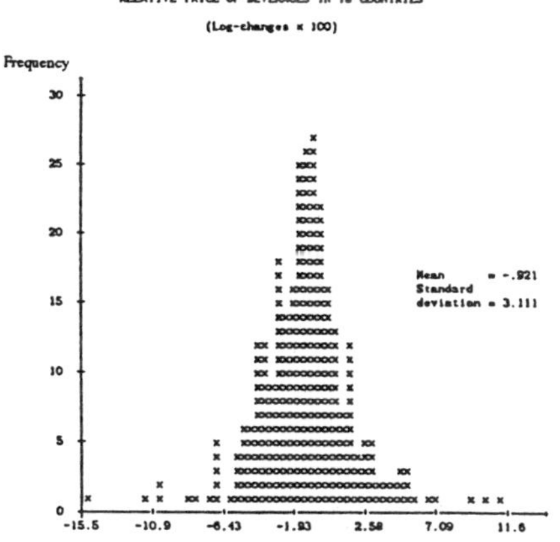

Figure 2.5

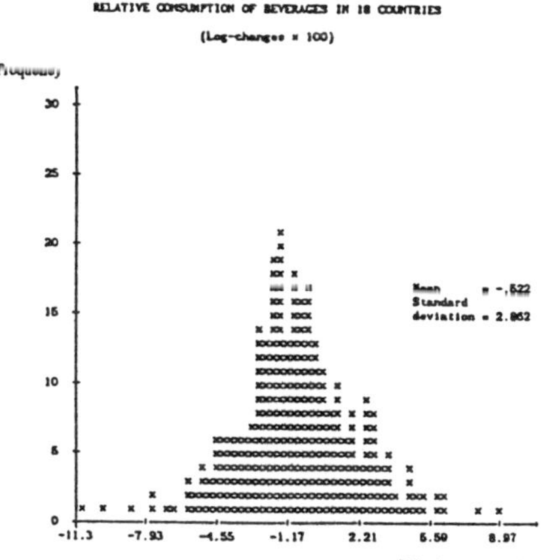

Figure 2.6

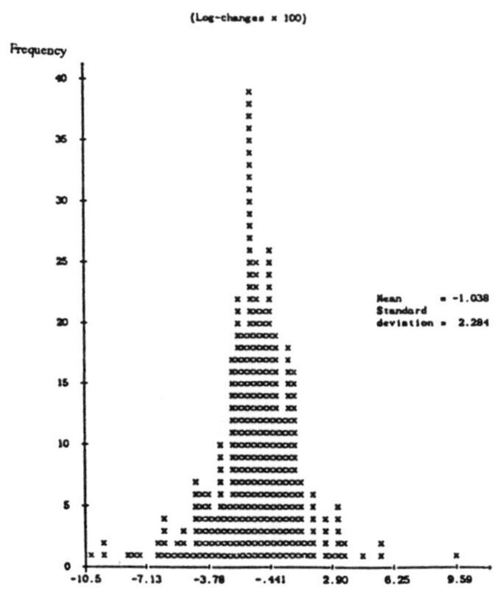

Figure 2.7

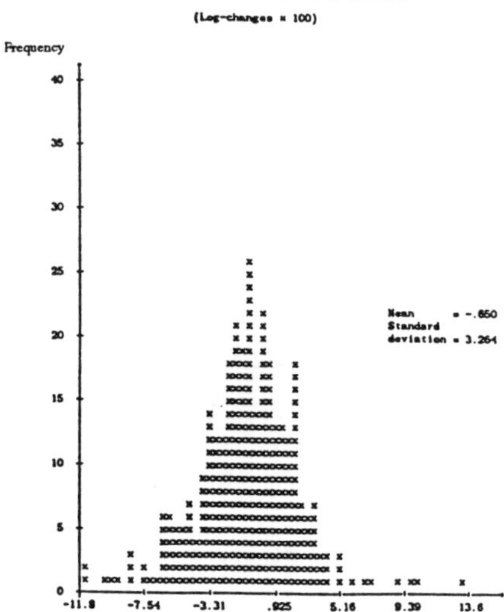

Figure 2.8

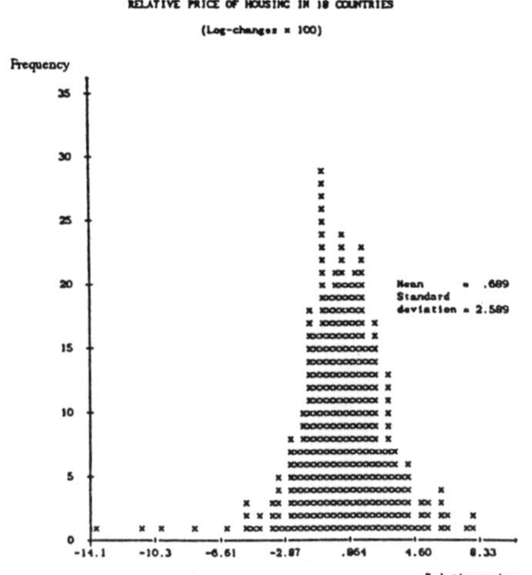

Figure 2.9

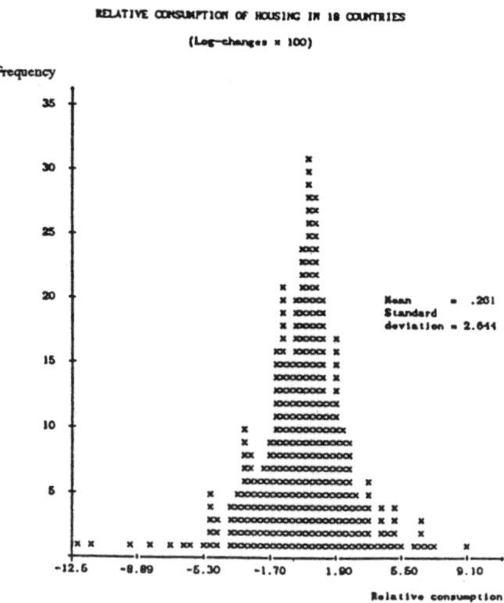

Figure 2.10

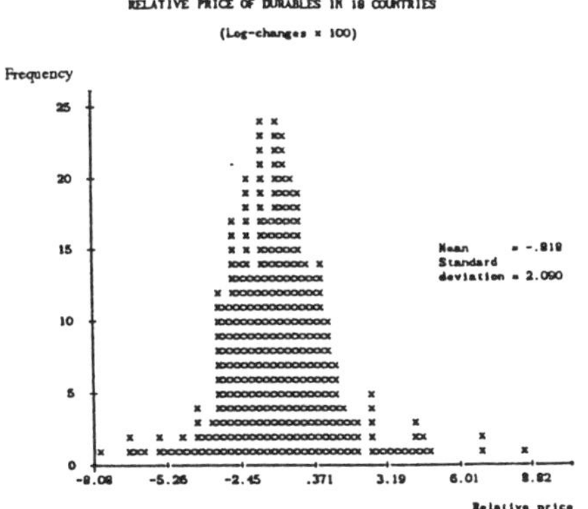

Figure 2.11

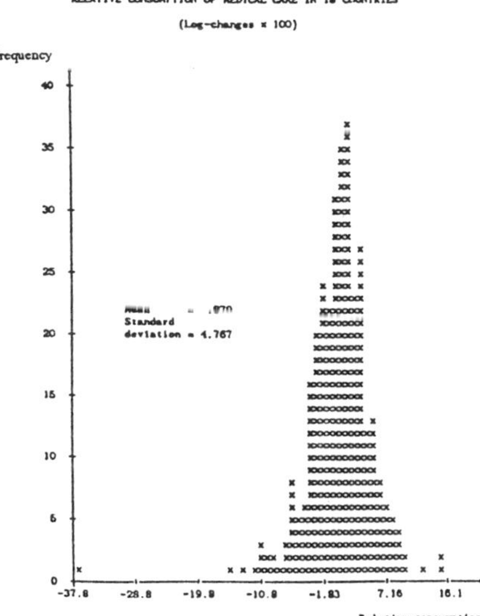

Figure 2.12

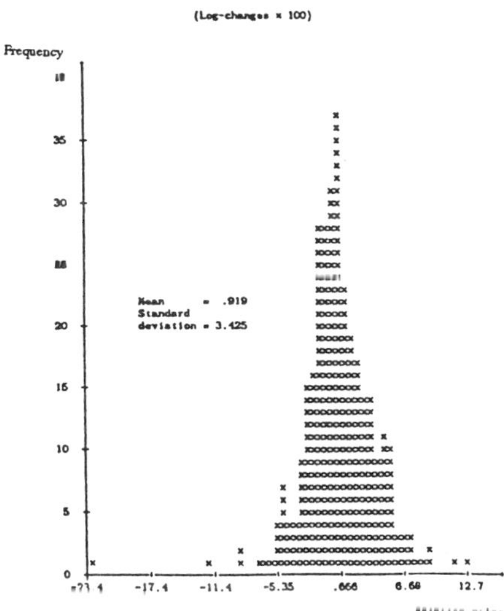

Figure 2.13

Figure 2.14

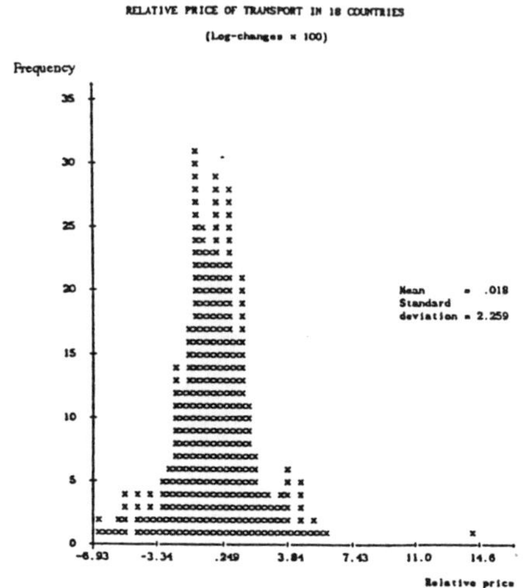

Figure 2.15

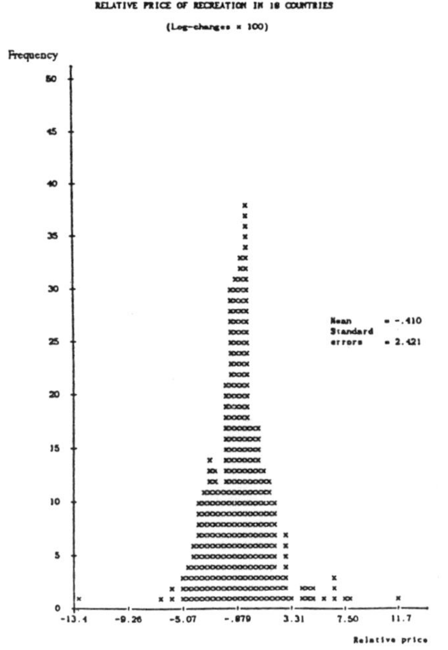

Figure 2.17

Figure 2.16

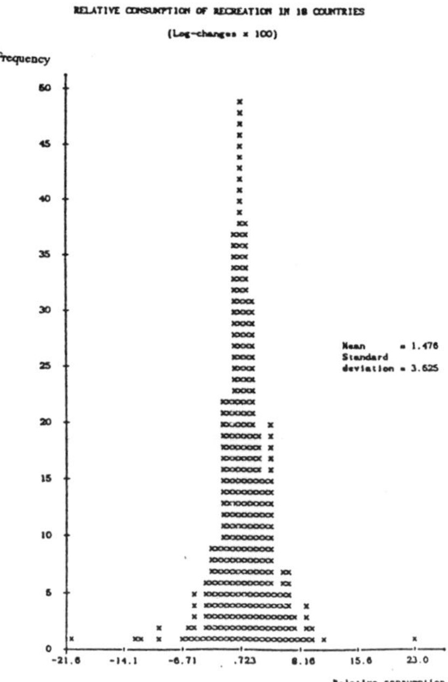

Figure 2.18

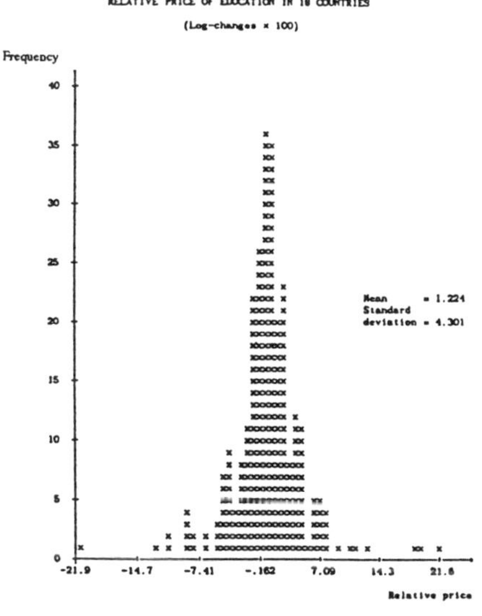

Figure 2.19

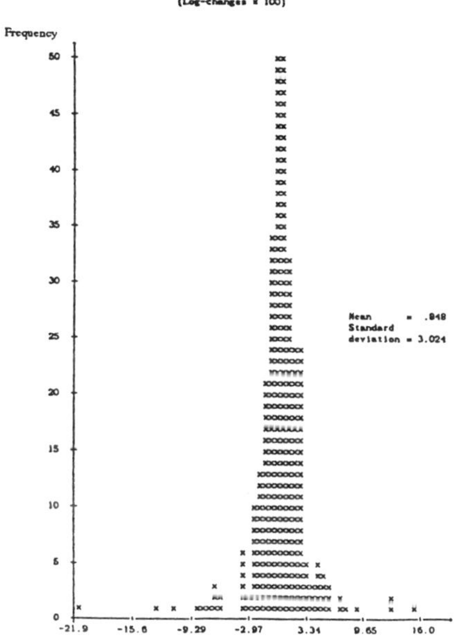

Figure 2.21

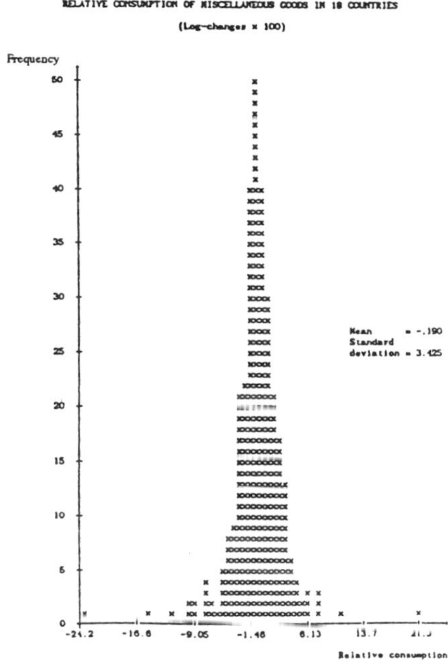

Figure 2.20

Figure 2.22

Table 2.11 presents the Kolmogorov-Smirnov test statistics for normality of the relative price and quantity log-changes and their critical values. As can be seen from the table, normality is not generally acceptable.

Table 2.12 presents the frequency distributions of the relative price and quantity log-changes (again, for all years and all countries). Columns 2-11 give the distributions for the 10 commodities individually and column 12 presents the figures for all goods. As can be seen from column 12, for an average OECD country, for all goods relative prices increased $31 + 11 + 7 = 49$ percent of the time while relative consumption decreased $10 + 13 + 25 = 48$ percent of the time.

2.6 DOUBLE-LOG DEMAND EQUATIONS

In this section we obtain preliminary estimates for the demand elasticities by estimating double-log demand equations. These double-log demand equations should be viewed as only a convenient way to summarize the data. In Chapter 3, we proceed more formally and estimate a more elaborate model and obtain a second set of elasticities; these elasticity values are then compared with the results of this section.

TABLE 2.11

KOLMOGOROV-SMIRNOV TEST STATISTICS FOR NORMALITY OF
RELATIVE PRICE AND QUANTITY LOG-CHANGES
FOR 10 COMMODITIES IN 18 COUNTRIES

Commodity	Relative Price Log-change	Relative Quantity Log-change	Critical values	
			5 percent	1 percent
(1)	(2)	(3)	(4)	(5)
1. Food	.077*	.054	.076	.091
2. Beverages	.083*	.059	.080	.096
3. Clothing	.101**	.055	.076	.091
4. Housing	.080*	.079**	.076	.091
5. Durables	.067	.068	.076	.091
6. Medical care	.074	.077*	.076	.091
7. Transport	.076*	.076	.076	.091
8. Recreation	.093**	.097**	.076	.091
9. Education	.116**	.070	.082	.099
10. Miscellaneous	.151**	.118**	.076	.091

The Kolmogorov-Smirnov test statistic is based on a comparison of the
observed sample cumulative relative frequency distribution (S) with the
hypothetical population cumulative distribution function specified by the null
hypothesis (F_0).   The Kolmogorov-Smirnov test statistic is given by
$D = \sup_x |F_0(x) - S(x)|$.   The test statistic D is normally distributed.   A
'*' denotes significant at the 5 percent level; and a '**' denotes significant at
the 1 percent level.

TABLE 2.12

FREQUENCY DISTRIBUTIONS OF RELATIVE PRICE AND QUANTITY LOG-CHANGES

FOR 10 COMMODITIES IN 18 COUNTRIES

(Percentages)

Range	Food	Beverages	Clothing	Housing	Durables	Medical care	Transport	Recreation	Education	Miscellaneous	All goods
(1)	(2)	(3)	(4)	(5)	(6)	(7)	(8)	(9)	(10)	(11)	(12)
					Relative Prices						
$(-\infty, -4]$	2	12	9	3	4	6	4	4	8	2	5
$(-4, -2]$	14	20	16	6	23	8	7	17	7	3	12
$(-2, 0]$	41	34	46	29	44	23	39	41	16	20	34
$(0, 2]$	29	22	22	36	22	32	36	28	34	51	31
$(2, 4]$	10	6	5	20	4	15	8	7	19	18	11
$(4, \infty)$	4	5	1	7	3	16	5	4	17	5	7
					Relative Quantities						
$(-\infty, -4]$	11	10	13	5	9	10	10	4	24	4	10
$(-4, -2]$	27	17	15	11	16	11	7	6	12	11	13
$(-2, 0]$	39	36	29	25	22	15	15	16	12	38	25
$(0, 2]$	19	20	24	38	25	23	21	37	16	29	26
$(2, 4]$	3	13	13	15	13	20	19	20	16	13	14
$(4, \infty)$	0	5	5	6	13	21	28	17	20	5	12

The ranges in column 1 are to be divided by 100.

Consider a double-log demand equation for commodity i in year t

$$Dq_{it} = \alpha_i + \eta_i DQ_t + \gamma_i Dp^*_{it} + \varepsilon_{it}, \qquad (6.1)$$

where α_i is an autonomous trend term; η_i is the income elasticity; γ_i is the Slutsky own-price elasticity; $Dp^*_{it} = Dp_{it} - DP_t$ is the log-change in the relative price of good i; and ε_{it} is a disturbance term. Note that (6.1) includes only the own price and not other prices.

We add a country superscript to everything in (6.1),

$$Dq^c_{it} = \alpha^c_i + \eta^c_i DQ^c_t + \gamma^c_i Dp^{*c}_{it} + \varepsilon^c_{it}, \qquad c=1,...,18. \qquad (6.2)$$

We assume that the ε^c_{it}'s are normally distributed with zero mean and are independent over time. As the dependent variable is the log-change in the volume of consumption, i.e. in first-difference form, serial correlation and heteroscedasticity are not likely to be major problems. We shall come back to this at the end of this section when we analyse the residuals.

We estimate equation (6.2) by least squares (LS) for $i=1,...,n^c$ goods and for each country separately. Tables 2.13-2.15 present the results. The first 18 rows present the estimates for the 18 countries and the second last row (labelled 'Mean') presents the means over the 18 countries. The last row of each table

TABLE 2.13

ESTIMATES OF THE AUTONOMOUS TRENDS FOR 10 COMMODITIES IN 18 COUNTRIES

(Standard errors are in parentheses)

Country	Food α_1^c	Beverages α_2^c	Clothing α_3^c	Housing α_4^c	Durables α_5^c	Medical care α_6^c	Transport α_7^c	Recreation α_8^c	Education α_9^c	Miscellaneous α_{10}^c
(1)	(2)	(3)	(4)	(5)	(6)	(7)	(8)	(9)	(10)	(11)
U.S.	.02	.40	-2.09	1.95	-2.90	3.84	-3.96	.39	.39	.50
	(.59)	(.52)	(.76)	(.21)	(.63)	(.65)	(.92)	(.82)	(1.80)	(.45)
Canada	-.80	1.19	-.11	3.20	-2.79	-6.76	-.76	-.02	4.32	.89
	(.49)	(.64)	(1.19)	(.49)	(.83)	(3.74)	(.91)	(1.16)	(3.07)	(.62)
Sweden	-.29	-2.12	-3.32	2.31	-2.23	2.10	-1.14	1.07	2.31	-2.66
	(.32)	(.89)	(1.41)	(.30)	(.64)	(1.00)	(.84)	(.85)	(1.53)	(.81)
Switzerland	-.34	-1.71	-4.18	1.53	-4.56	1.93	.10	.64		1.11
	(.35)	(.61)	(.89)	(.59)	(.57)	(.84)	(.93)	(.55)		(.40)
Denmark	-.43	-.37	-3.57	3.35	-3.36	1.24	-1.88	.81	8.49	-.65
	(.52)	(.50)	(1.21)	(.81)	(.65)	(1.16)	(.80)	(1.00)	(1.30)	(.56)
Australia	1.32	-1.00	-2.65	2.51	-1.86	.38	-.92	-2.15	-5.04	-.19
	(.34)	(.44)	(.81)	(.69)	(2.34)	(1.77)	(1.08)	(2.32)	(3.35)	(.59)
France	.07	-1.54	-2.70	1.36	-2.85	4.92	-1.55	1.67	3.27	.68
	(.43)	(.88)	(1.01)	(.88)	(1.73)	(1.62)	(1.37)	(1.03)	(5.08)	(.48)
Germany	-.33		-2.46	2.79	-1.56	1.01	-1.28	.70		1.71
	(.43)		(.60)	(.80)	(.67)	(.97)	(1.41)	(.71)		(.44)
Belgium	-.59	-.57	-3.49	1.12	-.73	2.78	1.97	.21	1.87	-5.82
	(.75)	(1.04)	(1.46)	(.92)	(1.84)	(1.29)	(.97)	(1.17)	(.32)	(2.62)
Norway	.62	.33	-1.81	3.20	-.45	2.01	-4.66	1.77	-.54	-1.08
	(.27)	(1.02)	(.67)	(.60)	(.82)	(1.43)	(1.05)	(.85)	(2.03)	(.63)
Netherlands	-.50	.74	-5.93	2.82	-.09	6.93	2.71	-.34	3.03	2.83
	(.87)	(1.65)	(1.36)	(1.15)	(2.23)	(1.70)	(1.63)	(1.75)	(2.05)	(1.16)
Iceland	-.26	.46	-2.30	2.91	-2.59	6.43	-3.88	-.06	6.58	-.27
	(1.09)	(1.67)	(2.01)	(.67)	(1.89)	(1.83)	(3.36)	(2.37)	(1.76)	(2.41)
Finland	.42	.05	-4.84	3.05	-1.15	4.36	-.88	-1.59	-8.36	2.95
	(.54)	(1.34)	(2.57)	(.43)	(1.51)	(1.41)	(2.28)	(1.58)	(4.04)	(.83)
Austria	.82	.42	-2.63	4.19	-4.17	5.41	-5.74	1.48	2.53	.60
	(.93)	(1.46)	(1.26)	(1.41)	(2.56)	(1.54)	(1.67)	(1.12)	(2.25)	(.62)
Japan	-.81		-3.94	4.10	-6.22	4.43	1.55	-.75		-.30
	(.64)		(1.36)	(.31)	(2.51)	(.96)	(1.57)	(1.26)		(1.36)
U.K.	-.43	-.46	-.43	1.49	-3.18	-1.20	-.33	.97	2.07	.05
	(.35)	(.81)	(.73)	(.43)	(.53)	(1.56)	(.97)	(.62)	(1.00)	(.43)
Spain	-.93	-1.09	-1.75	3.16	-.75	4.33	-1.70	1.65	4.99	2.69
	(1.54)	(2.23)	(1.68)	(.95)	(1.99)	(4.41)	(3.54)	(2.51)	(3.30)	(1.87)
Italy	-.73	-.34	-3.29	1.34	-1.62	2.86	.44	1.34	-.42	1.33
	(.40)	(1.09)	(.85)	(.31)	(1.55)	(1.58)	(1.45)	(.81)	(2.15)	(.71)
Mean	-.18	-.35	-2.86	2.58	-2.39	2.61	-1.22	.43	1.70	.24
	(.16)	(.29)	(.31)	(.17)	(.37)	(.44)	(.40)	(.33)	(.68)	(.27)
All countries	-.22	-.67	-2.67	2.66	-2.45	1.92	-1.24	.47	1.48	-.15
	(.12)	(.23)	(.26)	(.16)	(.27)	(.40)	(.33)	(.28)	(.48)	(.24)

All entries are to be divided by 100.

TABLE 2.14

ESTIMATES OF INCOME ELASTICITIES FOR 10 COMMODITIES IN 18 COUNTRIES

(Standard errors are in parentheses)

Country	Food η_1^c	Beverages η_2^c	Clothing η_3^c	Housing η_4^c	Durables η_6^c	Medical care η_6^c	Transport η_7^c	Recreation η_8^c	Education η_9^c	Miscellaneous η_{10}^c
(1)	(2)	(3)	(4)	(5)	(6)	(7)	(8)	(9)	(10)	(11)
U.S.	.29 (.20)	.41 (.18)	1.41 (.22)	.41 (.07)	1.55 (.21)	.52 (.22)	2.78 (.32)	1.27 (.23)	.98 (.33)	.70 (.14)
Canada	.79 (.14)	.36 (.19)	.75 (.32)	-.02 (.14)	1.59 (.21)	2.60 (1.11)	1.54 (.29)	1.94 (.30)	.94 (.74)	1.05 (.19)
Sweden	.37 (.13)	1.69 (.39)	1.40 (.32)	.24 (.12)	1.96 (.26)	.54 (.43)	2.04 (.34)	1.50 (.31)	.77 (.62)	1.13 (.27)
Switzerland	.82 (.13)	1.41 (.23)	1.96 (.28)	.27 (.21)	2.09 (.20)	.48 (.25)	1.65 (.34)	.97 (.19)		.60 (.17)
Denmark	.38 (.20)	.65 (.12)	1.55 (.29)	41 (.17)	1.43 (.23)	.19 (.38)	2.33 (.30)	1.16 (.27)	.04 (.41)	.99 (.17)
Australia	-.06 (.12)	.86 (.16)	1.25 (.30)	.59 (.24)	2.11 (.69)	.57 (.63)	1.80 (.40)	2.87 (.86)	2.46 (1.40)	.94 (.21)
France	.42 (.11)	.74 (.22)	1.02 (.26)	.86 (.21)	1.68 (.51)	.55 (.41)	1.92 (.34)	.87 (.25)	.11 (1.30)	.92 (.12)
Germany	.61 (.10)		1.49 (.16)	.16 (.19)	1.39 (.17)	.52 (.27)	2.29 (.39)	.96 (.19)		.74 (.11)
Belgium	.63 (.20)	.96 (.28)	1.59 (.34)	.56 (.25)	1.49 (.47)	.75 (.36)	.86 (.27)	1.20 (.33)	.04 (.09)	2.85 (.60)
Norway	.26 (.08)	.63 (.30)	1.07 (.19)	.08 (.17)	1.36 (.24)	.46 (.43)	3.29 (.30)	1.09 (.18)	.71 (.66)	.96 (.17)
Netherlands	.59 (.17)	.70 (.37)	1.93 (.28)	.40 (.23)	1.55 (.36)	.22 (.29)	.78 (.34)	1.11 (.38)	.76 (.34)	.65 (.22)
Iceland	.46 (.13)	.89 (.21)	1.39 (.26)	-.07 (.09)	1.79 (.27)	.43 (.25)	2.28 (.54)	1.39 (.34)	-.34 (.28)	1.70 (.31)
Finland	.44 (.10)	1.23 (.27)	1.71 (.48)	.09 (.08)	1.84 (.30)	.62 (.26)	1.92 (.47)	1.71 (.31)	1.94 (.81)	.78 (.17)
Austria	.27 (.23)	.40 (.38)	1.75 (.24)	.23 (.26)	1.93 (.50)	-.60 (.39)	3.40 (.41)	.69 (.30)	-.14 (.60)	.69 (.18)
Japan	.74 (.17)		1.74 (.34)	.25 (.08)	2.38 (.63)	.43 (.23)	1.13 (.35)	1.10 (.30)		1.55 (.29)
U.K.	.30 (.12)	.74 (.39)	1.21 (.20)	.38 (.12)	2.12 (.17)	1.30 (.58)	1.85 (.33)	1.31 (.21)	.79 (.38)	1.11 (.15)
Spain	.84 (.32)	1.12 (.43)	1.17 (.35)	.25 (.18)	1.10 (.41)	1.32 (.96)	2.52 (.82)	1.13 (.46)	.03 (.60)	.70 (.38)
Italy	.86 (.10)	.80 (.21)	1.83 (.21)	.43 (.09)	1.66 (.40)	.95 (.38)	1.60 (.35)	.49 (.20)	60 (.53)	.91 (.14)
Mean	.50 (.04)	.85 (.07)	1.46 (.07)	.31 (.04)	1.74 (.09)	.66 (.12)	2.00 (.10)	1.27 (.08)	.05 (.18)	1.05 (.06)
All countries	.53 (.03)	.85 (.06)	1.46 (.06)	.23 (.04)	1.76 (.07)	.75 (.10)	2.02 (.09)	1.22 (.07)	.32 (.12)	1.23 (.06)

TABLE 2.15

ESTIMATES OF PRICE ELASTICITIES FOR 10 COMMODITIES IN 18 COUNTRIES

(Standard errors are in parentheses)

Country	Food γ_1^c	Beverages γ_2^c	Clothing γ_3^c	Housing γ_4^c	Durables γ_5^c	Medical care γ_6^c	Transport γ_7^c	Recreation γ_8^c	Education γ_9^c	Miscellaneous γ_{10}^c
(1)	(2)	(3)	(4)	(5)	(6)	(7)	(8)	(9)	(10)	(11)
U.S	-.54	-.08	-.67	-.22	-1.46	-.59	.00	-.51	.51	-.73
	(.11)	(.11)	(.16)	(.16)	(.28)	(.28)	(.31)	(.24)	(1.21)	(.33)
Canada	-.63	-.62	-.77	-.28	-1.58	1.59	-.91	-.52	-.89	-.76
	(.09)	(.18)	(.32)	(.17)	(.47)	(1.46)	(.36)	(.32)	(.56)	(.22)
Sweden	-.61	-.20	-1.38	-.35	-.54	.00	-1.22	-1.04	-.27	-.13
	(.14)	(.29)	(.40)	(.14)	(.25)	(.13)	(.51)	(.48)	(.13)	(.37)
Switzerland	-.59	-.56	-.65	-.03	-1.05	-.05	-.70	-.61		.44
	(.13)	(.23)	(.43)	(.17)	(.20)	(.24)	(.47)	(.26)		(.26)
Denmark	-.25	-.39	-.83	-.27	-.90	-.58	-.47	-.69	-.02	-.04
	(.19)	(.15)	(.34)	(.22)	(.27)	(.32)	(.45)	(.43)	(.50)	(.31)
Australia	-.33	-.52	-.85	-.43	-.24	-.28	-.54	-.83	-1.77	-.09
	(.06)	(.07)	(.23)	(.16)	(.73)	(.33)	(.34)	(.41)	(.78)	(.10)
France	-.31	-.26	-1.03	.36	-.23	.43	-1.04	-.44	-.79	-.95
	(.09)	(.11)	(.27)	(.18)	(.60)	(.41)	(.28)	(.19)	(.75)	(.10)
Germany	-.60		-.47	-.04	-.76	-.74	-1.30	-.75		-.40
	(.19)		(.37)	(.22)	(.24)	(.21)	(.57)	(.27)		(.18)
Belgium	-.31	-.34	-1.06	-.09	-.37	.01	-.74	-.70	.04	-.04
	(.19)	(.30)	(.35)	(.19)	(.47)	(.22)	(.31)	(.34)	(.06)	(.23)
Norway	-.29	-1.05	-1.13	.12	-.49	-.92	-.35	-.51	-.14	.77
	(.12)	(.19)	(.31)	(.32)	(.39)	(.32)	(.40)	(.26)	(.67)	(.35)
Netherlands	-.40	-.52	-1.25	-.63	-.17	-.64	-2.03	-.29	-.65	-.64
	(.28)	(.33)	(.37)	(.19)	(.59)	(.22)	(.29)	(.44)	(.48)	(.51)
Iceland	-.21	-.28	-.42	.02	-.98	-.61	-1.67	-1.20	-.31	-.75
	(.21)	(.33)	(.30)	(.08)	(.40)	(.29)	(1.29)	(.34)	(.21)	(.29)
Finland	-.48	-.69	.14	-.17	.69	.42	-.48	-1.65	-.31	-.35
	(.17)	(.20)	(.71)	(.08)	(.49)	(.44)	(.32)	(.33)	(.54)	(.34)
Austria	-.26	-.26	-.72	-.30	-.86	-.23	.23	-.56	.10	-.69
	(.22)	(.19)	(.49)	(.38)	(.85)	(.28)	(.38)	(.32)	(.15)	(.24)
Japan	-.02		-.26	-.17	-.31	-.64	-1.14	-1.12		-1.12
	(.32)		(.29)	(.06)	(.45)	(.15)	(.45)	(.56)		(.80)
U.K.	-.08	-.59	-.31	-.16	-1.15	.90	-.17	-.54	-1.17	-.72
	(.15)	(.22)	(.14)	(.15)	(.24)	(.57)	(.38)	(.24)	(.30)	(.24)
Spain	-.23	-.06	-.34	.32	-.64	-.54	-.59	-.54	-.32	-.05
	(.31)	(.18)	(.34)	(.15)	(.26)	(.41)	(.38)	(.29)	(.30)	(.26)
Italy	-.11	-.27	-.07	.05	-.09	-.56	-.07	-1.14	-.18	-.48
	(.19)	(.15)	(.32)	(.09)	(.31)	(.26)	(.35)	(.28)	(.35)	(.25)
Mean	-.35	-.42	-.67	-.13	-.62	-.17	-.73	-.76	-.41	-.37
	(.04)	(.05)	(.09)	(.04)	(.11)	(.11)	(.12)	(.08)	(.14)	(.08)
All Countries	-.40	-.42	-.63	-.14	-.60	-.31	-.80	-.83	-.24	-.48
	(.04)	(.05)	(.07)	(.04)	(.08)	(.08)	(.10)	(.07)	(.08)	(.06)

will be discussed subsequently. Table 2.13 presents the estimates of the autonomous trend terms (α_i^c) for the 10 commodities in 18 countries.

Table 2.14 presents the estimates of the income elasticities. As can be seen, all except 6 of these elasticities are positive. However, the negative elasticities are all insignificant. All the elasticities in columns 2 and 5 are less than one, implying that food and housing are necessities in all countries. Looking at column 6 we see that all elasticities are greater than unity. Hence, durables arc a luxury in all countries. The second last row presents the mean over countries of the elasticities and its standard error for each commodity. As can be seen, on average, food, beverages, housing, medical care and education are necessities while the other five goods are luxuries.

All except 19 of the price elasticities presented in Table 2.15 are negative. However, among the 19 positive price elasticities only 2 are significant. With only a few exceptions, the price elasticities are all less than one in absolute value.

Next, we re-estimate model (6.2) under the assumption that the autonomous trends and the income and price elasticities are the same across countries. Thus, the model becomes

$$Dq_{it}^c = \alpha_i + \eta_i DQ_t^c + \gamma_i Dp_{it}^{*c} + \varepsilon_{it}^c, \tag{6.3}$$

where the ε_{it}^c's are normally distributed with zero mean and are independent over time and countries. Estimation of this model involves pooling the data across countries. The LS estimates are presented in the last rows (labelled 'All countries') of Tables 2.13-2.15. Comparing these estimates with the means presented in the second last rows of the tables, we see that they are similar. Next we relax the assumptions on the disturbances and estimate model (6.3) with full-cross-sectionally heteroscedastic and time-wise autoregressive errors. We use the POOL command in the SHAZAM econometric package for estimation. The results (not reported here) show that the estimates are close to those for 'All countries' and the standard errors are somewhat smaller.

In Appendix A2.1 we present the summary statistics for the estimated demand equations (6.2) and (6.3). In Appendix A2.2 we present the estimates and the summary statistics of these models with autonomous trend terms suppressed. As some of the values of the Durbin-Watson (DW) statistics presented in Tables A2.1 and A2.4 are in the indeterminant range, we compute the appropriate tail probabilities. If the computed value of the DW-statistic is $\bar{d}$ (say), then we compute $F(\bar{d})$, where F is the distribution function of the DW-statistic $\bar{d}$ under H_o: $\rho = 0$. We use the econometric software package SHAZAM to calculate the probability $P[d \leq \bar{d} \mid H_o: \rho = 0]$. If the alternative hypothesis is H_1: $\rho > 0$, then H_o will be rejected if this probability is less than .05 at the 5 percent level of significance (or if less than .01 at the 1 percent level). If the alternative hypothesis is H_1: $\rho \neq 0$, then H_o will be rejected if this probability is less than .025 or greater than .975 at the 5 percent level of significance (or if less than .005 or greater than .995 at the 1 percent level). The tail probabilities (labelled 'PROB') are presented in Tables A2.1 and A2.4. As can be seen, for H_1: $\rho \neq 0$ at the 5 percent level of significance, 157 out of 175 in Table A2.1 and 153 out of 175 in Table A2.4 (about 90 percent) of the DW-values fall outside the rejection region and almost all at the 1 percent level. Therefore, we can safely conclude that these results indicate no serial correlation.

2.7 A BIRD'S EYE VIEW OF THE ELASTICITIES

In Table 2.16 we summarize the autonomous trend and elasticity values in the form of cross-country frequency distributions. Columns 2 11 of Table 2.16 present the percentages of the estimates lying in certain ranges for the 10 commodities individually. Column 12 presents these percentages for all goods. The first part of the table presents the frequencies of the autonomous trends. Looking at the values for clothing and durables we see that the trend is always negative while for housing it is positive for all countries. The trends of other goods do not seem to have any particular sign.

The middle part of Table 2.16 presents the frequency distributions of the income elasticities. As can be seen from column 2 for food, 94 percent of the income elasticities lie between 0 and 1. This strongly supports the

TABLE 2.16

FREQUENCY DISTRIBUTIONS OF AUTONOMOUS TRENDS AND

INCOME AND PRICE ELASTICITIES FOR 10 COMMODITIES IN 18 COUNTRIES

(Percentages)

Range	Food	Beverages	Clothing	Housing	Durables	Medical care	Transport	Recreation	Education	Miscellaneous	All goods
(1)	(2)	(3)	(4)	(5)	(6)	(7)	(8)	(9)	(10)	(11)	(12)
Autonomous Trends ($\alpha_i^c \times 100$)											
$(-\infty,-1]$	0	25	89	0	78	11	50	11	13	17	30
$(-1, 0]$	67	31	11	0	22	0	22	22	13	22	21
$(0, 1]$	28	38	0	0	0	6	11	33	7	28	15
$(1, \infty)$	6	6	0	100	0	83	17	33	67	33	34
Income Elasticities (η_i^c)											
$(-\infty,-1]$	0	0	0	0	0	0	0	0	0	0	0
$(-1, 0]$	6	0	0	11	0	6	0	0	13	0	3
$(0, 1]$	94	75	6	89	0	78	11	28	73	67	52
$(1, \infty)$	0	25	94	0	100	17	89	72	13	33	45
Price Elasticities (η_i^c)											
$(-\infty,-1]$	0	6	28	0	22	0	33	28	13	6	14
$(-1, 0]$	100	94	67	72	72	66	62	72	67	83	75
$(0, 1]$	0	0	5	28	6	28	5	0	20	11	10
$(1, \infty)$	0	0	0	0	0	6	0	0	0	0	1

Engel's (1857) law that food is a necessity. The lower part of the table gives the results for the price elasticities. As can be seen from column 12, 14 + 75 = 89 percent of all the price elasticities are negative. This shows very clearly the tendency of the consumer to move away from those goods having above-average price increases. It can also be seen that 75 percent of the price elasticities are less than one in absolute value.

Table 2.17 presents the distributions of the absolute t-values of the three sets of parameter estimates. As can be seen from column 12 of the table, 35 percent of the intercept terms are highly insignificant $(|t| < 1)$; 25 percent are insignificant $(1 \leq |t| < 2)$; 16 percent are significant $(2 \leq |t| < 3)$; and 23 percent are highly significant $(3 \leq |t|)$. Among the income elasticities 76 percent have $|t|$-values greater than or equal to 2; while for the price elasticities 46 percent have $|t|$-values greater than or equal to 2. Consequently, the income elasticities tend to be estimated with greater precision than the autonomous trends and the price elasticities.

In Appendix A2.2 we present cross-country frequency distributions of the estimates when the autonomous trends are suppressed. In Sections 2.8 and 2.9 we consider the interrelationships between the elasticities and the autonomous trend terms.

TABLE 2.17

FREQUENCY DISTRIBUTIONS OF $|t|$-VALUES OF AUTONOMOUS TRENDS AND

INCOME AND PRICE ELASTICITIES FOR 10 COMMODITIES IN 18 COUNTRIES

(Percentages)

Range	Food	Beverages	Clothing	Housing	Durables	Medical care	Transport	Recreation	Education	Miscellaneous	All goods
(1)	(2)	(3)	(4)	(5)	(6)	(7)	(8)	(9)	(10)	(11)	(12)
Autonomous Trends ($\alpha_i^c \times 100$)											
[0 , 1)	67	69	11	0	33	17	50	56	27	28	35
[1 , 2)	22	12	17	11	22	28	22	39	40	39	25
[2 , 3)	6	19	44	17	11	17	11	6	13	17	16
[3 , ∞)	6	0	28	72	33	39	7	0	20	17	23
Income Elasticities (η_i^c)											
[0 , 1)	6	0	0	28	0	17	0	0	33	0	8
[1 , 2)	17	25	0	28	0	50	0	0	40	6	16
[2 , 3)	17	19	6	17	6	33	6	22	27	6	15
[3 , ∞)	61	56	94	28	94	0	94	78	0	89	61
Price Elasticities (γ_i^c)											
[0 , 1)	22	25	17	39	33	33	28	6	47	28	27
[1 , 2)	28	25	28	28	17	28	33	28	33	28	27
[2 , 3)	11	25	17	28	17	28	28	50	13	28	25
[3 , ∞)	39	25	39	6	33	11	11	17	7	17	21

2.8   IS THERE A RELATIONSHIP BETWEEN THE PRICE AND INCOME ELASTICITIES?

The size of the own-price elasticity reflects the availability of substitutes while the income elasticity indicates the luxuriousness of the good. As these refer to two distinct aspects of the good we would not expect there to be any particular relationship between the two sets of elasticities. However, the income and price elasticities in Tables 2.14 and 2.15 for a given country tend to be negatively correlated. This is illustrated in Figure 2.23 which gives a scatter plot of the weighted averages of the income and price elasticities for the 10 commodities, the weights being inversely proportional to the variances. This figure also contains the LS regression line. As can be seen, most of the points are not too far away from the regression line. The result is that those commodities which are more price elastic also tend to be more luxurious and vice versa.

The relationship between price and income elasticities was first considered by Pigou (1910) and is associated with preference independence. Under preference independence, the consumer's tastes can be described by a utility function which is the sum of n sub-utility functions, one for each good. Deaton (1974) shows that under preference independence, the own-price

Weighted Price Elasticities Against Weighted Income Elasticities

for 10 Commodities

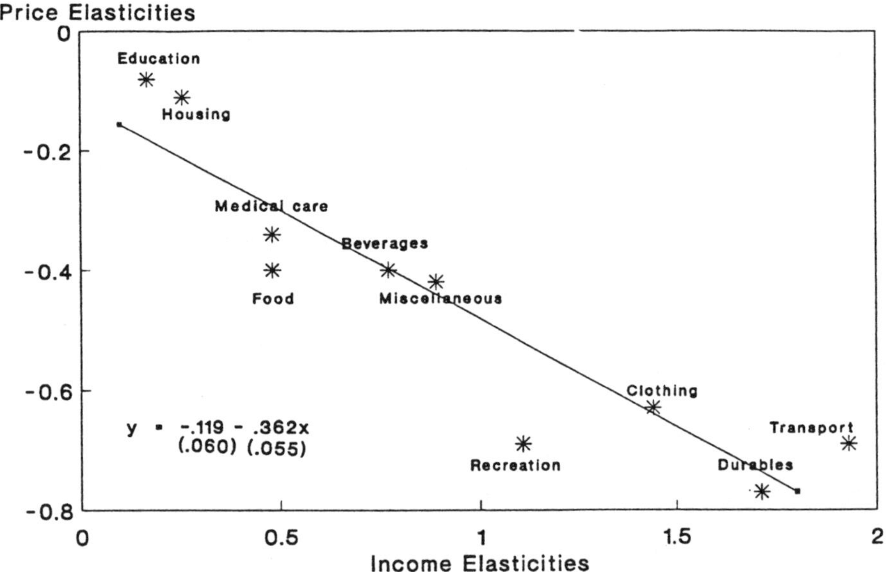

Figure 2.23

elasticities are approximately proportional to the income elasticities,

$$\gamma_i \simeq \phi\eta_i, \qquad\qquad i=1,...,n, \qquad\qquad (8.1)$$

where ϕ is a proportionality constant interpreted as the reciprocal of the income elasticity of the marginal utility of income, or the income flexibility for short.

Deaton (1974) failed to find any evidence for (8.1) using double-log demand

equations for the U.K. On the other hand, Clements et al. (1984) find support

for (8.1) using four sets of elasticities. They find that ϕ in (8.1) generally lies

between -.5 and -.6, a range consistent with estimates of the income flexibility

obtained using other methods (Theil, 1980). Are Deaton's results specific to his

sample? In this section we shed some light on this issue by using the OECD

elasticities to test hypothesis (8.1).

We estimate for each of the 18 countries

$$\gamma_i^c = \alpha^c + \phi^c \eta_i^c, \qquad\qquad i=1,\ldots,n^c, \qquad\qquad (8.2)$$

where α^c is the intercept term and ϕ^c is the slope. We use the income and

price elasticities presented in Tables 2.14 and 2.15 and estimate (8.2) by LS.

Table 2.18 presents the results. As can be seen from column 2, the intercepts

are insignificant for 15 countries. In column 4 we present F-statistics for testing

the null hypothesis that $\alpha^c = 0$ and $\phi^c = -.5$. (The value -.5 for the income

flexibility ϕ^c is in agreement with previous studies.) The conclusion is that we

may not reject this hypothesis for all countries except Austria, Spain and Italy

at the 5 percent level of significance. That is, the data support the

proportionality hypothesis for 15 countries at the 5 percent level and for 17

countries at the 1 percent level. The second last and the last rows of the table

TABLE 2.18

CROSS-COMMODITY REGRESSION RESULTS FOR PRICE AND INCOME ELASTICITIES

$$\gamma_i^c = \alpha^c + \phi^c \eta_i^c$$

(Standard errors are in parentheses)

Country	Intercept α^c	Slope ϕ^c	F-statistic for $\alpha^c=0,\ \phi^c=-.5$	t-statistic for $\phi^c=-.5$
(1)	(2)	(3)	(4)	(5)
U.S.	-.423 (.306) -	-.006 (.243) -.281 (.146)*	F(2,8) = 2.19	 t(9) = 1.49
Canada	-1.064 (.460)* -	.458 (.336) -.197 (.220)	F(2,8) = 4.08	 t(9) = 1.37
Sweden	-.163 (.301) -	-.352 (.228) -.461 (.103)*	F(2,8) = .21	 t(9) = .37
Switzerland	.200 (.201) -	-.546 (.154)** -.411 (.074)**	F(2,7) = 1.21	 t(8) = 1.19
Denmark	-.246 (.148) -	-.218 (.130) -.391 (.085)**	F(2,8) = 2.36	 t(9) = 1.28
Australia	-.232 (.247) -	-.259 (.149) -.375 (.083)**	F(2,8) = 1.57	 t(9) = 1.51
France	-.194 (.348) -	-.256 (.333) -.418 (.159)*	F(2,8) = .28	 t(9) = .52
Germany	-.205 (.163) -	-.421 (.136)** -.566 (.075)**	F(2,6) = 1.22	 t(7) = .89
Belgium	-.266 (.221) -	-.086 (.168) -.254 (.096)*	F(2,8) = 4.20	 t(9) = 2.57*
Norway	-.380 (.296) -	-.020 (.226) -.240 (.153)	F(2,8) = 2.38	 t(9) = 1.71
Netherlands	-.647 (.368) -	-.084 (.367) -.646 (.202)**	F(2,8) = 1.87	 t(9) = .72
Iceland	-.157 (.162) -	-.489 (.126)** -.583 (.080)**	F(2,8) = 1.01	 t(9) = 1.04
Finland	-.175 (.459) -	-.092 (.330) -.202 (.148)	F(2,8) = 1.91	 t(9) = 2.01
Austria	-.351 (.151)* -	-.005 (.107) -.157 (.103)	F(2,8) = 10.93**	 t(9) = 3.33**
Japan	-.530 (.364) -	-.059 (.272) -.402 (.145)*	F(2,6) = 1.33	 t(7) = .68
U.K.	-.226 (.444) -	-.155 (.358) -.318 (.153)*	F(2,8) = .78	 t(9) = 1.19
Spain	-.028 (.154) -	-.265 (.128)* -.285 (.064)**	F(2,8) = 4.97*	 t(9) = 3.33**
Italy	-.578 (.254)* -	.282 (.227) -.184 (.117)	F(2,8) = 7.91*	 t(9) = 2.70*
Mean	-.101 (.085) -	-.345 (.072)** -.422 (.033)**	F(2,8) = 3.59	 t(9) = 2.35*
All countries	-.145 (.080) -	-.328 (.069)** -.435 (.037)**	F(2,8) = 3.58	 t(9) = 1.77

A '*' denotes significant at the 5 percent level; and a '**' denotes significant at the 1 percent level.

present the regression results obtained using the corresponding values of the elasticities given in the second last and the last rows of Tables 2.14 and 2.15.

Column 3 of Table 2.18 also presents the estimates of ϕ^c with the constant α^c suppressed. As can be seen for 13 countries, the estimates are significantly different from zero at the 5 percent level. Column 5 presents the t-values for the null hypothesis that $\phi^c = -.5$ given $\alpha^c = 0$. As can be seen, we cannot reject the null hypothesis for all countries except Belgium, Austria, Spain and Italy at the 5 percent level; and at the 1 percent level, the hypothesis cannot be rejected for all except Austria and Spain. Taken as a whole, the results indicate that there is a distinct tendency for luxuries to be more price elastic than necessities. This finding provides some indirect evidence in favour of preference independence.

2.9 THE RELATIONSHIP BETWEEN THE AUTONOMOUS TRENDS AND INCOME AND PRICE ELASTICITIES

In this section we use Divisia indexes to analyse the relationships between the autonomous trends and the income and price elasticities. The autonomous trends for country c are α_i^c, $i=1,...,n^c$. The budget-share-weighted (or Divisia) mean of these is $\overline{\alpha}^c = \Sigma_{i=1}^{n^c} \overline{w}_i^c \alpha_i^c$, where $\overline{\overline{w}}_i^c = (1/T^c) \Sigma_{t=1}^{T^c} \overline{w}_{it}^c$ is the sample mean of $\overline{w}_{it}^c$. The Divisia variance of the autonomous trends is

$$V_{\alpha}^c = \sum_{i=1}^{n^c} \overline{\overline{w}}_i^c (\alpha_i^c - \overline{\alpha}^c)^2.$$

The Divisia variance of the income elasticities is

$$V_\eta^c = \sum_{i=1}^{n^c} \bar{w}_i^c (\eta_i^c - \bar{\eta}^c)^2,$$

where $\bar{\eta}^c = \sum_{i=1}^{n^c} \bar{w}_i^c \eta_i^c$ is the Divisia mean of the income elasticities. Similarly, the Divisia variance of the price elasticities is

$$V_\gamma^c = \sum_{i=1}^{n^c} \bar{w}_i^c (\gamma_i^c - \bar{\gamma}^c)^2,$$

where $\bar{\gamma}^c = \sum_{i=1}^{n^c} \bar{w}_i^c \gamma_i^c$ is the Divisia mean of the price elasticities.

We define the correlation between the autonomous trends and the income elasticities for country c as

$$\rho_{\alpha\eta}^c = \frac{V_{\alpha\eta}^c}{\sqrt{V_\alpha^c V_\eta^c}},$$

where $V_{\alpha\eta}^c = \sum_{i=1}^{n^c} \bar{w}_i^c (\alpha_i^c - \bar{\alpha}^c)(\eta_i^c - \bar{\eta}^c)$ is the Divisia covariance between $(\alpha_1^c,...,\alpha_{n^c}^c)$ and $(\eta_1^c,...,\eta_{n^c}^c)$. The trend-price elasticity correlation is

$$\rho_{\alpha\gamma}^c = \frac{V_{\alpha\gamma}^c}{\sqrt{V_\alpha^c V_\gamma^c}},$$

where $V_{\alpha\gamma}^c = \Sigma_{i=1}^{n^c} \bar{w}_i^c(\alpha_i^c - \bar{\alpha}^c)(\gamma_i^c - \bar{\gamma}^c)$ is the Divisia covariance between $(\alpha_1^c,...,\alpha_{n^c}^c)$ and $(\gamma_1^c,...,\gamma_{n^c}^c)$.

Column 2 of Table 2.19 presents the trend-income elasticity correlations. These are computed with the α_i^c's and η_i^c's from Tables 2.13 and 2.14. As can be seen, the autonomous trends and the income elasticities are highly negatively correlated. This indicates that those goods having a higher-than-average trend term have a lower-than-average income elasticity and vice versa. In other words, these two parameters act as substitutes for each other. The statistical explanation for this finding is that real income tends to grow according to a constant trend. Consequently, the income variable in the demand equation (6.2), DQ_t^c, is approximately a constant, which is obviously correlated with the constant term.

Column 3 of Table 2.19 gives the trend-price elasticity correlations. These correlations are mainly positive, but smaller (in absolute value) than most of the $\rho_{\alpha\eta}^c$'s. The conclusion is that there is much less of a relationship between the autonomous trends and the price elasticities.

2.10 A NONPARAMETRIC PICTURE OF PRICES AND QUANTITIES

The law of demand states that the demand curve slopes down. Thus, an increase in the relative price of a good causes its consumption to fall, other

TABLE 2.19

DIVISIA TREND-ELASTICITY CORRELATIONS IN 18 COUNTRIES

Country (1)	Trend-income elasticity correlation $\rho^c_{\alpha\eta}$ (2)	Trend-price elasticity correlation $\rho^c_{\alpha\gamma}$ (3)
U.S.	-.850	-.004
Canada	-.811	-.107
Sweden	-.655	.314
Switzerland	-.866	.711
Denmark	-.658	.563
Australia	-.746	.510
France	-.586	.616
Germany	-.741	.653
Belgium	-.850	.022
Norway	-.881	.140
Netherlands	-.805	.166
Iceland	-.810	.610
Finland	-.721	-.002
Austria	-.931	-.132
Japan	-.843	-.084
U.K.	-.565	.368
Spain	-.537	.495
Italy	-.641	-.437

things remaining unchanged. In this section we introduce a new nonparametric way of describing consumption data which provides further evidence on the validity of the law of demand. Existing nonparametric tests in demand analysis are mainly concerned with aspects of revealed preference; for a brief review, see Deaton (1984).

The log-change in the quantity consumed of good i from year t-1 to t is $Dq_{it} = \log q_{i,t} - \log q_{i,t-1}$. This Dq_{it} includes the effects of all the determinants of consumption, the effects of autonomous trends, income and relative prices. We commence by adjusting Dq_{it} to exclude the effects of the non-price determinants. To take account of the autonomous trends we subtract from Dq_{it} the constant term in the demand equation (6.1), α_i. Under the assumption of a unitary income elasticity, we can adjust for income by subtracting from Dq_{it} the log-change in real income, DQ_t. (This assumption will be relaxed in the next section.) Thus, adjusted consumption is

$$Dq_{it}^{*} = Dq_{it} - \alpha_i - DQ_t. \qquad (10.1)$$

This is the log-change in consumption of good i which results from change in relative prices and random factors only. For brevity, we shall subsequently refer to the adjusted consumption Dq_{it}^{*} as the 'relative consumption of i'. (Note that in Section 2.5 we called $Dq_{it} - DQ_t$ the log-change in the relative consumption of i; there should, however, be no confusion of terminology as now we will only use Dq_{it}^{*}.)

The law of demand predicts that Dq_{it}^{*} and the relative price change of good i, $Dp_{it}^{*} = Dp_{it} - DP_t$, would have opposite signs. Consider a 2×2 contingency table based on the signs of the pairs (Dq_{it}^*, Dp_{it}^*) for all goods in all years in all countries:

<table>
<tr><td rowspan="2"></td><td colspan="3" align="center">Sign of Relative Price, Dp_{it}^*</td></tr>
<tr><td align="center">Positive</td><td align="center">:</td><td align="center">Negative</td></tr>
<tr><td rowspan="2">Sign of Relative Consumption, Dq_{it}^* Positive</td><td align="center">I</td><td>:</td><td align="center">II</td></tr>
<tr><td align="center">IV</td><td>:</td><td align="center">III</td></tr>
</table>

If the law of demand were true, then most of the observations should lie in the off-diagonal cells, i.e. cells II and IV, implying that when the relative price of a good increases (decreases), its consumption grows less (more) rapidly than otherwise.

We implement (10.1) with the OECD data and use the estimates of the coefficients α_i given in Table 2.13. Table 2.20 presents the frequency distributions of the pairs of relative price and consumption changes. Rather than having four cells like the above 2×2 contingency table, Table 2.20 has four

TABLE 2.20

FREQUENCIES OF JOINT SIGNS OF RELATIVE CONSUMPTION AND

RELATIVE PRICES OF 10 COMMODITIES IN 18 COUNTRIES

In the table below, the first eleven data columns give **Positive relative prices** and the next eleven give **Negative relative prices**, each block ordered: Food, Beverages, Clothing, Housing, Durables, Medical care, Transport, Recreation, Education, Miscellaneous, All goods.

Country	Food	Beverages	Clothing	Housing	Durables	Medical care	Transport	Recreation	Education	Miscellaneous	All goods	Food	Beverages	Clothing	Housing	Durables	Medical care	Transport	Recreation	Education	Miscellaneous	All goods
Positive relative consumption																						
U.S.	1	1	4	2	3	3	7	4	12	1	38	3	4	14	1	15	1	11	15	0	1	65
Canada	1	0	1	1	4	9	1	3	11	2	33	6	3	9	1	17	8	15	16	0	2	77
Sweden	1	5	1	2	3	2	7	3	2	7	33	5	7	15	2	10	3	5	10	5	2	64
Switzerland	2	5	3	2	5	4	8	5		5	39	8	9	15	2	15	1	9	8		0	67
Denmark	1	0	1	3	2	2	3	2	3	5	22	5	9	12	1	7	6	9	7	3	4	63
Australia	0	2	3	1	1	6	6	9	7	3	38	2	7	14	1	16	2	11	9	5	5	72
France	0	1	1	6	1	1	11	0	2	1	24	1	5	9	1	14	0	4	7	0	2	43
Germany	0		6	1	3	3	6	5		1	25	6		11	1	13	3	9	8		3	54
Belgium	1	4	4	3	7	3	3	5	1	8	39	7	9	14	1	8	3	6	10	1	9	68
Norway	0	1	3	2	3	3	11	0	4	10	37	1	6	9	0	9	1	4	12	2	2	46
Netherlands	0	2	5	2	2	3	2	13	7	3	39	4	10	16	3	16	0	13	4	2	3	71
Iceland	2	0	2	1	3	2	1	3	1	3	18	0	5	5	2	7	1	7	5	2	7	41
Finland	1	4	3	0	8	2	4	4	10	2	38	1	6	8	2	6	1	7	9	1	2	43
Austria	0	0	0	1	1	1	9	0	3	2	17	1	5	17	0	12	0	7	5	1	2	50
Japan	2		3	1	1	1	1	1		4	14	1		5	1	7	3	4	6		1	28
U.K.	1	0	1	2	3	6	8	3	4	2	30	4	6	11	2	12	2	4	7	3	5	56
Spain	2	2	4	0	4	4	2	4		3	25	1	7	2	0	4	4	10	2	0	1	31
Italy	1	0	7	0	6	0	8	0	3	4	29	5	9	8	1	7	9	6	5	5	1	56
All countries	16	27	52	30	60	55	98	64	71	66	539	61	107	194	22	195	48	141	145	30	52	995
Negative relative consumption																						
U.S.	8	7	1	7	2	15	2	1	9	16	68	9	9	2	11	1	2	1	1	0	3	39
Canada	12	7	4	6	0	0	4	1	9	16	59	2	11	7	13	0	4	1	1	1	1	41
Sweden	7	5	0	10	2	7	4	1	6	8	50	4	0	1	3	2	5	1	3	4	0	23
Switzerland	5	3	1	11	1	13	2	5		13	54	6	4	2	6	0	3	2	3		3	29
Denmark	7	2	1	11	5	5	3	2	5	4	45	2	4	1	0	1	2	0	4	4	2	20
Australia	9	6	4	14	0	10	2	3	9	11	68	10	6	0	5	4	3	2	0	0	2	32
France	8	5	4	8	1	5	2	3	12	12	60	8	6	3	2	1	11	0	7	3	2	43
Germany	6		2	16	3	13	6	4		14	64	9		2	3	2	2	0	4		3	25
Belgium	6	4	1	5	1	9	8	6	5	4	49	7	4	2	12	5	6	4	0	14	0	54
Norway	7	6	5	5	4	9	1	2	6	3	48	9	4	0	10	1	4	1	3	5	2	39
Netherlands	11	2	3	13	1	19	8	6	14	15	92	10	11	1	7	6	3	2	2	2	4	48
Iceland	8	5	3	6	2	9	2	4	6	2	47	3	3	3	4	1	1	3	1	4	1	24
Finland	9	5	0	8	0	4	4	4	4	11	49	6	2	6	7	3	10	2	0	2	2	40
Austria	4	4	0	16	1	14	1	3	6	12	61	12	8	0	0	3	2	0	9	7	1	42
Japan	3		1	7	2	3	6	2		6	30	5		2	2	1	4	0	2		0	16
U.K.	4	5	2	12		5	2	3	9	9	52	8	6	3	1	1	4	3	4	1	1	32
Spain	4	1	6	4	5	4	1	6	10	5	46	6	3	1	9	0	1	0	1	3	4	28
Italy	4	3	2	12	2	5	2	4	7	12	53	7	5	0	4	2	3	1	8	2	0	32
All countries	122	70	40	171	38	149	60	60	117	173	995	123	86	36	99	34	70	23	53	52	31	607

quadrants. The first quadrant presents the number of pairs of relative prices and consumption that both have positive growth, disaggregated by commodity and country. The last row of this quadrant presents the frequency over all countries for each commodity and the last column presents the frequency over all goods for each country. The entries in the other three quadrants have the analogous interpretations.

To illustrate the working of Table 2.20, consider for example the U.S. The sample size for this country is 21 (see Table 2.2). Food consumption in the U.S. (adjusted for the autonomous trend) grows faster than income when its relative price increases only once during the sample period; this is indicated by the entry 1 in the first row of the first column of Table 2.20. Food consumption grows when the price falls in 3 years; consumption and the price both fall in 9 years; and consumption falls when the price increases in 8 years. These four entries in the table completely describe the 21 pairs of signs of the relative consumption and price of food in the U.S.

Next, consider the $21 \times 10 = 210$ pairs of signs of all goods in the U.S. Looking at the row totals in Table 2.20 for the U.S., $38 + 39 = 77$ pairs move in the same directions, while $65 + 68 = 133$ move in opposite directions. Overall, among the $\sum_{c=1}^{18} n^c T^c = 3135$ pairs of signs for all 18 countries (where, for country c, n^c is the number of commodities and T^c the number of observations), 538 of them have positive consumption and price growth; 995 have an increase in consumption and a fall in price; 607 have negative consumption and price growth; and 995 have a fall in consumption and a rise in price. This can be summarized as follows:

		Sign of Relative Price, Dp^*_{it}	
		Positive	Negative
Sign of Relative Consumption, Dq^*_{it}	Positive	538	995
	Negative	995	607

As can be seen, the off-diagonal entries are almost twice as large as the diagonals, so that this 2×2 matrix can be described as 'dominant non-diagonal'. This result gives clear support for the law of demand.

Table 2.21 presents the frequencies in Table 2.20 in percentage form. That is, the entries in the first quadrant of Table 2.21 are the percentages of the total number of observations having a simultaneous increase in relative prices and consumption, disaggregated by commodity and country. The entries in the other three quadrants have a similar interpretation. For example, for food in

INTERNATIONAL CONSUMPTION PATTERNS

TABLE 2.21

FREQUENCY DISTRIBUTIONS OF JOINT SIGNS OF RELATIVE CONSUMPTION AND

RELATIVE PRICES OF 10 COMMODITIES IN 18 COUNTRIES

(Percentages)

	Country	Positive relative prices											Negative relative prices										
		Food	Beverages	Clothing	Housing	Durables	Medical care	Transport	Recreation	Education	Miscellaneous	All goods	Food	Beverages	Clothing	Housing	Durables	Medical care	Transport	Recreation	Education	Miscellaneous	All goods
Positive relative consumption	U.S.	5	5	19	9	14	14	33	19	57	5	18	14	19	67	5	71	5	52	71	0	5	31
	Canada	5	0	5	5	19	43	5	14	52	9	16	29	14	43	5	81	38	71	76	0	10	37
	Sweden	6	29	6	12	18	12	41	18	12	41	19	29	41	88	12	59	18	29	59	29	12	38
	Switzerland	9	24	14	9	24	19	38	24		24	21	38	43	71	10	71	5	43	38		0	35
	Denmark	7	0	7	20	13	13	20	13	20	33	15	33	60	80	7	47	40	60	47	20	27	42
	Australia	0	9	14	5	5	29	29	43	33	14	18	10	33	67	5	76	10	52	43	24	24	34
	France	0	6	6	35	6	6	65	0	12	6	14	6	29	53	6	82	0	24	41	0	12	25
	Germany	0	0	29	5	14	14	29	24		5	15	29		52	5	62	14	43	38		14	32
	Belgium	5	19	19	14	33	14	14	24	5	38	19	33	43	67	5	38	14	29	48	5	43	32
	Norway	0	6	18	12	18	18	65	0	23	59	22	6	35	53	0	53	6	24	71	12	12	27
	Netherlands	0	8	20	8	8	12	8	52	28	12	16	16	40	64	12	64	0	52	16	8	12	28
	Iceland	15	0	15	8	23	15	8	23	8	23	14	0	39	39	15	54	8	54	39	15	54	32
	Finland	6	23	18	0	47	12	23	23	59	12	22	6	35	47	12	35	6	41	53	6	12	25
	Austria	0	0	0	6	6	6	53	0	18	12	10	6	29	100	0	71	0	41	29	6	12	29
	Japan	18		27	9	9	9	9	9		36	16	9		46	9	64	27	36	55		9	32
	U.K.	6	0	6	12	18	35	47	18	23	12	18	24	35	65	12	71	12	24	41	18	29	33
	Spain	15	15	31	0	31	31	15	31	0	23	19	8	54	15	0	31	31	77	15	0	8	24
	Italy	6	0	41	0	35	0	47	0	18	23	17	29	53	47	6	41	53	35	29	29	6	33
	All countries	5	9	16	9	19	17	30	20	26	20	17	19	37	60	7	61	15	44	45	11	16	32
Negative relative consumption	U.S.	38	33	5	33	10	71	10	5	43	76	32	43	43	9	52	5	9	5	5	0	14	19
	Canada	57	33	19	29	0	0	19	5	43	76	28	9	52	33	62	0	19	5	5	5	5	19
	Sweden	41	29	0	59	12	41	24	6	35	47	29	23	0	6	18	12	29	6	18	23	0	13
	Switzerland	24	14	5	52	5	62	10	24		62	29	29	19	9	29	0	14	9	14		14	15
	Denmark	47	13	7	73	33	33	20	13	33	27	30	13	27	7	0	7	13	0	27	27	13	13
	Australia	43	29	19	67	0	48	10	14	43	52	32	48	29	0	24	19	14	9	0	0	9	15
	France	47	29	24	47	6	29	12	18	71	71	35	47	35	18	12	6	65	0	41	18	12	25
	Germany	29		10	76	14	62	29	19		67	38	43		9	14	9	9	0	19		14	15
	Belgium	29	19	5	24	5	43	38	29	24	19	23	33	19	9	57	24	29	19	0	67	0	26
	Norway	41	35	29	29	24	53	6	12	35	18	28	53	23	0	59	6	23	6	18	29	12	23
	Netherlands	44	8	12	52	4	76	32	24	56	60	37	40	44	4	28	24	12	8	8	8	16	19
	Iceland	62	39	23	46	15	69	15	31	46	15	36	23	23	23	31	8	8	23	8	31	8	18
	Finland	53	29	0	47	0	24	24	24	24	65	29	35	12	35	41	18	59	12	0	12	12	23
	Austria	24	24	0	94	6	82	6	18	35	71	36	71	47	0	0	18	12	0	53	41	6	25
	Japan	27		9	64	18	27	55	18		55	34	45		18	18	9	36	0	18		0	18
	U.K.	24	29	12	71	6	29	12	18	53	53	31	47	35	18	6	6	23	18	23	6	6	19
	Spain	31	8	46	31	39	31	8	46	77	39	35	46	23	8	69	0	8	0	8	23	31	21
	Italy	24	18	12	71	12	29	12	24	41	71	31	41	29	0	23	12	18	6	47	12	0	19
	All countries	38	24	12	53	10	46	19	19	44	54	32	38	30	11	31	11	22	7	16	19	10	19

the U.S., relative prices and consumption move in the same directions for $5 + 43 = 48$ percent of the time, while they move in the opposite directions $14 + 38 = 52$ percent of the time. As can be seen from the 'All countries' rows and the 'All goods' columns, overall $32 + 32 = 64$ percent of the pairs of relative prices and consumption have opposite signs, while $17 + 19 = 36$ percent have the same signs.

Quadrants I and III of Table 2.21 refer to the situations where relative prices and consumption move in the same directions. Consequently, the information in these quadrants enables us to identify the major violators (commodities and countries) of the law of demand. If entries in the four quadrants of Table 2.21 occurred with equal probability, then each would be 25 percent. Thus using 30 percent as the cut-off value, the major villains in Table 2.21 are transport (30 percent of the cases are in quadrant I), food (38 percent in quadrant III), beverages (30 percent in quadrant III) and housing (31 percent in quadrant III). With respect to countries, there are none in quadrants I and III with more than 30 percent in the 'All goods' columns. Consequently, none of the countries individually is a major trouble-maker for the law of demand.

The entries in Table 2.20 are the number of occurrences of each sign pattern. In Table 2.22 we convert these count data to percentages within each quadrant. Thus, in the first quadrant, among the 538 occurrences of pairs of positive relative price and quantity changes (see Table 2.20), .2 percent of these

TABLE 2.22

FREQUENCY DISTRIBUTIONS OF 10 COMMODITIES IN 18 COUNTRIES

BY JOINT SIGNS OF RELATIVE CONSUMPTION AND RELATIVE PRICES

(Percentages)

Positive relative prices

Country	Food	Beverages	Clothing	Housing	Durables	Medical care	Transport	Recreation	Education	Miscellaneous	All goods
Positive relative consumption											
U.S.	.2	.2	.7	.4	.6	.6	1.3	.7	2.2	.2	7.1
Canada	.2	.0	.2	.2	.7	1.7	.2	.6	2.0	.4	6.1
Sweden	.2	.9	.2	.4	.6	.4	1.3	.6	.4	1.3	6.1
Switzerland	.4	.9	.6	.4	.9	.7	1.5	.9		.9	7.2
Denmark	.2	.0	.2	.6	.4	.4	.6	.4	.6	.9	4.1
Australia	.0	.4	.6	.2	.2	1.1	1.1	1.7	1.3	.6	7.1
France	.0	.2	.2	1.1	.2	.2	2.0	.0	.4	.2	4.5
Germany	.0		1.1	.2	.6	.6	1.1	.9		.2	4.6
Belgium	.2	.7	.7	.6	1.3	.6	.6	.9	.2	1.5	7.2
Norway	.0	.2	.6	.4	.6	.6	2.0	.0	.7	1.9	6.9
Netherlands	.0	.4	.9	.4	.4	.6	.4	2.4	1.3	.6	7.2
Iceland	.4	.0	.4	.2	.6	.4	.2	.6	.2	.6	3.3
Finland	.2	.7	.6	.0	1.5	.4	.7	.7	1.9	.4	7.1
Austria	.0	.0	.0	.2	.2	.2	1.7	.0	.6	.4	3.2
Japan	.4		.6	.2	.2	.2	.2	.2		.7	2.6
U.K.	.2	.0	.2	.4	.6	1.1	1.5	.6	.7	.4	5.6
Spain	.4	.4	.7	.0	.7	.7	.4	.7	.0	.6	4.6
Italy	.2	.0	1.3	.0	1.1	.0	1.5	.0	.6	.7	5.4
All countries	3.0	5.0	9.7	5.6	11.2	10.2	18.2	11.9	13.0	12.3	100.0
Negative relative consumption											
U.S.	.8	.7	.1	.7	.2	1.5	.2	.1	.9	1.6	6.8
Canada	1.2	.7	.4	.6	.0	.0	.4	.1	.9	1.6	5.9
Sweden	.7	.5	.0	1.0	.2	.7	.4	.1	.6	.8	5.0
Switzerland	.5	.3	.1	1.1	.1	1.3	.2	.5		1.3	5.4
Denmark	.7	.2	.1	1.1	.5	.5	.3	.2	.5	.4	4.5
Australia	.9	.6	.4	1.4	.0	1.0	.2	.3	.9	1.1	6.8
France	.8	.5	.4	.8	.1	.5	.2	.3	1.2	1.2	6.0
Germany	.6		.2	1.6	.3	1.3	.6	.4		1.4	6.4
Belgium	.6	.4	.1	.5	.1	.9	.8	.6	.5	.4	4.9
Norway	.7	.6	.5	.5	.4	.9	.1	.2	.6	.3	4.8
Netherlands	1.1	.2	.3	1.3	.1	1.9	.8	.6	1.4	1.5	9.2
Iceland	.8	.5	.3	.6	.2	.9	.2	.4	.6	.2	4.7
Finland	.9	.5	.0	.8	.0	.4	.4	.4	.4	1.1	4.9
Austria	.4	.4	.0	1.6	.1	1.4	.1	.3	.6	1.2	6.1
Japan	.3		.1	.7	.2	.3	.6	.2		.6	3.0
U.K.	.4	.5	.2	1.2	.1	.5	.2	.3	.9	.9	5.2
Spain	.4	.1	.6	.4	.5	.4	.1	.6	1.0	.5	4.6
Italy	.4	.3	.2	1.2	.2	.5	.2	.4	.7	1.2	5.3
All countries	12.3	7.0	4.0	17.2	3.3	15.0	6.0	6.0	11.8	17.4	100.0

Negative relative prices

Country	Food	Beverages	Clothing	Housing	Durables	Medical care	Transport	Recreation	Education	Miscellaneous	All goods
Positive relative consumption											
U.S.	.3	.4	1.4	.1	1.5	.1	1.1	1.5	.0	.1	6.5
Canada	.6	.3	.9	.1	1.7	.8	1.5	1.6	.0	.2	7.7
Sweden	.5	.7	1.5	.2	1.0	.3	.5	1.0	.5	.2	6.4
Switzerland	.8	.9	1.5	.2	1.5	.1	.9	.8		.0	6.7
Denmark	.5	.9	1.2	.1	.7	.6	.9	.7	.3	.4	6.3
Australia	.2	.7	1.4	.1	1.6	.2	1.1	.9	.5	.5	7.2
France	.1	.5	.9	.1	1.4	.0	.4	.7	.0	.2	4.3
Germany	.6		1.1	.1	1.3	.3	.9	.8		.3	5.4
Belgium	.7	.9	1.4	.1	.8	.3	.6	1.0	.1	.9	6.8
Norway	.1	.6	.9	.0	.9	.1	.4	1.2	.2	.2	4.6
Netherlands	.4	1.0	1.6	.3	1.6	.0	1.3	.4	.2	.3	7.1
Iceland	.0	.5	.5	.2	.7	.1	.7	.5	.2	.7	4.1
Finland	.1	.6	.8	.2	.6	.1	.7	.9	.1	.2	4.3
Austria	.1	.5	1.7	.0	1.2	.0	.7	.5	.1	.2	5.0
Japan	.1		.5	.1	.7	.3	.4	.6		.1	2.8
U.K.	.4	.6	1.1	.2	1.2	.2	.4	.7	.3	.5	5.6
Spain	.1	.7	.2	.0	.4	.4	1.0	.2	.0	.1	3.1
Italy	.5	.9	.8	.1	.7	.9	.6	.5	.5	.1	5.6
All countries	6.1	10.8	19.5	2.2	19.6	4.8	14.2	14.6	3.0	5.2	100.0
Negative relative consumption											
U.S.	1.5	1.5	.3	1.8	.2	.3	.2	.2	.0	.5	6.4
Canada	.3	1.8	1.2	2.1	.0	.7	.2	.2	.2	.2	6.8
Sweden	.7	.0	.2	.5	.3	.8	.2	.5	.7	.0	3.8
Switzerland	1.0	.7	.3	1.0	.0	.5	.3	.5		.5	4.8
Denmark	.3	.7	.2	.0	.2	.3	.0	.7	.7	.3	3.3
Australia	1.6	1.0	.0	.8	.7	.5	.3	.0	.0	.3	5.3
France	1.3	1.0	.5	.3	.2	1.8	.0	1.2	.5	.3	7.1
Germany	1.5		.3	.5	.3	.3	.0	.7		.5	4.1
Belgium	1.2	.7	.3	2.0	.8	1.0	.7	.0	2.3	.0	8.9
Norway	1.5	.7	.0	1.6	.2	.7	.2	.5	.8	.3	6.4
Netherlands	1.6	1.8	.2	1.2	1.0	.5	.3	.3	.3	.7	7.9
Iceland	.6	.5	.5	.7	.2	.2	.5	.2	.7	.2	4.0
Finland	1.0	.3	1.0	1.2	.5	1.6	.3	.0	.3	.3	6.6
Austria	2.0	1.3	.0	.0	.5	.3	.0	1.5	1.2	.2	6.9
Japan	.8		.3	.3	.2	.7	.0	.3		.0	2.6
U.K.	1.3	1.0	.5	.2	.2	.7	.5	.7	.2	.2	5.3
Spain	1.0	.5	.2	1.5	.0	.2	.0	.2	.5	.7	4.6
Italy	1.2	.8	.0	.7	.3	.5	.2	1.3	.3	.0	5.3
All countries	20.3	14.2	5.9	16.3	5.6	11.5	3.8	8.7	8.6	5.1	100.0

are for food in the U.S., .2 percent for beverages in the U.S. and so on. If we consider all goods, we see that 7.1 percent of the observations having this sign configuration are from the U.S, 6.1 percent from Canada and so on. Considering the 'All countries' row in the first quadrant, it can be seen that 3.0 percent of this sign configuration are from food, 5.0 percent from beverages etc. The other three quadrants are interpreted in a similar manner.

The row for 'All countries' in the first quadrant of Table 2.22 shows that transport is the main contributor to the violation of the law of demand in so far as this quadrant is concerned. Similarly we see that food, beverages and housing are the main deviants in quadrant III. However, looking at the 'All goods' columns in quadrants I and III we see that no individual country is a dominant contributor.

Table 2.23 presents a summary picture of Table 2.20. The upper half of Table 2.23 adds the corresponding entries in quadrants I and III of Table 2.20 to give the frequencies of the relative prices and consumption moving in the same directions. The lower half of the table presents the frequencies of those moving in the opposite directions; this lower half is constructed by adding the corresponding entries in quadrants II and IV of Table 2.20. Looking at the entries in column 12 for the U.S., we see that 77 of the pairs of relative prices and consumption move in the same directions, while 133 move in opposite directions. For all commodities and countries, among the 3135 pairs, 1990 pairs move in opposite directions, while the rest move in the same directions.

TABLE 2.23

SUMMARY OF FREQUENCIES OF JOINT SIGNS OF RELATIVE CONSUMPTION AND RELATIVE PRICES OF 10 COMMODITIES IN 18 COUNTRIES

Country	Food	Beverages	Clothing	Housing	Durables	Medical care	Transport	Recreation	Education	Miscellaneous	All goods
(1)	(2)	(3)	(4)	(5)	(6)	(7)	(8)	(9)	(10)	(11)	(12)
Relative consumption and relative prices move in the same directions											
U.S.	10	10	6	13	4	5	8	5	12	4	77
Canada	3	11	8	14	4	13	2	4	12	3	74
Sweden	5	5	2	5	5	7	8	6	6	7	56
Switzerland	8	9	5	8	5	7	10	8		8	68
Denmark	3	4	2	3	3	4	3	6	7	7	42
Australia	10	8	3	6	5	9	8	9	7	5	70
France	8	7	4	8	2	12	11	7	5	3	67
Germany	9		8	4	5	5	6	9		4	50
Belgium	8	8	6	15	12	9	7	5	15	8	93
Norway	9	5	3	12	4	7	12	3	9	12	76
Netherlands	10	13	6	9	8	6	4	15	9	7	87
Iceland	5	3	5	5	4	3	4	4	5	4	42
Finland	7	6	9	7	11	12	6	4	12	4	78
Austria	12	8	0	1	4	3	9	9	10	3	59
Japan	7		5	3	2	5	1	3		4	30
U.K.	9	6	4	3	4	10	11	7	5	3	62
Spain	8	5	5	9	4	5	2	5	3	7	53
Italy	8	5	7	4	8	3	9	8	5	4	61
All countries	139	113	88	129	94	125	121	117	122	97	1145
Relative consumption and relative prices move in opposite directions											
U.S.	11	11	15	8	17	16	13	16	9	17	133
Canada	18	10	13	7	17	8	19	17	9	18	136
Sweden	12	12	15	12	12	10	9	11	11	10	114
Switzerland	13	12	16	13	16	14	11	13		13	121
Denmark	12	11	13	12	12	11	12	9	8	8	108
Australia	11	13	18	15	16	12	13	12	14	16	140
France	9	10	13	9	15	5	6	10	12	14	103
Germany	12		13	17	16	16	15	12		17	118
Belgium	13	13	15	6	9	12	14	16	6	13	117
Norway	8	12	14	5	13	10	5	14	8	5	94
Netherlands	15	12	19	16	17	19	21	10	16	18	163
Iceland	8	10	8	8	9	10	9	9	8	9	88
Finland	10	11	8	10	6	5	11	13	5	13	92
Austria	5	9	17	16	13	14	8	8	7	14	111
Japan	4		6	8	9	6	10	8		7	58
U.K.	8	11	13	14	13	7	6	10	12	14	108
Spain	5	8	8	4	9	8	11	8	10	6	77
Italy	9	12	10	13	9	14	8	9	12	13	109
All countries	183	177	234	193	228	197	201	205	147	225	1990

Table 2.24 is the percentage version of Table 2.23. It is to be noted that in all countries prices and consumption move in opposite directions more than 50 percent of the time. Indeed, for most countries the figure is substantially above 50 percent.

2.11 MORE ON THE NONPARAMETRIC PICTURE

In the last section we defined the change in relative consumption of good i as the deviation of its quantity log-change from its autonomous trend and the Divisia volume index, $Dq_{it} - \alpha_i - DQ_t$. This assumes unitary income elasticities for all goods. In this section we relax this assumption by using our estimates of the income elasticities from the double-log demand equations. Thus we now define relative consumption as $Dq_{it} - \alpha_i - \eta_i DQ_t$, where η_i is the estimate of the income elasticity of good i presented in Table 2.14.

Table 2.25 presents the frequency distributions of the pairs of signs of relative prices and consumption. This table is to be compared with Table 2.20. Table 2.26 is the percentage version of Table 2.25 and is comparable with Table 2.21. As can be seen, overall, $18 + 17 = 35$ percent of the pairs of relative prices and consumption move in the same directions, while $34 + 31 = 65$ percent move in opposite directions. Looking at the 'All

TABLE 2.24

SUMMARY OF FREQUENCY DISTRIBUTIONS OF JOINT SIGNS OF RELATIVE

CONSUMPTION AND RELATIVE PRICES OF 10 COMMODITIES IN 18 COUNTRIES

(Percentages)

Country (1)	Food (2)	Beverages (3)	Clothing (4)	Housing (5)	Durables (6)	Medical care (7)	Transport (8)	Recreation (9)	Education (10)	Miscellaneous (11)	All goods (12)
Relative consumption and relative prices move in the same directions											
U.S.	48	48	29	62	19	24	38	24	57	19	37
Canada	14	52	38	67	19	62	9	19	57	14	35
Sweden	29	29	12	29	29	41	47	35	35	41	33
Switzerland	38	43	24	38	24	33	48	38		38	36
Denmark	20	27	13	20	20	27	20	40	47	47	28
Australia	48	38	14	29	24	43	38	43	33	24	33
France	47	41	23	47	12	71	65	41	29	18	39
Germany	43		38	19	24	24	29	43		19	30
Belgium	38	38	29	71	57	43	33	24	71	38	44
Norway	53	29	18	71	23	41	71	18	53	71	45
Netherlands	40	52	24	36	32	24	16	60	36	28	35
Iceland	38	23	38	38	31	23	31	31	38	31	32
Finland	41	35	53	41	65	71	35	23	71	23	46
Austria	71	47	0	6	23	18	53	53	59	18	35
Japan	64		45	27	18	45	9	27		36	34
U.K.	53	35	23	18	23	59	65	41	29	18	36
Spain	61	38	38	69	31	38	15	38	23	54	41
Italy	47	29	41	23	47	18	53	47	29	23	36
All countries	43	39	27	40	29	39	38	36	45	30	36
Relative consumption and relative prices move in opposite directions											
U.S.	52	52	71	38	81	76	62	76	43	81	63
Canada	86	48	62	33	81	38	90	81	43	86	65
Sweden	71	71	88	71	71	59	53	65	65	59	67
Switzerland	62	57	76	62	76	67	52	62		62	64
Denmark	80	73	87	80	80	73	80	60	53	53	72
Australia	52	62	86	71	76	57	62	57	67	76	67
France	53	59	76	53	88	29	35	59	71	82	61
Germany	57		62	81	76	76	71	57		81	70
Belgium	62	62	71	29	43	57	67	76	29	62	56
Norway	47	71	82	29	76	59	29	82	47	29	55
Netherlands	60	48	76	64	68	76	84	40	64	72	65
Iceland	61	77	61	61	69	77	69	69	61	69	68
Finland	59	65	47	59	35	29	65	76	29	76	54
Austria	29	53	100	94	76	82	47	47	41	82	65
Japan	36		54	73	82	54	91	73		64	66
U.K.	47	65	76	82	76	41	35	59	71	82	63
Spain	38	61	61	31	69	61	85	61	77	46	59
Italy	53	71	59	76	53	82	47	53	71	76	64
All countries	57	61	73	60	71	61	62	64	55	70	63

TABLE 2.25

FREQUENCIES OF JOINT SIGNS OF RELATIVE CONSUMPTION AND

RELATIVE PRICES OF 10 COMMODITIES IN 18 COUNTRIES:

NON-UNITARY INCOME ELASTICITIES

Country	Positive relative prices											Negative relative prices										
	Food	Beverages	Clothing	Housing	Durables	Medical care	Transport	Recreation	Education	Miscellaneous	All goods	Food	Beverages	Clothing	Housing	Durables	Medical care	Transport	Recreation	Education	Miscellaneous	All goods
Positive relative consumption																						
U.S.	4	4	2	3	2	6	5	2	12	3	43	7	5	12	7	13	2	6	11	0	4	67
Canada	1	1	2	1	1	8	0	2	10	2	28	7	10	11	8	14	6	12	11	0	2	81
Sweden	1	4	1	3	1	5	2	1	2	7	27	8	5	15	3	8	4	4	9	6	2	64
Switzerland	2	3	1	6	1	8	3	5		11	40	11	7	10	5	12	2	7	8		0	62
Denmark	2	0	1	4	2	3	3	0	4	5	24	6	11	11	1	7	6	4	7	4	4	61
Australia	3	3	3	4	1	9	1	4	5	4	37	8	10	10	2	10	2	8	6	4	5	65
France	1	1	1	9	1	5	2	2	4	1	27	8	9	9	2	8	3	3	10	2	3	57
Germany	3		4	7	2	6	3	5		5	35	12		10	3	12	4	8	8		3	60
Belgium	2	4	0	5	3	7	4	3	5	6	39	8	9	13	7	6	4	6	9	11	6	79
Norway	1	1	1	5	3	4	5	0	4	10	34	7	8	9	5	8	2	3	12	3	2	59
Netherlands	7	1	1	6	1	5	2	10	7	7	47	8	12	13	6	12	3	13	3	3	5	78
Iceland	5	0	2	3	2	3	1	3	1	1	21	1	7	4	3	6	1	5	4	4	6	41
Finland	3	3	1	4	3	3	2	2	7	5	33	5	6	7	5	2	5	6	7	1	2	46
Austria	1	2	0	7	1	5	4	0	3	5	28	8	11	11	0	11	1	3	9	2	2	58
Japan	2		1	2	0	1	1	1		2	10	2		3	3	5	6	4	6		1	30
U.K.	2	0	1	3	2	6	5	2	4	2	27	6	9	10	3	10	1	4	6	3	4	56
Spain	3	2	4	2	2	2	1	4	3	4	27	4	7	2	2	3	4	7	1	3	2	35
Italy	2	0	3	7	6	0	6	1	4	4	33	7	9	6	1	4	9	3	9	5	1	54
All countries	45	29	29	81	34	86	50	47	75	84	560	123	135	166	66	151	65	106	136	51	54	1053
Negative relative consumption																						
U.S.	5	4	3	6	3	12	4	3	9	14	63	5	8	4	5	3	1	6	5	0	0	37
Canada	12	6	3	6	3	1	5	2	10	16	64	1	4	5	6	3	6	4	6	1	1	37
Sweden	7	6	0	9	4	4	9	3	6	8	56	1	2	1	2	4	4	2	4	3	0	23
Switzerland	5	5	3	7	5	9	7	5		7	53	3	6	7	3	3	2	4	3		3	34
Denmark	6	2	1	10	5	4	3	4	4	4	43	1	2	2	0	1	2	5	4	3	2	22
Australia	6	5	4	11	0	7	7	8	11	10	69	4	3	4	4	10	3	5	3	1	2	39
France	7	5	4	6	1	1	11	1	10	12	57	1	2	3	1	7	8	1	4	1	1	29
Germany	3		4	10	4	10	9	4		10	54	3		3	1	3	1	1	4		3	19
Belgium	5	4	5	3	5	5	7	8	1	6	49	6	4	3	6	7	5	4	1	4	3	43
Norway	6	6	7	2	4	8	7	2	6	3	51	3	2	0	5	2	3	2	3	4	2	26
Netherlands	4	3	7	9	2	17	8	9	14	11	84	6	9	4	4	10	0	2	3	1	2	41
Iceland	5	5	3	4	3	8	2	4	6	4	44	2	1	4	3	2	1	5	2	2	2	24
Finland	7	6	2	4	5	3	6	6	7	8	54	2	2	7	4	7	6	3	2	2	2	37
Austria	3	2	0	10	1	10	6	3	6	9	50	5	2	6	0	4	1	4	5	6	1	34
Japan	3		3	6	3	3	6	2		8	34	4		4	0	3	1	0	2		0	14
U.K.	3	5	2	11	2	5	5	4	9	9	55	6	3	4	0	3	5	3	5	1	2	32
Spain	3	1	6	2	7	6	2	6	7	4	44	3	3	1	7	1	1	3	2	0	3	24
Italy	3	3	6	5	2	5	4	3	6	12	49	5	5	2	4	5	3	4	4	2	0	34
All countries	93	68	63	120	59	118	108	77	112	155	973	61	58	64	55	78	53	58	62	31	29	549

TABLE 2.26

FREQUENCY DISTRIBUTIONS OF JOINT SIGNS OF RELATIVE CONSUMPTION AND

RELATIVE PRICES OF 10 COMMODITIES IN 18 COUNTRIES:

NON-UNITARY INCOME ELASTICITIES

(Percentages)

Positive relative prices

Country	Food	Beverages	Clothing	Housing	Durables	Medical care	Transport	Recreation	Education	Miscellaneous	All goods
Positive relative consumption											
U.S.	19	19	9	14	9	29	24	9	57	14	20
Canada	5	5	9	5	5	38	0	9	48	9	13
Sweden	6	23	6	18	6	29	12	6	12	41	16
Switzerland	9	14	5	29	5	38	14	24		52	21
Denmark	13	0	7	27	13	20	20	0	27	33	16
Australia	14	14	14	19	5	43	5	19	24	19	18
France	6	6	6	53	6	29	12	12	23	6	16
Germany	14		19	33	9	29	14	24		24	21
Belgium	9	19	0	24	14	33	19	14	24	29	19
Norway	6	6	6	29	18	23	29	0	23	59	20
Netherlands	28	4	4	24	4	20	8	40	28	28	19
Iceland	38	0	15	23	15	23	8	23	8	8	16
Finland	18	18	6	23	18	18	12	12	41	29	19
Austria	6	12	0	41	6	29	23	0	18	29	16
Japan	18		9	18	0	9	9	9		18	11
U.K.	12	0	6	18	12	35	29	12	23	12	16
Spain	23	15	31	15	15	15	8	31	23	31	21
Italy	12	0	18	41	35	0	35	6	23	23	19
All countries	14	10	9	25	11	27	15	15	28	26	18
Negative relative consumption											
U.S.	24	19	14	29	14	57	19	14	43	67	30
Canada	57	29	14	29	14	5	24	9	48	76	30
Sweden	41	35	0	53	23	23	53	18	35	47	33
Switzerland	24	24	14	33	24	43	33	24		33	28
Denmark	40	13	7	67	33	27	20	27	27	27	29
Australia	29	24	19	52	0	33	33	38	52	48	33
France	41	29	23	29	6	6	65	6	59	71	33
Germany	14		19	48	19	48	43	19		48	32
Belgium	24	19	24	14	24	24	33	38	5	29	23
Norway	35	35	41	12	23	47	41	12	35	18	30
Netherlands	16	12	28	36	8	68	32	36	56	44	34
Iceland	38	38	23	31	23	61	15	31	46	31	34
Finland	41	35	12	23	29	18	35	35	41	47	32
Austria	18	12	0	59	6	59	35	18	35	53	29
Japan	27		27	54	27	27	54	18		73	39
U.K.	18	29	12	65	12	29	29	23	53	53	32
Spain	23	8	46	15	54	46	15	46	54	31	34
Italy	18	18	35	29	12	29	23	18	35	71	29
All countries	29	23	20	37	18	37	33	24	42	48	31

Negative relative prices

Country	Food	Beverages	Clothing	Housing	Durables	Medical care	Transport	Recreation	Education	Miscellaneous	All goods
Positive relative consumption											
U.S.	33	24	57	33	62	9	29	52	0	19	32
Canada	33	48	52	38	67	29	57	52	0	9	39
Sweden	47	29	88	18	47	23	23	53	35	12	38
Switzerland	52	33	48	24	57	9	33	38		0	33
Denmark	40	73	73	7	47	40	27	47	27	27	41
Australia	38	48	48	9	48	9	38	29	19	24	31
France	47	53	53	12	47	18	18	59	12	18	33
Germany	57		48	14	57	19	38	38		14	36
Belgium	38	43	62	33	29	19	29	43	52	29	38
Norway	41	47	53	29	47	12	18	71	18	12	35
Netherlands	32	48	52	24	48	12	52	12	12	20	31
Iceland	8	54	31	23	46	8	38	31	31	46	31
Finland	29	35	41	29	12	29	35	41	6	12	27
Austria	47	65	65	0	65	6	18	53	12	12	34
Japan	18		27	27	45	54	36	54		9	34
U.K.	35	53	59	18	59	6	23	35	18	23	33
Spain	31	54	15	15	23	31	54	8	23	15	27
Italy	41	53	35	6	23	53	18	53	29	6	32
All countries	38	47	52	20	47	20	33	42	19	17	34
Negative relative consumption											
U.S.	24	38	19	24	14	5	29	24	0	0	18
Canada	5	19	24	29	14	29	19	29	5	5	18
Sweden	6	12	6	12	23	23	12	23	18	0	13
Switzerland	14	29	33	14	14	9	19	14		14	18
Denmark	7	13	13	0	7	13	33	27	20	13	15
Australia	19	14	19	19	48	14	24	14	5	9	19
France	6	12	18	6	41	47	6	23	6	6	17
Germany	14		14	5	14	5	5	19		14	11
Belgium	29	19	14	29	33	24	19	5	19	14	20
Norway	18	12	0	29	12	18	12	18	23	12	15
Netherlands	24	36	16	16	40	0	8	12	4	8	16
Iceland	15	8	31	23	15	8	38	15	15	15	18
Finland	12	12	41	23	41	35	18	12	12	12	22
Austria	29	12	35	0	23	6	23	29	35	6	20
Japan	36		36	0	27	9	0	18		0	16
U.K.	35	18	23	0	18	29	18	29	6	12	19
Spain	23	23	8	54	8	8	23	15	0	23	18
Italy	29	29	12	23	29	18	23	23	12	0	20
All countries	19	20	20	17	24	16	18	19	11	9	17

countries' rows in quadrants I and III and using 30 percent as the cut-off value (as before), we see that now no individual good has a significant contribution to the violation of the law of demand. Thus, in this sense, the overall results improve slightly when we use non-unitary income elasticities.

APPENDICES TO CHAPTER 2

A2.1 SUMMARY STATISTICS FOR THE DEMAND EQUATIONS

Table A2.1 presents the values of R^2, the Durbin-Watson (DW) statistic and the standard error of estimate (SEE) implied by models (6.2) and (6.3) for the 18 countries. The format of this table is exactly the same as Tables 2.13-2.15. For brevity, we shall focus on the values of the summary statistics averaged over all countries; these are contained in the rows labelled 'Mean'. As can be seen, the fit of the model is satisfactory except for housing, medical care and education. The DW statistics indicates no serial correlation except for education. The standard errors of estimate range from 1.3 percent (for food) to 4.8 percent (education).

TABLE A2.1

SUMMARY STATISTICS FOR THE DEMAND EQUATIONS

WITH AUTONOMOUS TRENDS FOR 10 COMMODITIES IN 18 COUNTRIES

Country (1)		Food (2)	Beverages (3)	Clothing (4)	Housing (5)	Durables (6)	Medical care (7)	Transport (8)	Recreation (9)	Education (10)	Miscellaneous (11)
U.S.	R^2	.59	.23	.70	.67	.83	.30	.85	.62	.33	.63
	DW	1.42	1.27	2.75	1.64	1.32	1.38	2.14	1.75	.36	1.87
	PROB	.07	.03	.94	.15	.04	.05	.60	.20	.00	.33
	SEE	1.55	1.33	1.51	.55	1.65	1.69	2.18	1.68	2.51	1.08
Canada	R^2	.82	.54	.38	.14	.78	.25	.76	.70	.18	.65
	DW	1.67	1.44	2.16	1.42	1.21	1.13	1.83	1.88	.35	2.19
	PROB	.17	.07	.54	.05	.02	.01	.27	.28	.00	.59
	SEE	1.21	1.57	2.70	1.20	1.76	9.23	2.20	2.50	6.19	1.50
Sweden	R^2	.72	.67	.64	.35	.81	.11	.74	.68	.28	.56
	DW	1.83	1.29	1.22	1.98	2.28	1.66	2.34	1.23	1.92	2.51
	PROB	.31	.07	.03	.45	.69	.24	.75	.04	.31	.81
	SEE	.98	2.57	2.29	.87	1.89	3.02	2.52	2.33	4.61	1.96
Switzerland	R^2	.81	.74	.74	.08	.87	.18	.58	.59		.62
	DW	1.86	1.09	1.19	1.97	1.57	1.06	1.55	1.75		1.72
	PROB	.30	.01	.01	.43	.09	.00	.13	.25		.18
	SEE	.99	1.72	2.16	1.63	1.47	1.93	2.62	1.27		1.13
Denmark	R^2	.24	.75	.74	.40	.87	.24	.89	.64	.00	.73
	DW	2.65	1.62	2.33	1.09	2.43	1.40	2.81	1.34	2.44	2.79
	PROB	.90	.19	.72	.02	.79	.10	.95	.06	.76	.93
	SEE	1.64	1.28	3.10	1.84	2.24	3.99	2.70	2.84	4.18	1.85
Australia	R^2	.62	.82	.66	.49	.42	.07	.57	.44	.24	.54
	DW	2.12	1.91	1.65	1.23	1.31	2.44	2.13	2.64	.62	2.24
	PROB	.55	.42	.15	.03	.04	.82	.57	.93	.00	.72
	SEE	.73	.99	1.83	1.45	4.17	3.82	2.42	5.21	7.52	1.29
France	R^2	.58	.49	.67	.56	.55	.33	.84	.50	.07	.94
	DW	1.36	2.64	2.15	2.40	2.17	2.06	1.69	1.84	2.39	1.73
	PROB	.06	.91	.54	.75	.61	.50	.24	.33	.79	.23
	SEE	.54	1.09	1.33	1.07	2.22	1.69	1.63	1.19	6.66	.58
Germany	R^2	.68		.83	.04	.81	.43	.84	.61		.74
	DW	2.05		2.34	2.02	1.98	1.98	1.57	1.24		2.52
	PROB	.49		.70	.44	.39	.42	.10	.02		.86
	SEE	.83		1.36	1.66	1.49	2.28	2.62	1.60		.96
Belgium	R^2	.36	.41	.55	.29	.44	.20	.44	.42	.04	.68
	DW	2.17	2.14	2.52	2.37	2.50	1.80	2.09	2.93	1.08	2.23
	PROB	.61	.59	.87	.75	.83	.25	.53	.98	.01	.71
	SEE	1.43	2.46	2.30	1.97	2.94	3.08	2.32	2.39	.76	4.18
Norway	R^2	.53	.74	.78	.02	.71	.38	.90	.73	.08	.75
	DW	2.16	1.57	1.51	2.05	1.50	1.10	1.61	1.91	1.16	2.01
	PROB	.66	.22	.16	.55	.16	.02	.24	.40	.03	.51
	SEE	.70	2.62	1.71	1.50	2.12	3.67	2.65	1.43	5.16	1.45
Netherlands	R^2	.35	.35	.77	.38	.47	.30	.77	.29	.29	.32
	DW	2.07	2.65	3.03	1.73	2.50	1.82	2.20	1.47	2.42	1.60
	PROB	.53	.93	1.00	.20	.88	.30	.67	.08	.83	.15
	SEE	1.80	3.87	3.27	2.73	4.16	3.41	3.87	4.21	3.92	2.65
Iceland	R^2	.63	.64	.78	.07	.89	.37	.83	.67	.52	.76
	DW	2.45	2.56	1.57	1.58	2.59	2.20	1.44	.93	.85	2.74
	PROB	.73	.78	.16	.14	.79	.65	.15	.02	.01	.91
	SEE	2.59	4.56	5.43	1.80	5.17	4.96	8.65	6.30	4.41	6.49
Finland	R^2	.74	.66	.52	.26	.73	.39	.63	.77	.29	.61
	DW	2.29	1.98	2.56	1.75	1.71	1.88	1.75	2.52	.79	1.91
	PROB	.67	.43	.87	.27	.20	.35	.25	.82	.00	.35
	SEE	1.20	3.39	5.60	1.00	3.80	3.12	5.69	3.89	10.13	2.05
Austria	R^2	.13	.19	.79	.12	.52	.23	.86	.43	.04	.55
	DW	2.89	2.47	1.47	1.84	2.22	1.64	1.24	1.81	2.84	2.42
	PROB	.98	.83	.10	.30	.64	.17	.05	.33	.97	.80
	SEE	1.70	2.92	1.88	1.96	3.77	2.89	2.71	2.29	4.62	1.27
Japan	R^2	.77		.78	.63	.70	.74	.71	.72		.78
	DW	2.09		2.23	2.28	2.45	2.28	1.99	2.16		2.12
	PROB	.44		.64	.55	.71	.70	.53	.63		.54
	SEE	1.32		2.83	.63	5.56	2.14	3.25	2.78		2.68
U.K.	R^2	.32	.71	.73	.46	.92	.31	.72	.74	.53	.83
	DW	2.23	1.65	1.76	1.96	2.84	1.50	1.46	1.60	1.34	2.41
	PROB	.61	.23	.25	.38	.95	.11	.11	.15	.05	.72
	SEE	.97	2.44	1.48	1.02	1.38	4.91	2.70	1.79	3.12	1.30
Spain	R^2	.41	.44	.55	.53	.63	.22	.68	.62	.17	.33
	DW	1.66	1.94	1.68	2.17	1.50	1.43	1.99	2.34	1.36	1.75
	PROB	.21	.33	.24	.50	.15	.09	.50	.64	.08	.27
	SEE	1.83	2.33	2.13	1.01	2.43	5.70	4.44	2.52	2.87	2.03
Italy	R^2	.85	.51	.85	.74	.69	.43	.62	.64	.09	.80
	DW	1.61	1.93	2.18	2.29	1.12	1.47	1.78	2.49	1.19	2.54
	PROB	.15	.40	.62	.66	.02	.09	.30	.78	.02	.83
	SEE	.90	1.72	1.92	.68	2.94	3.56	3.18	1.84	4.97	1.26
Mean	R^2	.56	.55	.69	.35	.70	.30	.73	.60	.21	.66
	DW	2.03	1.88	2.02	1.88	1.96	1.68	1.87	1.88	1.41	2.18
	SEE	1.27	2.30	2.49	1.37	2.84	3.62	3.24	2.67	4.78	1.98

All SEEs are to be divided by 100.

A2.2 ESTIMATES OF THE DEMAND EQUATIONS
WITH THE AUTONOMOUS TRENDS SUPPRESSED

In this appendix we present the LS estimates of models (6.2) and (6.3) with the autonomous trend terms suppressed. Table A2.2 presents the estimates of the income elasticities. Again, this table has the same format as before. As can be seen, all elasticities are positive and the pooled estimates are similar to the mean values. Table A2.3 presents the price elasticities. Table A2.4 presents the values of the DW statistics and the SEEs implied by the models when the trend terms are omitted. This table is interpreted in the same way as Table A2.1.

Tables A2.5 and A2.6 present cross-country frequency distributions of the estimates and their $|t|$-values when the trend terms are omitted. These tables are interpreted in the same way as Tables 2.16 and 2.17.

TABLE A2.2

ESTIMATES OF INCOME ELASTICITIES FOR 10 COMMODITIES IN 18 COUNTRIES:

AUTONOMOUS TRENDS SUPPRESSED

(Standard errors are in parentheses)

Country	Food η_1^c	Beverages η_2^c	Clothing η_3^c	Housing η_4^c	Durables η_5^c	Medical care η_6^c	Transport η_7^c	Recreation η_8^c	Education η_9^c	Miscellaneous η_{10}^c
(1)	(2)	(3)	(4)	(5)	(6)	(7)	(8)	(9)	(10)	(11)
U.S.	.29 (.11)	.53 (.10)	.90 (.13)	.94 (.10)	.78 (.19)	1.44 (.26)	1.61 (.23)	1.36 (.13)	1.02 (.26)	.81 (.09)
Canada	.59 (.08)	.66 (.12)	.73 (.19)	.77 (.14)	1.05 (.17)	.93 (.65)	1.34 (.16)	1.93 (.18)	1.64 (.55)	1.24 (.14)
Sweden	.29 (.10)	1.03 (.31)	.96 (.29)	.74 (.23)	1.33 (.24)	1.14 (.35)	1.74 (.26)	1.73 (.26)	1.40 (.48)	.82 (.33)
Switzerland	.72 (.09)	.93 (.17)	1.11 (.31)	.69 (.16)	.84 (.25)	.87 (.21)	1.68 (.20)	1.15 (.10)		.90 (.16)
Denmark	.29 (.16)	.62 (.11)	1.25 (.34)	.70 (.24)	.92 (.35)	.37 (.34)	1.99 (.30)	1.25 (.24)	1.38 (.72)	.90 (.16)
Australia	.36 (.08)	.54 (.09)	.41 (.19)	1.35 (.15)	2.11 (.55)	.68 (.36)	1.51 (.19)	2.18 (.42)	.79 (.89)	.88 (.10)
France	.44 (.03)	.37 (.08)	.38 (.12)	1.16 (.09)	.89 (.20)	1.73 (.14)	1.55 (.11)	1.24 (.09)	.88 (.50)	1.08 (.04)
Germany	.54 (.05)		.94 (.11)	.68 (.15)	1.07 (.11)	.74 (.17)	1.96 (.16)	1.13 (.09)		1.10 (.08)
Belgium	.49 (.09)	.83 (.15)	.85 (.16)	.82 (.12)	1.32 (.17)	1.41 (.22)	1.32 (.15)	1.25 (.14)	.48 (.08)	1.42 (.28)
Norway	.40 (.06)	.71 (.18)	.66 (.15)	.81 (.18)	1.26 (.15)	.91 (.30)	2.24 (.28)	1.38 (.12)	.58 (.42)	.77 (.13)
Netherlands	.50 (.07)	.85 (.19)	.87 (.19)	.89 (.13)	1.53 (.21)	1.13 (.23)	1.28 (.17)	1.05 (.22)	1.18 (.20)	1.11 (.14)
Iceland	.44 (.09)	.93 (.16)	1.22 (.21)	.18 (.11)	1.58 (.23)	.92 (.29)	1.85 (.40)	1.38 (.24)	.39 (.28)	1.67 (.22)
Finland	.51 (.06)	1.23 (.16)	.97 (.30)	.57 (.10)	1.66 (.20)	1.28 (.19)	1.78 (.28)	1.46 (.19)	.72 (.62)	1.17 (.17)
Austria	.45 (.11)	.49 (.21)	1.39 (.19)	.81 (.22)	1.32 (.34)	.25 (.41)	2.12 (.23)	1.02 (.18)	.44 (.31)	.81 (.12)
Japan	.57 (.11)		.96 (.29)	1.04 (.21)	1.26 (.55)	1.20 (.28)	1.39 (.24)	.98 (.20)		1.52 (.23)
U.K.	.20 (.09)	.60 (.29)	1.12 (.13)	.60 (.13)	1.44 (.23)	1.01 (.44)	1.77 (.23)	1.52 (.17)	1.24 (.35)	1.12 (.11)
Spain	.65 (.10)	.93 (.14)	.84 (.15)	.81 (.09)	.96 (.14)	2.19 (.37)	2.16 (.32)	1.41 (.17)	.89 (.19)	1.22 (.13)
Italy	.72 (.06)	.75 (.11)	1.16 (.16)	.74 (.07)	1.29 (.19)	1.50 (.24)	1.68 (.19)	.74 (.13)	.52 (.29)	1.10 (.10)
Mean	.47 (.02)	.75 (.04)	.93 (.05)	.79 (.04)	1.26 (.07)	1.09 (.08)	1.72 (.06)	1.34 (.05)	.90 (.12)	1.09 (.04)
All countries	.49 (.02)	.72 (.04)	.97 (.05)	.74 (.04)	1.30 (.05)	1.12 (.07)	1.76 (.05)	1.32 (.04)	.60 (.08)	1.20 (.04)

TABLE A2.3

ESTIMATES OF PRICE ELASTICITIES FOR 10 COMMODITIES IN 18 COUNTRIES:

AUTONOMOUS TRENDS SUPPRESSED

(Standard errors are in parentheses)

Country	Food	Beverages	Clothing	Housing	Durables	Medical care	Transport	Recreation	Education	Miscellaneous
	γ_1^c	γ_2^c	γ_3^c	γ_4^c	γ_5^c	γ_6^c	γ_7^c	γ_8^c	γ_9^c	γ_{10}^c
(1)	(2)	(3)	(4)	(5)	(6)	(7)	(8)	(9)	(10)	(11)
U.S.	-.54	-.10	-.37	-.27	-1.27	-.22	-.59	-.59	.73	-.57
	(.11)	(.11)	(.14)	(.37)	(.39)	(.46)	(.39)	(.18)	(.63)	(.30)
Canada	-.65	-.59	-.75	-.32	-.76	1.54	-.96	-.52	-.43	-.70
	(.09)	(.19)	(.28)	(.30)	(.50)	(1.55)	(.35)	(.28)	(.47)	(.22)
Sweden	-.62	-.41	-.58	-.04	-.36	.03	-1.26	-1.29	-.27	-.85
	(.14)	(.32)	(.24)	(.30)	(.32)	(.14)	(.52)	(.44)	(.13)	(.39)
Switzerland	-.59	-.51	.39	.07	-.37	.27	-.71	-.79		.50
	(.12)	(.27)	(.53)	(.19)	(.39)	(.21)	(.46)	(.22)		(.30)
Denmark	-.19	-.32	-.16	.43	-.96	-.56	-.69	-.88	1.13	-.13
	(.17)	(.11)	(.32)	(.22)	(.47)	(.32)	(.51)	(.35)	(.95)	(.31)
Australia	-.39	-.51	-.82	-.23	.12	-.26	-.52	-.82	-1.70	-.10
	(.08)	(.08)	(.28)	(.18)	(.58)	(.31)	(.33)	(.41)	(.80)	(.10)
France	-.32	-.19	-.86	.49	-.54	-.36	-1.19	-.60	-.67	-.88
	(.08)	(.11)	(.31)	(.17)	(.60)	(.39)	(.25)	(.17)	(.71)	(.10)
Germany	-.52		-.09	.32	-.57	-.71	-1.62	-.83		-.16
	(.16)		(.49)	(.25)	(.26)	(.21)	(.45)	(.26)		(.22)
Belgium	-.21	-.31	-.43	.01	-.23	-.02	-.78	.71	.03	- 42
	(.15)	(.29)	(.26)	(.17)	(.31)	(.24)	(.33)	(.28)	(.10)	(.17)
Norway	-.31	-1.04	-1.09	.52	-.49	-.89	-.69	-.92	-.12	.51
	(.14)	(.18)	(.36)	(.52)	(.38)	(.33)	(.58)	(.19)	(.64)	(.34)
Netherlands	-.32	-.48	-1.32	-.56	-.15	-.13	-1.95	-.28	-.22	-.26
	(.23)	(.31)	(.49)	(.21)	(.44)	(.24)	(.29)	(.43)	(.39)	(.53)
Iceland	-.24	-.28	-.36	-.04	-.96	-.47	-2.18	-1.20	-.62	-.75
	(.17)	(.31)	(.30)	(.13)	(.42)	(.40)	(1.23)	(.31)	(.28)	(.27)
Finland	-.41	-.69	.84	-.39	.76	-.27	-.51	-1.56	-.53	-.01
	(.15)	(.20)	(.66)	(.14)	(.48)	(.48)	(.31)	(.32)	(.58)	(.44)
Austria	-.35	-.27	-.03	.53	.11	.19	-.57	-.61	.11	-.67
	(.20)	(.18)	(.39)	(.32)	(.64)	(.34)	(.40)	(.33)	(.15)	(.24)
Japan	-.16		.03	-.48	-.37	-.67	-.99	-1.09		-1.20
	(.30)		(.37)	(.24)	(.56)	(.26)	(.42)	(.53)		(.67)
U.K.	.00	-.62	-.24	.18	-.35	.88	-.23	-.69	-1.08	-.71
	(.13)	(.20)	(.09)	(.15)	(.36)	(.56)	(.33)	(.24)	(.33)	(.22)
Spain	-.16	-.01	-.42	.04	-.68	-.57	-.63	-.41	.01	.16
	(.28)	(.14)	(.33)	(.17)	(.24)	(.40)	(.35)	(.22)	(.21)	(.23)
Italy	-.03	-.23	-.37	-.08	-.27	-.68	-.04	-1.24	.17	- 16
	(.20)	(.10)	(.44)	(.13)	(.25)	(.26)	(.32)	(.29)	(.34)	(.21)
Mean	-.33	-.41	-.37	.01	-.41	-.16	-.89	-.84	-.25	-.30
	(.04)	(.05)	(.09)	(.06)	(.10)	(.12)	(.11)	(.07)	(.13)	(.08)
All countries	-.40	-.40	-.37	-.05	-.50	-.28	-.89	-.87	-.22	-.49
	(.04)	(.05)	(.07)	(.05)	(.09)	(.08)	(.09)	(.07)	(.08)	(.06)

TABLE A2.4

SUMMARY STATISTICS FOR THE DEMAND EQUATIONS FOR 10 COMMODITIES
IN 18 COUNTRIES: AUTONOMOUS TRENDS SUPPRESSED

Country		Food	Beverages	Clothing	Housing	Durables	Medical care	Transport	Recreation	Education	Miscellaneous
(1)		(2)	(3)	(4)	(5)	(6)	(7)	(8)	(9)	(10)	(11)
U.S.	DW	1.42	1.26	2.26	1.30	1.07	1.00	1.79	1.70	.38	1.78
	PROB	.09	.03	.67	.04	.01	.01	.32	.20	.00	.30
	SEE	1.50	1.32	1.76	1.30	2.37	2.80	3.02	1.64	2.45	1.08
Canada	DW	1.43	1.56	2.15	1.24	1.14	1.03	1.96	1.88	.37	1.80
	PROB	.09	.15	.61	.03	.02	.01	.44	.34	.00	.31
	SEE	1.26	1.67	2.63	2.16	2.18	9.77	2.18	2.43	6.34	1.54
Sweden	DW	1.91	.74	1.17	1.00	1.44	1.62	2.27	1.47	1.86	1.99
	PROB	.44	.00	.03	.01	.13	.28	.76	.13	.35	.48
	SEE	.97	2.94	2.61	1.92	2.49	3.34	2.60	2.38	4.81	2.53
Switzerland	DW	1.92	.58	.65	1.57	1.04	1.23	1.55	1.69		1.28
	PROB	.42	.00	.00	.17	.01	.02	.17	.23		.03
	SEE	.98	2.01	3.13	1.86	3.05	2.13	2.55	1.28		1.31
Denmark	DW	2.53	1.46	1.91	1.64	1.06	1.23	2.20	1.36	.87	2.47
	PROB	.90	.14	.45	.26	.04	.08	.74	.10	.01	.86
	SEE	1.62	1.25	3.91	2.76	3.86	4.01	3.13	2.80	8.57	1.88
Australia	DW	1.04	1.51	1.48	1.45	1.41	2.41	2.01	2.57	.51	2.24
	PROB	.01	.15	.09	.09	.07	.84	.52	.92	.00	.76
	SEE	.97	1.09	2.24	1.85	4.13	3.72	2.40	5.19	7.76	1.26
France	DW	1.40	2.16	1.72	2.77	1.82	1.82	2.08	2.24	2.53	1.53
	PROB	.09	.64	.24	.94	.36	.35	.58	.65	.89	.13
	SEE	.52	1.16	1.58	1.11	2.35	2.11	1.64	1.26	6.53	.60
Germany	DW	2.12		1.45	1.67	1.67	1.68	1.60	1.37		2.08
	PROB	.61		.08	.21	.20	.22	.15	.06		.58
	SEE	.82		1.85	2.09	1.65	2.29	2.61	1.60		1.28
Belgium	DW	2.10	2.03	2.62	2.33	2.50	1.87	2.10	2.93	1.16	2.35
	PROB	.59	.54	.92	.75	.86	.36	.60	.99	.02	.80
	SEE	1.41	2.41	2.57	1.99	2.88	3.36	2.50	2.33	1.27	4.59
Norway	DW	1.99	1.54	1.28	2.33	1.45	1.30	2.32	1.96	1.17	2.06
	PROB	.54	.21	.07	.78	.14	.07	.81	.48	.04	.59
	SEE	.79	2.54	2.04	2.52	2.07	3.78	3.97	1.58	5.00	1.54
Netherlands	DW	2.16	2.57	1.83	1.31	2.50	1.99	2.10	1.47	2.38	1.64
	PROB	.66	.92	.31	.03	.89	.48	.61	.09	.82	.20
	SEE	1.77	3.81	4.36	3.01	4.07	4.42	4.01	4.12	4.02	2.93
Iceland	DW	2.48	2.54	1.47	.85	2.18	1.42	1.47	.93	1.04	2.73
	PROB	.81	.84	.17	.01	.62	.19	.33	.03	.04	.95
	SEE	2.48	4.36	5.50	2.92	5.37	7.06	8.78	6.01	6.51	6.19
Finland	DW	2.13	1.98	1.90	1.49	1.62	1.63	1.76	2.36	.23	1.58
	PROB	.58	.51	.44	.14	.21	.22	.33	.78	.00	.19
	SEE	1.19	3.28	6.06	2.07	3.74	3.91	5.53	3.89	11.18	2.72
Austria	DW	2.90	2.46	1.13	2.25	2.06	1.35	1.90	1.91	2.23	2.33
	PROB	.98	.85	.02	.67	.54	.08	.42	.46	.71	.78
	SEE	1.69	2.83	2.08	2.42	3.97	3.83	3.56	2.34	4.66	1.27
Japan	DW	1.82		1.53	.66	1.75	1.25	1.76	1.97		2.15
	PROB	.36		.24	.00	.36	.12	.43	.59		.62
	SEE	1.36		3.83	2.85	6.97	3.84	3.24	2.68		2.53
U.K.	DW	2.08	1.75	1.71	1.81	1.45	1.36	1.51	1.82	.97	2.43
	PROB	.55	.35	.24	.32	.11	.09	.16	.34	.01	.80
	SEE	.98	2.39	1.45	1.34	2.53	4.85	2.62	1.88	3.45	1.26
Spain	DW	1.67	1.84	1.82	1.76	1.62	1.48	2.04	2.53	1.75	1.83
	PROB	.26	.30	.39	.25	.23	.16	.58	.83	.30	.34
	SEE	1.77	2.25	2.13	1.40	2.33	5.69	4.29	2.46	3.03	2.12
Italy	DW	1.49	1.93	1.76	2.19	1.28	1.50	1.84	2.42	1.16	2.69
	PROB	.13	.40	.33	.63	.05	.12	.37	.78	.03	.91
	SEE	.97	1.67	2.67	1.01	2.95	3.82	3.09	1.95	4.81	1.35
Mean	DW	1.92	1.74	1.66	1.65	1.61	1.51	1.91	1.92	1.24	2.05
	SEE	1.28	2.31	2.91	2.03	3.27	4.15	3.43	2.66	5.36	2.11

All SEEs are to be divided by 100.

TABLE A2.5

FREQUENCY DISTRIBUTIONS OF INCOME AND PRICE ELASTICITIES

FOR 10 COMMODITIES IN 18 COUNTRIES: AUTONOMOUS TRENDS SUPPRESSED

(Percentages)

Range	Food	Beverages	Clothing	Housing	Durables	Medical care	Transport	Recreation	Education	Miscellaneous	All goods
(1)	(2)	(3)	(4)	(5)	(6)	(7)	(8)	(9)	(10)	(11)	(12)
				Income Elasticities (η_i^c)							
$(-\infty, -1]$	0	0	0	0	0	0	0	0	0	0	0
$(-1, 0]$	0	0	0	0	0	0	0	0	0	0	0
$(0, 1]$	100	88	67	83	28	44	0	11	60	39	51
$(1, \infty)$	0	12	33	17	72	56	100	89	40	61	49
				Price Elasticities (γ_i^c)							
$(-\infty, -1]$	0	6	11	0	6	0	28	28	13	6	10
$(-1, 0]$	94	94	72	50	78	72	72	72	53	78	74
$(0, 1]$	6	0	17	50	17	22	0	0	27	17	15
$(1, \infty)$	0	0	0	0	0	6	0	0	7	0	1

TABLE A2.6

FREQUENCY DISTRIBUTIONS OF $|t|$-VALUES OF

INCOME AND PRICE ELASTICITIES FOR 10 COMMODITIES IN 18 COUNTRIES:

AUTONOMOUS TRENDS SUPPRESSED

(Percentages)

Range	Food	Beverages	Clothing	Housing	Durables	Medical care	Transport	Recreation	Education	Miscellaneous	All goods
(1)	(2)	(3)	(4)	(5)	(6)	(7)	(8)	(9)	(10)	(11)	(12)
Income Elasticities (η_i^c)											
[0 , 1)	0	0	0	0	0	6	0	0	7	0	1
[1 , 2)	6	0	0	6	0	17	0	0	47	0	7
[2 , 3)	17	12	6	6	11	6	0	0	13	6	7
[3 , ∞)	78	88	94	89	89	72	100	100	33	94	85
Price Elasticities (γ_i^c)											
[0 , 1)	22	19	33	44	44	50	11	6	60	39	32
[1 , 2)	28	38	22	39	28	28	50	17	13	22	29
[2 , 3)	11	12	39	17	22	17	22	33	20	22	22
[3 , ∞)	39	31	6	0	6	6	17	44	7	17	17

REFERENCES

Clements, K.W. (1982). 'Divisia Moments of Australian Consumption,' Economics Letters 9: 43-8.

——————————— (1983). 'The Demand for Energy used in Transport,' Australian Journal of Management 8: 27-56.

Clements, K.W., S. Kappelle and E.J. Roberts (1984). 'Are Luxuries More Price Elastic than Necessities?' McKethan-Matherly Discussion Paper MM6, Graduate School of Business, University of Florida, Gainesville.

Deaton, A. (1974). 'A Reconsideration of the Empirical Implications of Additive Preferences,' Economic Journal 84: 338-48.

——————— (1984). 'Demand Analysis,' in Z. Griliches and M.D. Intriligator (eds.), Handbook of Econometrics. Volume 3, Amsterdam: Elsevier Science Publishing Company.

Divisia (1925). 'L'indice Monétaire et la Théorie de la Monnaie,' Revue d'Economie Politique 39: 980-1008.

Engel, F. (1857). 'Die Productions - und Consumtionsverhältnisse des Könichreichs Sachsen,' Zeitschrift des Statistischen Büreaus des Königlich Sächsischen Ministeriums des Innern 8-9: 1-54. Reprinted in the Bulletin de l'Institut International de Statistique 9, 1895.

Meisner, J.F. (1979). 'Divisia Moments of U.S. Industry, 1947-1978,' Economics Letters 4: 239-42.

Pigou, A.C. (1910). 'A Method of Determining the Numerical Values of Elasticities of Demand,' Economic Journal 20: 636-40.

Selvanathan, E.A. (1987). Explorations in Consumer Demand. Ph.D. Thesis, Murdoch University, Western Australia.

Stening, K. (1985). 'OECD Consumption: A Database,' Unpublished manuscript, Department of Economics, The University of Western Australia.

Summers, R. and A. Heston (1984). 'Improved International Comparisons of Real Product and Its Composition: 1950-1980,' Review of Income and Wealth 30: 207-68.

Theil, H. (1967). Economics and Information Theory. Amsterdam: North-Holland Publishing Company.

Theil, H. (1980). The System-Wide Approach to Microeconomics. Chicago: The University of Chicago Press.

Theil, H. and F.E. Suhm (1981). International Consumption Comparisons: A System-Wide Approach. Amsterdam: North-Holland Publishing Company.

CHAPTER 3

DO OECD CONSUMERS OBEY DEMAND THEORY?

3.1 INTRODUCTION

Demand theory predicts that consumers do not suffer from money illusion and that the substitution effects are symmetric. These represent testable hypotheses known as demand homogeneity and Slutsky symmetry. In a review article on systems of consumer demand functions, Barten (1977) summarizes the results from various empirical applications which test the validity of these restrictions. These results show that homogeneity and symmetry are generally not acceptable. Barten suggests that one reason for these negative results is that since the test procedures are usually based on the asymptotic distribution of the test statistic without any adjustment for small-sample effects, they are biased towards rejection of the null hypothesis.

Using simulation experiments, Bera et al. (1981), Bewley (1983,1986), Laitinen (1978) and Meisner (1979) succeeded in showing that these asymptotic tests are indeed biased against the null, particularly for large systems. In view of these difficulties, Theil (1987) recently developed alternative testing procedures for homogeneity and symmetry which are distribution-free and hence do not require any asymptotic theory. These tests are based on Barnard's (1963) Monte Carlo simulation procedure.

In this chapter we apply Theil's new methodology to test homogeneity and symmetry for the 18 OECD countries described in Chapter 2. We also introduce a similar procedure to test preference independence, whereby goods exhibit no interaction in the consumer's utility function. The plan of this chapter is as follows. In Section 3.2 we present the demand model to be used for testing. In Section 3.3 we describe the asymptotic test of homogeneity and illustrate its application with the OECD data; we also present Laitinen's (1978) finite-sample test. Section 3.4 presents the asymptotic test of Slutsky symmetry and its application with OECD data. Our results show that, on the basis of the asymptotic tests, homogeneity and symmetry are in general rejected by the data.

The distribution-free Monte Carlo procedure and its application to homogeneity and symmetry are discussed in Section 3.5. In Sections 3.6 we discuss the problems associated with approximating the unknown error covariance matrix by its usual estimator and propose an alternative approach. Section 3.7 discusses the performance of the alternative approach. Sections 3.8-3.9 present the Monte Carlo test results for homogeneity and symmetry with the OECD data. On the basis of this approach, we find that homogeneity and symmetry are, in general, acceptable hypotheses. This result is in stark contrast to that based on the asymptotic tests.

In Section 3.10 we propose a Monte Carlo test of preference independence and present its application with OECD data. The finding is that there is some tentative support for preference independence in most countries. Sections 3.11 and 3.12 present the implied income and own-price elasticities. We also compare these elasticities with those obtained from the double-log demand equations in Chapter 2. We give our concluding comments in the last section.

3.2 THE DEMAND MODEL

Consider Working's model discussed in Section 1.11,

$$\overline{w}_{it}(Dq_{it} - DQ_t) = \beta_i DQ_t + \sum_{j=1}^{n} \pi_{ij} Dp_{jt} + \varepsilon_{it}, \qquad \begin{array}{l} i=1,...,n, \\ t=1,...,T, \end{array} \qquad (2.1)$$

where β_i is the ith income coefficient satisfying $\Sigma_{i=1}^{n} \beta_i = 0$; π_{ij} is the $(i,j)^{th}$ Slutsky coefficient with $\Sigma_{i=1}^{n} \pi_{ij} = 0$; ε_{it} is the disturbance term of the ith equation; and all other notation is as in Chapter 2. The error terms are normally distributed with mean zero and are independent over time.

Let $y_{it} = \overline{w}_{it}(Dq_{it} - DQ_t)$, $\gamma_i = [\beta_i \; \pi_{i1} \; ... \; \pi_{in}]'$ and $x_t =$

$[DQ_t \ Dp_{1t} \ ... \ Dp_{nt}]'$. Therefore (2.1) can be written as

$$y_i = X\gamma_i + \varepsilon_i, \qquad\qquad i=1,...,n, \qquad\qquad (2.2)$$

where $y_i = [y_{it}]$ is a T-vector; X is a $T \times (n+1)$ matrix whose t^{th} row is x_t'; and $\varepsilon_i = [\varepsilon_{it}]$ is a T-vector. It can be shown that the best linear unbiased estimators of the γ_i's in the system of equations (2.2) are the single-equation least squares (LS) estimators (Theil, 1971).

If we sum both sides of (2.1) over $i=1,...,n$, we get $\Sigma_{i=1}^{n} \ \varepsilon_{it} = 0$ for $t=1,...,T$, where we have used the properties that the income coefficients have zero sum and that $\Sigma_{i=1}^{n} \ \pi_{ij} = 0$. Therefore, the ε_{it}'s for $i=1,...,n$ are linearly dependent. Thus one of the equations in (2.2) is redundant and can be deleted. We delete the nth equation, and write (2.2) for $i=1,...,n-1$ as

$$y = (I \otimes X)\gamma + \varepsilon, \qquad\qquad (2.3)$$

where I is the identity matrix of order (n-1); and $y = [y_i]$, $\gamma = [\gamma_i]$ and $\varepsilon = [\varepsilon_i]$ are vectors consisting of (n-1) subvectors.

A point worth noting about the estimation of demand systems such as (2.1) is that traditionally prices are treated as exogenous as they are usually determined by the suppliers on the basis of cost considerations. Such a treatment is plausible in most cases except for agricultural goods. For many agricultural goods, because of the long gestation periods, the market supplies are fixed or predetermined in advance of current market prices; these supplies were determined by past prices, among other things. In such situations, the prices become endogenous so that the question is at what price can that fixed supply be sold? If prices are endogenous, then the least squares estimates of (2.1) are biased and inconsistent. One solution to this problem is to use instrumental variable estimates with quantities as instruments (for details, see Theil, 1976).

An alternative way of dealing with endogenous prices is by expressing prices as functions of quantities. These functions are called *inverse demand systems*. Such demand systems have been investigated by Anderson (1980), Deaton (1986), Hicks (1946), Huang (1983), Salvas-Bronsard et al. (1979), and Theil (1975/76). In our analysis, the commodity groups (listed in Table 2.1) are at a high level of aggregation and are not agricultural commodities. Furthermore, the data are annual. Consequently, we can fairly safely make the assumption that prices are exogenous.

3.3 DEMAND HOMOGENEITY

In the context of (2.1), demand homogeneity takes the form

$$\sum_{j=1}^{n} \pi_{ij} = 0, \qquad\qquad i=1,\ldots,n. \tag{3.1}$$

Let $\mathbf{a} = [0\ 1\ ...\ 1]'$. Then (3.1) can be written as

$$\mathbf{a}'\boldsymbol{\gamma}_i = 0, \qquad\qquad i=1,...,n.$$

For $i=1,...,n-1$, this can be expressed as

$$\mathbf{R}\boldsymbol{\gamma} = \mathbf{0}, \tag{3.2}$$

where $\mathbf{R} = \mathbf{I}_{n-1} \otimes \mathbf{a}'$.

The Asymptotic Test of Homogeneity

The test statistic for the homogeneity restriction (3.2) is

$$\frac{(\mathbf{R}\hat{\boldsymbol{\gamma}})'\boldsymbol{\Sigma}^{-1}(\mathbf{R}\hat{\boldsymbol{\gamma}})/\mathbf{a}'(\mathbf{X}'\mathbf{X})^{-1}\mathbf{a}}{\operatorname{tr}\boldsymbol{\Sigma}^{-1}\mathbf{S}}, \tag{3.3}$$

where $\hat{\boldsymbol{\gamma}}$ is the LS estimator of $\boldsymbol{\gamma}$, $\boldsymbol{\Sigma}$ is the error covariance matrix; and $\mathbf{S}$ is the LS residual moment matrix, an unbiased estimator of $\boldsymbol{\Sigma}$ (Theil, 1971). Under the null hypothesis, (3.3) is distributed as F with $(n-1)$ and $(n-1)(T-n-1)$ degrees of freedom. Usually, the error covariance matrix $\boldsymbol{\Sigma}$ is unknown and is replaced by its estimator $\mathbf{S}$. The test statistic for homogeneity then becomes

$$\Psi_H = \frac{(\mathbf{R}\hat{\boldsymbol{\gamma}})'\mathbf{S}^{-1}(\mathbf{R}\hat{\boldsymbol{\gamma}})}{\mathbf{a}'(\mathbf{X}'\mathbf{X})^{-1}\mathbf{a}}, \tag{3.4}$$

which has an asymptotic χ^2 distribution with (n-1) degrees of freedom under the null. Note that (3.4) involves S^{-1}, so that S must be non-singular. The necessary condition for S to be non-singular is that $T \geq 2n$ (Laitinen, 1978).

Now we apply this asymptotic test to the OECD data. Among the 18 OECD countries, only 7 satisfy the necessary condition for S to be non-singular; see columns 3 and 6 of Table 2.2. Therefore, we can compute (3.4) for these 7 countries only. Table 3.1 presents the results. The observed values of the test statistic are presented in column 5. Column 6 gives the critical values at the 5 percent level of significance. Comparing column 5 with column 6 we see that homogeneity is rejected at the 5 percent level for 6 countries. This agrees with the results from almost all previous studies. We shall discuss column 7 of Table 3.1 in the next subsection.

Laitinen's Exact Test of Homogeneity

Laitinen (1978) derived the exact finite-sample distribution for Ψ_H in (3.4). He showed that, under the null, Ψ_H is distributed as Hotelling's T^2, which itself is distributed as a constant multiple $(n-1)(T-n-1)/(T-2n+1)$ of $F(n-1,T-2n+1)$.

Based on this distribution, we present the critical values of the exact test in column 7 of Table 3.1 for the 7 OECD countries. Comparing the observed values of the test statistic in column 5 with these critical values, we can see that homogeneity is now acceptable for all countries except Germany. This points

TABLE 3.1

TESTING HOMOGENEITY IN 7 OECD COUNTRIES

(Based on $\mathbf{S}$)

Country	Number of commodities	Sample size		Test statistic	Asymptotic test critical value	Exact test critical value
	n	T	$T-2n$	Ψ_H	$\chi^2(n-1)$	T^2
(1)	(2)	(3)	(4)	(5)	(6)	(7)
1. U.S.	10	21	1	57.8*	16.9	872.1
2. Canada	10	21	1	19.1*	16.9	872.1
3. Switzerland	9	21	3	101.4*	15.5	132.9
4. Australia	10	21	1	133.4*	16.9	872.1
5. Germany	8	21	5	61.9**	14.1	58.9
6. Belgium	10	21	1	813.4*	16.9	872.1
7. Netherlands	10	25	5	10.7	16.9	86.1

A * denotes that we reject homogeneity at the 5 percent level on the basis of the asymptotic test. A ** denotes that we reject homogeneity at the 5 percent level on the basis of the asymptotic and the exact finite-sample test.

in the direction that the rejection of the homogeneity is due to the failure of the asymptotic theory.

3.4 SLUTSKY SYMMETRY

We now take homogeneity as given and consider Slutsky symmetry. The homogeneity-constrained version of model (2.1) is

$$y_{it} - \beta_i DQ_t + \sum_{j=1}^{n-1} \pi_{ij}(Dp_{jt} - Dp_{nt}) + \varepsilon_{it}, \qquad \begin{aligned} &i=1,\dots,n, \\ &t=1,\dots,T. \end{aligned} \qquad (4.1)$$

Let

$$\gamma_i^H = [\beta_i \; \pi_{i1} \; \dots \; \pi_{i,n-1}]'$$

and

$$x_t^H = [DQ_t \; Dp_{1t} - Dp_{nt} \; \dots \; Dp_{n-1,t} - Dp_{nt}]'.$$

Then (4.1) can be written as

$$y_i = x^H \gamma_i^H + \varepsilon_i, \qquad\qquad i=1,\dots,n, \qquad (4.2)$$

where $\mathbf{X}^H$ is a T×n matrix whose t^{th} row is $\mathbf{x}_t^{H\prime}$; and $\mathbf{y}_i$ and $\boldsymbol{\varepsilon}_i$ are as before. As for the unconstrained case, it can be shown that the best linear unbiased estimators of the γ_i^H's in (4.2) are the single- equation LS estimators (Theil, 1971).

As before, we delete the nth equation and write (4.2) in matrix form as

$$\mathbf{y} = (\mathbf{I} \otimes \mathbf{X}^H)\gamma^H + \boldsymbol{\varepsilon}, \tag{4.3}$$

where $\mathbf{I}$ is the identity matrix of order (n-1); $\gamma^H = [\gamma_i^H]$ is a vector consisting of (n-1) subvectors; and $\mathbf{y}$ and $\boldsymbol{\varepsilon}$ are as before. Let $\hat{\gamma}_i^H$ be the LS estimator of γ_i^H for i=1,...,n; and $\hat{\gamma}^H = [\hat{\gamma}_i^H]$ be the vector consisting of (n-1) subvectors. In terms of the parameters of (4.1), Slutsky symmetry takes the form

$$\pi_{ij} = \pi_{ji}, \qquad\qquad i,j=1,...,n-1. \tag{4.4}$$

In vector form this can be written as

$$\mathbf{R}\gamma^H = 0, \tag{4.5}$$

where $\mathbf{R}$ is a $q \times n(n-1)$ matrix with $q = \frac{1}{2}(n-1)(n-2)$ and each row of $\mathbf{R}$ consists of zeros except for a 1 and a -1 corresponding to π_{ij} and π_{ji} for some i≠j.

The test statistic for symmetry is

$$\frac{(\mathbf{R}\hat{\gamma}^H)' \{\mathbf{R}[\Sigma \otimes (\mathbf{X}^{H\prime}\mathbf{X}^H)^{-1}]\mathbf{R}'\}^{-1}(\mathbf{R}\hat{\gamma}^H)}{[q/(n-1)]\, \mathrm{tr}\, \Sigma^{-1}\mathbf{S}}, \tag{4.6}$$

where Σ is the error covariance matrix of model (4.1) for i=1,...,n-1 (Theil, 1971). Under the null, (4.6) is distributed as F with q and (n-1)(T-n) degrees of freedom. As before, we replace Σ by its estimator S (when S is non-singular) and the test statistic becomes

$$\Psi_S = (R\hat{\gamma}^H)' \{R[S \otimes (X^{H'}X^H)^{-1}]R'\}^{-1}(R\hat{\gamma}^H), \qquad (4.7)$$

which has an asymptotic χ^2 distribution with q degrees of freedom. We present the values of Ψ_S for the 7 OECD countries in column 4 of Table 3.2. As can be seen, symmetry is rejected for all countries at the 5 percent level. Most previous studies have reported similar results based on this asymptotic test.

Using simulation experiments, Meisner (1979) showed that the asymptotic test is biased against symmetry, particularly in large systems. Since (4.4) involves cross-equation restrictions, the exact distribution of Ψ_S is complicated and has not yet been derived.

3.5 THEIL'S MONTE CARLO TEST

As discussed in the previous two sections, the negative results of testing are at least in part due to the failure of the asymptotic tests. To overcome these problems, Theil (1987) develops distribution-free tests for homogeneity and symmetry. The basic idea is to simulate a large number of values of the

TABLE 3.2

TESTING SYMMETRY IN 7 OECD COUNTRIES

(Based on $\mathbf{S}$)

Country	Number of commodities	Degrees of freedom	Test statistic	Asymptotic test critical value
	n	q	Ψ_S	$\chi^2(q)$
(1)	(2)	(3)	(4)	(5)
1. U.S.	10	36	566.2*	49.8
2. Canada	10	36	172.3*	49.8
3. Switzerland	9	28	103.4*	41.3
4. Australia	10	36	71.4*	49.8
5. Germany	8	21	35.1*	32.7
6. Belgium	10	36	184.3*	49.8
7. Netherlands	10	36	169.9*	49.8

A * denotes that we reject symmetry at the 5 percent level.

test statistic under the null hypothesis to construct its empirical distribution. The observed value of the test statistic is then compared to this distribution, rather than its asymptotic counterpart. In this section, we set out Theil's methodology and its application.

The Monte Carlo Simulation Procedure

Switching to the standard notation, consider the system of equations $y = X\beta + \varepsilon$. Suppose we are interested in testing the null hypothesis $R\beta = b$ using a test statistic τ. Obviously τ is a function of the estimate of the parameter vector β. In general, Theil's Monte Carlo procedure can be summarized as follows:

Step 1:   Estimate the unrestricted model and obtain the data-based value τ_1 of τ.

Step 2:   Estimate the model under the null hypothesis $R\beta = b$ and obtain the estimate S of the covariance matrix Σ of the disturbances.

Step 3:   Generate quasi-normal error terms with zero means and covariance matrix S and use these errors together with the observed value of X and the restricted estimates to generate a new data set for y under the null. Use the generated data to estimate the unrestricted model.

Step 4:   Repeat Step 3 a certain number of times, N say, and in each case calculate the simulated value of the test statistic τ.

Step 5:   Let $\tau_2,...,\tau_M$ be the values of the test statistic τ obtained from the simulated data sets, where M=N+1. For a one-tailed test, we reject the null hypothesis for the observed sample at the α percent significance level if τ_1 is among the M' largest values of the τ_i's such that $(M'/M)\times 100 = \alpha$.

The number of replications (N) is usually chosen to be sufficiently large to reduce the 'blurring effect', which leads to loss of power (see Marriot, 1979). However, after a certain number of replications, the return for increased computing time diminishes. According to Besag and Diggle (1977), the suggested number of replications to reduce the 'blurring effect' for a 5 percent significance test is 99. If we use the $\alpha = 5$ percent significance level and $N = 99$ simulations, for a one-tailed test, we reject the null if the rank of τ_1 is 96,97,98,99 or 100. For a two-tailed test, we reject the null when the rank of τ_1 is 1,2,3,98,99 or 100.

Application to Homogeneity

Recall that homogeneity takes the form (3.1). Let $\hat{\pi}_{ij}$ be the LS estimate of π_{ij}. Then the test statistic for the homogeneity of the ith equation is

$$\hat{\tau}_i = \sum_{j=1}^{n} \hat{\pi}_{ij} \tag{5.1}$$

and the test statistic for the homogeneity of all n equations jointly is

$$\hat{\tau}_H = \sum_{i=1}^{n} |\hat{\tau}_i|. \tag{5.2}$$

[Since by construction $\sum_{i=1}^{n} \hat{\tau}_i = 0$, the sum of the absolute values of the $\hat{\tau}_i$'s are used in (5.2).]

For estimation, Theil (1987) uses the absolute price version of the Rotterdam model (see Section 1.9),

$$\bar{w}_{it}Dq_{it} \;=\; \theta_i DQ_t + \sum_{j=1}^{n} \pi_{ij}Dp_{jt} + \varepsilon_{it}, \qquad\qquad i=1,\dots,n, \qquad\qquad (5.3)$$
$$t=1,\dots,T,$$

where θ_i is the marginal share of i. For i=1,...,n-1, model (5.3) can also be written in the vector form (2.2), provided we redefine $y_i = [\bar{w}_{it}Dq_{it}]$ and $\gamma_i = [\theta_i\ \pi_{i1}\ \dots\ \pi_{in}]'$. The other terms in (2.2) retain their previous meanings. Column 2 of Table 3.3 gives the data-based values of the test statistics (5.1) and (5.2) for Dutch data consisting of n = 14 commodities. These results are from Theil (1987).

To assess the significance of the values of these test statistics, the Monte Carlo procedure is used. For this purpose, the homogeneity-constrained version of (5.3) is obtained by imposing restriction (3.1) on (5.3),

$$\bar{w}_{it}Dq_{it} \;=\; \theta_i DQ_t + \sum_{j=1}^{n-1} \pi_{ij}(Dp_{jt} - Dp_{nt}) + \varepsilon_{it}, \qquad i=1,\dots,n, \qquad (5.4)$$
$$t=1,\dots,T.$$

Theil estimates (5.4) by single-equation LS to obtain the data-based estimates of the parameters and an unbiased estimate of the contemporaneous covariance matrix of the ε_{it}'s; let this matrix be S_H. Then quasi-normal error terms are generated with zero means and covariance matrix S_H. These errors together

TABLE 3.3

MONTE CARLO TEST OF HOMOGENEITY: DUTCH DATA

(Standard errors are in parentheses)

Commodity (1)	$\hat{\tau}_i, \hat{\tau}_H$ (2)	Rank of the data-based test statistic (3)
1. Bread	-.006 (.005)	13
2. Groceries	-.002 (.010)	44
3. Dairy products	.017 (.011)	90
4. Vegetables, fruit	-.004 (.012)	38
5. Meat	.024 (.021)	90
6. Fish	.002 (.006)	64
7. Beverages	.019 (.008)	97
8. Tobacco	.007 (.007)	90
9. Pastry, ice cream	-.013 (.005)	1
10. Textiles	-.100 (.024)	1
11. Footwear	.005 (.004)	93
12. Other durables	.045 (.012)	100
13. Water, light, heat	.010 (.013)	82
14. Other non-durables	-.002 (.029)	44
All 14 goods	.256 (-)	98

with the constrained, data-based estimates of the parameters and the observed

values of the independent variables are used to generate simulated values for

the dependent variables from (5.4). This procedure is repeated 99 times and in

each case the unconstrained model (5.3) is estimated by single-equation LS and

the simulated values of the test statistics (5.1) and (5.2) are computed. Then

the data-based value of the test statistic is ranked among the simulated values.

Column 3 of Table 3.3 gives the results, from Theil (1987). As can be seen from the last entry in column 2 of the table, the value of the data-based test statistic for the homogeneity of the 14 equations jointly is $\hat{\tau}_H = .256$. Its rank is 98 and thus homogeneity is rejected at the 5 percent significance level but not at the 1 percent level (using a one-tail test as $\hat{\tau}_H > 0$). A two-tailed test for each of the individual equations at the 5 percent level shows that equations 9, 10 and 12 are the troublemakers; the rank for $\hat{\tau}_i$ for beverages is also on the high side.

Application to Symmetry

Given homogeneity, the demand model (5.3) takes the form (5.4). Let $\hat{\pi}_{ij}^H$ be the LS estimate of the π_{ij} in (5.4). That is, $\hat{\pi}_{ij}^H$ is the homogeneity-constrained LS estimate of π_{ij}. The test statistic for symmetry, given homogeneity, is

$$\hat{\tau}_S = \sum_{i=1}^{n} \sum_{j=1}^{n} \left| \hat{\pi}_{ij}^H - \hat{\pi}_{ji}^H \right|. \tag{5.5}$$

From Theil (1987), for Dutch data, the data-based value of $\hat{\tau}_S = 1.392$.

To apply the Monte Carlo procedure to assess the significance of this data-based value, the estimates of the symmetry-constrained version of (5.4) are required. In vector form, model (5.4) can be written as (4.3), where $\mathbf{y} = [\mathbf{y}_i]$ with $\mathbf{y}_i = [\bar{w}_{it} Dq_{it}]$; and $\boldsymbol{\gamma}^H = [\boldsymbol{\gamma}_i^H]$ with $\boldsymbol{\gamma}_i^H = [\theta_i \; \pi_{i1} \; ... \; \pi_{i,n-1}]'$. The symmetry constraint (4.4) is given by (4.5). It can be shown (Theil, 1971) that, under symmetry, the best linear unbiased estimator of γ^H in (4.3) is given by

$$\hat{\gamma}^S = \hat{\gamma}^H - C(\Sigma)R'[RC(\Sigma)R']^{-1}R\hat{\gamma}^H, \tag{5.6}$$

where $C(\Sigma) = \Sigma \otimes (X^{H'}X^H)^{-1}$; $\hat{\gamma}^H$ is the unconstrained LS estimator of γ^H in (4.3); and R is a $q \times n(n-1)$ matrix defined below (4.5). As before, the unknown Σ matrix is replaced with its homogeneity-constrained unbiased estimate; let this matrix be S_H. In words, S_H is an estimate of the contemporaneous covariance matrix of the ε_{it}'s in (5.4).

Then, quasi-normal error terms are generated with zero mean and covariance matrix S_S, the unbiased estimate of Σ under symmetry. These errors together with the observed values of the independent variables and the constrained parameter estimates are used to obtain simulated values of the dependent variables from equation (5.4). Next, model (5.4) without symmetry is estimated using the simulated data set and the simulated value of the test statistic (5.5) is computed. This procedure is repeated 99 times. Finally, the data-based value of the test statistic $\hat{\tau}_S$ is ranked among the simulated values.

For Dutch data, Theil (1987) finds this rank to be 16 in 99 simulations. Thus Slutsky symmetry may not be rejected at the 5 percent level for these data.

3.6 SPECIFYING THE COVARIANCE MATRIX

As discussed in Section 3.3, in general the covariance matrix Σ of the disturbance terms is unknown. It is common practice to approximate Σ by its unbiased estimator **S**, the matrix of mean squares and cross products of the LS residuals. As also noted in Section 3.3, since the inverse of **S** is required, this matrix must be non-singular. This is the case for only 7 of the 18 OECD countries.

Among the 18 countries the largest sample size is 25 (for Netherlands), but even this cannot be considered a large sample for a model with 10 equations. Therefore, even when S^{-1} exists, it would be unwise to rely on the large-sample tests of homogeneity or symmetry. Instead, we shall use the simulation procedure described in the previous section for those 7 countries with non-singular **S**. For the remaining countries, since **S** is singular, it cannot be used to generate quasi-normal error terms for the simulations. Therefore, as an alternative to **S**, following Deaton (1975) we specify a simple and plausible covariance structure as

$$\Sigma^{*} = \lambda^{2}\Omega, \tag{6.1}$$

where $\Omega = \overline{\overline{W}} - \overline{w}\,\overline{w}'$; $\overline{\overline{W}} = \text{diag}[\overline{\overline{w}}_{1},...,\overline{\overline{w}}_{n-1}]$; $\overline{w} = [\overline{\overline{w}}_{1} \; ... \; \overline{\overline{w}}_{n-1}]'$; $\overline{\overline{w}}_{i} = (1/T) \sum_{t=1}^{T} \overline{w}_{it}$; and λ^{2} is a parameter to be estimated. It can be easily shown that Ω is non-singular and that an unbiased LS estimator of λ^2 is

$$\hat{\lambda}^2 = \frac{1}{(T-K)(n-1)} \sum_{i=1}^{n-1} \sum_{j=1}^{n-1} \omega^{ij} \hat{\varepsilon}_i' \hat{\varepsilon}_j, \tag{6.2}$$

where K is the number of parameters in each equation; ω^{ij} is the $(i,j)^{th}$ element of Ω^{-1}; and $\hat{\varepsilon}_i$ is the LS residual vector of the ith equation.

Let $\Sigma^* = [\sigma^*_{ij}]$ and $\Omega = [\omega_{ij}]$. Then $\omega_{ii} = \bar{\bar{w}}_i(1 - \bar{\bar{w}}_i)$ and $\sigma^*_{ii} = \lambda^2 \omega_{ii}$. It can be easily seen that, for $0 \leq \bar{\bar{w}}_i \leq .5$, σ^*_{ii} increases with $\bar{\bar{w}}_i$. Therefore, since $\bar{\bar{w}}_i$ is less than .5 for all the OECD countries, σ^*_{ii} increases with $\bar{\bar{w}}_i$. Specification (6.1) thus allows for larger error variances for goods which occupy larger shares of the budget and the covarinace between commodities are proportional to the product of their average budget shares, which is plausible. See Barten and Theil (1964) for a multinomial interpretation of (6.1); see also E.A. Selvanathan (1985) for a previous application of (6.1).

3.7 THE PERFORMANCE OF ALTERNATIVE SPECIFICATIONS OF Σ

Theil (1987) considers two special cases of Σ^* to verify the merits of such specification. The two specifications considered by Theii are, $\Sigma^*_1 = I - (1/n)\iota\iota'$, where $\iota = [1 \ldots 1]'$ is an $(n-1)$-vector; and $\Sigma^*_2 = \bar{W} - \bar{w}\,\bar{w}'$, where $\bar{W}$ and $\bar{w}$ are defined below equation (6.1). He adopts Meisner's (1981) cross-country simulation design and uses Working's model [which is similar to (4.1)] for the fifteen-country data from Kravis et al. (1978) with eight commodity groups. A simulation experiment has the advantage that everything is known including the true error covariance matrix Σ. Therefore, it allows us to compare the performance of the specifications Σ_1^* and Σ_2^* with that when the true covariance matrix Σ is used.

Theil calculated the test statistic (4.6) for symmetry and reports the rejection percentages and his results for 500 simulations are given below.

	Significance levels			
	10 percent	5 percent	2.5 percent	1 percent
Using Σ	8.8	4.2	2.0	.4
Using S	91.4	89.4	86.6	82.4
Using Σ_1^*	9.2	5.4	2.4	1.2
Using Σ_2^*	11.4	7.2	3.4	1.0

As can be seen, the results are encouraging as the rejection percentages corresponding to Σ as well as the two specifications of Σ, Σ_1^* and Σ_2^*, are close to the significance levels. It is also worth noting the disastrous results when S is used. Accordingly, the conclusion is that the symmetry test works satisfactorily when either Σ_1^* or Σ_2^* are used for the disturbance covariance matrix. As Σ^* is a one-parameter generalization of Σ_2^*, it is reasonable to expect that it would also be satisfactory to use for testing.

To verify this further, we now perform the same experiment for specification (6.1), Σ^*, for testing homogeneity using the test statistic (3.3) for the seven OECD countries for which S is non-singular. Table 3.4 contains these results. As before, the results are very encouraging for all countries. The conclusion is that the homogeneity test works satisfactorily when Σ^* is used as an alternative specification for the error covariance matrix.

TABLE 3.4

REJECTIONS OF HOMOGENEITY BY THREE TESTS IN 7 COUNTRIES:
100 SIMULATIONS

| | Significance levels | | | | | | | | | | | |
| | 10 percent | | | 5 percent | | | 2.5 percent | | | 1 percent | | |
	S	Σ	Σ^*	S	Σ	Σ^*	S	Σ	Σ^*	S	Σ	Σ^*
1. U.S.	98	10	8	96	7	4	93	4	2	91	1	1
2. Canada	94	12	12	94	6	8	92	2	2	89	1	1
3. Switzerland	82	13	13	77	5	5	73	1	1	65	1	1
4. Australia	98	18	13	98	13	7	98	11	3	95	6	0
5. Germany	67	11	9	62	1	1	55	0	0	47	0	0
6. Belgium	94	24	13	94	20	6	94	16	2	92	13	1
7. Netherlands	73	7	8	66	3	4	61	1	2	56	0	0

3.8 MONTE CARLO TESTING OF HOMOGENEITY FOR THE OECD

In this section we use the methodology described in Section 3.5 to test homogeneity for the OECD countries. We do this in the context of Working's model, equation (2.1).

Seven Countries

For the 7 countries with non-singular S, we use the approach of the second subsection of Section 3.5; the only difference is that the model is now (2.1) rather than (5.3). The upper part of Table 3.5 summarizes the results. Columns 2-11 present the ranks of the data-based values of the test statistics for each equation. Columns 12 and 13 give the percentage which are significant over all equations for each country at the 5 and 1 percent levels. The rank of the data-based test statistic for the homogeneity of the n equations jointly is presented in column 14. The second last and last rows of the upper part of the tablepresent the rejection rate for each good.

Next, we include a constant term in each equation to account for the trend-like changes in tastes etc. The model with the constant terms can be derived from a utility function subject to additive random shocks; see Theil (1967, Section 7.1) for details. Let α_i be the constant term of equation i. When such a constant is included in equation (2.1), the parameter vector γ_i now has (n+2) elements, $\gamma_i = [\alpha_i \ \beta_i \ \pi_{i1} \ ... \ \pi_{in}]'$; and the X matrix is now of

TABLE 3.5

RANK OF THE DATA-BASED TEST STATISTIC FOR HOMOGENEITY

IN 99 SIMULATIONS FOR 7 COUNTRIES

(Based on S)

Country (1)	Food (2)	Beverages (3)	Clothing (4)	Housing (5)	Durables (6)	Medical care (7)	Transport (8)	Recreation (9)	Education (10)	Miscellaneous (11)	Percent significant at 5% level (12)	Percent significant at 1% level (13)	All goods (14)
No constant													
1. U.S.	9	67	56	97	4	100	29	6	82	71	10	10	91
2. Canada	66	2	68	76	21	74	15	47	39	39	10	0	45
3. Switzerland	46	19	1	97	1	65	5	100		100	44	44	99
4. Australia	77	2	51	42	75	66	27	29	2	97	20	0	35
5. Germany	12		2	100	13	90	18	95		97	25	10	100
6. Belgium	15	33	68	6	99	97	6	94	65	25	10	0	93
7. Netherlands	42	37	81	91	10	64	71	29	78	58	0	0	44
8. Percent significant at 5% level	0	33	28	14	28	14	0	14	20	14			28
9. Percent significant at 1% level	0	0	14	14	14	14	0	14	0	14			14
With constant													
10. U.S.	64	97	57	23	2	61	84	8	93	31	10	0	70
11. Canada	73	2	67	78	23	87	10	51	36	33	10	0	59
12. Switzerland	11	45	12	74	16	24	24	100		97	10	10	78
13. Australia	27	11	90	6	96	57	42	14	3	95	10	0	90
14. Germany	17		23	75	55	82	43	87		65	0	0	25
15. Belgium	12	28	75	5	98	93	6	90	67	34	10	0	92
16. Netherlands	42	37	92	95	8	46	48	32	69	37	0	0	52
17. Percent significant at 5% level	0	17	0	0	28	0	0	14	0	0			0
18. Percent significant at 1% level	0	0	0	0	0	0	0	14	0	0			0

order $T \times (n+2)$ with t^{th} row $x_t = [1 \; DQ_t \; Dp_{1t} \; ... \; Dp_{nt}]'$. Since the constant terms satisfy $\sum_{i=1}^{n} \alpha_i = 0$, one of the equations is still redundant. Everything else remains as before. We repeat the Monte Carlo procedure for the 7 countries and the lower part of Table 3.5 gives the results.

Looking at row 8 of Table 3.5, we see that the rejection rate for beverages, clothing and durables are on the high side at the 5 percent level. This finding is in agreement with Theil's results for the Netherlands given in Table 3.3, where textiles and durables arc significant and the rank of the test statistic for beverages is on the high side. As can be seen from the lower half of the table, when constant terms are included, homogeneity of the n equations jointly is acceptable at the 5 percent significance level for all 7 countries.

In Section 3.3 we found that homogeneity of the entire model is rejected by the asymptotic test for 6 of the 7 countries in question. Using Laitinen's exact test we found that it is acceptable for all countries except Germany. Since the model used in Section 3.3 is without constants, we compare these results with the Monte Carlo test results given in the upper half of Table 3.5. As can be seen from column 14 of this table, at the 5 percent level homogeneity is acceptable for 5 countries, while it is rejected for Switzerland and Germany. This shows that the Monte Carlo tests of homogeneity are similar to those from the exact test.

Eighteen Countries

To test homogeneity for the 11 countries with singular S, we use Σ^* instead of S. The estimator of the one unknown parameter in Σ^*, λ^2, is given by (6.2). For comparison, we also use Σ^* for the other 7 countries. We then follow the same procedure as before. Table 3.6 presents the results. As can be seen from the lower part of column 14 of the table, homogeneity of the entire model (with constant terms) is acceptable for all countries except Belgium at the 5 percent level and is acceptable for all countries at the 1 percent level.

Next, we compare the upper half of Table 3.6 with its lower half. As can be seen, at the 5 percent level, all the commodities except beverages, durables and recreation perform better when constants are added to the equations. Also, looking at the last column of the table we see that the homogeneity of the n equations jointly becomes more acceptable when constants are included. These findings point to the importance of including constants when testing homogeneity.

Tables 3.5 and 3.6 have 7 countries in common. A comparison of the results for all goods (column 14 of both tables) shows that for these countries things do not change much. For example, homogeneity is rejected at the 5 percent level for Switzerland and Germany when there are no constants, while it is accepted for both countries when constants are included irrespective of the choice of Σ. Consequently, there is no evidence that the use of Σ^* distorts the results.

TABLE 3.6

RANK OF THE DATA-BASED TEST STATISTIC FOR HOMOGENEITY

IN 99 SIMULATIONS FOR 18 COUNTRIES

(Based on Σ^M)

Country	Food	Beverages	Clothing	Housing	Durables	Medical care	Transport	Recreation	Education	Miscellaneous	Percent significant at 5% level	Percent significant at 1% level	All goods
(1)	(2)	(3)	(4)	(5)	(6)	(7)	(8)	(9)	(10)	(11)	(12)	(13)	(14)
						No constant							
1. U.S.	5	65	56	95	4	100	28	12	59	61	10	10	90
2. Canada	62	19	68	73	37	100	9	50	47	42	10	10	23
3. Sweden	88	57	43	81	31	69	3	90	53	6	10	0	87
4. Switzerland	45	27	1	100	2	59	8	100		97	44	30	100
5. Denmark	78	49	23	99	5	70	7	31	90	77	10	0	92
6. Australia	68	15	56	45	94	69	30	26	6	69	0	0	20
7. France	99	29	5	92	9	95	1	70	67	42	20	10	100
8. Germany	20		2	100	16	78	5	78		83	25	10	100
9. Belgium	10	44	62	3	100	96	23	80	53	13	20	10	100
10. Norway	77	39	23	95	68	79	2	80	41	35	10	0	83
11. Netherlands	45	39	00	82	1	64	68	24	64	66	10	10	25
12. Iceland	41	54	24	90	29	100	2	85	70	52	20	10	02
13. Finland	41	72	43	80	42	39	46	50	25	38	0	0	2
14. Austria	39	2	81	74	40	66	69	34	50	69	10	0	18
15. Japan	8		1	97	14	91	87	9		97	13	10	99
16. U.K.	16	59	39	67	20	32	44	71	50	88	0	0	25
17. Spain	60	55	68	35	54	61	35	69	37	26	0	0	1
18. Italy	12	60	1	77	20	95	99	84	55	77	20	10	99
19. Percent significant at 5% level	6	6	22	22	17	17	28	6	0	0			33
20. Percent significant at 1% level	0	0	17	11	11	17	6	6	0	0			22
						With constant							
21. U.S.	76	89	53	40	1	77	98	3	70	25	30	10	80
22. Canada	65	18	68	68	37	100	8	49	47	39	10	10	29
23. Sweden	91	74	95	24	35	49	2	58	48	37	10	0	75
24. Switzerland	16	45	17	92	29	40	16	96		94	0	0	82
25. Denmark	77	55	14	29	51	23	84	78	13	31	0	0	25
26. Australia	37	35	81	6	100	63	34	9	7	72	10	10	87
27. France	83	60	31	67	95	76	2	58	28	34	10	0	61
28. Germany	23		26	83	52	77	29	72		55	0	0	14
29. Belgium	10	37	70	3	100	93	25	79	55	29	20	10	99
30. Norway	83	1	77	76	61	12	70	63	51	27	10	10	01
31. Netherlands	39	38	92	91	2	55	55	26	59	45	10	0	37
32. Iceland	68	17	48	69	83	57	12	98	44	5	10	0	52
33. Finland	61	48	41	65	66	34	62	70	10	23	0	0	3
34. Austria	40	2	81	72	40	58	78	33	47	58	10	0	18
35. Japan	85		9	50	2	84	81	16		78	13	0	89
36. U.K.	19	81	74	25	85	41	20	64	50	83	0	0	43
37. Spain	63	56	73	35	51	58	37	76	32	25	0	0	2
38. Italy	20	52	11	33	73	95	87	55	32	55	0	0	29
39. Percent significant at 5% level	0	13	0	6	28	6	17	11	0	0			6
40. Percent significant at 1% level	0	6	0	0	17	6	0	0	0	0			0

3.9 MONTE CARLO TESTING OF SYMMETRY FOR THE OECD

In this section we take homogeneity as given and use Theil's methodology to test Slutsky symmetry for the OECD countries. As before, we use model (2.1) which becomes (4.1) under homogeneity.

For the 7 countries with non-singular S, the procedure is exactly the same as that of the third subsection of Section 3.5 with (4.1) replacing (5.4). When constant terms are included in model (4.1), obvious adjustments are to be made to the parameter vector γ^H and the matrix X^H of equation (4.3). Columns 2 and 3 of Table 3.7 give the results. The last two rows give the percentage of countries for which the test statistic is significant at the 5 and 1 percent levels. As can be seen, symmetry is acceptable at the 5 percent level for all 7 countries whether or not there are constant terms in the equations. This is in stark contrast to the results from the asymptotic test discussed in Section 3.4, where symmetry is rejected for all countries.

Next, we replace S by Σ^* and follow the same procedure as before. Columns 4 and 5 of Table 3.7 present the results. At the 5 percent level, symmetry is acceptable for all countries except the U.K. when there are no constants; and is acceptable for all countries except Switzerland when constants are included. Symmetry is acceptable for all countries at the 1 percent significance level whether or not there are constants.

TABLE 3.7

RANK OF THE DATA-BASED TEST STATISTIC FOR SYMMETRY IN 99 SIMULATIONS FOR 18 COUNTRIES

Country	Based on S		Based on Σ^*	
	No constant	With constant	No constant	With constant
(1)	(2)	(3)	(4)	(5)
1. U.S.	29	16	90	71
2. Canada	61	21	72	32
3. Sweden	..	..	51	14
4. Switzerland	54	59	95	96
5. Denmark	..	..	31	41
6. Australia	3	1	18	2
7. France	..	..	42	80
8. Germany	47	72	74	90
9. Belgium	17	5	56	30
10. Norway	..	..	85	11
11. Netherlands	46	20	91	56
12. Iceland	..	..	19	38
13. Finland	..	..	49	42
14. Austria	..	..	6	21
15. Japan	..	..	11	56
16. U.K.	..	..	96	30
17. Spain	..	..	28	87
18. Italy	..	..	47	49
19. Percent significant at 5% level	0	0	6	6
20. Percent significant at 1% level	0	0	0	0

To analyse the effects of using Σ^* rather than S, for the relevant countries we compare column 2 with 4 and column 3 with 5. This shows that the ranks increase in all cases when we use Σ^*. Comparing column 2 with 3 and 4 with 5, we see that, on the whole, adding constant terms to the model does not make any major difference to the results.

3.10   MONTE CARLO TESTING OF PREFERENCE INDEPENDENCE FOR THE OECD

Homogeneity and symmetry are the basic hypotheses of demand theory. The previous results of this chapter indicate that on the basis of the Monte Carlo tests, these hypotheses are not wildly inconsistent with the OECD data. Consequently, it would seem promising to keep proceeding and analyse the acceptability (or otherwise) of separability restrictions. We shall consider the strongest form of separability, preference independence. It should be recognized, however, that separability hypotheses are quite different to homogeneity and symmetry in the sense that the latter are part of demand theory in general, while the former are part of specialized versions of demand theory.

Let the consumer's utility function be $u(q_1,...,q_n)$. If this utility function can be written as the sum of n sub-utility functions, each involving one good only, then tastes are said to exhibit preference independence. Formally, the utility function is of the preference independent variety if

$$u(q_1,...,q_n) = \sum_{i=1}^{n} u_i(q_i),$$

so that the marginal utility of good i is independent of the consumption of j, $i \neq j$. The Klein-Rubin utility function discussed in Section 1.2 is a perfect example of preference independence. In this section we describe the Monte Carlo test of the preference independence hypothesis proposed by S. Selvanathan (1987) and then apply it to the OECD data.

Under preference independence the Slutsky coefficients take the form (see, e.g., Clements, 1987)

$$\pi_{ij} = \phi\theta_i(\delta_{ij} - \theta_j), \qquad i,j=1,...,n, \qquad (10.1)$$

where ϕ is the income flexibility (the reciprocal of the income elasticity of the marginal utility of income); θ_i is the marginal share of commodity i; and δ_{ij} is the Kronecker delta. Since the marginal shares sum to one, (10.1) satisfies homogeneity and symmetry. The marginal share of i implied by model (2.1) is $\theta_{it} = \overline{w}_{it} + \beta_i$. Therefore, (10.1) becomes

$$\pi_{ij} = \phi(\overline{w}_{it} + \beta_i)(\delta_{ij} - \overline{w}_{jt} - \beta_j). \qquad (10.2)$$

Substituting (10.2) for π_{ij} in (2.1), the substitution term becomes

$$\sum_{j=1}^{n} \pi_{ij} Dp_{jt} = \sum_{j=1}^{n} \phi(\overline{w}_{it} + \beta_i)(\delta_{ij} - \overline{w}_{jt} + \beta_j) Dp_{jt}$$

$$= \phi(\overline{w}_{it} + \beta_i) \sum_{j=1}^{n} (\delta_{ij} - \overline{w}_{jt} + \beta_j) Dp_{jt}$$

$$= \phi(\overline{w}_{it} + \beta_i) \left[Dp_{it} - \sum_{j=1}^{n} (\overline{w}_{jt} + \beta_j) Dp_{jt} \right].$$

Therefore the preference independence version of (2.1) is

$$\overline{w}_{it}(Dq_{it} - DQ_t) = \beta_i DQ_t + \phi(\overline{w}_{it} + \beta_i) \left[Dp_{it} - \sum_{j=1}^{n} (\overline{w}_{jt} + \beta_j) Dp_{jt} \right] + \varepsilon_{it}. \quad (10.3)$$

Since this model is nonlinear in the parameters, we use a maximum likelihood (ML) procedure for estimation. Details of the estimation procedure are presented in Appendices A3.1 and A3.2.

Let $\overset{\wedge S}{\pi}_{ij}$ be the homogeneity- and symmetry-constrained estimate of π_{ij}. Let $\overset{\wedge P}{\pi}_{ij}$ be the estimate under preference independence defined as

$$\overset{\wedge P}{\pi}_{ij} = \hat{\phi}(\overline{\overline{w}}_i + \hat{\beta}_i)(\delta_{ij} - \overline{\overline{w}}_j - \hat{\beta}_j), \quad (10.4)$$

where $\hat{\phi}$ and the $\hat{\beta}_i$'s are ML-estimates under preference independence; and $\bar{\bar{w}}_i = (1/T) \sum_{t=1}^{T} \bar{w}_{it}$ is the sample mean of $\bar{w}_{it}$. [Note that in going from (10.2) to (10.4) we have approximated $\bar{w}_{it}$ by $\bar{\bar{w}}_i$; this approximation will be satisfactory as long as there are not large changes in the budget shares.] We define the test statistic for preference independence as

$$\hat{\tau}_P = \sum_{i=1}^{n} \sum_{j \leq i} |\hat{\pi}_{ij}^S - \hat{\pi}_{ij}^P|. \tag{10.5}$$

To assess the significance of $\hat{\tau}_P$ we use the Monte Carlo procedure described in the first subsection of Section 3.5. To generate data sets under the null, we first calculate a consistent estimate of the contemporaneous covariance matrix of the ε_{it}'s in (10.3). This matrix is $S_P = [(1/T)\hat{\varepsilon}_i'\hat{\varepsilon}_j]$, where $\hat{\varepsilon}_i$ is the ML-residual vector for equation i. Then we generate quasi-normal error terms with zero means and covariance matrix S_P. We use these errors together with the observed values of the independent variables and the ML parameter estimates to obtain simulated values of the dependent variables from equation (10.3). This procedure is repeated a certain number of times and in each trial we use the generated data set to estimate the homogeneity- and symmetry-constrained model by (5.6). We then use these estimates to calculate the simulated value of the test statistic (10.5).

Columns 2 and 3 of Table 3.8 give the ranks in 99 simulations of the data-based values of the test statistics for the 7 countries with non-singular S

TABLE 3.8

RANK OF THE DATA-BASED TEST STATISTIC FOR
PREFERENCE INDEPENDENCE IN 99 SIMULATIONS
FOR 18 COUNTRIES

Country	Based on S		Based on Σ^*	
	No constant	With constant	No constant	With constant
(1)	(2)	(3)	(4)	(5)
1. U.S.	100	100	58	70
2. Canada	98	96	23	15
3. Sweden	..	..	22	89
4. Switzerland	91	86	95	82
5. Denmark	..	..	47	58
6. Australia	86	70	93	92
7. France	..	..	91	86
8. Germany	95	50	84	30
9. Belgium	99	100	43	49
10. Norway	..	..	97	93
11. Netherlands	98	99	39	25
12. Iceland	..	..	7	24
13. Finland	..	..	91	59
14. Austria	..	..	81	79
15. Japan	..	..	50	79
16. U.K.	..	..	43	5
17. Spain	..	..	56	36
18. Italy	..	..	84	77
19. Percent significant at 5% level	57	57	6	0
20. Percent significant at 1% level	14	29	0	0

matrix, with and without constants. As can be seen, in both cases preference independence is rejected at the 5 percent level for 4 out of 7 countries. Columns 4 and 5 of the table present the results when we use Σ^* for all 18 countries. When constants are included, preference independence may not be rejected at the 5 percent level for all countries.

In contrast to homogeneity and symmetry testing, for preference independence, there is notable difference between the results based on **S** and Σ^*; for Table 3.8 compare column 2 with 4 and column 3 with 5. Consider, for example, the U.S. where preference independence is rejected when we use **S** with and without the constants. However, when Σ^* is used the hypothesis becomes acceptable. One reason for this could be that the data-based and simulated values of the test statistics for homogeneity and symmetry do not depend on the covariance matrix; see equations (5.1), (5.2) and (5.5). The covariance matrix is used only to generate the error terms under the null and to obtain the restricted estimates for symmetry from (5.6). However, this is not the case for preference independence. As discussed in Appendices A3.1 and A3.2, the ML-estimates involve the disturbance covariance matrix, be it **S** or Σ^*. Therefore, the data-based and the simulated values of the test statistics are not the same for different specifications of the covariance matrix.

In Appendix A3.3 we explore further the effects of the choice of the covariance matrix estimator on the results for preference independence. In view of the effects of the covariance matrix, it would seem best to be cautious and conclude that the findings of this section give some tentative support to the hypothesis of preference independence.

3.11 THE IMPLIED DEMAND ELASTICITIES

In this section we present the income and own-price elasticities implied by the model under preference independence. We also present the estimates of the income flexibility for each country.

Let $\hat{\phi}$ and $\hat{\beta}_i$, i=1,...,n, be the ML-estimates of the parameters of model (10.3). The income elasticity of good i implied by (10.3) is

$$\eta_{it} = 1 + \frac{\hat{\beta}_i}{\bar{w}_{it}}. \tag{11.1}$$

When the budget shares are fairly stable over time, we can replace $\bar{w}_{it}$ by its sample mean $\bar{\bar{w}}_i = (1/T) \, \Sigma_{t=1}^{T} \, \bar{w}_{it}$ in (11.1) and write

$$\eta_i = 1 + \frac{\hat{\beta}_i}{\bar{\bar{w}}_i}. \tag{11.2}$$

Similarly, the Slutsky (or compensated) own-price elasticity of good i implied by (10.3) at means is

$$\eta_{ii} = \frac{\hat{\phi}(\bar{\bar{w}}_i + \hat{\beta}_i)(1 - \bar{\bar{w}}_i - \hat{\beta}_i)}{\bar{\bar{w}}_i}.$$

To calculate the elasticities, we use the ML-estimates of the parameters of model (10.3) with constant terms included and the covariance matrix specified as Σ^*. Columns 2-11 of Table 3.9 present the income elasticities and their root-mean-square errors obtained from 100 simulations. From the table we see that most of the income elasticities are highly significant and all but five of them are positive. We shall come back to these five in Section 3.12. In all countries food is a necessity. The income elasticities for food in Canada and Switzerland seem to be on the high side. In all countries except Canada clothing is a luxury. Housing is a necessity and durables a luxury in all countries. In almost all countries, medical care is a necessity and transport and recreation are luxuries.

Column 12 gives the estimate of income flexibility ϕ. As can be seen, all ϕ-estimates are negative, as they should be, and the average is -.45. This value is in broad agreement with previous studies (Theil, 1980; Theil and Brookes, 1970/71).

TABLE 3.9

INCOME ELASTICITIES OF 10 COMMODITIES AND INCOME FLEXIBILITY FOR 18 COUNTRIES

(Root-mean-square-errors are in parentheses)

Country (1)	Food (2)	Beverages (3)	Clothing (4)	Housing (5)	Durables (6)	Medical care (7)	Transport (8)	Recreation (9)	Education (10)	Miscellaneous (11)	Income flexibility ϕ (12)
1. U.S.	.61 (.14)	.28 (.32)	1.33 (.26)	.41 (.13)	1.74 (.24)	.37 (.24)	2.31 (.14)	1.22 (.29)	.82 (.49)	.70 (.18)	-.38 (.06)
2. Canada	.96 (.22)	.59 (.37)	.82 (.37)	.03 (.20)	1.57 (.35)	2.45 (.53)	1.56 (.21)	1.86 (.46)	1.05 (.67)	.93 (.29)	-.55 (.11)
3. Sweden	.55 (.12)	1.10 (.20)	1.45 (.31)	.16 (.15)	1.87 (.27)	.05 (.23)	2.01 (.19)	1.59 (.23)	.58 (.75)	1.03 (.27)	-.58 (.08)
4. Switzerland	.97 (.09)	1.35 (.17)	1.82 (.24)	.15 (.10)	2.10 (.27)	.30 (.24)	1.58 (.18)	1.01 (.24)		.61 (.26)	-.55 (.08)
5. Denmark	.36 (.16)	.69 (.19)	1.63 (.23)	.38 (.12)	1.59 (.16)	.49 (.46)	2.25 (.14)	1.24 (.23)	-.14 (.61)	.95 (.20)	-.46 (.08)
6. Australia	.26 (.21)	.83 (.27)	1.29 (.30)	.63 (.19)	2.22 (.35)	.70 (.41)	1.49 (.27)	2.25 (.46)	2.82 (1.66)	.54 (.27)	-.46 (.08)
7. France	.46 (.18)	.48 (.30)	1.29 (.25)	.44 (.16)	1.57 (.22)	.56 (.31)	2.21 (.23)	1.02 (.32)	.78 (1.27)	1.31 (.23)	-.53 (.08)
8. Germany	.62 (.11)		1.50 (.18)	.16 (.13)	1.44 (.20)	.83 (.35)	2.30 (.17)	1.00 (.23)		.71 (.21)	-.60 (.10)
9. Belgium	.49 (.18)	.98 (.37)	1.14 (.36)	.58 (.22)	1.49 (.27)	.58 (.41)	.88 (.28)	.94 (.50)	.06 (2.18)	2.37 (.38)	-.13 (.07)
10. Norway	.23 (.12)	1.14 (.20)	1.21 (.21)	.00 (.17)	1.29 (.22)	.79 (.34)	3.20 (.18)	1.03 (.30)	.52 (1.09)	.84 (.21)	-.48 (.09)
11. Netherlands	.50 (.15)	.62 (.18)	2.06 (.18)	.58 (.15)	1.41 (.27)	.60 (.19)	1.77 (.25)	.95 (.48)	.80 (.37)	.76 (.26)	-.84 (.11)
12. Iceland	.45 (.11)	.74 (.21)	1.34 (.16)	-.04 (.11)	1.89 (.19)	.76 (.28)	2.49 (.18)	1.44 (.35)	-.01 (1.30)	1.72 (.30)	-.69 (.09)
13. Finland	.55 (.14)	1.28 (.28)	1.67 (.32)	.15 (.21)	1.56 (.30)	.65 (.62)	1.80 (.19)	1.89 (.38)	1.16 (.64)	.71 (.32)	-.38 (.09)
14. Austria	.21 (.21)	.50 (.32)	1.79 (.25)	.18 (.24)	1.95 (.34)	-.73 (.53)	3.11 (.29)	.80 (.41)	-.40 (1.49)	.54 (.25)	-.15 (.10)
15. Japan	.62 (.15)		1.88 (.38)	.22 (.22)	2.08 (.35)	.78 (.25)	1.35 (.30)	1.15 (.32)		1.49 (.29)	-.37 (.10)
16. U.K.	.33 (.15)	1.03 (.17)	1.20 (.26)	.35 (.12)	2.14 (.22)	.61 (.59)	1.66 (.17)	1.34 (.25)	1.01 (.47)	1.17 (.15)	-.40 (.08)
17. Spain	.85 (.20)	.91 (.65)	1.29 (.34)	.19 (.30)	1.46 (.34)	.95 (.51)	2.37 (.35)	1.36 (.53)	.40 (.54)	.62 (.33)	-.29 (.08)
18. Italy	.86 (.10)	.70 (.26)	1.81 (.20)	.49 (.16)	1.53 (.23)	1.03 (.31)	1.42 (.18)	.67 (.25)	.62 (1.05)	.95 (.18)	-.18 (.07)
Mean	.55	.83	1.47	.28	1.72	.65	1.99	1.26	.67	1.00	-.45

Table 3.10 presents the own-price elasticities. With only a few exceptions, these elasticities are less than 1 in absolute value. Five of the elasticities are positive. It should be noted that these correspond to the five negative income elasticities.

In Chapter 2 we employed the OECD data to estimate income and own-price elasticities using double-log demand equations. Table 3.11 compares these elasticities with the current ones by presenting the cross-country means for both cases. The income elasticities are very close. The only exception is for education (.32 vs .67). The price elasticities are not as close as the income elasticities, but nevertheless seem to be broadly consistent.

3.12 MORE ON THE ELASTICITIES

We noted previously that five of the income elasticities in Table 3.9 are negative. Taken literally, these goods are inferior. However, none of these negative elasticities is significant, which is fortunate as the assumption of preference independence rules out inferior goods (Clements, 1987). We shall now re-estimate the model for the relevant countries with the constraint that all income elasticities are positive. To do this, we specify the coefficient β_i of good i with negative income elasticity to be $\beta_i = -\min_t \overline{w}_{it}$, so that the income elasticity $\eta_{it} = 1 + \beta_i/\overline{w}_{it}$ is now constrained to be positive.

TABLE 3.10

SLUTSKY OWN-PRICE ELASTICITIES OF 10 COMMODITIES FOR 18 COUNTRIES

(Root-mean-square-errors are in parentheses)

Country	Food	Beverages	Clothing	Housing	Durables	Medical care	Transport	Recreation	Education	Miscellaneous
(1)	(2)	(3)	(4)	(5)	(6)	(7)	(8)	(9)	(10)	(11)
1. U.S.	-.22	-.11	-.46	-.14	-.58	-.14	-.56	-.43	-.31	-.24
	(.05)	(.12)	(.12)	(.05)	(.11)	(.10)	(.09)	(.12)	(.18)	(.07)
2. Canada	-.45	-.32	-.42	-.02	-.75	-1.23	-.66	-.92	-.57	-.45
	(.11)	(.17)	(.21)	(.12)	(.24)	(.35)	(.14)	(.27)	(.35)	(.16)
3. Sweden	-.28	-.58	-.74	-.09	-.93	-.03	-.84	-.79	-.33	-.55
	(.07)	(.12)	(.18)	(.08)	(.16)	(.13)	(.13)	(.14)	(.41)	(.16)
4. Switzerland	-.42	-.65	-.88	-.08	-.97	-.16	-.72	-.50		-.32
	(.06)	(.11)	(.17)	(.06)	(.16)	(.13)	(.12)	(.14)		(.14)
5. Denmark	-.16	-.30	-.67	-.16	-.63	-.22	-.69	-.52	.06	-.40
	(.07)	(.09)	(.14)	(.06)	(.11)	(.21)	(.11)	(.13)	(.29)	(.11)
6. Australia	-.11	-.35	-.53	-.26	-.84	-.31	-.53	-.91	-1.28	-.23
	(.09)	(.12)	(.13)	(.08)	(.18)	(.18)	(.11)	(.19)	(.75)	(.12)
7. France	-.22	-.25	-.61	-.22	-.70	-.28	-.86	-.50	-.41	-.58
	(.09)	(.15)	(.14)	(.09)	(.14)	(.16)	(.14)	(.16)	(.64)	(.11)
8. Germany	-.31		-.76	-.09	-.72	-.49	-.97	-.56		-.40
	(.07)		(.15)	(.08)	(.14)	(.22)	(.15)	(.15)		(.11)
9. Belgium	-.06	-.12	-.13	-.07	-.15	-.07	-.10	-.11	-.01	-.22
	(.04)	(.09)	(.10)	(.04)	(.10)	(.07)	(.07)	(.10)	(.30)	(.11)
10. Norway	-.11	-.50	-.51	-.00	-.55	-.37	-.89	-.46	-.25	-.37
	(.06)	(.10)	(.13)	(.08)	(.14)	(.17)	(.17)	(.17)	(.53)	(.11)
11. Netherlands	-.36	-.50	-1.21	-.46	-.98	-.49	-1.32	-.78	-.66	-.59
	(.12)	(.15)	(.16)	(.12)	(.18)	(.15)	(.17)	(.42)	(.32)	(.22)
12. Iceland	-.28	-.49	-.80	.03	-1.07	-.50	-1.21	-.92	.01	-1.09
	(.07)	(.15)	(.12)	(.08)	(.16)	(.20)	(.16)	(.23)	(.91)	(.23)
13. Finland	-.18	-.43	-.54	-.06	-.52	-.24	-.51	-.64	-.43	-.25
	(.06)	(.14)	(.16)	(.09)	(.14)	(.25)	(.11)	(.18)	(.29)	(.13)
14. Austria	-.03	-.07	-.22	-.03	-.25	.12	-.28	-.12	.06	-.08
	(.04)	(.06)	(.15)	(.05)	(.17)	(.12)	(.17)	(.11)	(.24)	(.07)
15. Japan	-.19		-.59	-.08	-.66	-.27	-.44	-.38		-.43
	(.06)		(.21)	(.08)	(.16)	(.09)	(.13)	(.13)		(.14)
16. U.K.	-.12	-.38	-.43	-.13	-.71	-.24	-.51	-.47	-.39	-.37
	(.06)	(.07)	(.13)	(.05)	(.16)	(.22)	(.10)	(.12)	(.19)	(.08)
17. Spain	-.18	-.26	-.32	-.05	-.37	-.27	-.53	-.37	-.12	-.17
	(.06)	(.19)	(.12)	(.09)	(.12)	(.16)	(.13)	(.14)	(.17)	(.10)
18. Italy	-.12	-.12	-.28	-.09	-.25	-.18	-.22	-.12	-.11	-.15
	(.05)	(.08)	(.12)	(.04)	(.09)	(.09)	(.09)	(.06)	(.21)	(.07)
Mean	-.21	-.34	-.56	-.11	-.65	-.30	-.66	-.53	-.32	-.38

TABLE 3.11

TWO SETS OF DEMAND ELASTICITIES FOR 10 COMMODITIES

Model	Food	Beverages	Clothing	Housing	Durables	Medical care	Transport	Recreation	Education	Miscellaneous
(1)	(2)	(3)	(4)	(5)	(6)	(7)	(8)	(9)	(10)	(11)
<u>Income elasticities</u>										
1. Double-log	.53	.85	1.46	.23	1.76	.75	2.02	1.22	.32	1.23
2. Working's	.55	.83	1.47	.28	1.72	.65	1.99	1.26	.67	1.00
<u>Slutsky own-price elasticities</u>										
3. Double-log	-.40	-.42	-.63	-.14	-.60	-.31	-.80	-.83	-.24	-.48
4. Working's	-.21	-.34	-.56	-.11	-.65	-.30	-.66	-.53	-.32	-.38

All elasticities are cross-country means. Rows 1 and 3 are from Tables 2.14 and 2.15, respectively; and rows 2 and 4 are from Tables 3.9 and 3.10, respectively.

The countries involved are Denmark (for education), Iceland (housing and education) and Austria (medical care and education). It is to be noted that education is a troublemaker for all three countries; recall also that education is the only case in Table 3.11 where the two sets of income elasticities do not line up. This suggests that either there may be some problems with the data for education or that the model is not satisfactory for this good. For the three countries we specify the β_i's for the relevant commodities. All other parameters are estimated in the same way as before by ML using model (10.3) with constant terms included and the covariance matrix Σ^*. Table 3.12 presents the elasticities and the income flexibility with and without the restrictions. Comparing the two rows for each country, we see that the restrictions result in only minor changes for Denmark and Austria, while for Iceland the changes are somewhat larger.

To test the validity of the restrictions, we use the likelihood ratio statistic $-2 \log \lambda = -2[\log L_r - \log L_u]$, where L_r and L_u represent the log-likelihood values for the restricted and unrestricted models, respectively. This test statistic has an asymptotic χ^2 distribution with degrees of freedom equal to the number of restrictions. Table 3.13 presents for each country the log-likelihood values; the observed value of the test statistic; and the critical value at the 5 percent level. As can be seen, we are unable to reject the restrictions for all three countries. The conclusion is that the income elasticities jointly are not significantly negative. This agrees with the individual insignificance of the negative elasticities.

TABLE 3.12

UNRESTRICTED AND RESTRICTED DEMAND ELASTICITIES

FOR 10 COMMODITIES IN 3 COUNTRIES

(Root-mean-square-errors are in parentheses)

Country	Food	Beverages	Clothing	Housing	Durables	Medical care	Transport	Recreation	Education	Miscellaneous	ϕ Income flexibility
(1)	(2)	(3)	(4)	(5)	(6)	(7)	(8)	(9)	(10)	(11)	(12)
Income elasticities and income flexibility											
1. Denmark											
Unrestricted	.36	.69	1.63	.38	1.59	.49	2.25	1.24	-.14	.95	-.46
	(.16)	(.19)	(.23)	(.12)	(.16)	(.46)	(.14)	(.23)	(.61)	(.20)	(.08)
Restricted	.35	.69	1.63	.37	1.59	.48	2.24	1.24	.46	.95	-.47
	(.16)	(.19)	(.23)	(.12)	(.16)	(.46)	(.14)	(.23)	(-)	(.20)	(.08)
2. Iceland											
Unrestricted	.45	.74	1.34	-.04	1.89	.76	2.49	1.44	-.01	1.72	-.69
	(.11)	(.21)	(.16)	(.11)	(.19)	(.28)	(.18)	(.35)	(1.30)	(.30)	(.09)
Restricted	.40	.69	1.27	.23	1.82	.71	2.40	1.39	.11	1.65	-.72
	(.11)	(.22)	(.13)	(-)	(.19)	(.20)	(.18)	(.35)	( )	(.30)	(.09)
3. Austria											
Unrestricted	.21	.50	1.79	.18	1.95	-.73	3.11	.80	-.40	.54	-.15
	(.21)	(.32)	(.25)	(.24)	(.34)	(.53)	(.29)	(.41)	(1.49)	(.25)	(.10)
Restricted	.18	.43	1.77	.16	1.92	.27	3.03	.76	.31	.50	-.18
	(.21)	(.32)	(.25)	(.24)	(.35)	(-)	(.29)	(.42)	(-)	(.25)	(.10)
Slutsky own-price elasticities											
4. Denmark											
Unrestricted	-.16	-.30	-.67	-.16	-.63	-.22	-.69	-.52	.06	-.40	
	(.07)	(.09)	(.14)	(.06)	(.11)	(.21)	(.11)	(.13)	(.29)	(.11)	
Restricted	-.15	-.30	-.68	-.16	-.64	-.22	-.70	-.52	-.21	-.40	
	(.08)	(.09)	(.14)	(.05)	(.11)	(.18)	(.11)	(.12)	(-)	(.11)	
5. Iceland											
Unrestricted	-.28	-.49	-.80	.03	-1.07	-.50	-1.21	-.92	.01	-1.09	
	(.07)	(.15)	(.12)	(.08)	(.16)	(.20)	(.16)	(.23)	(.91)	(.23)	
Restricted	-.18	-.39	-.75	-.16	-1.10	-.56	-1.23	-.99	-.08	-1.14	
	(.08)	(.16)	(.12)	(-)	(.16)	(.20)	(.16)	(.26)	(-)	(.24)	
6. Austria											
Unrestricted	-.03	-.07	-.22	-.03	-.25	.12	-.28	-.12	.06	-.08	
	(.04)	(.06)	(.15)	(.05)	(.17)	(.12)	(.17)	(.11)	(.24)	(.07)	
Restricted	-.03	-.08	-.25	-.02	-.28	-.05	-.32	-.13	-.06	-.08	
	(.04)	(.07)	(.15)	(.06)	(.17)	(-)	(.17)	(.11)	(-)	(.07)	

For the restricted estimates, the income elasticities are constrained to be positive. The restrictions take the form $\beta_i = - \min_t \bar{w}_{it}$ for i = education in Denmark; housing and education in Iceland; and medical care and education in Austria. The unrestricted estimates are from Tables 3.9 and 3.10.

TABLE 3.13

TESTS OF RESTRICTIONS OF THE INCOME ELASTICITIES
FOR 3 COUNTRIESW

| Country | Log-likelihood values | | Likelihood ratio test statistic | Critical value at 5% level |
| | Unrestricted | Restricted | | |
(1)	(2)	(3)	(4)	(5)
1. Denmark	184.32	183.88	.89	3.84
2. Iceland	74.08	71.34	5.48	5.99
3. Austria	199.05	197.14	3.82	5.99

3.13 CONCLUDING COMMENTS

In this chapter we have presented an extensive application of Theil's (1987) distribution-free procedures to test the hypotheses of demand theory, homogeneity and symmetry. Using data for 18 OECD countries, we found that the hypotheses are acceptable in most cases. This is in stark contrast to almost all previous results based on the conventional asymptotic tests. The conclusion is that OECD consumers do indeed behave as if they obey demand theory.

We also introduced a similar distribution-free procedure to test the hypothesis of preference independence; i.e., that there is no interaction of commodities in the consumer's utility function. In most of the 18 countries, there is at least some tentative support for this hypothesis. Finally, the implications of the estimates were explored by tabulating and analysing the implied demand elasticities.

APPENDICES TO CHAPTER 3

A3.1   ESTIMATION UNDER PREFERENCE INDEPENDENCE

WITH THE USUAL COVARIANCE MATRIX

For convenience, we reproduce model (10.3),

$$\overline{w}_{it}(Dq_{it} - DQ_t) = \beta_i DQ_t + \phi(\overline{w}_{it} + \beta_i)\left[Dp_{it} - \sum_{j=1}^{n}(\overline{w}_{jt} + \beta_j)Dp_{jt}\right] + \varepsilon_{it}. \qquad (A1.1)$$

Since $\sum_{j=1}^{n}(\overline{w}_{jt} + \beta_j) = 1$, we can eliminate β_n from (A1.1) to give

$$\overline{w}_{it}(Dq_{it} - DQ_t) = \beta_i DQ_t + \phi(\overline{w}_{it} + \beta_i)\left[Dp_{it}^* - \sum_{j=1}^{n-1}(\overline{w}_{jt} + \beta_j)Dp_{jt}^*\right] + \varepsilon_{it}, \qquad (A1.2)$$

where $Dp^*_{it} = Dp_{it} - Dp_{nt}$. We write equation (A1.2) in the form

$$y_{it} = \beta_i DQ_t + \phi z_{it} + \varepsilon_{it}, \qquad (A1.3)$$

where $y_{it} = \overline{w}_{it}(Dq_{it} - DQ_t)$ and

$$z_{it} = (\overline{w}_{it} + \beta_i)\left[Dp^*_{it} - \sum_{j=1}^{n-1} (\overline{w}_{jt} + \beta_j)Dp^*_{jt}\right].$$

For reasons described in Section 3.2, we confine ourselves to (A1.3) for $i=1,...,n-1$. In vector form (A1.3) can be written as

$$\mathbf{y}_t = \mathbf{X}_t \theta + \varepsilon_t, \qquad (A1.4)$$

where $\mathbf{y}_t = [y_{it}]$; $\mathbf{X}_t = [DQ_t \mathbf{I} \; z_t]$, $\mathbf{I}$ being the identity matrix of order $n-1$; $z_t = [z_{it}]$; $\theta = [\beta' \; \phi]' = [\beta_1 \; ... \; \beta_{n-1} \; \phi]'$; and $\varepsilon_t = [\varepsilon_{it}]$.

Assuming that the ε_t's are independent normal vectors with zero mean and non-singular covariance matrix Σ, the log-likelihood function of the $\mathbf{y}_t$'s is given by

$$L(\theta,\Sigma;y) = C + \frac{T}{2} \log |\Sigma^{-1}| - \frac{1}{2} \sum_{t=1}^{T} (\mathbf{y}_t - \mathbf{X}_t \theta)' \Sigma^{-1}(\mathbf{y}_t - \mathbf{X}_t \theta), \qquad (A1.5)$$

where C is a constant; and T is the sample size. The first-order conditions for a maximum of (A1.5) are

$$\frac{\partial L}{\partial \Sigma^{-1}} = \frac{T}{2}\Sigma - \frac{1}{2}\sum_{t=1}^{T}(y_t - X_t\theta)(y_t - X_t\theta)' = 0 \qquad (A1.6)$$

and

$$\frac{\partial L}{\partial \theta'} = \sum_{t=1}^{T}(y_t - X_t\theta)'\Sigma^{-1}\frac{\partial X_t\theta}{\partial \theta'} = 0, \qquad (A1.7)$$

where

$$\frac{\partial X_t\theta}{\partial \theta'} = \left[DQ_t I + \phi\frac{\partial z_t}{\partial \beta'} \quad z_t\right]; \qquad (A1.8)$$

$$\frac{\partial z_t}{\partial \beta'} = \left[\frac{\partial z_{it}}{\partial \beta_j}\right];$$

and

$$\frac{\partial z_{it}}{\partial \beta_j} = -(\overline{w}_{it} + \beta_i)Dp^*_{jt} + \delta_{ij}\left[Dp^*_{it} - \sum_{k-1}^{n-1}(\overline{w}_{kt} + \beta_k)Dp^*_{kt}\right].$$

From the first-order condition (A1.6), we have

$$\hat{\Sigma} = \frac{1}{T}\sum_{t=1}^{T}(y_t - X_t\hat{\theta})(y_t - X_t\hat{\theta})'.$$

This is the usual ML estimator of Σ. In Section 3.10 we denote this estimator by S_P.

It follows from (A1.7) that

$$\frac{\partial^2 L}{\partial \Sigma^{-1} \partial \boldsymbol{\theta}'} = \sum_{t=1}^{T} (\mathbf{y}_t - \mathbf{X}_t \boldsymbol{\theta}) \left[\frac{\partial \mathbf{X}_t \boldsymbol{\theta}}{\partial \boldsymbol{\theta}'} \right]' . \tag{A1.9}$$

Since $E[(\mathbf{y}_t - \mathbf{X}_t \boldsymbol{\theta})] = E[\boldsymbol{\varepsilon}_t] = 0$, the expected value of the right-hand side of (A1.9) vanishes, so that the information matrix of the ML procedure is block-diagonal with respect to $\boldsymbol{\theta}$ and Σ^{-1}. From (A1.7) we also have

$$\frac{\partial^2 L}{\partial \boldsymbol{\theta} \partial \boldsymbol{\theta}'} = - \sum_{t=1}^{T} \frac{\partial (\mathbf{X}_t \boldsymbol{\theta})'}{\partial \boldsymbol{\theta}} \Sigma^{-1} \frac{\partial (\mathbf{X}_t \boldsymbol{\theta})}{\partial \boldsymbol{\theta}'} + \sum_{t=1}^{T} (\mathbf{y}_t - \mathbf{X}_t \boldsymbol{\theta})' \Sigma^{-1} \frac{\partial^2 (\mathbf{X}_t \boldsymbol{\theta})}{\partial \boldsymbol{\theta} \partial \boldsymbol{\theta}'} .$$

The second term on the right-hand side has zero expectation. Therefore, the asymptotic covariance matrix of the ML estimator of $\boldsymbol{\theta}$ is

$$\mathbf{V} = - \left[E \left[\frac{\partial^2 L}{\partial \boldsymbol{\theta} \partial \boldsymbol{\theta}'} \right] \right]^{-1} = \left[\sum_{t=1}^{T} \frac{\partial (\mathbf{X}_t \boldsymbol{\theta})'}{\partial \boldsymbol{\theta}} \Sigma^{-1} \frac{\partial (\mathbf{X}_t \boldsymbol{\theta})}{\partial \boldsymbol{\theta}'} \right]^{-1} . \tag{A1.10}$$

The ML estimator of $\boldsymbol{\theta}$ is obtained by means of Newton's iterative scheme based on successive estimates of $\mathbf{V}$ and Σ. The asymptotic standard errors are the square roots of the diagonal elements of $\mathbf{V}$ with ML-estimates substituted for the unknown parameters in $\mathbf{V}$.

When constant terms (α_i) are included in the model, (A1.3) becomes

$$y_{it} = \alpha_i + \beta_i DQ_t + \phi z_{it} + \varepsilon_{it}.$$

This can be written in vector form as equation (A1.4) provided we redefine the parameter vector θ as $[\boldsymbol{\beta}'\ \phi\ \boldsymbol{\alpha}']'$, with $\boldsymbol{\alpha}' = [\alpha_1 \ldots \alpha_{n-1}]$; $\mathbf{X}_t$ as $[DQ_t I\ z_t\ I]$; and all other notation remains the same. The only modification is that equation (A1.8) becomes

$$\frac{\partial \mathbf{X}_t \boldsymbol{\theta}}{\partial \boldsymbol{\theta}'} = \left[DQ_t I + \phi \frac{\partial z_t}{\partial \boldsymbol{\beta}'}\ \ z_t\ \ I \right].$$

The rest of the procedure is as before.

A3.2   ESTIMATION UNDER PREFERENCE INDEPENDENCE WITH THE ALTERNATIVE COVARIANCE MATRIX

When the covariance matrix is specified as $\Sigma^* = \lambda^2 \Omega$, the log-likelihood function (A1.5) becomes

$$L(\boldsymbol{\theta},\lambda^2;y) = C + \frac{T}{2} \log \lambda^{-2(n-1)} - \frac{1}{2\lambda^2} \sum_{t=1}^{T} (\mathbf{y}_t - \mathbf{X}_t \boldsymbol{\theta})' \Omega^{-1}(\mathbf{y}_t - \mathbf{X}_t \boldsymbol{\theta}). \qquad (A2.1)$$

The first-order conditions for a maximum of (A2.1) are

$$\frac{\partial L}{\partial \lambda^2} = -\frac{T(n-1)}{2\lambda^2} + \frac{1}{2\lambda^4} \sum_{t=1}^{T} (\mathbf{y}_t - \mathbf{X}_t\boldsymbol{\theta})' \boldsymbol{\Omega}^{-1} (\mathbf{y}_t - \mathbf{X}_t\boldsymbol{\theta}) = 0 \qquad (A2.2)$$

and

$$\frac{\partial L}{\partial \boldsymbol{\theta}'} = \frac{1}{\lambda^2} \sum_{t=1}^{T} (\mathbf{y}_t - \mathbf{X}_t\boldsymbol{\theta})' \boldsymbol{\Omega}^{-1} \frac{\partial \mathbf{X}_t\boldsymbol{\theta}}{\partial \boldsymbol{\theta}'} = 0, \qquad (A2.3)$$

where $\partial(\mathbf{X}_t\boldsymbol{\theta})/\partial\boldsymbol{\theta}'$ is given by (A1.8).

The first-order condition (A2.2) implies

$$\hat{\lambda}^2 = \frac{1}{T(n-1)} \sum_{t=1}^{T} (\mathbf{y}_t - \mathbf{X}_t\hat{\boldsymbol{\theta}})' \boldsymbol{\Omega}^{-1} (\mathbf{y}_t - \mathbf{X}_t\hat{\boldsymbol{\theta}}).$$

This is the ML estimator of λ^2. Note that the estimator of λ^2 presented in (6.2) is the LS version.

From (A2.3),

$$\frac{\partial^2 L}{\partial \lambda^2 \partial \boldsymbol{\theta}'} = -\frac{1}{\lambda^4} \sum_{t=1}^{T} (\mathbf{y}_t - \mathbf{X}_t\boldsymbol{\theta})' \boldsymbol{\Omega}^{-1} \frac{\partial \mathbf{X}_t\boldsymbol{\theta}}{\partial \boldsymbol{\theta}'},$$

which has zero expectation. Thus the information matrix is block-diagonal with respect to $\boldsymbol{\theta}$ and λ^2. From (A2.3) we also have

$$\frac{\partial^2 L}{\partial\theta\partial\theta'} = -\frac{1}{\lambda^2} \sum_{t=1}^{T} \frac{\partial(\mathbf{X}_t\theta)'}{\partial\theta} \Omega^{-1} \frac{\partial(\mathbf{X}_t\theta)}{\partial\theta'} + \frac{1}{\lambda^2} \sum_{t=1}^{T} (\mathbf{y}_t - \mathbf{X}_t\theta)' \Omega^{-1} \frac{\partial^2(\mathbf{X}_t\theta)}{\partial\theta\partial\theta'}.$$

The second term on the right-hand side has zero expectation. Therefore, the asymptotic covariance matrix of the ML estimator of θ is

$$\mathbf{V}^* = -\left[E\left[\frac{\partial^2 L}{\partial\theta\partial\theta'}\right]\right]^{-1} = \left[\frac{1}{\lambda^2} \sum_{t=1}^{T} \frac{\partial(\mathbf{X}_t\theta)'}{\partial\theta} \Omega^{-1} \frac{\partial(\mathbf{X}_t\theta)}{\partial\theta'}\right]^{-1}.$$

The ML estimator of θ is obtained by means of Newton's scheme based on successive estimates of $\mathbf{V}^*$ and λ^2. The asymptotic standard errors are the square roots of the diagonal elements of $\mathbf{V}^*$ with ML-estimates substituted for the unknown parameters in $\mathbf{V}^*$.

When constants are included, the adjustments are exactly the same as those presented at the end of Appendix A3.1.

A3.3 FURTHER RESULTS ON PREFERENCE INDEPENDENCE

As noted in Section 3.10, the results for testing the hypothesis of preference independence seem to be dependent on whether we use S or Σ^* for the covariance matrix. In the procedure described in Section 3.10, the covariance matrix is used at 3 stages:

1. To obtain the data-based homogeneity- and symmetry-constrained parameter estimates, where we use the covariance matrix of the error terms given homogeneity $(S_H; \Sigma_H^*)$; see equation (5.6). These parameter estimates are used to compute the test statistic (10.5); see the next stage.

2. To obtain the parameter estimates under preference independence (the null hypothesis) and to generate error terms under the null. Here we use the covariance matrix under preference independence $(S_P; \Sigma_P^*)$. At this stage we also compute the data-based value of the test statistic τ, defined by equation (10.5).

3. To obtain simulated homogeneity- and symmetry-constrained parameter estimates, where we use the covariance matrix of the error terms under homogeneity $(S_H; \Sigma_H^*)$. At this stage we apply (5.6) to the simulated data. Here we also compute the simulated values of the test statistic.

To see whether the results are systematically affected by the choice of the covariance matrix at a particular stage, we replace S by Σ^* (or vice versa) at the 3 stages of the procedure. Table A3.1 summarizes four combinations of S and Σ^*. For each of these combinations, we test the preference independence hypothesis for the 7 countries with non-singular covariance matrix. In Table A3.2, we present the ranks of the data-based test statistics in 99 simulations for the four combinations of S and Σ^*. The upper half of columns 2 and 5 are the relevant parts of columns 2 and 4 of Table 3.8; and

TABLE A3.1

COMBINATIONS OF S AND Σ^* AT DIFFERENT STAGES
OF THE PREFERENCE INDEPENDENCE TEST

Combination	Stage 1 Data-based estimation with homogeneity and symmetry	Stage 2 Data-based estimation with preference independence and data-based value of τ	Stage 3 Simulated value of τ
1	S	S	S
2	S	S	Σ^*
3	S	Σ^*	Σ^*
4	Σ^*	Σ^*	Σ^*

the lower half of these columns are the relevant parts of columns 3 and 5 of Table 3.8. As can be seen from rows 8 and 16 of Table A3.2, the number of rejections falls as we move from the left to the right of the table. Moving to the right in this table corresponds to going down in Table A3.1, from a lower to a higher combination in which Σ^* plays a more important role in the procedure. Consequently, there is a tendency for the hypothesis to be more acceptable when we use Σ^* instead of S.

TABLE A3.2

RANK OF THE DATA-BASED TEST STATISTIC FOR
PREFERENCE INDEPENDENCE WITH DIFFERENT COMBINATIONS OF
S AND Σ^* IN 99 SIMULATIONS FOR 7 COUNTRIES

Country	Combination			
	1	2	3	4
(1)	(2)	(3)	(4)	(5)
No constant				
1. U.S.	100	96	45	58
2. Canada	98	89	5	23
3. Switzerland	91	44	76	95
4. Australia	86	80	55	93
5. Germany	95	74	22	84
6. Belgium	99	99	79	43
7. Netherlands	98	97	58	39
8. Percent significant at 5% level	57	43	0	0
With constant				
9. U.S.	100	99	47	70
10. Canada	96	94	7	15
11. Switzerland	86	90	37	82
12. Australia	70	57	46	92
13. Germany	50	32	2	30
14. Belgium	100	100	86	49
15. Netherlands	99	100	86	25
16. Percent significant at 5% level	57	43	0	0

See Table A3.1 for the definitions of the 4 combinations.

REFERENCES

Anderson, R.W. (1980). 'Some Theory of Inverse Demand for Applied Demand Analysis,' <u>European Economic Review</u> 14: 281-90.

Barnard, G.A. (1963). 'Comment,' <u>Journal of the Royal Statistical Society</u>, Series B, 25: 294.

Barten, A.P. (1977). 'The Systems of Consumer Demand Functions Approach: A Review,' <u>Econometrica</u> 45: 23-51.

Bera, A.K., R.P. Byron and C.M. Jarque (1981). 'Further Evidence on Asymptotic Tests for Homogeneity and Symmetry in Large Demand Systems,' <u>Economics Letters</u> 8: 101-5.

Besag, J. and D.J. Diggle (1977). 'Simple Monte Carlo Tests of Spatial Pattern,' <u>Applied Statistics</u> 26: 327-333.

Bewley, R.A. (1983). 'Tests of Restrictions in Large Demand Systems,' <u>European Economic Review</u> 20: 257-69.

———— (1986). <u>Allocation Models: Specification, Estimation and Applications</u>. Cambridge, Mass.: Ballinger Publishing Company.

Clements, K.W. (1987). 'Alternative Approaches to Consumption Theory,' Chapter 1 in H. Theil and K.W. Clements, <u>Applied Demand Analysis: Results from System-Wide Approaches</u>. Cambridge, Mass.: Ballinger Publishing Company, pp.1-35.

Deaton, A. (1975).   Models and Projections of Demand in Post-War Britain. London: Chapman and Hall.

——————— (1986).   'Demand Analysis,' Chapter 30 in Handbook of Econometrics, Vol.3, Z. Griliches and M.D. Intriligator (eds.), Amsterdam: North Holland Publishing Company.

Hicks, J.R. (1946).   Value and Capital.   Second Edition. Oxford: Oxford University Press.

Huang, K.S. (1983).   'The Family of Inverse Demand Systems,' European Economic Review 23: 329-37.

Kravis, I.B., A.W. Heston and R. Summers (1978).   International Comparisons of Real Product and Purchasing Power. Baltimore, Md: The Johns Hopkins University Press.

Laitinen, K. (1978).   'Why is Demand Homogeneity So Often Rejected?' Economics Letters 1: 187-91.

Marriot, F.H.C. (1979).   'Barnard's Monte Carlo Tests: How Many Simulations?' Applied Statistics 28: 75-77.

Meisner, J.F. (1979).   'The Sad Fate of the Asymptotic Slutsky Symmetry Test for Large Systems,' Economics Letters 2: 231-33.

——————— (1981).   Appendix to International Consumption Comparisons: A System- Wide Approach, by H. Theil and F.E. Suhm. Amsterdam: North-Holland Publishing Company.

Salvas-Bronsard, L., D. Leblanc and C. Bronsard (1977). 'Estimating Demand Equations: The Converse Approach,' _European Economic Review_ 9: 301-21.

Selvanathan, E.A. (1985). 'An Even Simpler Differential Demand System,' _Economics Letters_ 19: 343-7.

Selvanathan, S. (1987). 'A Monte Carlo Test of Preference Independence,' _Economics Letters_ 25: 259-61.

Theil, H. (1967). _Economics and Information Theory_. Amsterdam: North-Holland Publishing Company.

——— (1971). _Principles of Econometrics_. New York: John Wiley and Sons.

——— (1975/76). _Theory and Measurement of Consumer Demand_. Two volumes. Amsterdam: North Holland Publishing Company.

——— (1980). _The System-Wide Approach to Microeconomics_. Chicago: University of Chicago Press.

——— (1987). 'The Econometrics of Demand Systems,' Chapter 3 in H. Theil and K.W. Clements, _Applied Demand Analysis: Results from System-Wide Approaches_. Cambridge, Mass.: Ballinger Publishing Company, pp.101-62.

Theil, H. and R.B. Brooks (1970/71). 'How Does the Marginal Utility of Income Change When Real Income Changes?' _European Economic Review_ 2: 218-40.

CHAPTER 4

HOW SIMILAR ARE OECD CONSUMERS?

4.1 INTRODUCTION

Stigler and Becker (1977) hypothesize that tastes neither change capriciously nor differ importantly between people. In an international context, this hypothesis amounts to stating that consumers in different countries are similar irrespective of differences in language, culture and geography. In an innovative paper, Pollak and Wales (1987) formally tested this hypothesis. They use the quadratic expenditure system with time-series/cross-country data for Belgium, the U.K. and the U.S. On the basis of likelihood ratio and nonparametric (revealed preference) tests, they conclude that the data from these countries cannot be pooled to estimate a common demand system. That is, they reject the hypothesis of identical tastes.

In this chapter we test this hypothesis using the consumption data for the OECD countries described in Chapter 2. In Chapter 3 we allowed the consumers in different countries to be idiosyncratic by estimating 18 separate systems of demand equations, one for each country. We commence this chapter by presenting these estimates. We then specify that consumers in different countries are the same and take the parameters of the demand equations to be the same across countries. This involves pooling the data and estimating a common demand system for all countries. An analysis of the predictions from the demand equations shows that the pooled model performs quite well. This finding points in the direction of there being more similarities than differences in tastes across countries. This is in contrast to the results of Pollack and Wales (1987).

In addition, we analyse in this chapter the extent to which Theil's (1987) cross-country demand system for 30 countries can explain the OECD time-series data. We also use our estimates to investigate the extent to which the parameters of the demand equations vary with income and prices. This includes a test of the Frisch's (1959) famous conjecture about the income dependence of the income elasticity of the marginal utility of income.

4.2   MODEL I: A DEMAND SYSTEM FOR EACH OF THE 15 COUNTRIES

We discussed Working's (1943) model under preference independence in Section 3.10. With a country superscript (c) added, this model for commodity i takes the form

$$y^c_{it} = \alpha^c_i + \beta^c_i DQ^c_t + \phi^c z^c_{it} + \varepsilon^c_{it},\qquad(2.1)$$

where $y^c_{it} = \overline{w}^c_{it}(Dq^c_{it} - DQ^c_t)$;

$$z^c_{it} = (\beta^c_i + \overline{w}^c_{it})\left[Dp^{*c}_{it} - \sum_{j=1}^{9} (\beta^c_j + \overline{w}^c_{jt})Dp^{*c}_{jt}\right],$$

$Dp^{*c}_{it} = Dp^c_{it} - Dp^c_{10,t}$; and ε^c_{it} is a disturbance term. All other notation is as before. The α^c_i's and β^c_i's satisfy $\sum_{i=1}^{n^c} \alpha^c_i - \sum_{i=1}^{n^c} \beta^c_i = 0$, where n^c is the number of commodities in country c.

In Chapter 3 we estimated model (2.1) for $i=1,...,n^c$ for 18 OECD countries by maximum likelihood (ML). All except 3 countries have 10 commodities and, for comparability, in this chapter we omit those 3 countries. It is to be noted that model (2.1) has the restrictions of homogeneity, symmetry and preference independence built in. We tested these restrictions in Chapter 3 and found that they are not at total variance with the data for most countries. As the parameters of (2.1) take different values for each country, we shall refer to this model as the individual country model or Model I.

Table 4.1 presents the estimates of the income coefficients (β^c_i) and the income flexibilities (ϕ^c) for the 15 countries. In Section 1.10 we noted that various previous estimates of Working's β_i for food lie in the range -.13 to -.18.

As can be seen from column 2 of Table 4.1, among the 15 estimates 12 lie either within this range or are not significantly different from values in the range. The last row of the table presents the arithmetic means of the parameters across countries. We present the estimates of the constants (α_i^c) in Appendix A4.1. We will evaluate the performance of this model in Section 4.6.

4.3   MODEL II: COMMON DEMAND PARAMETERS

Next, we analyse informally the extent to which the estimates of the individual country models differ across countries. This will provide some preliminary evidence regarding the similarity (or lack thereof) of consumers. Technical details of this section are presented in Appendix A4.2.

Let $\beta^c = [\beta_1^c \ \ldots \ \beta_{10}^c]'$ be the vector of estimates of the 10 income coefficients for country c given in Table 4.1. Consider a matrix-weighted mean of $\beta^1,\ldots,\beta^{15}$,

$$\tilde{\beta} = \sum_{c=1}^{15} A^c \beta^c. \tag{3.1}$$

It can be easily shown that (3.1) defines an optimal combination of the β^c's when the weight matrices $A^1,\ldots,A^{15}$ are proportional to the inverses of the

TABLE 4.1

INCOME COEFFICIENTS FOR 10 COMMODITIES AND INCOME FLEXIBILITY FOR 15 COUNTRIES

(Standard errors are in parentheses)

Country	Food β_1^c	Beverages β_2^c	Clothing β_3^c	Housing β_4^c	Durables β_5^c	Medical care β_6^c	Transport β_7^c	Recreation β_8^c	Education β_9^c	Miscellaneous β_{10}^c	Income flexibility ϕ^c
(1)	(2)	(3)	(4)	(5)	(6)	(7)	(8)	(9)	(10)	(11)	(12)
1. U.S.	−.055 (.019)	−.031 (.014)	.027 (.021)	−.115 (.026)	.054 (.017)	−.059 (.021)	.209 (.024)	.014 (.018)	−.003 (.009)	−.041 (.023)	−.384 (.066)
2. Canada	−.007 (.037)	−.025 (.022)	−.015 (.029)	−.183 (.041)	.050 (.034)	.055 (.020)	.084 (.036)	.051 (.027)	.001 (.011)	−.011 (.044)	−.554 (.120)
3. Sweden	−.094 (.025)	.008 (.015)	.038 (.022)	−.190 (.032)	.067 (.021)	−.022 (.005)	.138 (.026)	.054 (.021)	−.001 (.001)	.002 (.021)	−.580 (.088)
4. Denmark	−.123 (.032)	−.028 (.018)	.044 (.016)	−.130 (.024)	.053 (.017)	−.010 (.008)	.188 (.023)	.019 (.018)	−.009 (.005)	−.005 (.018)	−.465 (.081)
5. Australia	−.144 (.037)	−.015 (.025)	.027 (.030)	−.059 (.033)	.100 (.031)	−.018 (.025)	.074 (.040)	.072 (.024)	.013 (.012)	−.050 (.027)	−.463 (.077)
6. France	−.115 (.034)	−.024 (.014)	.024 (.023)	−.081 (.024)	.059 (.022)	−.047 (.033)	.146 (.025)	.001 (.020)	−.001 (.003)	.039 (.024)	−.527 (.077)
7. Belgium	−.119 (.044)	−.001 (.025)	.011 (.028)	−.066 (.033)	.070 (.039)	−.028 (.025)	−.012 (.030)	−.002 (.021)	−.002 (.005)	.150 (.041)	−.127 (.069)
8. Norway	−.180 (.029)	.010 (.015)	.021 (.021)	−.145 (.024)	.026 (.020)	−.009 (.014)	.293 (.024)	.002 (.022)	−.003 (.006)	−.016 (.022)	−.484 (.088)
9. Netherlands	−.132 (.040)	−.024 (.013)	.157 (.028)	−.046 (.019)	.051 (.029)	−.027 (.014)	.051 (.016)	−.002 (.017)	−.006 (.012)	−.023 (.025)	−.842 (.107)
10. Iceland	−.129 (.025)	−.020 (.016)	.037 (.018)	−.198 (.022)	.089 (.018)	−.015 (.017)	.181 (.020)	.023 (.017)	−.004 (.006)	.036 (.014)	−.695 (.089)
11. Finland	−.126 (.037)	.024 (.025)	.055 (.027)	−.122 (.032)	.042 (.023)	−.009 (.015)	.109 (.029)	.053 (.021)	.002 (.010)	−.028 (.027)	−.378 (.081)
12. Austria	−.175 (.041)	−.036 (.023)	.090 (.031)	−.099 (.030)	.085 (.028)	−.060 (.018)	.282 (.034)	−.011 (.021)	−.005 (.005)	−.071 (.036)	−.154 (.093)
13. U.K.	−.127 (.027)	.002 (.011)	.017 (.020)	−.118 (.023)	.068 (.018)	−.003 (.005)	.087 (.020)	.027 (.018)	.000 (.009)	.027 (.023)	−.396 (.071)
14. Spain	−.049 (.061)	−.003 (.024)	.031 (.036)	−.111 (.045)	.039 (.030)	−.002 (.024)	.130 (.032)	.015 (.020)	−.012 (.012)	−.034 (.028)	−.291 (.073)
15. Italy	−.044 (.029)	−.017 (.016)	.077 (.018)	−.067 (.023)	.036 (.015)	.001 (.012)	.044 (.019)	−.024 (.016)	−.002 (.004)	−.006 (.021)	−.184 (.074)
Mean	−.108 (.009)	−.012 (.005)	.043 (.007)	−.116 (.008)	.061 (.006)	−.017 (.005)	.134 (.007)	.019 (.005)	−.002 (.002)	−.002 (.007)	−.435 (.022)

relevant covariance matrices. The derivation of the covariance matrix of $\tilde{\beta}$ is presented in Appendix A4.2.

Next, consider the 15 estimates of the income flexibility presented in Table 4.1, $\phi^1,...,\phi^{15}$. We proceed as before and define a weighted mean,

$$\tilde{\phi} = \sum_{c=1}^{15} a^c \phi^c, \tag{3.2}$$

where $a^c = (1/\text{var } \phi^c)/\left[\sum_{d=1}^{15} (1/\text{var } \phi^d) \right]$ is the optimal value of the weight for country c. We refer to the model with the common demand parameters, $\tilde{\beta}_i$, i=1,...,10 and $\tilde{\phi}$, as Model II.

The first row of Table 4.2 presents the weighted means of the income coefficients and the income flexibility and the second row gives their standard errors. Note that these weighted means are not too different from their unweighted counterparts given at the bottom of Table 4.1. Consequently, the weights do not seem to play a vital role. The root-mean-square error (RMSE) of the β_i^c's around the weighted mean $\tilde{\beta}_i$ and corresponding measure for the ϕ^c's are

$$\left[\frac{1}{15} \sum_{c=1}^{15} (\beta_i^c - \tilde{\beta}_i)^2 \right]^{\frac{1}{2}} \quad \text{and} \quad \left[\frac{1}{15} \sum_{c=1}^{15} (\phi^c - \tilde{\phi})^2 \right]^{\frac{1}{2}}.$$

The third row of Table 4.2 presents these RMSEs.

TABLE 4.2

WEIGHTED MEANS OF INCOME COEFFICIENTS FOR 10 COMMODITIES

AND INCOME FLEXIBILITY, AND THE ROOT-MEAN-SQUARE ERRORS

(1)	Food β_1 (2)	Beverages β_2 (3)	Clothing β_3 (4)	Housing β_4 (5)	Durables β_5 (6)	Medical care β_6 (7)	Transport β_7 (8)	Recreation β_8 (9)	Education β_9 (10)	Miscellaneous β_{10} (11)	Income flexibility ϕ (12)
1. Weighted means	-.102	-.013	.042	-.110	.058	-.013	.121	.017	-.001	.001	-.404
2. SEs	.008	.004	.006	.007	.005	.003	.006	.005	.001	.006	.021
3. RMSEs	.048	.017	.039	.047	.021	.027	.084	.027	.006	.051	.193

Figures 4.1-4.10 plot the income coefficients and their weighted means for the 10 commodities. Figure 4.11 presents the analogous plot for the income flexibility. The figures also give the two-standard-error bands constructed using the RMSEs presented in Table 4.2. Among the 165 points in the 11 plots, all except 8 lie within the two-standard-error bands. That is, more than 95 percent of the estimates lie within the band. This evidence points in the direction of the similarity of consumers (as measured by the coefficients β_i and ϕ) in countries.

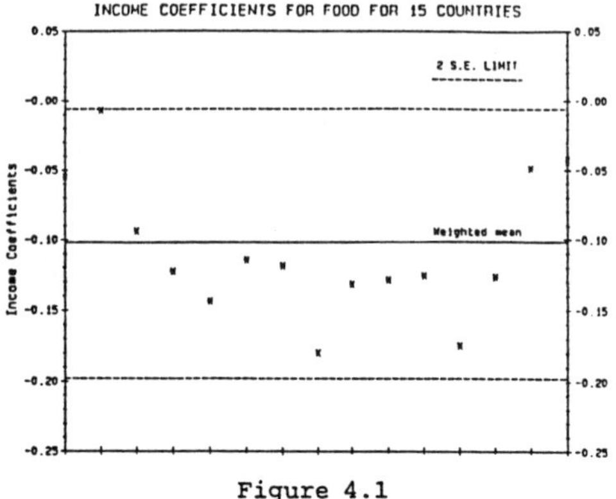

Figure 4.1

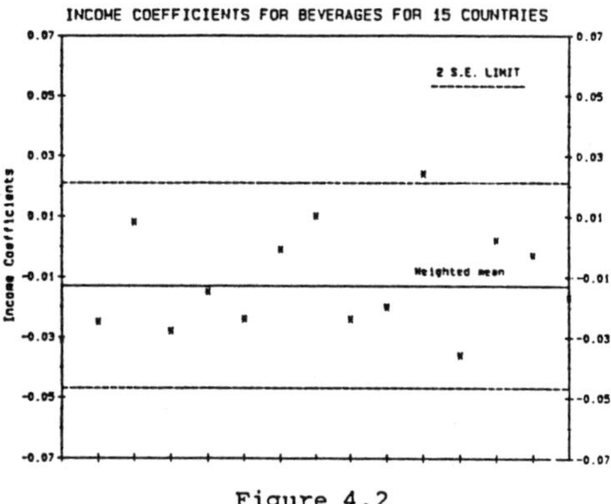

Figure 4.2

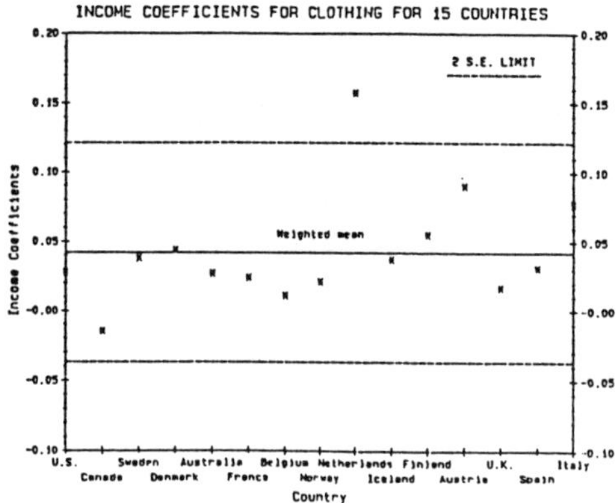

Figure 4.3

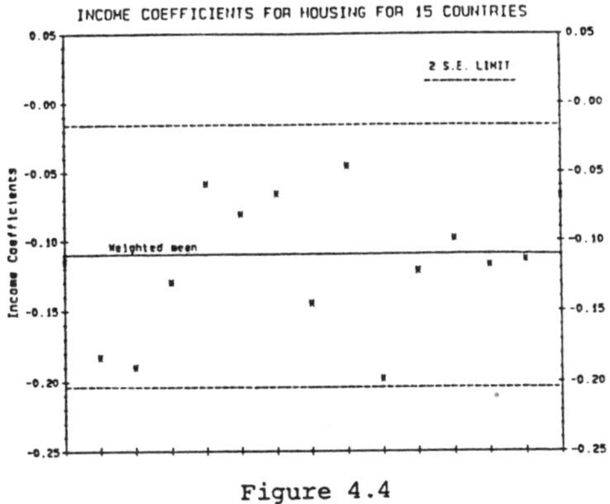

Figure 4.4

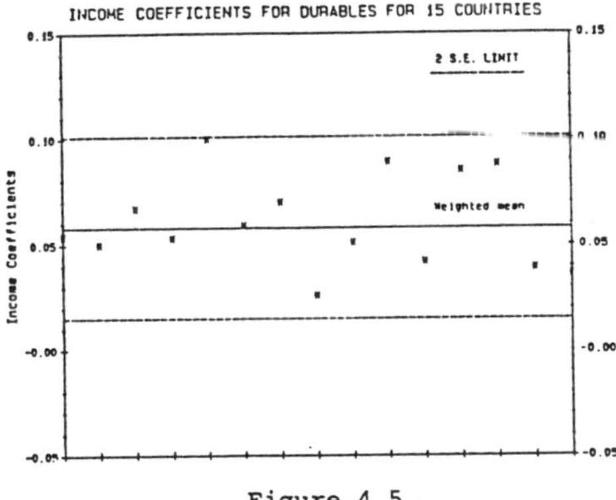

Figure 4.5

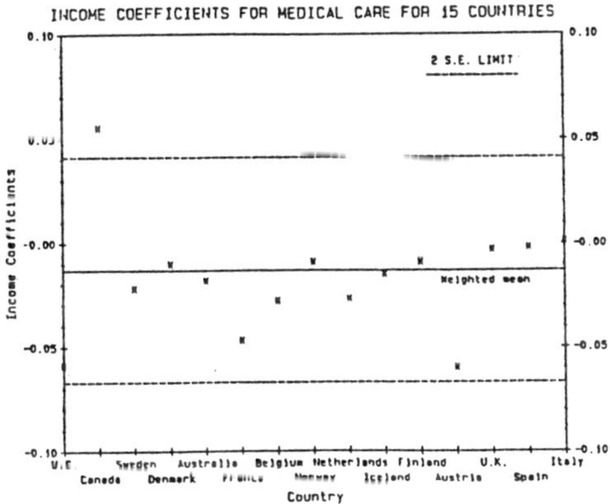

Figure 4.6

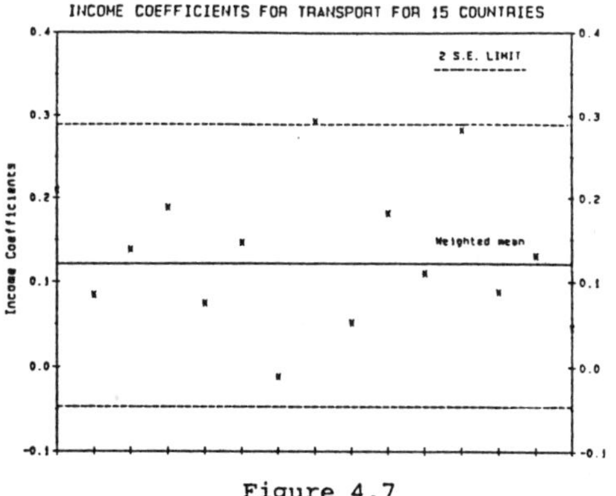

Figure 4.7

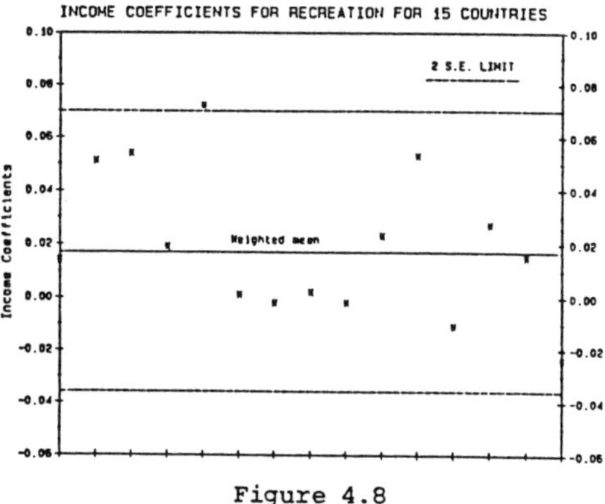

Figure 4.8

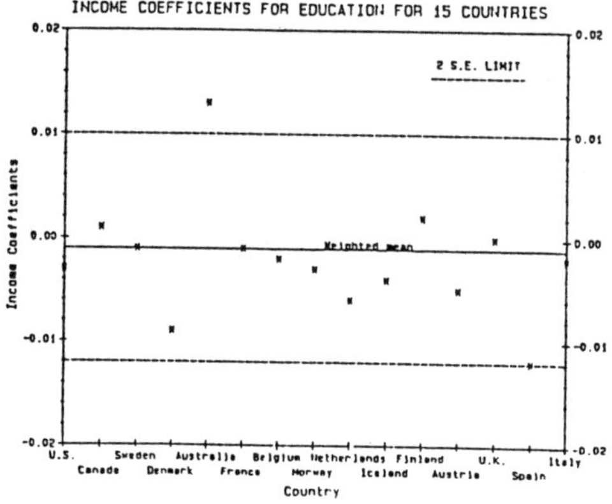

Figure 4.9

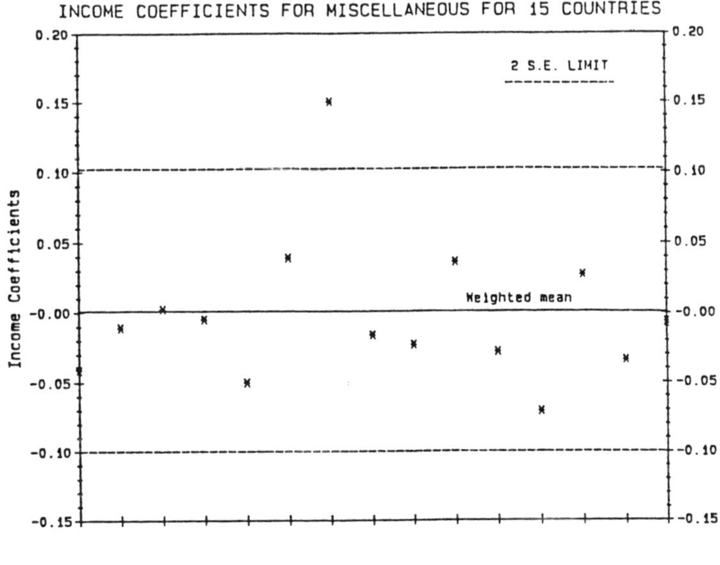

Figure 4.10

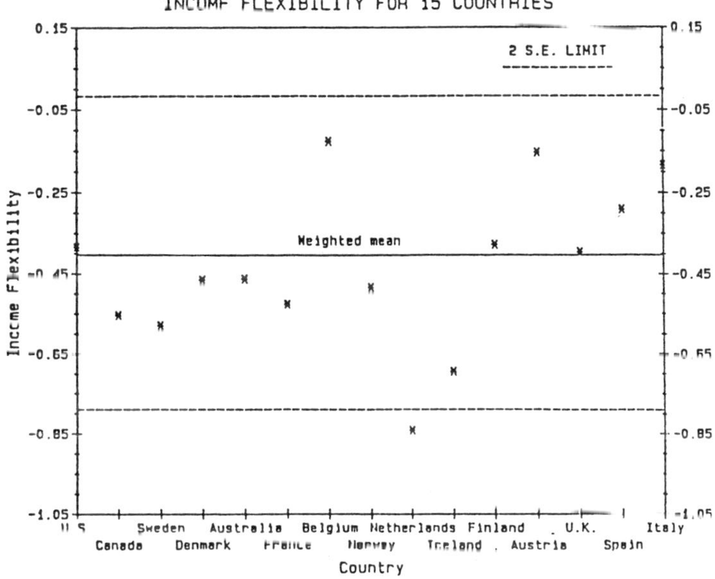

Figure 4.11

4.4 MODEL III: A FORMALLY POOLED DEMAND SYSTEM

In this section we specify that the coefficients of the demand equations are the same in all countries and pool the data to estimate a common system for all 15 countries. That is, we now assume that $\beta_i^c = \beta_i$, $\phi^c = \phi$, i=1,...,10 commodities; c=1,...,15 countries. As the constant terms (α_i^c) take account of non-economic factors, they have a somewhat different status, so we allow them to vary over countries. Thus (2.1) becomes

$$y_{it}^c = \alpha_i^c + \beta_i DQ_t^c + \phi z_{it}^c + \varepsilon_{it}^c, \qquad \begin{array}{l} i=1,...,10; \\ t=1,...,T_c; \\ c=1,...,15, \end{array} \qquad (4.1)$$

where $z_{it}^c = (\beta_i + \overline{w}_{it}^c)\left[Dp_{it}^{*c} - \sum_{j=1}^{9}(\beta_j + \overline{w}_{jt}^c)Dp_{jt}^{*c}\right]$; T_c is the sample size of country c; and all other notation is as before. The error terms, ε_{it}^c's, are assumed to be normally distributed with zero means and independent over time and countries. We shall refer model (4.1) as the pooled model or Model III.

The first two rows of Table 4.3 present the ML-estimates of the income coefficients and the income flexibility for model (4.1) and their asymptotic standard errors. Details of the ML estimation procedure and the estimates of the constants are presented in Appendix A4.3. For comparison, in the next two rows of the table we reproduce from Table 4.2 the weighted means of the individual-country estimates and their standard errors. As can be seen, the two sets of estimates are very similar. We test this similarity using a likelihood ratio test. We take the pooled model as the unrestricted model, while the restricted model is that the income coefficients and the income flexibility are known and equal to the weighted means from row 3 of Table 4.3. That is, the null hypothesis is that $\beta_i = \tilde{\beta}_i$, i=1,...,10; and $\phi = \tilde{\phi}$. Under the null, $-2(L_r - L_u)$ has an asymptotic $\chi^2(10)$ distribution, where L_r is the restricted log-likelihood value and L_u is the unrestricted value. The observed value of the test statistic is 6.8, less than the critical value of 18.3 at the 5 percent level. Consequently, the test confirms the similarity of the pooled estimates and the weighted means.

Recall the result from the previous section that more than 95 percent of the individual-country estimates lie within the two-standard-error bands. As the pooled estimates are so close to the weighted means, we can conclude that the pooled estimates also are not too different from those of the individual country model. Since the estimates of Model II and Model III are not significantly different from each other, in what follows we shall concentrate on Model III, equation (4.1).

Now we shall formally test the restrictions of the pooled model against the individual country model by means of a likelihood ratio test. When the model is estimated for each country separately, we estimate 15×9 free constant terms (α_i^c), 15×9 free income coefficients (β_i^c) and 15×1 income flexibilities (ϕ^c). Under pooling, we continue to estimate 15×9 free constants, so there are no restrictions here. When we pool, however, β_i takes the same

TABLE 4.3

POOLED ESTIMATES AND WEIGHTED MEANS OF INCOME COEFFICIENTS

FOR 10 COMMODITIES AND INCOME FLEXIBILITY

(1)	Food β_1 (2)	Beverages β_2 (3)	Clothing β_3 (4)	Housing β_4 (5)	Durables β_5 (6)	Medical care β_6 (7)	Transport β_7 (8)	Recreation β_8 (9)	Education β_9 (10)	Miscellaneous β_{10} (11)	Income flexibility ϕ (12)
1. Pooled estimates	-.097	-.011	.040	-.114	.054	-.012	.122	.017	-.002	.004	-.449
2. ASEs of pooled estimates	.008	.005	.006	.008	.006	.003	.007	.005	.001	.006	.022
3. Weighted means	-.102	-.013	.042	-.110	.058	-.013	.121	.017	-.001	.001	-.404
4. SEs of weighted means	.008	.004	.006	.007	.005	.003	.006	.005	.001	.006	.021

value in each country, so that we have only 9 free income coefficients. Consequently, pooling involves $15 \times 9 - 9 = 126$ restrictions on the income coefficients. Also, the income flexibility is taken to be the same for all countries when we pool, which involves a further 14 restrictions. Relative to the 15 individual country models, pooling therefore involves a total of $126 + 14 = 140$ restrictions.

Under the null hypothesis of pooling, the test statistic $-2(L_r - L_u)$ has an asymptotic $\chi^2(140)$ distribution, where L_r and L_u are the restricted and the unrestricted log-likelihood values, respectively. Under the assumption that the observations are independent across countries, the unrestricted log-likelihood value is the sum of the log-likelihood values for the 15 countries individually (L_u^c), $L_u = \Sigma_{c=1}^{15} L_u^c = 3037.1$. Under pooling, the restricted log-likelihood value $L_r = 2844.4$. Thus the value of the test statistic $-2(L_r - L_u)$ is $-2(2844.4 - 3037.1) = 385.4$. As this value is too high for $\chi^2(140)$, we are unable to accept the pooled model on the basis of the likelihood ratio test. In light of our previous findings regarding the cross-country similarities of parameters, this result is puzzling. It may be that the asymptotic test is not performing satisfactorily, as has been found to be the case for homogeneity and symmetry testing (see Sections 3.3 and 3.4). Accordingly, in what follows we shall keep an open mind about the status of the restrictions of the pooled model.

4.5 MODEL IV: THEIL'S CROSS-COUNTRY DEMAND SYSTEM

The application of model (4.1) involves the use of time-series data. Theil (1987), however, develops another version of this model in which countries play the role of time periods. He estimates this model with data pertaining to 30 countries from Kravis et al. (1982). Theil uses the same 10 commodity groups as we do. Although the unit of observation is now different (countries rather than years), the parameters of the cross-country model have exactly the same interpretation as those of the time-series version. In this section we present Theil's estimates, which we refer to as Model IV, and in Section 4.6 analyse how these estimates perform in explaining the OECD time-series data. It should be noted that among the 15 OECD countries considered in this chapter only 9 are included in the 30 countries used by Theil.

Theil's ML-estimates are presented in column 2 of Table 4.4. For comparison, in column 3 we reproduce from Table 4.3 the pooled estimates and their asymptotic standard errors. As can be seen, the estimates are not similar.

It may be objected that the two models are not strictly comparable as Model III has constant terms which allow for trend-like changes in tastes etc.; Theil's model contains no similar terms. To put the two models on a more equal footing, we re-estimate Model III [equation (4.1)] with the constant terms suppressed. Column 4 of Table 4.4 contains the results. While the new estimates are a bit 'closer' to Theil's, differences still remain. In what follows we use Model III with the constants since (i) more than 75 percent of their estimates are significant (see Table A4.2, Appendix A4.3); and (ii) the model with constants tends to be more compatible with the data than when they are suppressed (see Chapter 3).

TABLE 4.4

THREE SETS OF INCOME COEFFICIENTS AND INCOME FLEXIBILITY

(Standard errors are in parentheses)

Commodity	Income coefficient β_i		
	Model IV: Theil's	Model III: Pooled model	
		With constants	No constants
(1)	(2)	(3)	(4)
1. Food	-.154 (.010)	-.097 (.008)	-.109 (.006)
2. Beverages	.001 (.005)	-.011 (.005)	-.013 (.003)
3. Clothing	-.005 (.005)	.040 (.006)	-.005 (.004)
4. Housing	.032 (.006)	-.114 (.008)	-.021 (.005)
5. Durables	.025 (.004)	.054 (.006)	.021 (.004)
6. Medical Care	.024 (.003)	-.012 (.003)	.006 (.003)
7. Transport	.030 (.006)	.122 (.007)	.086 (.004)
8. Recreation	.019 (.003)	.017 (.005)	.023 (.003)
9. Education	-.004 (.005)	-.002 (.001)	-.001 (.001)
10. Miscellaneous	.033 (.006)	.004 (.006)	.012 (.005)
Income flexibility	-.526 (.037)	-.449 (.022)	-.382 (.022)

4.6 COMPARISON OF THE MODELS

Model I [equation (2.1)] allows consumers in different countries to be
idiosyncratic as all the parameters differ across countries. Model III [equation
(4.1)] and model IV [the cross-country version of equation (4.1)] assume that

consumers in different countries are the same in the sense that the income coefficients and the income flexibility take common values internationally. However, consumers can still be country specific in Models III and IV because (i) the constant terms vary over countries to account for differences in non-economic factors; and (ii) the error terms take different values across countries to allow for unexplained random factors. Subsequently, we refer to Models III and IV as implying that tastes are identical internationally. It is to be understood, however, that this is to be interpreted as referring to the β_i- and ϕ-parameters of the demand equations; tastes can still differ due to (i) and (ii) above. In this section we compare the ability of the models to explain the data. This comparison allows us to analyse the extent to which consumers in different countries are similar.

We compare the models on the basis of a goodness-of-fit criterion, the information inaccuracy, defined as

$$I_t^c = \sum_{i=1}^{10} w_{it}^c \log \left[\frac{w_{it}^c}{\hat{w}_{it}^c} \right], \tag{6.1}$$

where w_{it}^c is the observed value of the budget share of commodity i in year t in country c; and $\hat{w}_{it}^c$ is the predicted budget share implied by the demand model. The information inaccuracy is zero when the fit of the model is perfect and increases as it becomes worse.

Columns 6-8 of Table 4.5 present the information inaccuracies (6.1) of the three models averaged over $t=1,...,T_c$ and adjusted for degrees of freedom. The degrees of freedom adjustment allows for the differing number of unknown parameters in each model. Technical details are presented in Appendix A4.4. Column 9 gives the information inaccuracy for a naive model of no-change extrapolation, whereby the prediction of w_{it}^c is specified as $w_{i,t-1}^c$. Looking at rows 1-15 of columns 6 and 7 (which refer to Models I and III), we see that the two sets of inaccuracies display similarities across countries. For example, for both models France has the best fit; U.S. the second best; and U.K. the third best. All countries have the same ranking for the two models except Denmark, Australia, Norway, Austria and Spain, but even these differences are small. The conclusion is that the same general patterns emerge whether or not we specify the parameters of the demand equations to be the same across countries. This points in the direction of cross-country similarities of tastes.

Looking at columns 8 and 9 of Table 4.5, we see that for all countries except Canada the inaccuracies of Theil's model and the naive model are higher than those for Models I and III. (Recall that we also noted some problems for Canada in Chapter 3.) Interestingly, in all cases except Canada Theil's model performs much better than no-change extrapolation of the budget shares. This is a striking result as Theil's sample of 30 countries includes only 9 of the OECD countries.

TABLE 4.5

POPULATION, GDP AND AVERAGE INFORMATION INACCURACIES

IN 15 COUNTRIES FOR FOUR DEMAND MODELS

Country	Mid-year population in 1975 (millions)	Per capita GDP in 1975 international dollars	GDP in 1975 international dollars (billions)	GDP weights × 100	Average information inaccuracy			
					Model I: Individual country model	Model III: Pooled model	Model IV: Theil's estimates	Naive model
(1)	(2)	(3)	(4)	(5)	(6)	(7)	(8)	(9)
* 1. U.S.	215.97	7132	1540.30	51.34	1.36	1.48	2.33	3.18
2. Canada	22.73	6788	154.29	5.14	4.99	5.51	6.01	5.45
3. Sweden	8.19	6749	55.27	1.84	1.76	1.82	3.30	4.05
* 4. Denmark	5.10	5969	30.44	1.01	2.33	2.34	4.16	7.48
5. Australia	13.89	5919	82.22	2.74	2.90	3.02	3.30	5.15
* 6. France	52.71	5864	309.09	10.30	.96	.96	1.19	3.52
* 7. Belgium	9.80	5554	54.43	1.81	3.35	3.75	4.04	6.16
8. Norway	4.01	5419	21.73	.72	2.15	2.76	4.06	4.98
* 9. Netherlands	13.65	5321	72.65	2.42	5.13	6.40	6.61	8.23
10. Iceland	.22	5201	1.14	.04	11.03	12.47	21.69	27.73
11. Finland	4.71	5192	24.46	.82	6.77	6.72	8.15	10.65
*12. Austria	7.52	4994	37.56	1.25	2.74	3.12	4.28	7.09
*13. U.K.	55.89	4601	257.15	8.57	1.56	1.61	2.31	4.05
*14. Spain	35.60	4032	143.52	4.78	2.71	2.62	3.22	7.40
*15. Italy	55.83	3870	216.06	7.20	1.77	2.26	2.43	4.21
16. Unweighted mean					3.43	3.79	5.14	7.29
17. GDP-weighted mean					1.87	2.04	2.73	4.10
18. RMS percentage prediction error					1.93	2.02	2.34	2.86

A * denotes that the country is included in Theil's (1987) sample. Populations are from Stening (1985). Per capita GDP's in international dollars are from Summers and Heston (1984). The GDP in column 4 is obtained by multiplying the per capita GDP given in column 3 by the corresponding population in column 2. The GDP weights given in column 5 are obtained by dividing the entries in column 4 by their total. All entries in columns 6-9 of rows 1-17 are to be divided by 10^4.

For a given row in Table 4.5, as we move across from column 6 to column 9, in general the inaccuracy increases, indicating that the predictions get worse. This is to be expected as this move corresponds to more restrictions being placed on the data. Rows 16 and 17 present the cross-country unweighted and GDP-weighted means of the inaccuracies. As can be seen, the GDP-weighted means ($\times 10^4$) for Models I and III are 1.87 and 2.04, which are not too different. A similar result also holds for the unweighted means (3.43 versus 3.79). The conclusion is that the pooled model is almost as good as the individual country model.

To facilitate further the comparison of the models, we present the root-mean-squared (RMS) percentage prediction error,

$$\text{RMS percentage prediction error} = 100 \sqrt{\sum_{i=1}^{10} w_{it}^c \left[\frac{\hat{w}_{it}^c - w_{it}^c}{w_{it}^c}\right]^2}. \qquad (6.2)$$

In words, (6.2) is 100 times the square root of the budget-share- weighted mean of the squared relative prediction errors of the budget share. In Appendix A4.5 we show that $100\sqrt{2I_t^c}$ is approximately equal to (6.2). Row 18 of Table 4.5 gives 100 times the square root of twice the GDP-weighted means of the inaccuracies; these have the RMS error interpretation. As can be seen, the RMS error is 1.93 percent for the individual country model and 2.02 percent for the pooled model. That is, the average deterioration in the quality of the predictions when tastes are taken to be identical is 2.02 - 1.93 = .09 percentage points. This is clearly quite modest and again points in the direction that tastes are not too dissimilar across countries. The RMS errors for Theil's model and the naive model are 2.34 and 2.86 percent, respectively, higher than before.

In Appendix A4.6, we measure the goodness-of-fit of the models with respect to each commodity using the Strobel (1982) decomposition of the information inaccuracy. The results indicate that no individual commodity dominates the lack of fit of the models.

4.7   MORE ON THE COMPARISON

Column 5 of Table 4.5 gives the country weights. These are used to compute the weighted averages of the information inaccuracies. Comparing columns 5 and 6, we see that the U.S. has a largest weight of 51 percent and an inaccuracy of 1.36, which is the second lowest; France has the second largest weight of 10 percent and the lowest inaccuracy (.96); and the third largest country is the U.K. with weight 9 percent and inaccuracy 1.56, which is the third smallest. All other countries have smaller weights and higher inaccuracies. Consequently, the larger countries have better-fitting demand equations. To what extent is our finding of cross-country similarities dependent on the weighting scheme which gives more weight to the better-fitting countries?

Table 4.6 pursues this matter by presenting the RMS errors with some countries excluded. Rows 2-4 exclude the three countries mentioned above. As is to be expected, the RMS errors increase as the better-fitting countries are excluded. The deterioration of fit when we take tastes to be the same increases from 2.02-1.93 = .09 percentage points when all countries are included (row 1 of Table 4.6) to 2.66-2.52 = .14 percentage points when the three countries are excluded (row 4).   Although the deterioration of fit increases, it is still fair to describe this deterioration of .14 percentage points as quite modest.

Next, consider ranking the countries in the order of decreasing total GDP,

1. U.S.	(51)	8. Netherlands	(2)
2. France	(10)	9. Sweden	(2)
3. U.K.	(9)	10. Belgium	(2)
4. Italy	(7)	11. Austria	(1)
5. Canada	(5)	12. Denmark	(1)
6. Spain	(5)	13. Finland	(1)
7. Australia	(3)	14. Norway	(1)
		15. Iceland	(0),

where the numbers in parentheses are the GDP weights in percentage form. (Note that elsewhere in the book countries are listed in the order of decreasing per capita GDP.)   In row 5 of Table 4.5 we present the RMS errors with

TABLE 4.6

RMS PERCENTAGE PREDICTION ERRORS FOR

THE INDIVIDUAL COUNTRY AND THE POOLED DEMAND MODELS

Country	Model I: Individual country model	Model III: Pooled model
(1)	(2)	(3)
1. All countries	1.93	2.02
2. All countries excluding U.S.	2.20	2.30
3. All countries excluding U.S. and France	2.37	2.49
4. All countries excluding U.S., France and U.K.	2.52	2.66
5. Excluding the 7 countries with larger weights	2.66	2.84
6. Excluding the 8 countries with smaller weights	1.84	1.91

When all countries are included, the weights are from column 5 of Table 4.5;
when countries are excluded, the weights are renormalized versions of the
previous ones.   The RMS percentage prediction errors are computed as
100 times square root of twice the GDP-weighted means of the average
information inaccuracies.

the 7 largest countries excluded (i.e., the U.S. to Australia). Here the deterioration of fit due to the assumption of identical tastes is 2.84 - 2.66 = .18 percentage points, which is still not substantial. Finally, row 6 of the table shows that the deterioration of fit is 1.91 - 1.84 = .07 percentage points when the 8 smallest countries are excluded (i.e., Netherlands to Iceland).

The results of this section show that the weighting scheme plays little or no role in our conclusion that tastes are not too dissimilar internationally. Another way of making this point is by using the unweighted cross-country means of the inaccuracies given in row 16 of Table 4.5. The RMS percentage prediction errors corresponding to the unweighted means for Models I and III are $\sqrt{2 \times 3.43}$ = 2.62 percent and $\sqrt{2 \times 3.79}$ = 2.75 percent, respectively. Consequently, on this basis the deterioration of fit is 2.75 - 2.62 = .13 percentage points. As this is not too far from its GDP-weighted counterpart of .09 percentage points, we see again that the weights do not have a substantial influence on the results.

4.8   DO THE DEMAND PARAMETERS DEPEND ON INCOME AND PRICES?

The conclusion of the previous two sections is that the demand parameters do not seem to vary across countries. This conclusion was reached by a comparison of the predictions of the pooled model with those of the individual country model in which the coefficients are completely free to vary across countries. Rather than allowing the parameters to vary arbitrarily across countries, it is interesting to inquire whether they change internationally in response to systematic differences in economic characteristics. The economic characteristics we shall consider are per capita GDP and relative prices.

Column 2 of Table 4.7 presents per capita GDP in 1980 expressed in international dollars for the 15 countries. Columns 3-12 present the relative prices of the 10 commodity groups in the 15 countries, where the overall price level in each country (P^c) is equal to 100. (See Appendix A4.7, for the data source and further details.) To analyse the effect of income and prices on the income coefficients, we regress these coefficients from the individual country models (presented in Table 4.1) on the logarithm of the per capita GDP (y^c), and the logarithm of the relative price of commodity i, $\tilde{p}_i^c = \log (p_i^c/P^c)$,

$$\beta_i^c = v_i + \gamma_i y^c + \lambda_i \tilde{p}_i^c + \varepsilon_i^c, \qquad c=1,...,15, \qquad (8.1)$$

where v_i, γ_i and λ_i are parameters to be estimated; and ε_i^c is an independent disturbance term with mean zero. We use weighted least squares (WLS) to estimate (8.1), where the weights are inversely proportional to the asymptotic standard errors of the income coefficients.

TABLE 4.7

PER CAPITA GDP AND RELATIVE PRICES OF 10 COMMODITIES

IN 1980 FOR 15 COUNTRIES

Country	Per capita GDP in international dollars	Relative prices									
		Food	Beverages	Clothing	Housing	Durables	Medical care	Transport	Recreation	Education	Miscellaneous
(1)	(2)	(3)	(4)	(5)	(6)	(7)	(8)	(9)	(10)	(11)	(12)
1. U.S.	8089	89	97	88	104	87	134	89	93	117	105
2. Canada	7521	89	99	87	95	101	129	93	94	121	98
3. Sweden	7142	99	102	111	95	110	90	119	106	110	95
4. Denmark	6746	108	114	132	101	97	100	122	104	105	96
5. Australia	6308	99	102	111	95	110	90	119	106	110	95
6. France	6678	98	80	125	102	119	89	117	108	105	93
7. Belgium	6293	95	84	121	106	103	88	112	109	86	92
8. Norway	6825	110	122	134	91	131	72	151	114	160	94
9. Netherlands	5856	88	72	104	97	99	89	119	88	137	94
10. Iceland	5836	99	102	111	95	110	90	119	106	110	95
11. Finland	5939	112	157	105	93	111	66	136	132	174	97
12. Austria	6052	103	106	116	85	117	73	123	104	119	89
13. U.K.	4990	98	124	99	94	118	72	139	99	53	99
14. Spain	4264	97	88	111	101	111	93	117	103	59	95
15. Italy	4661	106	82	117	72	130	85	121	126	94	92

Per capita GDP's in column 2 are from Summers and Heston (1984).

The first 10 rows of column 2 of Table 4.8 present the F-statistics for the null hypothesis that $\gamma_i = \lambda_i = 0$ for each commodity. All except one of the F-values are insignificant at the 5 percent level; all are insignificant at the 1 percent level. That is, the income coefficients are not related to income and relative prices. The first 10 rows of column 3 of Table 4.8 present the WLS-estimates of α_i in (8.1) under the restriction $\gamma_i = \lambda_i = 0$. These estimates are similar to the weighted averages of the parameter estimates presented in row 1 of Table 4.2.

Next, we analyse the effect of income on the income flexibility by estimating

$$\phi^c = \eta_0 + \eta_1 y^c + \xi^c, \qquad c=1,...,15, \qquad (8.2)$$

where η_0 and η_1 are parameters to be estimated; and ξ^c is an independent disturbance term with mean zero. We use the income flexibilities from the individual country model (presented in Table 4.1) to estimate (8.2) by WLS. The last row of Table 4.8 presents the F-value for the null hypothesis that $\eta_1 = 0$. As the F-value is insignificant, we conclude that ϕ is independent of real income. The restricted estimates of η_0 in (8.2) is given as the last entry of column 3. Again this is similar to the weighted mean presented in row 1 of Table 4.2.

TABLE 4.8

F-STATISTICS AND RESTRICTED WEIGHTED LEAST SQUARES

ESTIMATES OF DEMAND PARAMETERS

(Standard errors are in parentheses)

β_i, ϕ	F-statistics	Restricted estimates
(1)	(2)	(3)
1. Food	2.64	-.104 (.012)
2. Beverages	4.30*	-.012 (.004)
3. Clothing	0.84	.042 (.009)
4. Housing	0.51	-.111 (.013)
5. Durables	0.35	.059 (.006)
6. Medical Care	1.71	-.013 (.004)
7. Transport	3.34	.127 (.022)
8. Recreation	0.67	.016 (.007)
9. Education	0.49	-.002 (.001)
10. Miscellaneous	0.22	-.000 (.010)
11. Income flexibility	1.37	-.404 (.047)

Critical value at the 5 percent level for the F-statistics of the income
coefficients in rows 1-10 of column 2 is $F(2,12) = 3.88$; and for the income
flexibility in the last row of column 2 the critical value is $F(1,13) = 4.67$.
A * denotes significant at the 5 percent level.

The finding that ϕ is unrelated to real income is, of course, at variance

with Frisch's (1959) famous conjecture. He argues that ϕ should increase in

absolute value as the consumer (or country) becomes more affluent. Our

rejection of Frisch, however, agrees with the previous results of Clements and

Theil (1979), Theil (1980), Theil (1987) and Theil and Brooks (1970/71). We shall further analyse Frisch's conjecture in Chapter 6.

To summarize, the income coefficients and income flexibility seem to be unrelated to income and prices. The constancy of these coefficients suggests that they are fundamental parameters characterizing tastes which are invariant in a wide variety of economic circumstances.

4.9   CONCLUDING COMMENTS

Stigler and Becker (1977) argue that we may treat tastes as stable over time and similar among people. In this chapter we verified their claim using data for 15 OECD countries. We have presented four demand systems to explain time-series consumption data for the 15 countries. Model I allows consumers in different countries to be idiosyncratic; Model II is obtained by taking weighted averages of the parameter estimates of Model I; and in Model III consumers are taken to be the same across countries by specifying that the demand parameters are identical in different countries.

We found that about 95 percent of the parameter estimates of Model I lie within the two-standard-error bands of the estimates from Models II and III. This finding points in the direction of similarities of consumers internationally. However, on the basis of a likelihood ratio test we found that the hypothesis of identical tastes is not acceptable. Using a goodness-of-fit criterion, the information inaccuracy, we analysed the relative performance of the models. We found that Model III (identical consumers) performed quite well, again implying that OECD consumers are not too dissimilar. It needs to be emphasized, however, that this finding relates to the broad aggregates comprising 10 commodity groups. If commodities were further disaggregated, it may well be the case that there would be more disparities in tastes.

We also used Theil's (1987) cross-country demand system to analyse the extent to which it explains the OECD time-series data; this is Model IV. The result is that Models I-III explain the data better than does Theil's. However, Theil's model still does very well given that the 30 countries used to estimate it (from Kravis et al., 1982) include only 9 of our OECD countries. We also found that the demand parameters are unrelated to systematic differences in income and prices across countries; and that our data did not support Frisch's (1959) famous conjecture about the income dependence of the income elasticity of the marginal utility of income.

APPENDICES TO CHAPTER 4

A4.1   THE CONSTANT TERMS FOR THE INDIVIDUAL COUNTRY MODEL

Table A4.1 gives the ML-estimates of the constants for the individual country model.

A4.2   THE WEIGHTED MEANS OF THE INDIVIDUAL COUNTRY ESTIMATES

In this appendix we derive the weighted means of the income coefficients and income flexibilities which are presented in Section 4.3.

The Income Coefficients

Let $\beta^c = [\beta_1^c \; ... \; \beta_{10}^c]'$ be the vector of the estimates of the 10 income coefficients for country c. The constraint $\Sigma_{i=1}^{10} \beta_i^c = 0$ implies that $\Omega_c = \text{var } \beta^c$ is singular. Let $\beta^{*c} = [\beta_1^c \; ... \; \beta_9^c]'$ and $\Omega_c^* = \text{var } \beta^{*c}$. The 9×9 covariance matrix Ω_c^* is non-singular.

Consider the generalized sum of squares

$$L = \sum_{c=1}^{15} \varepsilon_c^{*'} \Omega_c^{*-1} \varepsilon_c^* = \sum_{c=1}^{15} (\beta^{*c} - \tilde{\beta}^*)' \Omega_c^{*-1} (\beta^{*c} - \tilde{\beta}^*), \qquad (A2.1)$$

TABLE A4.1

CONSTANT TERMS FOR 10 COMMODITIES IN 15 COUNTRIES: INDIVIDUAL COUNTRY MODEL

(Standard errors are in parentheses)

Country	Food α_1^c	Beverages α_2^c	Clothing α_3^c	Housing α_4^c	Durables α_5^c	Medical care α_6^c	Transport α_7^c	Recreation α_8^c	Education α_9^c	Miscellaneous α_{10}^c
(1)	(2)	(3)	(4)	(5)	(6)	(7)	(8)	(9)	(10)	(11)
1. U.S.	−.121	.033	−.131	.384	−.203	.351	−.418	.040	.028	.037
	(.060)	(.039)	(.069)	(.078)	(.052)	(.053)	(.074)	(.058)	(.023)	(.063)
2. Canada	−.213	.046	.014	.581	−.177	−.300	−.103	−.026	.047	.136
	(.124)	(.085)	(.120)	(.144)	(.125)	(.073)	(.133)	(.109)	(.038)	(.119)
3. Sweden	−.099	−.073	−.156	.507	−.142	.067	−.108	.110	.004	−.110
	(.071)	(.046)	(.081)	(.067)	(.051)	(.024)	(.065)	(.058)	(.006)	(.041)
4. Denmark	−.065	−.010	−.228	.649	−.286	.017	−.209	.084	.070	−.022
	(.080)	(.004)	(.050)	(.072)	(.055)	(.025)	(.071)	(.057)	(.016)	(.054)
5. Australia	.122	−.074	−.227	.377	−.234	.017	−.015	−.031	−.041	.106
	(.112)	(.074)	(.087)	(.087)	(.111)	(.053)	(.111)	(.066)	(.022)	(.071)
6. France	−.011	−.027	−.280	.510	−.299	.475	−.311	.060	.001	−.118
	(.133)	(.062)	(.094)	(.080)	(.093)	(.131)	(.097)	(.092)	(.011)	(.087)
7. Belgium	−.008	−.036	−.073	.164	−.087	.238	.170	.045	.004	−.426
	(.161)	(.092)	(.105)	(.121)	(.146)	(.088)	(.110)	(.074)	(.017)	(.155)
8. Norway	.160	−.073	−.204	.502	−.026	.018	−.550	.148	.000	.024
	(.103)	(.059)	(.075)	(.083)	(.070)	(.044)	(.085)	(.087)	(.018)	(.068)
9. Netherlands	.049	.085	−.896	.228	−.129	.316	−.045	.046	.095	.250
	(.197)	(.082)	(.148)	(.091)	(.174)	(.057)	(.089)	(.062)	(.048)	(.106)
10. Iceland	.033	.106	−.262	.536	−.272	.289	−.472	.015	.020	.006
	(.187)	(.133)	(.159)	(.185)	(.152)	(.108)	(.160)	(.112)	(.034)	(.110)
11. Finland	−.065	−.008	−.441	.419	−.077	.095	−.075	−.090	−.058	.300
	(.183)	(.125)	(.135)	(.169)	(.119)	(.077)	(.118)	(.109)	(.045)	(.124)
12. Austria	.247	.042	−.222	.158	−.270	.158	−.569	.092	.010	.053
	(.156)	(.095)	(.125)	(.105)	(.115)	(.059)	(.147)	(.083)	(.019)	(.127)
13. U.K.	−.090	−.046	−.066	.280	−.216	−.002	.055	.080	.015	−.010
	(.073)	(.039)	(.069)	(.058)	(.053)	(.015)	(.059)	(.050)	(.022)	(.063)
14. Spain	−.349	−.016	−.235	.406	−.216	.220	−.155	.009	.054	.282
	(.287)	(.125)	(.159)	(.229)	(.137)	(.105)	(.156)	(.085)	(.050)	(.128)
15. Italy	−.225	.023	−.301	.161	−.083	.114	.109	.114	−.002	.090
	(.121)	(.072)	(.073)	(.089)	(.002)	(.050)	(.076)	(.066)	(.017)	(.081)

All entries in columns 2-11 are to be divided by 100.

where $\varepsilon_c^* = \beta^{*c} - \tilde{\beta}^*$; and $\tilde{\beta}^* = [\tilde{\beta}_i^*]$ is a vector of 9 unknown elements. Using the first-order condition for a minimum of L with respect to $\tilde{\beta}^*$ yields

$$\tilde{\beta}^* = \sum_{c=1}^{15} A^{*c} \beta^{*c}, \tag{A2.2}$$

where

$$A^{*c} = \left[\sum_{d=1}^{15} \Omega_d^{*-1} \right]^{-1} \Omega_c^{*-1}$$

is a weight matrix which satisfies $\sum_{c=1}^{15} A^{*c} = I_9$ (the identity matrix of order 9).

The covariance matrix of $\tilde{\beta}^*$ is

$$\begin{aligned}
\operatorname{cov} \tilde{\beta}^* &= \left[\sum_{d=1}^{15} \Omega_d^{*-1} \right]^{-1} \sum_{c=1}^{15} \Omega_c^{*-1} \operatorname{cov} \beta^{*c} \, \Omega_c^{*-1} \left[\sum_{d=1}^{15} \Omega_d^{*-1} \right]^{-1} \\
&= \left[\sum_{d=1}^{15} \Omega_d^{*-1} \right]^{-1} \sum_{c=1}^{15} \Omega_c^{*-1} \Omega_c^* \Omega_c^{*-1} \left[\sum_{d=1}^{15} \Omega_d^{*-1} \right]^{-1} \\
&= \left[\sum_{d=1}^{15} \Omega_d^{*-1} \right]^{-1},
\end{aligned}$$

where we have assumed that the parameters are independent across countries.

The standard errors of the $\tilde{\beta}_i$'s are the square roots of the diagonal elements of $\text{cov } \tilde{\beta}^*$.

Recall that β^{*c} and $\tilde{\beta}^*$ involve only 9 income coefficients. We use the constraint $\Sigma_{i=1}^{10} \tilde{\beta}_i = 0$ to obtain

$$\tilde{\beta}_{10} = - \sum_{i=1}^{9} \tilde{\beta}_i \quad \text{and} \quad \text{SE}[\tilde{\beta}_{10}] = \left[\sum_{i=1}^{9} \sum_{j=1}^{9} \text{cov}[\tilde{\beta}_i, \tilde{\beta}_j] \right]^{\frac{1}{2}}. \quad (A2.3)$$

Let

$$A^c = \begin{bmatrix} A^{*c} & 0 \\ & \\ -\iota' A^{*c} & 0 \end{bmatrix},$$

where $\iota = [1 \ ... \ 1]'$ is a vector of 9 unit elements. Combining (A2.2) and (A2.3), we have

$$\tilde{\beta} = \sum_{c-1}^{15} A^c \beta^c,$$

where $\tilde{\beta}$ is a 10-element vector of common income coefficients.

Following Barten (1969), it can also be easily shown that

$$\varepsilon_c^{*\prime} \Omega_c^{*-1} \varepsilon_c^* = \varepsilon_c'(\Omega_c + \frac{1}{10} u')^{-1} \varepsilon_c, \quad (A2.4)$$

where $\varepsilon_c = \beta^c - \tilde{\beta}$; and $\iota = [1 \ldots 1]'$ is now a vector of 10 unit elements. The expression on the left-hand side of (A2.4) involves only the first 9 commodities, whereas the right-hand side involves all 10. Any commodity can be taken as the 10th and (A2.4) would still be valid. Since the right-hand side of (A2.4) includes all 10 commodities and is invariant to which commodity is dropped in the left-hand side, it follows that equation (A2.1) also does not depend on the commodity deleted to form ε_c^*. This implies that the values of $\tilde{\beta}^*$ and $\tilde{\beta}_{10}$ do not depend on which commodity is dropped.

Next, consider the role of the constraint $\Sigma_{i=1}^{10} \tilde{\beta}_i = 0$, which we write in the form $\iota'\tilde{\beta} = 0$. We form the Lagrangean function

$$L = \varepsilon_c'\left(\Omega_c + \frac{1}{10} u'\right)^{-1}\varepsilon_c + \lambda\,\iota'\tilde{\beta} \qquad (A2.5)$$

$$= \sum_{c=1}^{15} \varepsilon_c^{*\prime}\,\Omega_c^{*-1}\,\varepsilon_c^* + \lambda\,\iota'\tilde{\beta},$$

where λ is a Lagrangean multiplier. The first-order condition for a minimum with respect to the last element of $\tilde{\beta}$, $\tilde{\beta}_{10}$, is

$$\frac{\partial L}{\partial \tilde{\beta}_{10}} = \lambda = 0.$$

As the value of the multiplier λ is zero, $\tilde{\beta}_{10}$ is a free parameter in (A2.5). This shows that minimizing $\varepsilon_c'[\Omega_c + (1/10)\iota\iota']^{-1}\varepsilon_c$ subject to the constraint $\iota'\tilde{\beta} = 0$ is equivalent to the unconstrained minimization of $\Sigma_{c=1}^{15} \varepsilon_c^{*'}\Omega_c^{*-1}\varepsilon_c^{*}$.

The Income Flexibility

To obtain the weighted mean $\tilde{\phi}$ of the income flexibilities ϕ^c, c=1,...,15, we minimize the weighted sum of squares

$$L = \sum_{c=1}^{15} \left[\frac{1}{\text{var } \phi^c}\right](\phi^c - \tilde{\phi})^2. \qquad (A2.6)$$

The first-order condition for a minimum of (A2.6) is

$$\frac{\partial L}{\partial \tilde{\phi}} = -2 \sum_{c=1}^{15} \left[\frac{1}{\text{var } \phi^c}\right](\psi^c - \tilde{\phi}) = 0$$

which yields

$$\tilde{\phi} = \sum_{c=1}^{15} a^c \phi^c,$$

where

$$a^c = \left[\sum_{d=1}^{15} \left[\frac{1}{\text{var } \phi^d}\right]\right]^{-1} \frac{1}{\text{var } \phi^c}.$$

It can be easily verified that the standard error of $\widetilde{\phi}$ is

$$SE[\widetilde{\phi}] = \left[\sum_{d=1}^{15} \left[\frac{1}{\text{var } \phi^d} \right] \right]^{-\frac{1}{2}}.$$

A4.3   ESTIMATION OF THE POOLED DEMAND SYSTEM

For convenience, we reproduce the pooled model (4.1),

$$y_{it}^c = \alpha_i^c + \beta_i DQ_t^c + \phi z_{it}^c + \varepsilon_{it}^c, \qquad \begin{array}{l} i=1,\ldots,10; \\ t=1,\ldots,T_c; \\ c=1,\ldots,15. \end{array} \qquad (A3.1)$$

As one equation is redundant for each country, the number of free parameters to be estimated in (A3.1) is $15 \times 9 = 135$ constant terms, 9 income coefficients and 1 income flexibility. That is, we have a total of $135 + 9 + 1 = 145$ free parameters to be estimated. As this is very large, we eliminate the constants by using deviations from means. This reduces the number of parameters to be estimated to 10.

Let $\bar{y}_{it}^c$, $\overline{DQ}_t^c$, $\bar{z}_i^c$ and $\bar{\varepsilon}_i^c$ be the sample means of y_{it}^c, DQ_t^c, z_{it}^c and ε_{it}^c, respectively. Since the disturbances will be assumed to have zero means, without loss of generality we can take $\bar{\varepsilon}_i^c = 0$. Taking the sum of both sides of

(A3.1) over $t=1,...,T_c$ and dividing through by T_c we get

$$\bar{y}_i^c = \alpha_i^c + \beta_i . D\bar{Q}^c + \phi \bar{z}_i^c, \qquad \begin{array}{l} i=1,...,10; \\ c=1,...,15. \end{array} \qquad \text{(A3.2)}$$

From equations (A3.1) and (A3.2) we have

$$y_{it}^{*c} = \beta_i . DQ_t^{*c} + \phi z_{it}^{*c} + \varepsilon_{it}^c, \qquad \begin{array}{l} i=1,...,10; \\ t=1,...,T_c; \\ c=1,...,15, \end{array} \qquad \text{(A3.3)}$$

where $y_{it}^{*c} = y_{it}^c - \bar{y}_i^c$; $DQ_t^{*c} = DQ_t^c - D\bar{Q}^c$; and $z_{it}^{*c} = z_{it}^c - \bar{z}_i^c$. Since for each country c, $\Sigma_{i=1}^{10} \varepsilon_{it}^c = 0$, for $t=1,...,T_c$, the ε_{it}^c's are linearly dependent. Thus one of the equations is redundant and can be deleted. Therefore we confine ourselves to (A3.3) for $i=1,...,9$.

Let $\mathbf{y}_t^{*c} = [y_{it}^{*c}]$, $\mathbf{z}_t^{*c} = [z_{it}^{*c}]$, $\boldsymbol{\varepsilon}_t^c = [\varepsilon_{it}^c]$ and $\boldsymbol{\beta} = [\beta_1 \ldots \beta_9]'$ be vectors of 9 elements. Then for $i=1,...,9$, (A3.3) can be written in vector form as

$$\mathbf{y}_t^{*c} = DQ_t^{*c}\boldsymbol{\beta} + \phi \mathbf{z}_t^{*c} + \boldsymbol{\varepsilon}_t^c, \qquad \begin{array}{l} t=1,...,T_c; \\ c=1,...,15. \end{array} \qquad \text{(A3.4)}$$

We assume that the disturbances ε_{it}^c's are normally distributed with zero means and $\mathrm{cov}[\varepsilon_{it}^{c}, \varepsilon_{jt}^{c}] = \sigma_{ij}^{c}$, and are independent over time and countries. That is,

$$E[\varepsilon_{it}^{c}\, \varepsilon_{js}^{d}] \;=\; \sigma_{ij}^{c}\delta_{ts}\delta_{cd}, \qquad\qquad \begin{aligned} &i,j=1,\dots,9; \\ &t,s=1,\dots,T_{c}; \\ &c,d=1,\dots,15, \end{aligned}$$

where δ_{ts} is the Kronecker delta. Let $\Sigma_{c} = [\sigma_{ij}^{c}]$. Then

$$E[\varepsilon_{t}^{c}\varepsilon_{s}^{c\,\prime}] \;=\; \delta_{ts}\Sigma_{c}. \qquad\qquad\qquad (A3.5)$$

Let $\boldsymbol{\theta} = [\boldsymbol{\beta}' \quad \phi]'$ be a vector of 10 parameters. Then (A3.4) can be expressed as

$$\mathbf{y}_{t}^{*c} \;=\; [DQ_{t}^{*c}I_{9} \quad \mathbf{z}_{t}^{*c}]\boldsymbol{\theta} + \boldsymbol{\varepsilon}_{t}^{c}$$

$$\;=\; \mathbf{X}_{t}^{*c}\boldsymbol{\theta} + \boldsymbol{\varepsilon}_{t}^{c}, \qquad\qquad \begin{aligned} &t=1,\dots,T_{c}; \\ &c=1,\dots,15, \end{aligned}$$

where $\mathbf{X}_{t}^{*c} = [DQ_{t}^{*c}I_{9} \quad \mathbf{z}_{t}^{*c}]$ is a matrix of order 9×10, with I_{9} the identity matrix of order 9. For $t=1,\dots,T_{c}$, this can be written as

$$\mathbf{y}^{*c} \;=\; \mathbf{X}^{*c}\boldsymbol{\theta} + \boldsymbol{\varepsilon}^{c}, \qquad\qquad c=1,\dots,15, \qquad\qquad (A3.6)$$

where $\mathbf{y}^{*c} = [\mathbf{y}_{t}^{*c}]$ and $\boldsymbol{\varepsilon}^{c} = [\boldsymbol{\varepsilon}_{t}^{c}]$ are vectors of $9T_{c}$ elements; and $\mathbf{X}^{*c} = [\mathbf{X}_{t}^{*c}]$

is a matrix of order $9T_c \times 10$. It follows from (A3.5) that

$$E[\varepsilon^c \varepsilon^{c\,\prime}] \;=\; I_{T_c} \otimes \Sigma_c, \qquad\qquad c=1,...,15. \qquad\qquad (A3.7)$$

For c=1,...,15, (A3.6) can be written as

$$y^* \;=\; X^* \theta + \varepsilon, \qquad\qquad (A3.8)$$

where $y^* = [y^{*c}]$ and $\varepsilon = [\varepsilon^c]$ are vectors of 9T elements, with $T = \Sigma_{c=1}^{15} T_c$; and $X^* = [X^{*c}]$ is a matrix of order $9T \times 10$. The vector of disturbances ε has expectation zero and covariance matrix

$$E[\varepsilon\varepsilon'] = \mathrm{diag}\left[(I_{T_1} \otimes \Sigma_1),..., (I_{T_{15}} \otimes \Sigma_{15}) \right] = \Sigma \;\text{(say)}, \qquad (A3.9)$$

where we have used (A3.7) and assumed that the disturbances are independent across countries.

Under normality, the log-likelihood function is

$$L^*(\theta,\Sigma;y^*) = C^* + \frac{1}{2}\log|\Sigma^{-1}| - \frac{1}{2}\left[(y^* - X^*\theta)'\Sigma^{-1}(y^* - X^*\theta) \right], \qquad (A3.10)$$

where C^* is a constant. Consider the term in the square brackets on the right-hand side of (A3.10). From (A3.8) and (A3.9),

$$(\mathbf{y}^* - \mathbf{X}^*\theta)'\Sigma^{-1}(\mathbf{y}^* - \mathbf{X}^*\theta) = \varepsilon'\Sigma^{-1}\varepsilon$$

$$= \sum_{c=1}^{15} \varepsilon^{c\,\prime}\left[(I_{T_c} \otimes \Sigma_c)^{-1}\right]\varepsilon^c = \sum_{c=1}^{15}\sum_{t=1}^{T_c} \varepsilon_t^{c\,\prime}\Sigma_c^{-1}\varepsilon_t^c$$

$$= \sum_{c=1}^{15}\sum_{t=1}^{T_c} (\mathbf{y}_t^{*c} - \mathbf{X}_t^{*c}\theta)'\Sigma_c^{-1}(\mathbf{y}_t^{*c} - \mathbf{X}_t^{*c}\theta).$$

We also have

$$\log\,|\Sigma^{-1}| = \log\left[\prod_{c=1}^{15}\,|I_{T_c} \otimes \Sigma_c^{-1}|\right]$$

$$= \sum_{c=1}^{15} \log\,|I_{T_c} \otimes \Sigma_c^{-1}| = \sum_{c=1}^{15} \log\left[|\Sigma_c^{-1}|\right]^{T_c}$$

$$= \sum_{c=1}^{15} T_c \log\,|\Sigma_c^{-1}|.$$

Substituting these in (A3.10), the log-likelihood function takes the form

$$L^* = C^* + \frac{1}{2}\sum_{c=1}^{15} T_c \log\,|\Sigma_c^{-1}| - \frac{1}{2}\sum_{c=1}^{15}\sum_{t=1}^{T_c} (\mathbf{y}_t^{*c} - \mathbf{X}_t^{*c}\theta)'\Sigma_c^{-1}(\mathbf{y}_t^{*c} - \mathbf{X}_t^{*c}\theta)$$

$$= \sum_{c=1}^{15}\left[C^{*c} + \frac{T_c}{2}\log\,|\Sigma_c^{-1}| - \frac{1}{2}\sum_{t=1}^{T_c} (\mathbf{y}_t^{*c} - \mathbf{X}_t^{*c}\theta)'\Sigma_c^{-1}(\mathbf{y}_t^{*c} - \mathbf{X}_t^{*c}\theta)\right]$$

$$= \sum_{c=1}^{15} L^{*c}, \qquad\qquad\qquad (A3.11)$$

where

$$L^{*c} = C^{*c} + \frac{T_c}{2} \log |\Sigma_c^{-1}| - \frac{1}{2} \sum_{t=1}^{T_c} (y_t^{*c} - X_t^{*c}\theta)' \Sigma_c^{-1}(y_t^{*c} - X_t^{*c}\theta) \qquad (A3.12)$$

is the log-likelihood function of country c; and C^{*c} is a constant term satisfying $C^* = \Sigma_{c=1}^{15} C^{*c}$.

In general the covariance matrix Σ_c is unknown. For reasons described in Chapter 3, we specify the following covariance structure:

$$\Sigma_c = \lambda_c^2 \Omega_c,$$

where λ_c^2 is a constant to be estimated;

$$\Omega_c = \overline{\overline{W}}^c - \overline{w}^c \overline{w}^c{}';$$

$$\overline{\overline{W}}^c = \text{diag}[\overline{\overline{w}}_1^c \ldots \overline{\overline{w}}_9^c]; \quad \overline{w}^c = [\overline{w}_1^c \ldots \overline{w}_9^c]'; \text{ and } \overline{w}_i^c = (1/T_c) \sum_{t=1}^{T_c} \overline{w}_{it}^c, \; i=1,\ldots,9.$$

Therefore, from (A3.9) we have

$$\Sigma = \text{diag}\left[\lambda_1^2(I_{T_1} \otimes \Omega_1),\ldots, \lambda_{15}^2(I_{T_{15}} \otimes \Omega_{15})\right]. \qquad (A3.13)$$

With the covariance matrix specified as (A3.13), the log-likelihood function for country c, (A3.12), takes the form

$$L^{*c} = C_1^{*c} - \frac{9T_c}{2} \log \lambda_c^2 - \frac{1}{2\lambda_c^2} \sum_{t=1}^{T_c} (y_t^{*c} - X_t^{*c}\theta)' \Omega_c^{-1} (y_t^{*c} - X_t^{*c}\theta), \qquad (A3.14)$$

where C_1^{*c} is a constant.

The first-order conditions for a maximum of (A3.11) with respect to λ_c^2, c=1,...,15, and θ' are

$$\frac{\partial L^*}{\partial \lambda_c^2} = \frac{\partial L^{*c}}{\partial \lambda_c^2}$$

$$= -\frac{9T_c}{2\lambda_c^2} + \frac{1}{2\lambda_c^4} \sum_{t=1}^{T_c} (y_t^{*c} - X_t^{*c}\theta)' \Omega_c^{-1} (y_t^{*c} - X_t^{*c}\theta) = 0 \qquad (A3.15)$$

and

$$\frac{\partial L^*}{\partial \theta'} = \sum_{c=1}^{15} \frac{\partial L^{*c}}{\partial \theta'}$$

$$= \sum_{c=1}^{15} \left[\frac{1}{\lambda_c^2} \sum_{t=1}^{T_c} (y_t^{*c} - X_t^{*c}\theta)' \Omega_c^{-1} \frac{\partial (X_t^{*c}\theta)}{\partial \theta'} \right] = 0, \qquad (A3.16)$$

where

$$\frac{\partial(X_t^{*c}\theta)}{\partial\theta'} = \left[\frac{\partial(X_t^{*c}\theta)}{\partial\beta'} \quad \frac{\partial(X_t^{*c}\theta)}{\partial\phi}\right]$$

$$= \left[DQ_t^{*c}I_9 + \phi\frac{\partial z_t^{*c}}{\partial\beta'} \quad z_t^{*c}\right];$$

$$\frac{\partial z_t^{*c}}{\partial\beta'} = \left[\frac{\partial z_{it}^{*c}}{\partial\beta_j}\right];$$

and

$$\frac{\partial z_{it}^{*c}}{\partial\beta_j} = \frac{\partial(z_{it}^c - \bar{z}_i^c)}{\partial\beta_j}$$

$$= \frac{\partial z_{it}^c}{\partial\beta_j} - \frac{1}{T_c}\sum_{s=1}^{T_c}\frac{\partial z_{is}^c}{\partial\beta_j}$$

$$= -(\beta_i + \bar{w}_{it}^c)Dp_{jt}^{*c} + \delta_{ij}\left[Dp_{it}^{*c} - \sum_{k=1}^{9}(\beta_k + \bar{w}_{kt}^c)Dp_{kt}^{*c}\right]$$

$$+ \frac{1}{T_c}\sum_{s=1}^{T_c}\left[(\beta_i + \bar{w}_{is}^c)Dp_{js}^{*c} - \delta_{ij}\left[Dp_{is}^{*c} - \sum_{k=1}^{9}(\beta_k + \bar{w}_{ks}^c)Dp_{ks}^{*c}\right]\right].$$

From (A3.16), for $c=1,\dots,15$,

$$\frac{\partial^2 L^*}{\partial \lambda_c^2 \partial \theta'} = -\frac{1}{\lambda_c^4} \sum_{t=1}^{T_c} (y_t^{*c} - X_t^{*c}\theta)' \Omega_c^{-1} \frac{\partial(X_t^{*c}\theta)}{\partial \theta'} . \qquad (A3.17)$$

Since $E[y_t^{*c} - X_t^{*c}\theta] = E[\varepsilon_t^c] = 0$, from (A3.17), the information matrix of the ML procedure is block-diagonal with respect to θ and λ_c^2, c=1,...,15. From (A3.16) we also have

$$\frac{\partial^2 L^*}{\partial\theta\partial\theta'} = \sum_{c=1}^{15} \left[-\frac{1}{\lambda_c^2} \sum_{t=1}^{T_c} \frac{\partial(X_t^{*c}\theta)'}{\partial\theta} \Omega_c^{-1} \frac{\partial(X_t^{*c}\theta)}{\partial\theta'} \right.$$
$$\left. + \frac{1}{\lambda_c^2} \sum_{t=1}^{T_c} (y_t^{*c} - X_t^{*c}\theta)' \Omega_c^{-1} \frac{\partial^2(X_t^{*c}\theta)}{\partial\theta\partial\theta'} \right] .$$

The second term on the right-hand side has zero expectation. Therefore, the asymptotic covariance matrix of the ML estimator of θ is

$$V^* = -\left[E\left[\frac{\partial^2 L^*}{\partial\theta\partial\theta'} \right] \right]^{-1} = \left[\sum_{c=1}^{15} \frac{1}{\lambda_c^2} \sum_{t=1}^{T_c} \frac{\partial(X_t^{*c}\theta)'}{\partial\theta} \Omega_c^{-1} \frac{\partial(X_t^{*c}\theta)}{\partial\theta'} \right]^{-1} .$$

The ML estimator of θ is obtained by means of Newton's iterative scheme based on successive estimates of V^* and λ_c^2, c=1,...,15. The asymptotic standard errors are the square roots of the diagonal elements of V^* with ML-estimates substituted for the unknown parameters in V^*.

Using the ML estimator of θ, $\hat{\theta}$, we obtain the ML estimators of α_i^c,

$i=1,...,10$, $c=1,...,15$, from (A3.2),

$$\hat{\alpha}_i^c = \bar{y}_i^c - \hat{\beta}_i D\bar{Q}^c - \hat{\phi}\bar{z}_i^c. \qquad\qquad (A3.18)$$

$$= \bar{y}_i^c - [0 \ ... \ D\bar{Q}^c \ ... \ 0 \ \ \bar{z}_i^c]\hat{\theta}$$

$$= \bar{y}_i^c - \mathbf{a}_i^{c\,\prime}\hat{\theta}$$

$$= \alpha_i^c(\hat{\theta}),$$

where $\mathbf{a}_i^c = [0 \ ... \ D\bar{Q}^c \ ... \ 0 \ \ \bar{z}_i^c]'$ is a vector of 10 elements with $D\bar{Q}^c$ as the ith element, $\bar{z}_i^c$ as the 10th and all other elements zero. Therefore $\hat{\alpha}_i^c$ is a totally differentiable nonlinear function of $\hat{\theta}$. Thus $\sqrt{T_c}\ [\alpha_i^c(\hat{\theta}) - \alpha_i^c(\theta)]$ converges in distribution to a normal random variate with mean zero and asymptotic variance $[\partial\alpha_i^c/\partial\hat{\theta}']\hat{\Sigma}_\theta[\partial\alpha_i^c/\partial\hat{\theta}]$, where $\hat{\Sigma}_\theta = \text{var}\ \hat{\theta}$. Consequently, the asymptotic standard errors of the $\hat{\alpha}_i^c$'s are given by

$$\text{ASE}[\hat{\alpha}_i^c] = \left[\frac{\partial\hat{\alpha}_i^c}{\partial\hat{\theta}'}\ \hat{\Sigma}_\theta\ \frac{\partial\hat{\alpha}_i^c}{\partial\hat{\theta}}\right]^{\frac{1}{2}},$$

where

$$\frac{\partial\hat{\alpha}_i^c}{\partial\hat{\theta}'} = -\left[\mathbf{a}_i^{c\,\prime} \ \mid \ \hat{\theta}'\ \frac{\partial\mathbf{a}_i^c}{\partial\hat{\theta}'}\right].$$

Table A4.2 presents the estimates of the constants for the pooled model.

TABLE A4.2

CONSTANT TERMS FOR 10 COMMODITIES IN 15 COUNTRIES: POOLED MODEL

(Standard errors are in parentheses)

Country (1)	Food α_1^c (2)	Beverages α_2^c (3)	Clothing α_3^c (4)	Housing α_4^c (5)	Durables α_5^c (6)	Medical care α_6^c (7)	Transport α_7^c (8)	Recreation α_8^c (9)	Education α_9^c (10)	Miscellaneous α_{10}^c (11)
1. U.S.	−.025 (.019)	−.013 (.011)	−.181 (.019)	.381 (.018)	−.208 (.014)	.264 (.006)	−.213 (.015)	.022 (.015)	.026 (.002)	−.053 (.019)
2. Canada	−.013 (.019)	.006 (.013)	−.161 (.020)	.388 (.020)	−.173 (.017)	−.100 (.008)	−.194 (.017)	.111 (.017)	.043 (.002)	.091 (.024)
3. Sweden	−.098 (.013)	−.045 (.007)	−.131 (.017)	.411 (.008)	−.129 (.009)	.046 (.006)	−.114 (.009)	.188 (.010)	.005 (.001)	−.133 (.022)
4. Denmark	−.100 (.011)	−.047 (.010)	−.217 (.015)	.644 (.006)	−.288 (.008)	.019 (.004)	−.128 (.009)	.088 (.010)	.063 (.001)	−.033 (.024)
5. Australia	.007 (.020)	−.085 (.010)	−.260 (.015)	.477 (.014)	−.079 (.018)	.006 (.005)	−.131 (.014)	.080 (.011)	−.020 (.002)	.004 (.021)
6. France	−.066 (.030)	−.077 (.018)	−.328 (.024)	.604 (.022)	−.260 (.021)	.353 (.011)	−.229 (.022)	.004 (.022)	.004 (.003)	−.006 (.026)
7. Belgium	−.085 (.026)	−.011 (.015)	−.207 (.022)	.324 (.020)	−.072 (.018)	.204 (.008)	−.210 (.018)	−.016 (.016)	.003 (.004)	.071 (.025)
8. Norway	−.061 (.022)	−.012 (.012)	−.253 (.017)	.422 (.019)	−.098 (.015)	.025 (.006)	−.106 (.016)	.104 (.018)	−.001 (.002)	−.020 (.020)
9. Nethrelands	−.110 (.036)	.030 (.021)	−.335 (.027)	.451 (.028)	−.042 (.028)	.218 (.009)	−.345 (.029)	−.044 (.019)	.058 (.004)	.119 (.031)
10. Iceland	−.166 (.035)	.057 (.023)	−.235 (.037)	.148 (.037)	−.038 (.032)	.246 (.012)	−.194 (.034)	.011 (.024)	.009 (.005)	.162 (.035)
11. Finland	−.162 (.028)	.124 (.017)	−.387 (.026)	.383 (.033)	−.137 (.023)	.106 (.012)	−.128 (.024)	.049 (.022)	−.044 (.003)	.197 (.029)
12. Austria	−.022 (.028)	−.088 (.018)	−.110 (.024)	.509 (.016)	−.225 (.021)	.054 (.005)	.010 (.020)	−.023 (.019)	.000 (.004)	−.104 (.032)
13. U.K.	−.147 (.016)	−.021 (.010)	−.144 (.019)	.283 (.007)	−.150 (.011)	.013 (.005)	.019 (.011)	.096 (.010)	.019 (.001)	.032 (.022)
14. Spain	−.152 (.037)	.014 (.025)	−.253 (.025)	.402 (.038)	−.261 (.023)	.264 (.011)	−.196 (.033)	.022 (.018)	.025 (.004)	.134 (.037)
15. Italy	−.069 (.028)	−.036 (.021)	−.175 (.020)	.316 (.023)	−.136 (.018)	.150 (.012)	−.104 (.020)	−.052 (.019)	−.001 (.004)	.108 (.028)

All entries in columns 2-11 are to be divided by 100.

A4.4   THE GOODNESS-OF-FIT OF THE MODELS

This and the next two appendices provide the technical details for the material in Section 4.6.

The Information Inaccuracy

For country c, let w_{it}^c be the observed value of the budget share of commodity i in year t and $\hat{w}_{it}^c$ be the predicted share implied by the demand model. Then as a measure of poorness of fit of the model with respect to the observed shares, we use the information inaccuracy of the predictions defined as

$$I_t^c = \sum_{i=1}^{10} w_{it}^c \log \left[\frac{w_{it}^c}{\hat{w}_{it}^c} \right]. \tag{A4.1}$$

Clearly $I_t^c \geq 0$ for all $t=1,\dots,T_c$ and $c=1,\dots,15$. When the predictions are perfect (i.e., $\hat{w}_{it}^c = w_{it}^c$ for $i=1,\dots,10$), $I_t^c = 0$. Usually, $\hat{w}_{it}^c$ will be positive. In practical applications, although we cannot absolutely guarantee that $\hat{w}_{it}^c$ is always positive, it is likely to be so. As an empirical matter, none of the (about 3,000) fitted shares were negative. We shall discuss the budget share forecasts for each model later in this appendix.

The average information inaccuracy for each country is given by

$$\bar{I}_c = \frac{1}{T_c} \sum_{t=1}^{T_c} I_t^c.$$

Table A4.3 presents the average information inaccuracies for the 15 countries for Models I, III, IV and the naive model. In contrast to the information inaccuracies in Table 4.5, these inaccuracies are not adjusted for degrees of freedom; later in this appendix we present such an adjustment. Comparing columns 6-9 of Table 4.5 with columns 2-5 of Table A4.3, we see that both tables display similar patterns. For example, looking at columns 2 and 3 (which refer to Models I and III), we see that France has the lowest inaccuracy; the U.S. has the second lowest; and the U.K. has the third lowest in both models. This is exactly the same ranking as that displayed in columns 6 and 7 of Table 4.5.

In Section 4.6 we analysed the deterioration of fit when we take tastes to be identical. This was carried out by comparing the differences between the degrees-of-freedom-adjusted inaccuracies of Models I and III (given in columns 6 and 7 of Table 4.5). For comparison, now we do the same thing before the degrees of freedom adjustment. The unadjusted inaccuracies are given in columns 2 and 3 of Table A4.3. Comparing the increase in the inaccuracy when going from Model I to Model III before and after the degrees of freedom adjustment [i.e., comparing the differences between column 3 and column 2 of Table A4.3 with that between columns 7 and 6 of Table 4.5], we see that the increase is smaller after the adjustment. For example, for the U.S.,

TABLE A4.3

UNADJUSTED AVERAGE INFORMATION INACCURACIES IN 15 COUNTRIES
FOR FOUR DEMAND MODELS

Country (1)	Model I: Individual country model (2)	Model III: Pooled model (3)	Model IV: Theil's estimates (4)	Naive model (5)
* 1. U.S.	1.22	1.39	2.19	3.18
2. Canada	4.49	5.18	5.65	5.45
3. Sweden	1.54	1.71	3.10	4.05
* 4. Denmark	2.00	2.20	3.91	7.48
5. Australia	2.61	2.84	3.10	5.15
* 6. France	.84	.89	1.12	3.52
* 7. Belgium	3.01	3.53	3.80	6.16
8. Norway	1.88	2.59	3.82	4.98
* 9. Netherlands	4.70	6.02	6.22	8.23
10. Iceland	9.24	11.72	20.39	27.73
11. Finland	5.93	6.32	7.66	10.65
*12. Austria	2.40	2.93	4.02	7.09
*13. U.K.	1.37	1.51	2.17	4.05
*14. Spain	2.27	2.46	3.03	7.40
*15. Italy	1.55	2.12	2.28	4.21
16. Unweighted mean	3.00	3.56	4.83	7.29
17. GDP-weighted mean	1.67	1.92	2.57	4.10

A * denotes that the country is included in Theil's (1987) sample. All entries in columns 2-5 are to be divided by 10^4. The weights for the GDP-weighted means in the last row are from column 5 of Table 4.5.

the increase ($\times 10^{-4}$) is $1.39 - 1.22 = .17$ before the adjustment and $1.48 - 1.36 = .12$ after the adjustment. The inaccuracies associated with Theil's model also move closer to those of Models I and III after the adjustment.

The Predictions from Model I: The Individual Country Model

The individual country model is equation (2.1) which we write as

$$y_{it}^c = \alpha_i^c + \beta_i^c DQ_t^c + \phi^c(\beta_i^c + \overline{w}_{it}^c)\left[Dp_{it}^{*c} - \sum_{j=1}^{9}(\beta_j^c + \overline{w}_{jt}^c)Dp_{jt}^{*c}\right] + \varepsilon_{it}^c, \quad (A4.2)$$

where $y_{it}^c = \overline{w}_{it}^c(Dq_{it}^c - DQ_t^c)$; and $Dp_{it}^{*c} = Dp_{it}^c - Dp_{10,t}^c$. Let $\hat{\alpha}_i^c$, $\hat{\beta}_i^c$ and $\hat{\phi}^c$ be the ML-estimates of α_i^c, β_i^c and ϕ^c, respectively. Then the ML-residual of the ith equation for country c is

$$\hat{\varepsilon}_{it}^c = y_{it}^c - \hat{\alpha}_i^c - \hat{\beta}_i^c DQ_t^c - \hat{\phi}^c(\hat{\beta}_i^c + \overline{w}_{it}^c)\left[Dp_{it}^{*c} - \sum_{j=1}^{9}(\hat{\beta}_j^c + \overline{w}_{jt}^c)Dp_{jt}^{*c}\right]. \quad (A4.3)$$

Thus the predicted value of y_{it}^c is

$$\hat{y}_{it}^c = y_{it}^c - \hat{\varepsilon}_{it}^c. \quad (A4.4)$$

Our objective is to transform this prediction into a budget share prediction, $\hat{w}_{it}^{c}$. It can be shown that (see Selvanathan, 1988)

$$\hat{w}_{it}^{c} = w_{it}^{c} - \hat{\varepsilon}_{it}^{c}.$$

Therefore, by substituting for $\hat{\varepsilon}_{it}^{c}$ from (A4.3) we can obtain the predicted value of w_{it}^{c}. However, since $\bar{w}_{it}^{c}$ occurs on the right-hand side of (A4.3), assuming that $\bar{w}_{it}^{c}$ is known to obtain $\hat{\varepsilon}_{it}^{c}$ is not really legitimate. This is because $\bar{w}_{it}^{c}$ is the average of w_{it}^{c} and $w_{i,t-1}^{c}$, and w_{it}^{c} is unknown since it is the object of prediction. Theil (1967) notes that this problem can be handled by using the following iterative procedure. We first replace $\bar{w}_{it}^{c}$ by $w_{i,t-1}^{c}$ which leads to a forecast $w_{it}^{c\,\prime}$ of w_{it}^{c}. Then we replace $\bar{w}_{it}^{c}$ in (A4.3) by the average of $w_{it}^{c\,\prime}$ and $w_{i,t-1}^{c}$, which leads to a new forecast of w_{it}^{c}, and so on until convergence is reached. This is the procedure we use.

The Predictions from Model III: The Pooled Model

The pooled model (4.1) is exactly the same as the individual country model (A4.2) except that the income coefficients β_i and the income flexibility ϕ now do not have a country superscript. Therefore, to obtain the budget share predictions of the pooled model we follow the same procedure described for the individual country model.

The Predictions from Model IV: Theil's Cross-Country Demand System

Table 4.4 gives the estimates of Theil's (1987) cross-country demand system. To apply these estimates to time-series data we add constant terms for each good and each country. We estimate these as the means of the time-series residuals,

$$\hat{\alpha}_i^{cT} = \frac{1}{T_c} \sum_{t=1}^{T_c} \hat{\xi}_{it}^c,$$

where

$$\hat{\xi}_{it}^c = y_{it}^c - \hat{\beta}_i^{cT} DQ_t^c - \hat{\phi}^{cT} z_{it}^c$$

is the ith residual in year t for country c; and the superscript T denotes a Theil estimate. We use the same procedure described for the pooled model to obtain the budget share predictions for this model.

The Predictions from the Naive Model

The naive model of no-change extrapolation is $\hat{w}_{it}^c = w_{i,t-1}^c$. Using these one-step ahead forecasts of the budget shares in (A4.1) we then obtain the average information inaccuracies for the 15 countries.

Correction for Degrees of Freedom

In the individual country model, each observation yields n-1 = 9 degrees of freedom. Therefore, the total number of degrees of freedom supplied by T_c observations is $(n-1)T_c = 9T_c$, where T_c is the sample size for country c. The unconstrained coefficients are n-1 constants, n-1 income coefficients and 1 income flexibility, a total of $2(n-1) + 1 = (2 \times 9) + 1 = 19$. Therefore, due to the statistical adjustment of the coefficients of the model, the correction of the average information inaccuracy for country c is (Theil, 1980)

$$\frac{(n-1)T_c}{(n-1)T_c - [2(n-1) + 1]} = \frac{9T_c}{9T_c - 19} . \tag{A4.5}$$

Rows 1-15 of column 2 of Table A4.4 give T_c for the 15 countries, while column 3 gives (A4.5).

For the pooled model, the total number of degrees of freedom is $(n-1) \sum_{c=1}^{15} T_c = 9 \times 269 = 2421$. The unconstrained parameters are 15(n-1) constants, n-1 income coefficients and 1 income flexibility, a total of $15(n-1) + (n-1) + 1 = 135 + 9 + 1 = 145$. Thus the correction factor for the average information inaccuracy for the pooled model is

$$\frac{(n-1) \sum_{c=1}^{15} T_c}{(n-1) \sum_{c=1}^{15} T_c - [16(n-1) + 1]} = \frac{2421}{2421 - 145} = 1.06.$$

TABLE A4.4

SAMPLE SIZES AND DEGREES OF FREEDOM CORRECTION FACTORS

FOR THE INDIVIDUAL COUNTRY MODELS AND THE POOLED MODEL

Country	Sample size	Correction factor
(1)	(2)	(3)
1. U.S.	21	1.11
2. Canada	21	1.11
3. Sweden	17	1.14
4. Denmark	15	1.16
5. Australia	21	1.11
6. France	17	1.14
7. Belgium	21	1.11
8. Norway	17	1.14
9. Netherlands	25	1.09
10. Iceland	13	1.19
11. Finland	17	1.14
12. Austria	17	1.14
13. U.K.	17	1.14
14. Spain	13	1.19
15. Italy	17	1.14
Pooled model	269	1.06

The correction for Theil's model is the same as that for the pooled
model, while no adjustment is needed for the naive model. Columns 6-9 of
Table 4.5 of the text are derived from columns 2-5 of Table A4.3 by
multiplying by the corresponding correction factors. That is, column 6 of
Table 4.5 is column 2 of Table A4.3 multiplied by the correction factors for
each country presented in Table A4.4; columns 7 and 8 are columns 3 and 4 of

Table A4.3 multiplied by the correction factor for the pooled model, 1.06; and column 9 is column 5 of Table A4.3.

A4.5   INTERPRETATION OF THE INFORMATION INACCURACY

In Section 4.6 we defined the information inaccuracy in period t for country c as

$$I_t^c = \sum_{i=1}^{10} w_{it}^c \log \left[\frac{w_{it}^c}{\hat{w}_{it}^c} \right]. \tag{A5.1}$$

Using a Taylor series expansion of the logarithm in the sum and dropping third and higher-order terms, we obtain

$$\log \left[\frac{w_{it}^c}{\hat{w}_{it}^c} \right] \simeq - \frac{\hat{w}_{it}^c - w_{it}^c}{w_{it}^c} + \tfrac{1}{2} \left[\frac{\hat{w}_{it}^c - w_{it}^c}{w_{it}^c} \right]^2 .$$

Substituting this in (A5.1) yields,

$$I_t^c \simeq \sum_{i=1}^{10} w_{it}^c \left[- \frac{\hat{w}_{it}^c - w_{it}^c}{w_{it}^c} + \tfrac{1}{2} \left[\frac{\hat{w}_{it}^c - w_{it}^c}{w_{it}^c} \right]^2 \right]$$

$$= - \sum_{i=1}^{10} \hat{w}_{it}^c + \sum_{i=1}^{10} w_{it}^c + \tfrac{1}{2} \sum_{i=1}^{10} w_{it}^c \left[\frac{\hat{w}_{it}^c - w_{it}^c}{w_{it}^c} \right]^2$$

$$= \tfrac{1}{2} \sum_{i=1}^{10} w_{it}^c \left[\frac{\hat{w}_{it}^c - w_{it}^c}{w_{it}^c} \right]^2 , \qquad (A5.2)$$

where for the last step we have used $\sum_{i=1}^{10} w_{it}^c = \sum_{i=1}^{10} \hat{w}_{it}^c = 1$.

Multiplying both sides of (A5.2) by 2 and taking the square-root we have

$$\sqrt{2I_t^c} \simeq \left[\sum_{i=1}^{10} w_{it}^c (r_{it}^c)^2 \right]^{\frac{1}{2}} , \qquad (A5.3)$$

where

$$r_{it}^c = \frac{\hat{w}_{it}^c - w_{it}^c}{w_{it}^c}$$

is the proportionate prediction error for the ith budget share. Since $\sum_{i=1}^{10} w_{it}^c r_{it}^c = 0$, the right-hand side of (A5.3) is the square root of the budget-share-weighted mean of the squared relative prediction errors of the budget shares. We refer to this as the root-mean-squared (RMS) proportionate prediction error. Thus, when multiplied by 100, $\sqrt{2I^c_t}$ can be interpreted as the RMS percentage prediction error.

A4.6 THE RELATIVE STROBEL MEASURES AND THEIR ENTROPY

The information inaccuracy defined in equation (A4.1) refers to all 10 commodities jointly. It is also possible to consider the goodness-of-fit of the model with respect to each commodity. Strobel (1982) proposes the following decomposition of the information inaccuracy:

$$I^c_{it} = \hat{w}^c_{it} - w^c_{it} + w^c_{it}\log\left[\frac{w^c_{it}}{\hat{w}^c_{it}}\right]. \tag{A6.1}$$

The inaccuracy $I^c_{it} \geq 0$ and vanishes only when the prediction is perfect. Summing both sides of (A6.1) over $i=1,...,10$, and using (A4.1) and the fact that $\Sigma^{10}_{i=1} w^c_{it} = \Sigma^{10}_{i=1} \hat{w}^c_{it} = 1$, we get

$$\sum_{i=1}^{10} I^c_{it} = \sum_{i=1}^{10} \hat{w}^c_{it} - \sum_{i=1}^{10} w^c_{it} + \sum_{i=1}^{10} w^c_{it}\log\left[\frac{w^c_{it}}{\hat{w}^c_{it}}\right] = I^c_t.$$

We also have that $0 \leq I^c_{it} \leq I^c_t$ for every i. Therefore the Strobel measure provides a simple decomposition of the information inaccuracy of the model over the individual commodity groups. We analyse the fit of the model with respect to commodity i by examining the ratio I^c_{it}/I^c_t which is the proportion of the inaccuracy of the model due to the misfit of the demand equation for commodity i. This ratio is called the relative Strobel measure.

The entropy of the relative Strobel measures is defined as

$$H^c_t = - \sum_{i=1}^{10} \left[\frac{I^c_{it}}{I^c_t}\right] \log \left[\frac{I^c_{it}}{I^c_t}\right].$$

The measure H^c_t varies between 0 and log 10 $\simeq$ 2.30, where 10 is the number of commodities. It takes a higher value when all commodities contribute more equally to the information inaccuracy; and it takes a lower value when the lack of fit of the model is dominated by one commodity (i.e., when $I^c_{it}/I^c_t \simeq 1$ for some i and the rest are approximately zero).

Columns 2-11 of Table A4.5 present the average relative Strobel measures for the 15 countries for each commodity for Models I, III, IV and the naive model. These measures are averaged over the T_c observations. As can be seen from the four rows labelled 'Mean', in all models transport is consistently the largest contributor to the misfit of the models. We also see that education is the smallest contributor. However, there is not too much difference between the contributions of the 10 commodities to the misfit of any of the four models.

TABLE A4.5

AVERAGE RELATIVE STROBEL MEASURES FOR 10 COMMODITIES

AND THEIR ENTROPY IN 15 COUNTRIES FOR FOUR MODELS

Country (1)	Food (2)	Beverages (3)	Clothing (4)	Housing (5)	Durables (6)	Medical care (7)	Transport (8)	Recreation (9)	Education (10)	Miscellaneous (11)	Entropy (12)
Model I: Individual country model											
U.S.	20	3	8	4	12	12	22	5	6	7	1.56
Canada	6	4	6	5	5	34	11	7	16	4	1.45
Sweden	11	13	14	6	9	19	16	12	1	8	1.55
Denmark	10	3	16	12	8	6	19	13	5	8	1.57
Australia	5	2	8	7	23	14	13	16	7	6	1.50
France	5	5	10	14	21	15	14	5	5	5	1.53
Belgium	8	6	9	9	14	11	13	5	0	24	1.59
Norway	3	22	9	7	9	12	21	4	4	9	1.53
Netherlands	8	10	16	8	10	7	16	6	4	7	1.69
Iceland	11	9	12	8	10	7	23	12	1	9	1.64
Finland	3	9	20	2	12	2	27	12	11	3	1.61
Austria	11	12	10	11	19	7	17	4	1	7	1.67
U.K.	7	11	7	8	0	9	24	8	8	10	1.60
Spain	14	8	8	8	11	17	15	7	4	8	1.70
Italy	7	5	11	3	13	15	24	10	5	7	1.63
Mean	9	8	11	7	13	12	18	8	5	8	1.59
Model III: Pooled model											
U.S.	19	3	7	4	12	11	30	3	1	6	1.51
Canada	12	4	6	5	4	28	12	8	16	5	1.66
Sweden	13	15	13	6	9	7	16	13	1	7	1.59
Denmark	11	4	15	12	8	6	17	13	6	8	1.52
Australia	6	2	8	7	21	15	11	15	7	5	1.40
France	4	5	11	14	21	14	13	5	6	6	1.49
Belgium	7	6	5	8	14	10	15	4	0	30	1.49
Norway	4	18	8	5	10	10	29	3	4	8	1.41
Netherlands	6	9	18	11	17	6	20	4	4	6	1.67
Iceland	9	7	14	6	10	7	25	10	2	9	1.50
Finland	3	9	20	2	12	2	26	12	10	4	1.55
Austria	8	11	11	8	16	10	23	5	2	7	1.69
U.K.	7	11	8	8	9	9	22	8	8	9	1.68
Spain	14	7	8	8	12	15	16	7	6	8	1.70
Italy	7	4	10	4	13	11	33	9	3	5	1.56
Mean	9	8	11	7	13	11	20	8	5	8	1.56
Model IV: Theil's cross-country demand system											
U.S.	16	3	7	8	9	11	33	4	3	7	1.47
Canada	15	3	5	11	4	28	12	7	13	3	1.60
Sweden	12	9	8	12	9	14	17	10	3	6	1.60
Denmark	7	4	14	17	8	10	19	9	4	8	1.53
Australia	4	2	8	9	24	16	13	14	6	5	1.45
France	3	7	10	21	17	12	16	5	5	4	1.43
Belgium	6	5	6	15	15	11	9	4	0	29	1.51
Norway	2	15	9	14	8	11	28	3	3	8	1.42
Netherlands	6	8	20	8	18	10	15	4	4	7	1.66
Iceland	7	5	9	23	8	9	29	5	1	5	1.50
Finland	3	5	21	12	10	4	24	9	8	5	1.65
Austria	6	11	11	11	14	10	25	4	1	6	1.63
U.K.	4	11	7	13	8	14	22	8	6	6	1.62
Spain	14	7	7	16	10	10	15	5	4	12	1.65
Italy	9	4	13	10	18	10	??	9	3	7	1.62
Mean	8	7	10	13	12	12	20	7	4	8	1.56
Naive model											
U.S.	17	7	8	6	6	20	24	5	3	4	1.52
Canada	10	6	9	13	7	12	13	9	15	5	1.58
Sweden	13	11	8	19	7	7	16	11	1	6	1.58
Denmark	10	8	10	30	10	3	13	5	7	5	1.62
Australia	15	5	10	14	18	11	10	9	4	5	1.56
France	19	10	10	20	9	16	11	2	1	1	1.62
Belgium	13	6	5	15	13	11	8	3	0	26	1.49
Norway	15	6	10	11	6	8	31	4	2	8	1.54
Netherlands	16	7	17	7	17	12	10	4	4	6	1.68
Iceland	13	6	11	19	9	6	24	6	1	6	1.59
Finland	12	5	17	8	11	2	26	7	0	6	1.59
Austria	14	10	6	19	10	7	27	2	2	3	1.50
U.K.	16	7	10	16	11	4	23	6	3	4	1.55
Spain	18	7	4	9	3	22	11	6	5	10	1.71
Italy	15	10	9	7	11	9	24	4	2	9	1.56
Mean	14	7	10	14	10	10	18	6	4	7	1.58

All entries in columns 2-11 are to be divided by 100.

Column 12 of Table A4.5 gives the average entropy of the relative Strobel measures for each country for the four models. For Model I, the entropy takes values between 1.45 (Canada) and 1.70 (Spain) with an average of 1.59. For Model III the entropy has a cross-country average of 1.56, for Model IV it is also 1.56 and for the naive model it is 1.58. As these values are not too close to zero, we conclude that on average no individual commodity dominates the lack of fit of any model. The entries for the individual countries in column 12 also indicate that this result also holds for each country.

A4.7   THE RELATIVE PRICE DATA

In this appendix we give the data source for relative prices used in Section 4.8 of the text. These data are derived from Tables B2 and J of the Statistical Appendix of Ward (1985). In Ward's paper, beverages are split into beverages and tobacco; recreation into equipment/recreation and cultural services/recreation; and education into books/magazines and education. To aggregate these into relative prices for our 10 groups, we take conditional budget-share-weighted- averages of these three pairs.

Sweden, Australia and Iceland are excluded from Ward's (1985) study. For these three countries we use the relative prices averaged over the 12 included countries. The per capita GDP data used in Sections 4.6 and 4.7 are the 1975 values in international dollars. However, in Section 4.8 we use per capita GDPs for 1980 since the relative price data refer to that year.

REFERENCES

Barten, A.P. (1969). 'Maximum Likelihood Estimation of a Complete System of Demand Equations,' European Economic Review 1: 7-73.

Clements, K.W. (1987). 'Alternative Approaches to Consumption Theory,' Chapter 1 in H. Theil and K.W. Clements, Applied Demand Analysis: Results from System-Wide Approaches. Cambridge, Mass.: Ballinger Publishing Company, pp.1-35.

Clements, K.W. and H. Theil (1979). 'A Cross-Country Analysis of Consumption Patterns,' Report 7924, Centre for Mathematical Studies in Business and Economics, University of Chicago.

Frisch, R. (1959). 'A Complete Scheme for Computing All Direct and Cross Demand Elasticities in a Model with Many Sectors,' Econometrica 27: 177-96.

Kravis, I.B., A.W. Heston, R. Summers (1982) World Product and Income: International Comparisons of Real Gross Product. Baltimore, Md.: The Johns Hopkins University Press.

Laitinen, K. (1978). 'Why is Demand Homogeneity So Often Rejected?'
Economics Letters 1: 187-91.

Meisner, J.F. (1979). 'The Sad Fate of the Asymptotic Slutsky Test for Large
Systems,' Economics Letters 2: 231-3.

Pollak, R.A. and T.J. Wales (1987). 'Pooling International Consumption Data,'
Review of Economics and Statistics 69: 90-99.

Selvanathan, S. (1988). A System-Wide Analysis of International and
Interregional Consumption Patterns. Ph.D. Thesis, The University of
Western Australia.

Stening, K. (1985). 'OECD Consumption: A Database,' Unpublished
manuscript, Department of Economics, The University of Western
Australia.

Stigler, G.J. and G.S. Becker (1977). 'De Gustibus Non Est Disputandum,'
American Economic Review 67: 76-90.

Strobel, D. (1982). 'Determining Outliers in Multivariate Surveys by
Decomposition of a Measure of Information,' Proceedings of the
American Statistical Association, Business and Economic Statistics
Section: 31-5.

Summers, R. and A. Heston (1984). 'Improved International Comparisons of
Real Product and Its Composition: 1950-80,' Review of Income and
Wealth 30: 207-68.

Theil, H. (1967). _Economics and Information Theory_. Amsterdam: North-Holland Publishing Company.

——————— (1980). _The System-Wide Approach to Microeconomics_. Chicago: The University of Chicago Press.

——————— (1987). 'Evidence from International Consumption Comparisons,' Chapter 2 in H. Theil and K.W. Clements, _Applied Demand Analysis: Results from System-Wide Approaches_. Cambridge, Mass.: Ballinger Publishing Company, pp.37-100.

Theil, H. and R.B. Brooks (1970/71). 'How Does the Marginal Utility of Income Change When Real Income Changes?' _European Economic Review_ 2: 218-40.

Ward, M. (1985). _Purchasing Power Parities and Real Expenditures in the OECD_. OECD, Paris.

Working, H. (1943). 'Statistical Laws of Family Expenditure,' _Journal of the American Statistical Association_ 38: 43-56.

CHAPTER 5

THE RELIABILITY OF ML ESTIMATORS OF SYSTEMS OF

DEMAND EQUATIONS

5.1   INTRODUCTION

Maximum likelihood (ML) estimators of systems of demand equations are consistent and asymptotically efficient. As these properties are asymptotic, their application in small-sample situations is, however, open to question (see Barten, 1977; Bera et al., 1981; Bewley, 1983; Bewley, 1986; Byron, 1970; Deaton, 1972; Laitinen, 1978; and Meisner, 1979). Much progress has recently been made in analysing this question; these developments have been synthesized and extended by Theil (1987). Theil shows that, in large systems, when the unknown error covariance matrix Σ is approximated by its usual ML-estimator S, the matrix of mean squares and cross products of the residuals, the estimates suffer from two problems. The first is that the asymptotic standard errors severely understate the true sampling variability of the estimates. The second problem is that the ML coefficient estimates have an impaired efficiency. Theil refers to these difficulties as the 'two perils' of estimating large demand models. He shows that the cause of the two perils is not knowing the true value of Σ. (By contrast, however, E.A. Selvanathan, 1987, finds that the two perils are not so serious for smaller demand systems.)

In Chapter 3 we estimated Working's (1943) model under preference independence for 10 commodities using ML for 18 OECD countries. As the number of annual observations is less than 25 and the number of equations in the model is 10 for most countries, the model can probably be considered to be large. In an attempt to avoid the above-mentioned two perils, rather than using $\mathbf{S}$ in Section 3.6 we proposed an alternative specification for the covariance matrix. The main aim of this chapter is to verify whether or not this alternative specification avoids the two perils. To do this we follow Theil (1987) and use Monte Carlo simulation procedures. The results of this chapter are 4-dimensional (4-D). Usually, demand analysis is 2-D, involving time and commodities. When countries are added as a third dimension and all this is then embedded in the simulation framework, we have a 4-D approach.

The structure of this chapter is as follows. Section 5.2 gives the estimates of the demand equations for the 18 individual countries and for the pooled model. Sections 5.3-5.6 describe the simulation procedure and discuss the results. Finally, in Section 5.7 we give our concluding comments.

5.2   THE ESTIMATES

In Section 4.2 we presented the individual country model. In this model the demand equation for commodity i during period t for country c is

$$y_{it}^c = \alpha_i^c + \beta_i^c DQ_t^c + \phi^c(\overline{w}_{it}^c + \beta_i^c)\left[Dp_{it}^c - \sum_{j=1}^{n^c} (\overline{w}_{jt}^c + \beta_j^c)Dp_{jt}^c\right] + \varepsilon_{it}^c, \qquad (2.1)$$

where all the notation is as before. Let Σ^c be the contemporaneous covariance matrix of the ε_{it}^c's. In Chapter 3 we considered two estimators of Σ^c. The first is S^c, the usual ML estimator. The second is

$$\Sigma^{*c} = \lambda^{c2}\Omega^c, \qquad (2.2)$$

where λ^{c2} is a parameter to be estimated and Ω^c is a known matrix. In Section 3.10 we estimated (2.1) by ML for the 18 countries with Σ^{*c}. For comparison, we also estimated (2.1) by ML with S^c for 7 countries. [In Section 3.6 we showed that 11 of the 18 countries have undersized samples for some versions of the model. The 7 for which we use S^c constitute the remaining countries.]

Table 5.1 presents the estimates of the income coefficients (β_i^c), the income flexibility (ϕ^c) and the constants (α_i^c) for 7 countries when $\Sigma^c = S^c$. [Note that this is the first time in the book that these estimates have been presented; see Section 2.2 for a description of the data.] Tables 5.2 and

TABLE 5.1

ML ESTIMATES OF DEMAND PARAMETERS FOR 10 COMMODITIES IN 7 COUNTRIES

(Based on S)

(Standard errors are in parentheses)

Country	Food	Beverages	Clothing	Housing	Durables	Medical care	Transport	Recreation	Education	Miscellaneous	Income flexibility ϕ^c
(1)	(2)	(3)	(4)	(5)	(6)	(7)	(8)	(9)	(10)	(11)	(12)
Income coefficients β_i^c and income flexibility ϕ^c											
1. U.S.	−.058	−.034	.058	−.111	.072	−.078	.149	.041	−.007	−.032	−.689
	(.017)	(.004)	(.015)	(.011)	(.010)	(.014)	(.034)	(.011)	(.004)	(.014)	(.053)
2. Canada	−.011	−.027	.007	−.172	.078	.025	.032	.069	−.004	.005	−.904
	(.013)	(.006)	(.014)	(.014)	(.014)	(.036)	(.020)	(.013)	(.006)	(.019)	(.070)
3. Switzerland	−.020	.045	.058	−.181	.087	−.042	.083	−.000		−.030	−.589
	(.019)	(.015)	(.015)	(.022)	(.011)	(.010)	(.030)	(.013)		(.015)	(.050)
4. Australia	−.139	−.009	.016	−.005	.052	.053	−.013	.074	.002	−.031	−.404
	(.019)	(.010)	(.020)	(.024)	(.041)	(.026)	(.035)	(.028)	(.008)	(.015)	(.046)
5. Germany	−.101		.056	−.131	.049	−.009	.162	−.001		−.024	−.627
	(.025)		(.014)	(.021)	(.016)	(.005)	(.028)	(.011)		(.008)	(.082)
6. Belgium	−.092	−.001	.042	−.104	.194	−.046	−.020	.005	−.002	.025	−.608
	(.021)	(.013)	(.014)	(.010)	(.026)	(.010)	(.021)	(.010)	(.000)	(.017)	(.050)
7. Netherlands	−.138	−.017	.132	−.046	.058	−.010	.051	.011	−.016	−.024	−.782
	(.031)	(.010)	(.027)	(.015)	(.037)	(.010)	(.015)	(.010)	(.007)	(.018)	(.084)
Constant terms α_i^c ($\times 100$)											
8. U.S.	−.102	.043	−.264	.383	−.255	.397	−.229	−.065	.041	.050	
	(.062)	(.015)	(.055)	(.034)	(.038)	(.040)	(.117)	(.040)	(.011)	(.042)	
9. Canada	−.153	.048	−.098	.552	−.299	−.213	.039	−.143	.077	.190	
	(.062)	(.029)	(.071)	(.062)	(.055)	(.149)	(.093)	(.060)	(.027)	(.059)	
10. Switzerland	−.070	−.148	−.267	.381	−.329	.168	.030	.077		.159	
	(.060)	(.047)	(.046)	(.068)	(.031)	(.022)	(.080)	(.036)		(.033)	
11. Australia	.104	−.099	−.213	.249	−.077	−.111	.177	−.057	−.028	.055	
	(.068)	(.033)	(.063)	(.074)	(.153)	(.069)	(.118)	(.080)	(.017)	(.044)	
12. Germany	−.086		−.264	.451	−.186	.004	−.140	.060		.162	
	(.099)		(.053)	(.066)	(.062)	(.018)	(.110)	(.043)		(.028)	
13. Belgium	−.103	−.043	−.229	.308	−.562	.300	.227	.027	.004	.071	
	(.097)	(.054)	(.061)	(.071)	(.126)	(.051)	(.081)	(.036)	(.001)	(.117)	
14. Netherlands	.067	.046	−.786	.223	−.157	.285	−.045	.005	.118	.245	
	(.163)	(.067)	(.153)	(.078)	(.224)	(.056)	(.096)	(.044)	(.029)	(.083)	

and 5.3 present the estimation results for all 18 countries when $\Sigma^c = \Sigma^{*c}$. An entry-by-entry comparison of the estimates for the seven countries common to these three tables shows that in most cases they are not too different. Consequently, the use of Σ^{*c} does not seem to have any radical, systematic implications. We also tested for serial correlation based on the Durbin-Watson statistics and the results show that in most cases, we do not reject the null hypothesis of zero correlation of the error terms.

We introduced in Section 4.4 the pooled model for the 15 countries with 10 commodity groups. Here the income and price responses are identical across countries (i.e., $\beta_i^c = \beta_i$, $\phi^c = \phi$, i=1,...,10; c=1,...,15). The demand equation for commodity i in this model is

$$y_{it}^c = \alpha_i^c + \beta_i DQ_t^c + \phi(\overline{w}_{it}^c + \beta_i)\left[Dp_{it}^c - \sum_{j=1}^{10} (\overline{w}_{jt}^c + \beta_j)Dp_{jt}^c\right] + \varepsilon_{it}^c. \qquad (2.3)$$

Note that the constant terms (α_i^c) are allowed to vary over countries in (2.3). In Section 4.4 we estimated the pooled model by ML with covariance matrix given by equation (A3.9) of Appendix A4.3, which is block-diagonal and involves the alternative specification (2.2) for the individual countries. Table 5.4 gives the estimates of the pooled model (2.3).

TABLE 5.2

ML ESTIMATES OF THE INCOME COEFFICIENTS FOR 10 COMMODITIES

AND THE INCOME FLEXIBILITY IN 18 COUNTRIES

(Based on Σ^{*})

(Standard errors are in parentheses)

Country	Food β_1^c	Beverages β_2^c	Clothing β_3^c	Housing β_4^c	Durables β_5^c	Medical care β_6^c	Transport β_7^c	Recreation β_8^c	Education β_9^c	Miscellaneous β_{10}^c	Income flexibility ϕ^c
(1)	(2)	(3)	(4)	(5)	(6)	(7)	(8)	(9)	(10)	(11)	(12)
1. U.S.	−.055	−.031	.027	−.115	.054	−.059	.209	.014	−.003	−.041	−.384
	(.019)	(.014)	(.021)	(.026)	(.017)	(.021)	(.024)	(.018)	(.009)	(.023)	(.066)
2. Canada	−.007	−.025	−.015	−.183	.050	.055	.084	.051	.001	−.011	−.554
	(.037)	(.022)	(.029)	(.041)	(.034)	(.020)	(.036)	(.027)	(.014)	(.044)	(.120)
3. Sweden	−.094	.008	.038	−.190	.067	−.022	.138	.054	−.001	.002	−.580
	(.025)	(.015)	(.022)	(.032)	(.021)	(.005)	(.026)	(.021)	(.001)	(.021)	(.088)
4. Switzerland	−.007	.033	.055	−.153	.086	−.046	.063	.001		−.033	−.551
	(.025)	(.017)	(.016)	(.020)	(.019)	(.014)	(.021)	(.023)		(.022)	(.075)
5. Denmark	−.123	−.028	.044	−.130	.053	−.010	.188	.019	−.009	−.005	−.465
	(.032)	(.018)	(.016)	(.024)	(.017)	(.008)	(.023)	(.018)	(.005)	(.018)	(.084)
6. Australia	−.144	−.015	.027	−.059	.100	−.018	.075	.072	.013	−.050	−.463
	(.037)	(.025)	(.030)	(.033)	(.031)	(.025)	(.040)	(.024)	(.012)	(.027)	(.077)
7. France	−.115	−.024	.024	−.081	.059	−.047	.146	.001	−.001	.039	−.527
	(.034)	(.014)	(.023)	(.024)	(.022)	(.033)	(.025)	(.020)	(.003)	(.024)	(.077)
8. Germany	−.113		.052	−.133	.053	−.005	.171	.000		−.025	−.602
	(.031)		(.020)	(.020)	(.020)	(.010)	(.021)	(.017)		(.017)	(.100)
9. Belgium	−.119	−.001	.011	−.066	.070	−.028	−.012	−.002	−.002	.150	−.127
	(.044)	(.025)	(.028)	(.033)	(.039)	(.025)	(.030)	(.021)	(.005)	(.041)	(.069)
10. Norway	−.180	.010	.021	−.145	.026	−.009	.293	.002	−.003	−.016	−.484
	(.029)	(.015)	(.021)	(.024)	(.020)	(.014)	(.024)	(.022)	(.006)	(.022)	(.088)
11. Netherlands	−.132	−.024	.157	−.046	.051	−.027	.051	−.002	−.006	−.023	−.842
	(.040)	(.013)	(.028)	(.019)	(.029)	(.014)	(.016)	(.017)	(.012)	(.025)	(.107)
12. Iceland	−.129	−.020	.037	−.198	.089	−.015	.181	.023	−.004	.036	−.695
	(.025)	(.016)	(.018)	(.022)	(.018)	(.017)	(.020)	(.017)	(.006)	(.014)	(.089)
13. Finland	−.126	.024	.055	−.122	.042	−.009	.109	.053	.002	−.028	−.378
	(.037)	(.025)	(.027)	(.032)	(.023)	(.015)	(.029)	(.021)	(.010)	(.027)	(.081)
14. Austria	−.175	−.036	.090	−.099	.085	−.060	.282	−.011	−.005	−.071	−.154
	(.041)	(.023)	(.031)	(.030)	(.028)	(.018)	(.034)	(.021)	(.005)	(.036)	(.093)
15. Japan	−.105		.069	−.130	.073	−.020	.031	.013		.070	−.370
	(.039)		(.031)	(.038)	(.022)	(.023)	(.026)	(.026)		(.035)	(.101)
16. U.K.	−.127	.002	.017	−.118	.088	−.003	.087	.027	.000	.027	−.396
	(.027)	(.011)	(.020)	(.023)	(.018)	(.005)	(.020)	(.018)	(.009)	(.023)	(.071)
17. Spain	−.049	−.003	.031	−.114	.039	−.002	.130	.015	−.012	−.034	−.291
	(.061)	(.024)	(.036)	(.045)	(.030)	(.024)	(.032)	(.020)	(.012)	(.028)	(.073)
18. Italy	−.044	−.017	.077	−.067	.036	.001	.044	−.024	−.002	−.006	−.184
	(.029)	(.016)	(.018)	(.023)	(.015)	(.012)	(.019)	(.016)	(.004)	(.021)	(.074)

The estimates are from Table 4.1 for all countries except Switzerland, Germany and Japan. The estimates for these three countries are new; see Section 2.2 for a description of the data for these countries.

TABLE 5.3

ML ESTIMATES OF THE CONSTANT TERMS FOR 10 COMMODITIES IN 18 COUNTRIES

(Based on Σ^*)

(Standard errors are in parentheses)

Country (1)	Food α_1^c (2)	Beverages α_2^c (3)	Clothing α_3^c (4)	Housing α_4^c (5)	Durables α_5^c (6)	Medical care α_6^c (7)	Transport α_7^c (8)	Recreation α_8^c (9)	Education α_9^c (10)	Miscellaneous α_{10}^c (11)
1. U.S.	-.121 (.060)	.033 (.039)	-.131 (.069)	.384 (.078)	-.203 (.052)	.351 (.053)	-.418 (.074)	.040 (.058)	.028 (.023)	.037 (.063)
2. Canada	-.218 (.124)	.046 (.085)	.014 (.120)	.581 (.144)	-.177 (.125)	-.300 (.073)	-.103 (.133)	-.026 (.109)	.047 (.038)	.136 (.119)
3. Sweden	-.099 (.071)	-.073 (.046)	-.156 (.081)	.507 (.067)	-.142 (.051)	.067 (.024)	-.108 (.065)	.110 (.058)	.004 (.006)	-.110 (.041)
4. Switzerland	-.100 (.071)	-.122 (.050)	.258 (.050)	.342 (.053)	-.327 (.053)	.169 (.031)	.063 (.054)	.074 (.060)		.159 (.045)
5. Denmark	-.065 (.080)	-.010 (.064)	-.228 (.059)	.049 (.072)	.086 (.055)	.017 (.025)	-.209 (.071)	.084 (.057)	.070 (.016)	-.022 (.054)
6. Australia	.122 (.112)	-.074 (.074)	-.227 (.087)	.377 (.087)	-.234 (.111)	.017 (.053)	-.015 (.111)	-.031 (.066)	-.041 (.022)	.106 (.071)
7. France	-.011 (.133)	-.027 (.062)	-.280 (.094)	.510 (.080)	-.299 (.093)	.475 (.131)	-.311 (.097)	.060 (.092)	.001 (.011)	-.118 (.087)
8. Germany	-.013 (.120)		-.251 (.074)	.455 (.060)	-.200 (.081)	-.007 (.028)	-.172 (.001)	.055 (.063)		.161 (.055)
9. Belgium	-.008 (.161)	-.036 (.092)	-.073 (.105)	.164 (.121)	-.087 (.146)	.238 (.088)	.179 (.110)	.045 (.074)	.004 (.017)	-.426 (.155)
10. Norway	.160 (.103)	-.073 (.059)	-.204 (.075)	.502 (.083)	-.026 (.070)	.018 (.044)	-.550 (.085)	.148 (.087)	.000 (.018)	.024 (.068)
11. Netherlands	.049 (.197)	.085 (.082)	-.896 (.148)	.228 (.091)	-.129 (.174)	.316 (.057)	-.045 (.089)	.046 (.062)	.095 (.048)	.250 (.106)
12. Iceland	.033 (.187)	.106 (.133)	-.262 (.159)	.536 (.185)	-.272 (.152)	.289 (.108)	-.472 (.160)	.015 (.112)	.020 (.034)	.006 (.110)
13. Finland	-.065 (.183)	-.008 (.125)	-.441 (.135)	.419 (.169)	-.077 (.119)	.095 (.077)	-.075 (.148)	-.090 (.109)	-.058 (.045)	.300 (.124)
14. Austria	.247 (.156)	.042 (.095)	-.222 (.125)	.458 (.105)	-.270 (.115)	.150 (.059)	.560 (.147)	.092 (.083)	.010 (.019)	.053 (.127)
15. Japan	-.140 (.173)		-.335 (.120)	.711 (.160)	-.403 (.099)	.300 (.109)	.015 (.108)	-.052 (.117)		-.106 (.136)
16. U.K.	-.090 (.073)	-.046 (.039)	-.066 (.069)	.280 (.058)	-.216 (.053)	-.002 (.015)	.055 (.059)	.080 (.050)	.015 (.022)	-.010 (.063)
17. Spain	-.349 (.287)	-.016 (.125)	-.235 (.159)	.406 (.229)	-.216 (.137)	.220 (.105)	-.155 (.156)	.009 (.085)	.054 (.050)	.282 (.128)
18. Italy	-.225 (.121)	.023 (.072)	-.301 (.073)	.161 (.089)	-.083 (.062)	.114 (.050)	.109 (.070)	.114 (.060)	-.002 (.017)	.090 (.081)

All entries are to be divided by 100. The estimates are from Table A4.1 for all countries except Switzerland, Germany and Japan. The estimates for these three countries are new; see Section 2.2 for a description of the data for these countries.

TABLE 5.4

ML ESTIMATES OF THE POOLED DEMAND MODEL FOR 15 COUNTRIES

(Standard errors are in parentheses)

Country (1)	Food (2)	Beverages (3)	Clothing (4)	Housing (5)	Durables (6)	Medical care (7)	Transport (8)	Recreation (9)	Education (10)	Miscellaneous (11)	Income flexibility ϕ (12)
Income coefficients β_i and income flexibility ϕ											
1. All countries	−.097	−.011	.040	−.114	.054	−.012	.122	.017	−.002	.004	−.449
	(.008)	(.005)	(.006)	(.008)	(.006)	(.003)	(.007)	(.005)	(.001)	(.006)	(.022)
Constant terms α_i^c ($\times 100$)											
2. U.S.	−.025	−.013	−.181	.381	−.208	.264	−.213	.022	.026	−.053	
	(.019)	(.011)	(.019)	(.018)	(.014)	(.006)	(.015)	(.015)	(.002)	(.019)	
3. Canada	−.013	.006	−.161	.388	−.173	−.100	−.194	.111	.043	.091	
	(.019)	(.013)	(.020)	(.020)	(.017)	(.008)	(.017)	(.017)	(.002)	(.024)	
4. Sweden	−.098	−.045	−.131	.411	−.129	.046	−.114	.188	.005	−.133	
	(.013)	(.007)	(.017)	(.008)	(.009)	(.006)	(.009)	(.010)	(.001)	(.022)	
5. Denmark	−.100	−.047	−.217	.644	−.288	.019	−.128	.088	.063	−.033	
	(.011)	(.010)	(.015)	(.006)	(.008)	(.004)	(.009)	(.010)	(.001)	(.024)	
6. Australia	.007	−.085	−.260	.477	−.079	.006	−.131	.080	−.020	.004	
	(.020)	(.010)	(.015)	(.014)	(.018)	(.005)	(.014)	(.011)	(.002)	(.021)	
7. France	−.066	−.077	−.328	.604	−.260	.353	−.229	.004	.004	−.006	
	(.030)	(.018)	(.024)	(.022)	(.021)	(.011)	(.022)	(.022)	(.003)	(.026)	
8. Belgium	−.085	−.011	−.207	.324	−.072	.204	−.210	−.016	.003	.071	
	(.026)	(.015)	(.022)	(.020)	(.018)	(.008)	(.018)	(.016)	(.004)	(.025)	
9. Norway	−.061	−.012	−.253	.422	−.098	.025	−.106	.104	−.001	−.020	
	(.022)	(.012)	(.017)	(.019)	(.015)	(.006)	(.016)	(.018)	(.002)	(.020)	
10. Netherlands	−.110	.030	−.335	.451	−.042	.218	−.345	−.044	.058	.119	
	(.036)	(.021)	(.027)	(.028)	(.028)	(.009)	(.029)	(.019)	(.004)	(.031)	
11. Iceland	−.166	.057	−.235	.148	−.038	.246	−.194	.011	.009	.162	
	(.035)	(.023)	(.037)	(.037)	(.032)	(.012)	(.034)	(.024)	(.005)	(.035)	
12. Finland	−.162	.124	−.387	.383	−.137	.106	−.128	.049	−.044	.197	
	(.028)	(.017)	(.026)	(.033)	(.023)	(.012)	(.024)	(.022)	(.003)	(.029)	
13. Austria	−.022	−.088	−.110	.509	−.225	.054	.010	−.023	.000	−.104	
	(.028)	(.018)	(.024)	(.016)	(.021)	(.005)	(.020)	(.019)	(.004)	(.032)	
14. U.K.	−.147	−.021	−.144	.283	−.150	.013	.019	.096	.019	.032	
	(.016)	(.010)	(.019)	(.007)	(.011)	(.005)	(.011)	(.010)	(.001)	(.022)	
15. Spain	−.152	.014	−.253	.402	−.261	.264	−.196	.022	.025	.134	
	(.037)	(.025)	(.025)	(.038)	(.023)	(.011)	(.033)	(.018)	(.004)	(.037)	
16. Italy	−.069	−.036	−.175	.316	−.136	.150	−.104	−.052	−.001	.108	
	(.028)	(.021)	(.020)	(.023)	(.018)	(.012)	(.020)	(.019)	(.004)	(.028)	

The estimates of the income coefficients and the income flexibility are from Table 4.3; and the estimates of the constant terms are from Table A4.2.

5.3 THE SIMULATION PROCEDURE

In this section we describe the Monte Carlo simulation procedure to be used to analyse the reliability of the estimates. We start with the ML-estimates $(\hat{\alpha}_i^c, \hat{\beta}_i^c, \hat{\phi}^c)$ of model (2.1) for $i=1,...,n^c$, the number of goods for country c. We shall refer to these estimates as the true parameter values for the simulation experiment. Let $\hat{\Sigma}^c$ be a data-based consistent estimator of Σ^c. (Subsequently we shall specify $\hat{\Sigma}^c$ to be S^c or Σ^{*c}.) To obtain data sets for the simulation experiment, we generate pseudo-normal random error vectors with mean zero and covariance matrix $\hat{\Sigma}^c$. Then we use these values together with the true values of the parameters and the observed values of the independent variables to obtain new values for the dependent variables from equation (2.1) for $i=1,...,n^c$. These values and the observed values of the independent variables are then used to re-estimate model (2.1) by ML. This procedure is repeated 100 times.

In the above simulation experiment we assume that Σ^c is unknown for each trial. That is, we re-estimate Σ^c as well as the demand parameters in each trial. Recognizing the fact that in a simulation experiment Σ^c is known and equal to its data-based estimate $\hat{\Sigma}^c$, we repeat the simulation experiment with known Σ^c.

To assess the reliability of the pooled estimates, we use the same simulation procedure with the pooled model (2.3) and the ML-estimates $(\hat{\alpha}_i^c, \hat{\beta}_i, \hat{\phi})$.

5.4   THE SIMULATION RESULTS FOR SEVEN COUNTRIES
WITH THE USUAL COVARIANCE MATRIX

In this section we apply the simulation procedure described in the last section using $\hat{\Sigma}^c = S^c$ for 7 countries. Table 5.5 presents the simulation results for the U.S. Column 2 of the table presents the data-based ML-estimates (the true values) from Table 5.1. Columns 3-6 give the results when S^c is treated as unknown at each iteration in the ML procedure. In column 3 we present the means over the 100 trials of the estimates obtained using the simulated data. As can be seen, these estimates are quite close to the corresponding true values given in column 2. To test for any bias, we use the test statistic

$$|\text{bias}| \times \sqrt{\frac{\text{Number of trials}}{\text{RMSE}}}, \tag{4.1}$$

where RMSE is the root-mean-squared error computed around the true value; the RMSEs are given in column 4. The test statistic (4.1) has a t-distribution with (number of trials - 1) = 99 degrees of freedom. Using this test we conclude that the ML estimates are unbiased.

Column 5 of the table presents the root-mean-squared asymptotic standard errors (RMSASEs). The RMSASEs are obtained by summing each diagonal element of the asymptotic covariance matrix over the 100 trials,

TABLE 5.5

MONTE CARLO SIMULATION RESULTS WITH S^c FOR 100 TRIALS, U.S.

Commodity (1)	True value (2)	S^c unknown				S^c known			
		Mean (3)	RMSE (4)	RMSASE (5)	(5)/(4) (6)	Mean (7)	RMSE (8)	RMSASE (9)	(9)/(8) (10)
					Income coefficients β_i^c				
1. Food	−.058	−.057	.021	.012	.566	−.059	.016	.017	1.036
2. Beverages	−.034	−.035	.006	.003	.444	−.034	.004	.004	.882
3. Clothing	.058	.057	.022	.011	.498	.058	.014	.015	1.019
4. Housing	−.111	−.111	.016	.009	.544	−.110	.011	.011	.981
5. Durables	.072	.070	.013	.008	.579	.070	.011	.010	.909
6. Medical care	−.078	−.080	.021	.010	.486	−.078	.013	.014	1.068
7. Transport	.149	.152	.047	.025	.544	.152	.036	.034	.927
8. Recreation	.041	.041	.013	.008	.588	.040	.010	.011	1.021
9. Education	−.007	−.007	.005	.003	.560	−.007	.003	.004	1.098
10. Miscellaneous	−.032	−.030	.019	.011	.562	−.032	.013	.014	1.075
					Income flexibility ϕ^c				
11.	−.689	−.701	.088	.038	.428	−.695	.061	.053	.864
					Constant terms α_i^c ($\times 100$)				
12. Food	−.102	−.105	.065	.056	.861	−.100	.055	.062	1.133
13. Beverages	.043	.045	.018	.013	.732	.043	.016	.015	.902
14. Clothing	−.264	−.257	.068	.045	.662	−.260	.050	.055	1.091
15. Housing	.383	.382	.042	.030	.716	.380	.035	.034	.978
16. Durables	−.255	−.249	.044	.033	.764	−.249	.040	.038	.936
17. Medical care	.397	.401	.044	.036	.820	.398	.037	.039	1.051
18. Transport	−.229	−.244	.133	.103	.776	−.245	.118	.117	.989
19. Recreation	−.065	−.062	.042	.033	.790	−.060	.038	.040	1.047
20. Education	.041	.041	.013	.010	.793	.041	.012	.011	.906
21. Miscellaneous	.050	.048	.047	.036	.767	.051	.038	.042	1.091
22. Mean					.642				1.000

dividing by 100 and then taking the square root. Comparing column 4 with column 5 we see that the RMSASEs are always less than the RMSEs. To facilitate this comparison, column 6 gives the ratio RMSASE/RMSE. Row 22 presents the mean of these ratios. As can be seen, all entries in column 6 are far below 1. Consequently, when S^c is used the asymptotic standard errors provide an overly optimistic picture of the true sampling variability of the point estimates. This confirms that these estimates do indeed suffer from Theil's (1987) first peril.

Columns 7-10 of Table 5.5 present the results when S^c is treated as known for each iteration. As before, bias is not a problem. As can be seen from column 10, the RMSASE/RMSE ratios now fluctuate around unity. This shows that the source of the first peril is in estimating the error covariance matrix. Note also that the RMSEs in column 4 are substantially higher than those in column 8. This indicates that there is a substantial loss of efficiency when the covariance matrix is estimated. This is Theil's (1987) second peril. See Appendix A5.1 for the detailed results of the other 6 countries where S^c is used.

Columns 2-11 of Table 5.6 presents the RMSASE/RMSE ratios for the income coefficients for the 10 commodities in the 7 countries. Column 12 gives the means of these ratios for each country. Column 13 presents the ratios for the income flexibility. The upper half of the table presents the results when S^c is re-estimated in each trial; the lower half presents the results when this

TABLE 5.6

RMSASE/RMSE RATIOS FOR INCOME COEFFICIENTS FOR 10 COMMODITIES AND INCOME FLEXIBILITY IN 7 COUNTRIES: 100 TRIALS WITH S^c

Country (1)	Food β_1^c (2)	Beverages β_2^c (3)	Clothing β_3^c (4)	Housing β_4^c (5)	Durables β_5^c (6)	Medical care β_6^c (7)	Transport β_7^c (8)	Recreation β_8^c (9)	Education β_9^c (10)	Miscellaneous β_{10}^c (11)	Mean (12)	Income flexibility ϕ^c (13)
					S^c unknown for each trial							
1. U.S.	.57	.44	.50	.54	.58	.49	.54	.59	.56	.56	.54	.43
2. Canada	.51	.59	.53	.62	.61	.53	.53	.51	.61	.56	.56	.48
3. Switzerland	.68	.64	.69	.63	.68	.68	.63	.69		.63	.66	.53
4. Australia	.63	.53	.57	.57	.56	.58	.51	.53	.49	.59	.56	.40
5. Germany	.73		.74	.80	.77	.58	.65	.63		.68	.70	.56
6. Belgium	.45	.41	.47	.13	.40	.43	.55	.55	.46	.48	.46	.41
7. Netherlands	.60	.67	.66	.59	.64	.60	.63	.55	.74	.68	.64	.59
8. Mean	.60	.55	.59	.60	.61	.56	.58	.58	.57	.60	.59	.49
					S^c known for each trial							
9. U.S.	1.04	.88	1.02	.98	.91	1.07	.93	1.02	1.10	1.08	1.00	.86
10. Canada	.99	1.01	1.11	1.03	1.07	1.14	1.04	.92	1.08	1.08	1.05	1.00
11. Switzerland	.98	1.02	.96	1.07	.99	1.04	.96	1.05		.88	.99	1.04
12. Australia	1.10	.87	.87	1.04	.96	1.01	.92	.98	.88	1.06	.97	.92
13. Germany	.97		.93	1.03	1.05	.98	.97	.90		1.01	.98	.99
14. Belgium	1.06	.94	1.10	.99	1.01	.97	1.13	.99	.92	1.05	1.02	.93
15. Netherlands	1.00	1.02	.96	1.00	.91	1.02	1.12	1.04	1.09	1.02	1.02	1.07
16. Mean	1.02	.96	.99	1.02	.99	1.03	1.01	.99	1.01	1.02	1.00	.97

The ratios in columns 2-11 and 13 are from columns 6 and 10 of Tables 5.5 and A5 1-A5.6.

matrix is treated as known. Rows 8 and 16 present the ratios averaged over countries for the two cases. As can be seen, the ratios are well below unity when S^c is unknown, while they are very close to one when S^c is known. This clearly shows the existence of the first peril in all 7 countries when the covariance matrix is estimated in the usual way. It should also be noted that the first peril tends to be a bit more of a problem for the ϕ-estimates than for the β_i-estimates. On average, the asymptotic standard errors of the ϕ's are understated by about 50 percent when S^c is treated as unknown; for the β_i's the understatement is about 40 percent (see row 8 of columns 12 and 13).

Table 5.7 presents same ratios for the constant terms. While these results have the same general pattern as those of Table 5.6, the upper-half ratios (S^c unknown) are a bit closer to unity.

5.5   THE SIMULATION RESULTS FOR EIGHTEEN COUNTRIES
WITH THE ALTERNATIVE COVARIANCE MATRIX

In this section we assess the reliability of the ML-estimates of the individual country models obtained with the covariance matrix specification (2.2).

Table 5.8 presents the simulation results for the U.S. when Σ^c is specified as Σ^{*c}. Column 2 presents the data-based estimates from Tables 5.2

TABLE 5.7

RMSASE/RMSE RATIOS FOR THE CONSTANT TERMS

FOR 10 COMMODITIES IN 7 COUNTRIES: 100 TRIALS WITH S^c

Country	Food α_1^c	Beverages α_2^c	Clothing α_3^c	Housing α_4^c	Durables α_5^c	Medical care α_6^c	Transport α_7^c	Recreation α_8^c	Education α_9^c	Miscellaneous α_{10}^c	Mean
(1)	(2)	(3)	(4)	(5)	(6)	(7)	(8)	(9)	(10)	(11)	(12)
S^c unknown for each trial											
1. U.S.	.86	.73	.66	.72	.76	.82	.78	.79	.79	.77	.77
2. Canada	.88	.75	.70	.80	.74	.69	.76	.62	1.18	.70	.78
3. Switzerland	.82	.85	.79	.81	.73	.95	.76	.77		.82	.81
4. Australia	.80	.63	.69	.73	.62	.81	.77	.69	.66	.75	.72
5. Germany	.85		.83	.92	.85	.81	.83	.71		.80	.03
6. Belgium	.70	.57	.62	.85	.65	.86	.65	.65	.72	.90	.72
7. Netherlands	.73	.90	.81	.73	.76	.90	.75	.83	.87	.78	.81
8. Mean	.81	.74	.73	.79	.73	.83	.76	.72	.85	.79	.78
S^c known for each trial											
9. U.S.	1.13	.90	1.09	.98	.94	1.05	.99	1.05	.91	1.09	1.01
10. Canada	1.07	1.00	1.09	.98	1.06	1.04	1.07	.91	1.18	.92	1.03
11. Switzerland	1.00	1.04	.96	.88	.97	1.03	1.00	1.04		.98	.99
12. Australia	1.02	.87	.98	.97	.96	1.07	1.02	1.01	.97	1.04	.99
13. Germany	1.04		.98	1.02	1.05	1.00	1.17	.93		1.14	1.04
14. Belgium	1.14	.97	1.13	1.02	.94	1.01	1.00	1.02	1.08	1.05	1.04
15. Netherlands	1.07	1.14	1.03	.98	1.05	1.01	1.01	1.11	1.07	.99	1.05
16. Mean	1.07	.99	1.04	.98	.90	1.03	1.04	1.01	1.04	1.03	1.02

The ratios in columns 2–11 are from columns 6 and 10 of Tables 5.5 and
A5.1–A5.6.

TABLE 5.8

MONTE CARLO SIMULATION RESULTS WITH Σ^{*c} FOR 100 TRIALS, U.S.

Commodity	True value	Σ^{*c} unknown				Σ^{*c} known			
		Mean	RMSE	RMSASE	(5)/(4)	Mean	RMSE	RMSASE	(9)/(8)
(1)	(2)	(3)	(4)	(5)	(6)	(7)	(8)	(9)	(10)
Income coefficients β_i^c									
1. Food	−.055	−.056	.019	.018	.978	−.056	.019	.019	1.030
2. Beverages	−.031	−.027	.015	.013	.873	−.027	.015	.014	.919
3. Clothing	.027	.024	.021	.020	.954	.024	.021	.021	1.003
4. Housing	−.115	−.116	.026	.025	.978	−.116	.026	.026	1.028
5. Durables	.054	.051	.016	.016	.976	.051	.016	.017	1.026
6. Medical care	−.059	−.060	.019	.020	1.040	−.060	.019	.021	1.093
7. Transport	.209	.211	.022	.023	1.040	.211	.022	.024	1.094
8. Recreation	.014	.013	.018	.017	.944	.013	.018	.018	.992
9. Education	−.003	−.003	.009	.008	.980	−.003	.009	.009	1.031
10. Miscellaneous	−.041	−.038	.021	.022	1.027	−.038	.021	.023	1.080
Income flexibility ϕ^c									
11.	−.384	−.384	.063	.063	.996	−.384	.063	.066	1.047
Constant terms α_i^c (×100)									
12. Food	−.121	−.121	.053	.057	1.077	−.121	.053	.060	1.133
13. Beverages	.033	.025	.044	.037	.850	.025	.044	.039	.894
14. Clothing	−.131	−.120	.066	.065	.984	−.120	.066	.069	1.034
15. Housing	.384	.384	.078	.074	.945	.384	.078	.078	.994
16. Durables	−.203	−.197	.052	.050	.958	−.197	.052	.052	1.008
17. Medical care	.351	.351	.052	.050	.966	.351	.052	.053	1.016
18. Transport	−.418	−.425	.064	.070	1.091	−.425	.064	.074	1.147
19. Recreation	.040	.042	.053	.056	1.039	.042	.053	.058	1.092
20. Education	.028	.027	.022	.022	.991	.027	.022	.023	1.042
21. Miscellaneous	.037	.033	.062	.060	.973	.033	.062	.063	1.024
Proportionality constant λ^{c2} (×10⁴)									
22.	.269	.243	.038						
23. Mean					.984				1.035

and 5.3. Columns 3-6 give the results when Σ^{*c} is treated as unknown. In column 3 we present the means over 100 trials of the estimates obtained using the simulated data. As can be seen, these estimates are also quite close to the corresponding true values in column 2. Using the test statistic (4.1), we conclude that the estimates are unbiased. Comparing the RMSEs given in column 4 with the RMSASEs in column 5 we see that the latter are in general slightly lower. Row 23 presents the mean of the RMSASE/RMSE ratios. This mean shows that the RMSASEs are about $1\frac{1}{2}$ percent less than the RMSEs on average. Therefore, we conclude that while the asymptotic standard errors still tend to understate the sampling variability of the estimates, the first peril is not nearly such a problem when we use Σ^{*c}. (Compare column 6 of Table 5.8 with the same column of Table 5.5.)

Columns 7-10 of the Table 5.8 present the results when Σ^{*c} is treated as known. As λ^{c2} is the only unknown parameter in Σ^{*c} [see equation (2.2)], this amounts to fixing this one parameter at its data-based ML value. Comparing column 10 with column 6, we see that the RMSASE/RMSE ratios have now slightly increased. However, the ratios are all close to unity in both cases. It can also be seen that the RMSEs in column 4 are virtually equal to the RMSEs in column 8. This indicates that the second peril is also not a problem when we use Σ^{*c}. We present the detailed results for the remaining 17 countries in Appendix A5.2.

Tables 5.9 and 5.10 present the RMSASE/RMSE ratios for all 18 countries. The upper half of the tables present the results when Σ^{*c} (i.e., $\lambda^{c}2$) is re-estimated in each trial and the lower half presents the results when this matrix is treated as known. Rows 19 and 38 of the tables present the cross-country means. As can be seen from row 19 the ratios are now only a bit below unity when Σ^{*c} is treated as unknown. The ratios move even closer to unity when Σ^{*c} is specified as being known in each trial, as can be seen from the lower halves of Tables 5.9 and 5.10.

In a typical application, the error covariance matrix Σ^{c} will be unknown and has to be estimated. To compare the effects of using Σ^{*c} rather than S^{c}, we should consequently focus on the contrast between upper halves of Tables 5.9 and 5.10, on the one hand, and Tables 5.6 and 5.7, on the other. This contrast is stark indeed. Using Σ^{*c} leads to a spectacular improvement in the results in all cases.

5.6 THE SIMULATION RESULTS FOR THE POOLED MODEL

Table 5.11 presents the summary results of the simulations for the pooled model with the specified covariance matrix, described below equation (2.3). Column 2 reproduces the data-based estimates from Table 5.4. Columns 3-6 present the results for 100 trials when the covariance matrix is

TABLE 5.9

RMSASE/RMSE RATIOS FOR INCOME COEFFICIENTS FOR 10 COMMODITIES AND INCOME FLEXIBILITY IN 18 COUNTRIES: 100 TRIALS WITH Σ^{*c}

Country	Food β_1^c	Beverages β_2^c	Clothing β_3^c	Housing β_4^c	Durables β_5^c	Medical care β_6^c	Transport β_7^c	Recreation β_8^c	Education β_9^c	Miscellaneous β_{10}^c	Mean	Income flexibility ϕ^c
(1)	(2)	(3)	(4)	(5)	(6)	(7)	(8)	(9)	(10)	(11)	(12)	(13)
Σ^{*c} _unknown for each trial_												
1. U.S.	.98	.87	.95	.98	.98	1.04	1.04	.94	.98	1.03	.98	1.00
2. Canada	1.00	.90	.98	.89	1.02	1.01	.89	.88	.95	.97	.95	.93
3. Sweden	.98	.93	.86	.87	.90	.95	.83	1.02	1.00	.98	.93	.84
4. Switzerland	.94	.98	.90	.96	.97	.95	.82	.92		.90	.93	.88
5. Denmark	.93	.92	1.02	1.03	.91	.95	.88	.99	.86	.94	.94	.87
6. Australia	1.04	.89	.83	.92	.92	.97	.96	.88	.88	1.00	.93	.88
7. France	.90	.93	.89	.92	1.00	.90	.85	.96	.77	.97	.91	.85
8. Germany	.94		.89	.94	.97	.96	.97	.92		1.05	.96	1.02
9. Belgium	.93	.88	1.05	1.00	.90	1.01	1.03	.95	1.00	1.09	.98	1.01
10. Norway	.92	.80	.90	.93	.95	1.01	.93	1.01	.91	.94	.94	.99
11. Netherlands	.88	.88	.97	.90	.89	1.06	.98	1.00	1.00	.93	.95	.97
12. Iceland	1.02	.84	.85	.74	.88	.88	.85	.81	.80	.96	.86	.88
13. Finland	.95	.86	.94	.90	.90	.88	1.00	1.04	.85	1.07	.94	.85
14. Austria	.98	.87	.96	.91	.89	1.10	.91	1.00	.86	.93	.94	.81
15. Japan	.80		.89	.93	.88	.81	.87	.95		1.03	.89	.82
16. U.K.	.86	.97	.97	.97	.94	.91	.84	.99	1.00	1.03	.95	.89
17. Spain	.83	.78	.92	.87	.86	.75	.89	.81	.92	1.04	.87	.84
18. Italy	.90	.81	1.01	.81	.90	.07	.98	1.04	.91	1.02	.94	1.00
19. Mean	.93	.89	.93	.91	.93	.95	.92	.95	.91	.99	.93	.91
Σ^{*c} _known for each trial_												
20. U.S.	1.03	.92	1.00	1.03	1.03	1.09	1.09	.99	1.03	1.08	1.03	1.05
21. Canada	1.05	.95	1.03	.94	1.08	1.07	.94	.93	1.00	1.02	1.00	.98
22. Sweden	1.04	.99	.92	.92	.96	1.01	.89	1.08	1.06	1.04	.99	.89
23. Switzerland	1.00	1.04	.95	1.01	1.02	1.01	.87	.98		.95	.98	.93
24. Denmark	.99	.98	1.10	1.11	.97	1.02	.94	1.05	.92	1.01	1.01	.93
25. Australia	1.10	.94	.88	.97	.97	1.02	1.01	.93	.93	1.06	.98	.93
26. France	.95	.98	.94	.98	1.06	.96	.90	1.03	.82	1.03	.97	.90
27. Germany	.99		.93	.99	1.02	1.01	1.02	.97		1.10	1.00	1.07
28. Belgium	.98	.92	1.10	1.05	.94	1.07	1.09	1.00	1.06	1.15	1.03	1.06
29. Norway	.98	.92	.97	.99	1.01	1.07	.99	1.08	.97	.99	1.00	1.05
30. Netherlands	.92	.92	1.01	.91	1.03	1.11	1.02	1.05	1.05	.97	.99	1.01
31. Iceland	1.11	.91	.93	.80	.96	.96	.92	.89	.87	1.05	.94	.96
32. Finland	1.01	.92	1.00	.95	.96	.94	1.06	1.11	.91	1.14	1.00	.90
33. Austria	1.04	.92	1.02	.96	.95	1.17	.97	1.06	.91	.99	1.00	.86
34. Japan	.90		.99	1.04	.98	.91	.97	1.06		1.15	1.00	.92
35. U.K.	.92	1.03	1.03	1.03	1.00	.97	.89	1.05	1.06	1.10	1.01	.95
36. Spain	.91	.85	.99	.94	.94	.81	.97	.88	1.00	1.13	.94	.91
37. Italy	.96	.87	1.08	.86	1.02	1.03	1.04	1.10	.97	1.08	1.00	1.06
38. Mean	.99	.94	.99	.97	.99	1.01	.98	1.01	.97	1.06	.99	.96

The ratios in columns 2–11 and 13 are from columns 6 and 10 of Tables 5.8 and A5.7–A5.23.

TABLE 5.10

RMSASE/RMSE RATIOS FOR THE CONSTANT TERMS FOR 10 COMMODITIES
IN 18 COUNTRIES: 100 TRIALS WITH Σ^{*c}

Country	Food α_1^c	Beverages α_2^c	Clothing α_3^c	Housing α_4^c	Durables α_5^c	Medical care α_6^c	Transport α_7^c	Recreation α_8^c	Education α_9^c	Miscellaneous α_{10}^c	Mean
(1)	(2)	(3)	(4)	(5)	(6)	(7)	(8)	(9)	(10)	(11)	(12)
Σ^{*c} unknown for each trial											
1. U.S.	1.08	.85	.98	.94	.96	.97	1.09	1.04	.99	.97	.99
2. Canada	1.03	.91	.98	.87	1.04	.94	.89	.90	1.04	.99	.96
3. Sweden	1.03	1.04	.84	.90	.88	.98	.89	.98	1.00	.84	.94
4. Switzerland	.96	1.00	.92	.85	1.01	.95	.98	.96		.96	.95
5. Denmark	.92	.98	.99	.91	.88	1.00	.97	1.03	1.03	.86	.96
6. Australia	.98	.88	.93	.84	.94	1.07	1.00	.89	.95	.97	.95
7. France	.93	.92	.91	.88	1.03	.88	.84	.96	.84	.94	.91
8. Germany	1.00		.94	.99	.97	1.05	1.08	.88		1.10	1.00
9. Belgium	1.03	.89	1.03	.94	.92	.98	1.03	.94	1.02	1.04	.98
10. Norway	.94	.90	.89	.94	.98	1.09	1.00	.96	.93	.93	.96
11. Netherlands	.95	.93	1.00	.92	1.03	1.07	.95	.92	1.01	.90	.97
12. Iceland	.97	.97	.76	.86	.95	.97	.91	.88	.89	.88	.91
13. Finland	1.00	.92	.89	.96	.90	1.00	1.02	1.04	.88	1.02	.96
14. Austria	.91	.93	.95	.84	.94	1.06	.88	.96	.82	.94	.92
15. Japan	.81	.00	.85	.88	.90	.88	.85	.93	.00	.87	.87
16. U.K.	.91	1.14	.99	.90	.87	.87	.88	.91	1.03	.88	.94
17. Spain	.86	.79	.95	.88	.84	.79	.96	.85	.90	1.04	.88
18. Italy	.91	.85	1.01	.82	1.01	.99	1.02	1.00	.94	.97	.95
19. Mean	.96	.93	.93	.89	.95	.97	.96	.95	.95	.95	.94
Σ^{*c} known for each trial											
20. U.S.	1.13	.89	1.03	.99	1.01	1.02	1.15	1.09	1.04	1.02	1.04
21. Canada	1.09	.96	1.03	.92	1.10	.99	.94	.95	1.10	1.04	1.01
22. Sweden	1.10	1.11	.89	.95	.93	1.04	.95	1.04	1.06	.90	1.00
23. Switzerland	1.01	1.06	.97	.90	1.07	1.00	1.03	1.02	.00	1.02	1.01
24. Denmark	.99	1.05	1.06	.97	.95	1.07	1.04	1.11	1.10	.92	1.02
25. Australia	1.03	.93	.98	.89	.99	1.13	1.06	.94	1.01	1.02	1.00
26. France	.99	.98	.97	.94	1.10	.94	.89	1.02	.89	.99	.97
27. Germany	1.05	.00	.99	1.03	1.01	1.10	1.13	.92	.00	1.16	1.05
28. Belgium	1.09	.93	1.08	.99	.96	1.03	1.08	.99	1.08	1.09	1.03
29. Norway	1.00	.96	.94	.99	1.04	1.16	1.06	1.02	.99	.99	1.02
30. Netherlands	1.00	.97	1.05	.96	1.08	1.12	1.00	.97	1.06	.94	1.01
31. Iceland	1.06	1.06	.83	.94	1.04	1.06	.99	.96	.97	.96	.99
32. Finland	1.07	.98	.95	1.02	.96	1.06	1.09	1.11	.94	1.09	1.03
33. Austria	.97	.99	1.01	.89	1.00	1.13	.93	1.02	.87	.99	.98
34. Japan	.91	.00	.95	.98	1.00	.99	.95	1.03	.00	.98	.97
35. U.K.	.96	1.22	1.05	.95	.93	.92	.94	.97	1.10	.94	1.00
36. Spain	.93	.85	1.03	.95	.91	.86	1.04	.93	.98	1.13	.96
37. Italy	.96	.90	1.07	.87	1.07	1.05	1.09	1.06	.99	1.03	1.01
38. Mean	1.02	.99	.99	.95	1.01	1.04	1.02	1.01	1.01	1.01	1.01

The ratios in columns 2-11 are from columns 6 and 10 of Tables 5.8 and
A5.7-A5.23.

unknown.   As before, the estimates are unbiased.   As can be seen from column 6, the RMSASEs are in general slightly less than the RMSEs, but the differences are very small.

Columns 7-10 of Table 5.11 present the results when the covariance matrix is treated as known.   In most cases, the RMSEs fall while the RMSASEs increase, so that the ratios move closer to unity.   However, the changes are again very small, as can be seen from the means of the RMSASE/RMSE ratios: .983 (covariance matrix unknown) and .998 (covariance matrix known).   (The estimation procedure for the pooled model uses data deviated from means and hence calculates the constant terms from the income coefficient and income flexibility estimates.   To reduce what would otherwise be an enormous amount of computing time, the simulated values of the constant terms were not calculated.)

The above results clearly show that the two perils are not a problem when the pooled demand model is estimated with the specified covariance matrix.   Therefore, we conclude that the ML-estimates of this model and the standard errors presented in Table 5.4 are reliable.

TABLE 5.11

ML ESTIMATION: SUMMARY RESULTS FOR 100 TRIALS,

POOLED MODEL FOR 15 COUNTRIES

Commodity	True value	Covariance matrix unknown				Covariance matrix known			
		Mean	RMSE	RMSASE	(5)/(4)	Mean	RMSE	RMSASE	(9)/(8)
(1)	(2)	(3)	(4)	(5)	(6)	(7)	(8)	(9)	(10)
Income coefficients β_i									
1. Food	-.097	-.097	.0841	.0836	.993	-.097	.0863	.0843	.977
2. Beverages	-.011	-.011	.0461	.0450	.977	-.011	.0462	.0455	.985
3. Clothing	.040	.039	.0654	.0628	.961	.039	.0642	.0634	.987
4. Housing	-.114	-.114	.0707	.0747	1.056	-.114	.0703	.0754	1.072
5. Durables	.054	.053	.0494	.0568	1.150	.053	.0492	.0573	1.166
6. Medical care	-.012	-.012	.0287	.0291	1.015	-.012	.0285	.0294	1.034
7. Transport	.122	.122	.0761	.0658	.864	.121	.0753	.0663	.881
8. Recreation	.017	.018	.0560	.0526	.940	.018	.0551	.0531	.964
9. Education	-.002	-.002	.0109	.0105	.965	-.002	.0108	.0106	.983
10. Miscellaneous	.004	.004	.0602	.0596	.990	.004	.0598	.0601	1.004
Income flexibility ϕ									
11.	-.449	-.452	.2381	.2147	.901	-.451	.2352	.2167	.921
12. Mean					.983				.998

All entries in columns 4, 5, 8 and 9 are to be divided by 10.

5.7 CONCLUDING COMMENTS

Theil (1987) demonstrates that there are problems with the usual ML estimator when applied to large demand systems. In particular, when the error covariance matrix is replaced by its usual ML-estimator S, the matrix of mean squares and cross products of the residuals, the estimates suffer from two problems. First, the asymptotic standard errors severely understate the sampling variability of the estimates, so that the precision of the estimates is overstated. Second, the efficiency of the coefficient estimates is greatly impaired. Theil refers to these problems as the 'two perils' of estimating large systems.

If the estimator is working satisfactorily, the root-mean- squared asymptotic standard errors (RMSASEs) of the parameters from a Monte Carlo simulation should be approximately equal to the root-mean-squared errors (RMSEs). That is, the RMSASE/RMSE ratios should be close to unity. However, if we used S in a large system the first peril implies that these ratios will be substantially below unity. In this chapter we initially used S to estimate by ML large systems for 7 countries. The results of simulations for these countries are illustrated by column 2 of Table 5.12. This column presents the RMSASE/RMSE ratios averaged over all parameters for the 7 countries and their cross-country mean. As can be seen, the ratios are all well below unity, confirming that the estimates suffer from the first peril.

Column 3 of Table 5.12 presents the ratios when S is treated as known in each trial of the simulation. Comparing columns 2 and 3, we see that, on average, knowledge of the S matrix causes the ratios to increase from .67 to 1.01. The satisfactory performance of the estimates when S is known indicates that the cause of the first peril is estimating S. Other results in this chapter also clearly showed the existence of the second peril when S was used.

We then analysed whether the two perils can be avoided by using an alternative specification for the error covariance matrix. This matrix, denoted by Σ^*, contains only one unknown parameter. To analyse the performance of Σ^*, again we used Monte Carlo simulations, but now with data from 18 countries. To illustrate these results, columns 4-5 of Table 5.12 present the average RMSASE/RMSE ratios. The ratios in column 4 are now all slightly less than unity. The ratios increase a bit when Σ^* is treated as known for each trial; however, they are close to unity in both cases.

It will usually be the case that the error covariance matrix is unknown and has to be estimated. To compare the effects of using Σ^* rather than S, we should thus focus on the contrast between columns 4 and 2 of Table 5.12. This contrast shows very clearly that Σ^* leads to a marked improvement in all cases. In other words, the first peril can be virtually avoided by using Σ^*. The reason for this is that Σ^* contains only one unknown parameter, whereas the S matrix contains $\frac{1}{2}n(n-1)$, n being the number of equations in the model. Our other results indicate that Σ^* avoids the second peril also.

TABLE 5.12

ML ESTIMATION: SUMMARY RESULTS OF MONTE CARLO SIMULATIONS

FOR 18 COUNTRIES

Country	Average RMSASE/RMSE ratio with error covariance matrix specified as			
	S^c		Σ^{*c}	
	S^c unknown in each trial	S^c known in each trial	Σ^{*c} unknown in each trial	Σ^{*c} known in each trial
(1)	(2)	(3)	(4)	(5)
1. U.S.	.64	1.00	.98	1.04
2. Canada	.66	1.04	.95	1.01
3. Sweden			.93	.99
4. Switzerland	.73	.99	.94	.99
5. Denmark			.95	1.01
6. Australia	.62	.98	.94	.99
7. France			.91	.97
8. Germany	.75	1.01	.98	1.03
9. Belgium	.58	1.02	.08	1.04
10. Norway			.95	1.01
11. Netherlands	.72	1.03	.96	1.00
12. Iceland			.89	.96
13. Finland			.95	1.01
14. Austria			.93	.98
15. Japan			.88	.98
16. U.K.			.94	1.00
17. Spain			.87	.95
18. Italy			.95	1.01
19. Mean	.67	1.01	.94	1.00
20. Pooled			.98	1.00

S^c is the usual ML estimator of the error covariance matrix for country c; and Σ^{*c} is the alternative estimator, defined by (2.2). This table draws on Tables 5.5, A5.1–A5.6, 5.8, A5.7–A5.23 and 5.11.

Finally, we used a similar procedure with the pooled model, where the parameters are the same across countries. Row 20 of Table 5.12 presents the mean ratios from this model. These ratios are approximately equal to unity when the covariance matrix is both unknown and known, again indicating the satisfactory performance of the alternative specification of the covariance matrix.

Based on these results, we conclude that the ML estimates and their asymptotic standard errors present a fairly realistic picture for the 18 countries when Σ^* is used for the error covariance matrix. Consequently, the results of this chapter clearly demonstrate that the alternative specification Σ^* is a viable way to avoid the two perils.

APPENDICES TO CHAPTER 5

A5.1 SIMULATION RESULTS FOR SIX COUNTRIES WITH THE USUAL COVARIANCE MATRIX

Section 5.4 of the text presents the detailed simulation results for the U.S with $\hat{\Sigma}^c = S^c$, the usual ML estimator. Tables A5.1-A5.6 of this appendix give the detailed results for the remaining 6 countries.

A5.2 SIMULATION RESULTS FOR SEVENTEEN COUNTRIES WITH THE ALTERNATIVE COVARIANCE MATRIX

Section 5.5 of the text presents the detailed simulation results for the U.S. with $\hat{\Sigma}^c = \Sigma^{*c}$, the alternative estimator defined in equation (2.2). Tables A5.7-A5.23 of this appendix present the detailed results for the remaining 17 countries.

TABLE A5.1

MONTE CARLO SIMULATION RESULTS WITH S^c FOR 100 TRIALS, CANADA

Commodity	True value	S^c unknown				S^c known			
		Mean	RMSE	RMSASE	(5)/(4)	Mean	RMSE	RMSASE	(9)/(8)
(1)	(2)	(3)	(4)	(5)	(6)	(7)	(8)	(9)	(10)
Income coefficients β_i^c									
1. Food	-.011	-.012	.018	.009	.514	-.011	.013	.013	.994
2. Beverages	-.027	-.027	.008	.005	.594	-.026	.006	.006	1.008
3. Clothing	.007	.004	.019	.010	.532	.005	.013	.014	1.108
4. Housing	-.172	-.174	.017	.011	.616	-.174	.014	.014	1.027
5. Durables	.078	.075	.018	.011	.614	.075	.013	.014	1.068
6. Medical care	.025	.024	.051	.027	.530	.024	.032	.037	1.143
7. Transport	.032	.034	.028	.015	.530	.032	.019	.020	1.042
8. Recreation	.069	.070	.019	.010	.509	.071	.014	.013	.918
9. Education	-.004	-.003	.008	.005	.611	-.004	.006	.007	1.076
10. Miscellaneous	.005	.009	.024	.014	.565	.009	.018	.019	1.076
Income flexibility ϕ^c									
11.	-.904	-.902	.099	.048	.482	-.898	.069	.069	1.003
Constant terms α_i^c ($\times 100$)									
12. Food	-.153	-.154	.064	.056	.878	-.156	.058	.062	1.072
13. Beverages	.048	.045	.034	.025	.750	.044	.029	.029	.998
14. Clothing	-.098	-.081	.085	.060	.703	-.085	.065	.071	1.091
15. Housing	.552	.558	.071	.057	.801	.557	.064	.063	.980
16. Durables	-.299	-.290	.063	.047	.742	-.289	.052	.055	1.057
17. Medical care	-.213	-.213	.184	.126	.687	-.212	.144	.149	1.037
18. Transport	.039	.027	.107	.082	.761	.034	.087	.093	1.072
19. Recreation	-.143	-.148	.081	.050	.622	-.148	.066	.061	.914
20. Education	.077	.075	.023	.027	1.183	.075	.023	.027	1.184
21. Miscellaneous	.190	.180	.073	.051	.697	.181	.065	.059	.917
22. Mean					.663				1.037

TABLE A5.2

MONTE CARLO SIMULATION RESULTS WITH S^c FOR 100 TRIALS, SWITZERLAND

Commodity	True value	S^c unknown				S^c known			
		Mean	RMSE	RMSASE	(5)/(4)	Mean	RMSE	RMSASE	(9)/(8)
(1)	(2)	(3)	(4)	(5)	(6)	(7)	(8)	(9)	(10)
		Income coefficients β_i^c							
1. Food	−.020	−.018	.023	.016	.680	−.018	.020	.019	.977
2. Beverages	.045	.045	.019	.012	.638	.045	.015	.015	1.018
3. Clothing	.058	.056	.018	.012	.686	.058	.015	.015	.963
4. Housing	−.181	−.181	.026	.017	.633	−.181	.020	.022	1.065
5. Durables	.087	.087	.014	.009	.678	.088	.011	.011	.992
6. Medical care	−.042	−.043	.012	.008	.682	−.043	.009	.010	1.037
7. Transport	.083	.083	.038	.024	.631	.083	.031	.030	.958
8. Recreation	−.000	.000	.016	.011	.685	.000	.013	.013	1.048
9. Education									
10. Miscellaneous	−.030	−.029	.019	.012	.632	−.030	.018	.015	.877
		Income flexibility ϕ^c							
11.	−.589	−.597	.068	.036	.534	−.593	.048	.050	1.040
		Constant terms α_i^c (×100)							
12. Food	−.070	−.074	.066	.055	.822	−.074	.060	.060	1.000
13. Beverages	−.148	−.146	.050	.042	.852	−.145	.045	.047	1.045
14. Clothing	−.267	−.261	.052	.041	.785	−.264	.048	.046	.965
15. Housing	.381	.372	.080	.064	.808	.373	.077	.068	.883
16. Durables	−.329	−.329	.038	.027	.729	−.330	.032	.031	.970
17. Medical care	.168	.166	.022	.021	.946	.166	.021	.022	1.030
18. Transport	.030	.036	.093	.071	.762	.037	.080	.080	.999
19. Recreation	.077	.080	.041	.032	.775	.080	.035	.036	1.037
20. Education									
21. Miscellaneous	.159	.155	.036	.030	.824	.156	.034	.033	.979
22. Mean					.725				.994

TABLE A5.3

MONTE CARLO SIMULATION RESULTS WITH S^c FOR 100 TRIALS, AUSTRALIA

Commodity	True value	S^c unknown				S^c known			
		Mean	RMSE	RMSASE	(5)/(4)	Mean	RMSE	RMSASE	(9)/(8)
(1)	(2)	(3)	(4)	(5)	(6)	(7)	(8)	(9)	(10)
Income coefficients β_i^c									
1. Food	−.139	−.141	.022	.014	.633	−.140	.017	.019	1.101
2. Beverages	−.009	−.009	.014	.008	.527	−.007	.012	.010	.872
3. Clothing	.016	.019	.027	.015	.568	.018	.023	.020	.867
4. Housing	−.005	−.009	.032	.018	.570	−.003	.023	.024	1.043
5. Durables	.052	.052	.058	.032	.557	.048	.043	.041	.958
6. Medical care	.053	.052	.031	.018	.585	.054	.025	.026	1.007
7. Transport	−.013	−.011	.050	.025	.510	−.016	.038	.035	.920
8. Recreation	.074	.075	.038	.020	.530	.074	.028	.028	.979
9. Education	.002	.003	.011	.006	.489	.003	.009	.008	.883
10. Miscellaneous	−.031	−.032	.018	.011	.586	−.032	.014	.015	1.061
Income flexibility ϕ^c									
11.	−.404	−.417	.077	.031	.404	−.405	.049	.045	.921
Constant terms α_i^c (×100)									
12. Food	.104	.109	.073	.059	.798	.106	.067	.068	1.019
13. Beverages	−.099	−.101	.044	.028	.630	−.106	.038	.033	.870
14. Clothing	−.213	−.217	.077	.053	.687	−.216	.064	.063	.978
15. Housing	.249	.254	.088	.064	.733	.241	.076	.074	.973
16. Durables	−.077	−.082	.205	.128	.621	−.064	.160	.153	.956
17. Medical care	−.111	−.107	.074	.060	.814	−.114	.065	.070	1.073
18. Transport	.177	.171	.134	.103	.767	.180	.116	.119	1.025
19. Recreation	−.057	−.056	.096	.066	.690	−.055	.080	.080	1.007
20. Education	−.028	−.030	.022	.015	.659	−.030	.018	.018	.969
21. Miscellaneous	.055	.058	.050	.038	.755	.058	.043	.044	1.036
22. Mean					.624				.977

TABLE A5.4

MONTE CARLO SIMULATION RESULTS WITH S^c FOR 100 TRIALS, GERMANY

Commodity	True value	S^c unknown				S^c known			
		Mean	RMSE	RMSASE	(5)/(4)	Mean	RMSE	RMSASE	(9)/(8)
(1)	(2)	(3)	(4)	(5)	(6)	(7)	(8)	(9)	(10)
Income coefficients β_i^c									
1. Food	−.101	−.099	.029	.021	.732	−.101	.026	.025	.973
2. Beverages									
3. Clothing	.056	.055	.017	.012	.741	.056	.015	.014	.931
4. Housing	−.131	−.133	.022	.018	.795	−.131	.021	.021	1.030
5. Durables	.049	.050	.017	.013	.770	.050	.015	.016	1.046
6. Medical care	−.009	−.010	.008	.004	.584	−.009	.006	.005	.976
7. Transport	.162	.164	.036	.023	.652	.163	.029	.028	.968
8. Recreation	−.001	−.003	.015	.009	.627	−.003	.012	.011	.903
9. Education									
10. Miscellaneous	−.024	−.024	.010	.007	.678	−.025	.008	.008	1.010
Income flexibility ϕ^c									
11.	−.627	−.640	.111	.062	.558	−.630	.083	.082	.990
Constant terms α_i^c (×100)									
12. Food	−.086	−.089	.103	.088	.848	−.082	.096	.099	1.036
13. Beverages									
14. Clothing	−.264	−.256	.057	.047	.834	−.260	.053	.053	.984
15. Housing	.451	.455	.066	.061	.915	.452	.064	.066	1.022
16. Durables	−.180	.103	.064	.055	.853	−.190	.059	.062	1.054
17. Medical care	.004	.005	.020	.016	.805	.004	.018	.018	1.004
18. Transport	−.140	−.152	.118	.098	.833	−.151	.095	.110	1.166
19. Recreation	.060	.066	.052	.037	.715	.064	.046	.042	.931
20. Education									
21. Miscellaneous	.162	.163	.031	.025	.801	.164	.025	.028	1.142
22. Mean					.749				1.010

TABLE A5.5

MONTE CARLO SIMULATION RESULTS WITH S^c FOR 100 TRIALS, BELGIUM

Commodity	True value	S^c unknown				S^c known			
		Mean	RMSE	RMSASE	(5)/(4)	Mean	RMSE	RMSASE	(9)/(8)
(1)	(2)	(3)	(4)	(5)	(6)	(7)	(8)	(9)	(10)
Income coefficients β_i^c									
1. Food	-.092	-.093	.029	.013	.448	-.092	.020	.021	1.062
2. Beverages	-.001	-.002	.021	.009	.414	.000	.014	.013	.941
3. Clothing	.042	.042	.020	.009	.467	.041	.013	.014	1.096
4. Housing	-.104	-.105	.015	.007	.430	-.105	.010	.010	.994
5. Durables	.194	.191	.040	.016	.403	.190	.025	.026	1.014
6. Medical care	-.046	-.047	.014	.006	.433	-.046	.010	.010	.971
7. Transport	-.020	-.018	.028	.016	.545	-.017	.019	.022	1.127
8. Recreation	.005	.007	.013	.007	.551	.006	.010	.010	.986
9. Education	-.002	-.002	.000	.000	.461	-.002	.000	.000	.921
10. Miscellaneous	.025	.028	.025	.012	.481	.026	.017	.017	1.051
Income flexibility ϕ^c									
11.	-.608	-.612	.074	.030	.409	-.610	.054	.050	.933
Constant terms α_i^c (×100)									
12. Food	-.103	-.100	.115	.080	.697	-.104	.085	.098	1.144
13. Beverages	-.043	-.043	.079	.045	.573	-.047	.056	.054	.971
14. Clothing	-.229	-.222	.077	.048	.624	-.219	.054	.061	1.133
15. Housing	.308	.304	.080	.067	.845	.304	.069	.071	1.020
16. Durables	-.562	-.546	.163	.106	.652	-.543	.135	.126	.935
17. Medical care	.300	.297	.055	.047	.857	.294	.051	.052	1.006
18. Transport	.227	.221	.101	.066	.655	.218	.081	.081	.998
19. Recreation	.027	.020	.045	.029	.650	.023	.035	.036	1.017
20. Education	.004	.004	.001	.001	.721	.004	.001	.001	1.079
21. Miscellaneous	.071	.066	.124	.112	.899	.069	.111	.117	1.054
23. Mean					.582				1.022

TABLE A5.6

MONTE CARLO SIMULATION RESULTS WITH S^c FOR 100 TRIALS, NETHERLANDS

Commodity	True value	S^c unknown				S^c known			
		Mean	RMSE	RMSASE	(5)/(4)	Mean	RMSE	RMSASE	(9)/(8)
(1)	(2)	(3)	(4)	(5)	(6)	(7)	(8)	(9)	(10)
Income coefficients β_i^c									
1. Food	−.138	−.143	.040	.024	.603	−.139	.031	.031	.997
2. Beverages	−.017	−.017	.011	.008	.674	−.017	.009	.010	1.016
3. Clothing	.132	.132	.034	.022	.661	.134	.028	.027	.964
4. Housing	−.046	−.046	.020	.012	.588	−.048	.015	.015	1.002
5. Durables	.058	.061	.047	.030	.644	.060	.040	.037	.909
6. Medical care	−.010	−.011	.012	.007	.600	−.011	.010	.010	1.019
7. Transport	.051	.052	.020	.012	.627	.051	.014	.015	1.119
8. Recreation	.011	.010	.013	.007	.552	.009	.009	.010	1.042
9. Education	−.016	−.017	.008	.006	.744	−.017	.006	.007	1.092
10. Miscellaneous	−.021	−.021	.022	.015	.681	−.021	.018	.018	1.020
Income flexibility ϕ^c									
11.	−.782	.782	.103	.061	.591	−.785	.078	.084	1.074
Constant terms α_i^c (×100)									
12. Food	.067	.088	.186	.136	.733	.072	.152	.163	1.072
13. Beverages	.046	.046	.067	.061	.900	.046	.059	.068	1.140
14. Clothing	−.786	−.784	.168	.135	.806	−.795	.148	.153	1.029
15. Housing	.223	.221	.096	.070	.732	.228	.080	.078	.975
16. Durables	−.157	−.169	.249	.100	.759	−.164	.213	.223	1.048
17. Medical care	.285	.284	.057	.052	.905	.286	.056	.056	1.011
18. Transport	−.045	−.046	.114	.085	.745	−.039	.095	.096	1.012
19. Recreation	.005	.006	.047	.039	.831	.010	.040	.044	1.114
20. Education	.118	.120	.031	.027	.872	.119	.027	.029	1.066
21. Miscellaneous	.245	.234	.094	.073	.779	.236	.084	.083	.991
22. Mean					.716				1.034

TABLE A5.7

MONTE CARLO SIMULATION RESULTS WITH Σ^{*c} FOR 100 TRIALS, CANADA

| Commodity | True value | Σ^{*c} unknown | | | | Σ^{*c} known | | | |
| | | Mean | RMSE | RMSASE | (5)/(4) | Mean | RMSE | RMSASE | (9)/(8) |
(1)	(2)	(3)	(4)	(5)	(6)	(7)	(8)	(9)	(10)
Income coefficients β_i^c									
1. Food	-.007	-.008	.034	.034	1.000	-.008	.034	.036	1.055
2. Beverages	-.025	-.022	.023	.021	.904	-.022	.023	.022	.953
3. Clothing	-.015	-.017	.028	.028	.983	-.017	.028	.029	1.035
4. Housing	-.183	-.183	.043	.039	.892	-.183	.043	.041	.940
5. Durables	.050	.041	.031	.032	1.025	.041	.031	.034	1.078
6. Medical care	.055	.053	.019	.019	1.015	.053	.019	.020	1.069
7. Transport	.084	.083	.038	.034	.892	.083	.038	.036	.940
8. Recreation	.051	.055	.029	.026	.884	.055	.029	.027	.930
9. Education	.001	.002	.014	.014	.952	.002	.014	.014	1.004
10. Miscellaneous	-.011	-.004	.043	.042	.967	-.004	.043	.044	1.017
Income flexibility ϕ^c									
11.	-.554	-.560	.120	.112	.928	-.560	.120	.117	.976
Constant terms α_i^c ($\times 100$)									
12. Food	-.218	-.220	.114	.117	1.029	-.220	.114	.123	1.085
13. Beverages	.046	.035	.089	.081	.908	.035	.089	.086	.957
14. Clothing	.014	.029	.116	.114	.980	.029	.116	.119	1.032
15. Housing	.581	.577	.157	.136	.868	.577	.157	.143	.915
16. Durables	-.177	-.153	.114	.119	1.041	-.153	.114	.125	1.095
17. Medical care	-.300	-.295	.073	.069	.943	-.295	.073	.072	.992
18. Transport	-.103	-.104	.141	.126	.893	-.104	.141	.133	.940
19. Recreation	-.026	-.038	.114	.103	.901	-.038	.114	.108	.948
20. Education	.047	.044	.036	.037	1.039	.044	.036	.039	1.095
21. Miscellaneous	.136	.124	.115	.114	.989	.124	.115	.120	1.042
Proportionality constant λ^{c2} ($\times 10^4$)									
22.	.978	.883	.139						
23. Mean					.954				1.005

TABLE A5.8

MONTE CARLO SIMULATION RESULTS WITH Σ^{*c} FOR 100 TRIALS, SWEDEN

Commodity	True value	Σ^{*c} unknown				Σ^{*c} known			
		Mean	RMSE	RMSASE	(5)/(4)	Mean	RMSE	RMSASE	(9)/(8)
(1)	(2)	(3)	(4)	(5)	(6)	(7)	(8)	(9)	(10)
Income coefficients β_i^c									
1. Food	-.094	-.095	.024	.023	.981	-.095	.024	.025	1.044
2. Beverages	.008	.011	.015	.014	.931	.011	.015	.015	.991
3. Clothing	.038	.040	.024	.021	.861	.040	.024	.022	.916
4. Housing	-.190	-.189	.035	.030	.866	-.189	.035	.032	.921
5. Durables	.067	.067	.022	.020	.905	.067	.022	.021	.962
6. Medical care	-.022	-.022	.005	.004	.947	-.022	.005	.005	1.008
7. Transport	.138	.135	.030	.025	.834	.135	.030	.026	.887
8. Recreation	.054	.055	.019	.019	1.016	.055	.019	.021	1.080
9. Education	-.001	-.001	.001	.001	.997	-.001	.001	.001	1.061
10. Miscellaneous	.002	-.001	.020	.019	.977	-.001	.020	.021	1.038
Income flexibility ϕ^c									
11.	-.500	-.572	.098	.082	.842	-.572	.098	.088	.895
Constant terms α_i^c ($\times 100$)									
12. Food	-.099	-.096	.065	.067	1.033	-.096	.065	.071	1.098
13. Beverages	-.073	-.077	.042	.043	1.042	-.077	.042	.046	1.108
14. Clothing	-.156	-.155	.090	.076	.839	-.155	.090	.080	.892
15. Housing	.507	.498	.071	.063	.896	.498	.071	.067	.953
16. Durables	-.142	-.140	.055	.048	.876	-.140	.055	.051	.931
17. Medical care	.067	.068	.023	.022	.975	.068	.023	.024	1.037
18. Transport	-.108	-.104	.068	.061	.895	-.104	.068	.064	.952
19. Recreation	.110	.109	.056	.055	.981	.109	.056	.058	1.043
20. Education	.004	.004	.006	.006	1.000	.004	.006	.006	1.064
21. Miscellaneous	-.110	-.108	.046	.039	.843	-.108	.046	.041	.897
Proportionality constant λ^{c2} ($\times 10^4$)									
22.	.343	.303	.058						
23. Mean					.930				.989

TABLE A5.9

MONTE CARLO SIMULATION RESULTS WITH Σ^{*c} FOR 100 TRIALS, SWITZERLAND

Commodity	True value	Σ^{*c} unknown				Σ^{*c} known			
		Mean	RMSE	RMSASE	(5)/(4)	Mean	RMSE	RMSASE	(9)/(8)
(1)	(2)	(3)	(4)	(5)	(6)	(7)	(8)	(9)	(10)
Income coefficients β_i^c									
1. Food	−.007	−.003	.025	.023	.941	−.003	.025	.025	.995
2. Beverages	.033	.034	.017	.016	.982	.034	.017	.017	1.039
3. Clothing	.055	.055	.017	.015	.900	.055	.017	.016	.952
4. Housing	−.153	−.154	.020	.019	.959	−.154	.020	.020	1.014
5. Durables	.086	.086	.018	.018	.967	.086	.018	.019	1.024
6. Medical care	−.046	−.048	.014	.013	.953	−.048	.014	.014	1.009
7. Transport	.063	.063	.024	.019	.823	.063	.024	.020	.870
8. Recreation	.001	.000	.023	.022	.924	.000	.023	.023	.978
9. Education									
10. Miscellaneous	−.033	−.033	.023	.021	.898	−.033	.023	.022	.950
Income flexibility ϕ^c									
11.	−.551	−.558	.080	.070	.880	−.558	.080	.075	.932
Constant terms α_i^c (×100)									
12. Food	−.100	−.107	.070	.067	.959	−.107	.070	.071	1.015
13. Beverages	−.122	−.122	.047	.048	1.001	−.122	.047	.050	1.060
14. Clothing	−.258	−.255	.052	.047	.917	−.255	.052	.050	.971
15. Housing	.342	.338	.060	.050	.847	.338	.060	.053	.896
16. Durables	−.327	−.330	.049	.050	1.009	−.330	.049	.052	1.068
17. Medical care	.169	.168	.031	.030	.946	.168	.031	.031	1.001
18. Transport	.063	.067	.052	.051	.977	.067	.052	.054	1.033
19. Recreation	.074	.080	.058	.056	.964	.080	.058	.060	1.021
20. Education									
21. Miscellaneous	.159	.160	.044	.042	.961	.160	.044	.045	1.017
Proportionality constant λ^{c2} (×10⁴)									
22.	.280	.250	.042						
23. Mean				.937					.992

TABLE A5.10

MONTE CARLO SIMULATION RESULTS WITH Σ^{*c} FOR 100 TRIALS, DENMARK

Commodity	True value	Σ^{*c} unknown				Σ^{*c} known			
		Mean	RMSE	RMSASE	(5)/(4)	Mean	RMSE	RMSASE	(9)/(8)
(1)	(2)	(3)	(4)	(5)	(6)	(7)	(8)	(9)	(10)
Income coefficients β_i^c									
1. Food	-.123	-.123	.032	.030	.927	-.123	.032	.032	.992
2. Beverages	-.028	-.029	.018	.017	.916	-.029	.018	.018	.981
3. Clothing	.044	.045	.015	.015	1.025	.045	.015	.016	1.098
4. Housing	-.130	-.128	.022	.022	1.032	-.128	.022	.024	1.105
5. Durables	.053	.055	.017	.015	.908	.055	.017	.017	.972
6. Medical care	-.010	-.010	.007	.007	.952	-.010	.007	.008	1.020
7. Transport	.188	.189	.024	.021	.877	.189	.024	.022	.939
8. Recreation	.019	.015	.017	.016	.985	.015	.017	.019	1.055
9. Education	-.009	-.009	.006	.005	.860	-.009	.006	.005	.921
10. Miscellaneous	-.005	-.005	.018	.017	.943	-.005	.018	.018	1.010
Income flexibility ϕ^c									
11.	.165	-.478	.089	.077	.869	-.478	.089	.083	.930
Constant terms α_i^c (×100)									
12. Food	-.065	-.063	.081	.075	.920	-.063	.081	.080	.985
13. Beverages	-.010	-.011	.061	.060	.977	-.011	.061	.064	1.046
14. Clothing	-.228	-.228	.056	.055	.986	-.228	.056	.059	1.056
15. Housing	.649	.641	.075	.068	.906	.641	.075	.073	.970
16. Durables	-.286	-.285	.058	.051	.884	-.285	.058	.055	.947
17. Medical care	.017	.015	.024	.024	.996	.015	.024	.025	1.067
18. Transport	-.209	-.210	.068	.066	.968	-.210	.068	.071	1.037
19. Recreation	.084	.090	.051	.053	1.034	.090	.051	.057	1.107
20. Education	.070	.069	.015	.015	1.027	.069	.015	.016	1.100
21. Miscellaneous	-.022	-.018	.058	.050	.859	-.018	.058	.054	.920
Proportionality constant λ^{c2} (×10⁴)									
22.	.444	.387	.076						
23. Mean					.945				1.012

TABLE A5.11

MONTE CARLO SIMULATION RESULTS WITH Σ^{*c} FOR 100 TRIALS, AUSTRALIA

Commodity	True value	Σ^{*c} unknown				Σ^{*c} known			
		Mean	RMSE	RMSASE	(5)/(4)	Mean	RMSE	RMSASE	(9)/(8)
(1)	(2)	(3)	(4)	(5)	(6)	(7)	(8)	(9)	(10)
Income coefficients β_i^c									
1. Food	-.144	-.141	.033	.035	1.045	-.141	.033	.036	1.102
2. Beverages	-.015	-.011	.027	.024	.895	-.011	.027	.025	.943
3. Clothing	.027	.026	.034	.028	.834	.026	.034	.030	.880
4. Housing	-.059	-.058	.034	.031	.916	-.058	.034	.033	.966
5. Durables	.100	.097	.032	.029	.919	.097	.032	.031	.969
6. Medical care	-.018	-.018	.024	.023	.972	-.018	.024	.024	1.025
7. Transport	.075	.071	.039	.037	.962	.071	.039	.040	1.014
8. Recreation	.072	.072	.026	.023	.878	.072	.026	.024	.925
9. Education	.013	.014	.012	.011	.878	.014	.012	.011	.926
10. Miscellaneous	-.050	-.051	.025	.025	1.002	-.051	.025	.027	1.057
Income flexibility ϕ^c									
11.	-.463	-.471	.080	.071	.883	-.471	.080	.075	.932
Constant terms α_i^c (×100)									
12. Food	.122	.116	.108	.106	.979	.116	.108	.112	1.032
13. Beverages	-.074	-.085	.079	.070	.885	-.085	.079	.074	.933
14. Clothing	-.227	-.219	.088	.082	.930	-.219	.088	.087	.981
15. Housing	.377	.373	.098	.083	.843	.373	.098	.088	.889
16. Durables	-.234	-.229	.111	.104	.943	-.229	.111	.110	.994
17. Medical care	.017	.015	.047	.051	1.068	.015	.047	.053	1.126
18. Transport	-.015	-.009	.105	.105	1.002	-.009	.105	.111	1.057
19. Recreation	-.031	-.030	.070	.062	.891	-.030	.070	.065	.939
20. Education	-.041	-.042	.022	.021	.955	-.042	.022	.022	1.007
21. Miscellaneous	.106	.109	.070	.068	.966	.109	.070	.072	1.018
Proportionality constant λ^{c2} (×10⁴)									
22.	.569	.513	.081						
23. Mean					.936				.986

TABLE A5.12

MONTE CARLO SIMULATION RESULTS WITH Σ^{*c} FOR 100 TRIALS, FRANCE

Commodity	True value	Σ^{*c} unknown				Σ^{*c} known			
		Mean	RMSE	RMSASE	(5)/(4)	Mean	RMSE	RMSASE	(9)/(8)
(1)	(2)	(3)	(4)	(5)	(6)	(7)	(8)	(9)	(10)
Income coefficients β_i^c									
1. Food	−.115	−.118	.036	.032	.898	−.118	.036	.034	.955
2. Beverages	−.024	−.022	.015	.014	.925	−.022	.015	.014	.982
3. Clothing	.024	.021	.024	.021	.888	.021	.024	.023	.945
4. Housing	−.081	−.077	.025	.023	.924	−.077	.025	.024	.982
5. Durables	.059	.057	.021	.021	1.000	.057	.021	.022	1.064
6. Medical care	−.047	−.047	.034	.031	.904	−.047	.034	.033	.963
7. Transport	.146	.146	.028	.024	.849	.146	.028	.025	.904
8. Recreation	.001	.003	.020	.020	.904	.003	.020	.021	1.026
9. Education	−.001	−.001	.004	.003	.772	−.001	.004	.003	.820
10. Miscellaneous	.039	.038	.023	.022	.970	.038	.023	.024	1.032
Income flexibility ϕ^c									
11.	−.527	−.521	.083	.070	.848	−.521	.083	.075	.904
Constant terms α_i^c (×100)									
12. Food	−.011	.000	.135	.125	.926	.000	.135	.133	.985
13. Beverages	−.027	−.036	.064	.059	.924	−.036	.064	.063	.983
14. Clothing	−.280	−.264	.097	.088	.908	−.264	.097	.094	.967
15. Housing	.510	.491	.087	.076	.881	.491	.087	.081	.936
16. Durables	−.299	−.291	.084	.087	1.036	−.291	.084	.093	1.102
17. Medical care	.475	.476	.138	.122	.883	.476	.138	.130	.911
18. Transport	−.311	−.315	.108	.091	.841	−.315	.108	.097	.895
19. Recreation	.060	.055	.091	.087	.956	.055	.091	.092	1.018
20. Education	.001	.000	.012	.010	.840	.000	.012	.011	.891
21. Miscellaneous	−.118	−.117	.088	.082	.935	−.117	.088	.087	.994
Proportionality constant λ^{c2} (×10⁴)									
22.	.184	.162	.031						
23. Mean					.908				.966

TABLE A5.13

MONTE CARLO SIMULATION RESULTS WITH Σ^{*c} FOR 100 TRIALS, GERMANY

Commodity	True value	Σ^{*c} unknown				Σ^{*c} known			
		Mean	RMSE	RMSASE	(5)/(4)	Mean	RMSE	RMSASE	(9)/(8)
(1)	(2)	(3)	(4)	(5)	(6)	(7)	(8)	(9)	(10)
Income coefficients β_i^c									
1. Food	-.113	-.111	.031	.030	.941	-.111	.031	.031	.987
2. Beverages									
3. Clothing	.052	.052	.022	.019	.888	.052	.022	.020	.932
4. Housing	-.133	-.134	.020	.019	.945	-.134	.020	.020	.991
5. Durables	.053	.054	.020	.019	.971	.054	.020	.020	1.019
6. Medical care	-.005	-.004	.010	.009	.960	-.004	.010	.010	1.006
7. Transport	.171	.172	.021	.020	.970	.172	.021	.021	1.018
8. Recreation	.000	-.002	.018	.016	.922	-.002	.018	.017	.967
9. Education									
10. Miscellaneous	-.025	-.026	.015	.016	1.048	-.026	.015	.016	1.099
Income flexibility ϕ^c									
11.	-.602	-.605	.093	.095	1.018	-.605	.093	.099	1.069
Constant terms α_i^c ($\times 100$)									
12. Food	-.043	-.045	.114	.114	1.000	-.045	.114	.120	1.049
13. Beverages									
14. Clothing	-.251	-.248	.075	.071	.945	-.248	.075	.074	.991
15. Housing	.455	.459	.058	.058	.987	.459	.058	.060	1.035
16. Durables	-.200	-.206	.079	.077	.966	-.206	.079	.080	1.014
17. Medical care	-.007	-.008	.026	.027	1.047	-.008	.026	.028	1.098
18. Transport	-.172	-.178	.071	.077	1.080	-.178	.071	.081	1.132
19. Recreation	.055	.058	.068	.060	.878	.058	.068	.062	.921
20. Education									
21. Miscellaneous	.161	.168	.048	.053	1.102	.168	.048	.055	1.156
Proportionality constant λ^{c2} ($\times 10^4$)									
22.	.292	.266	.041						
23. Mean					.980				1.028

TABLE A5.14

MONTE CARLO SIMULATION RESULTS WITH Σ^{*c} FOR 100 TRIALS, BELGIUM

Commodity	True value	Σ^{*c} unknown				Σ^{*c} known			
		Mean	RMSE	RMSASE	(5)/(4)	Mean	RMSE	RMSASE	(9)/(8)
(1)	(2)	(3)	(4)	(5)	(6)	(7)	(8)	(9)	(10)
Income coefficients β_i^c									
1. Food	−.119	−.119	.045	.042	.932	−.119	.045	.044	.980
2. Beverages	−.001	.002	.027	.024	.879	.002	.027	.025	.924
3. Clothing	.011	.009	.025	.027	1.048	.009	.025	.028	1.102
4. Housing	−.066	−.068	.032	.031	.997	−.068	.032	.033	1.047
5. Durables	.070	.056	.041	.037	.897	.056	.041	.039	.943
6. Medical care	−.028	−.026	.023	.024	1.013	−.026	.023	.025	1.065
7. Transport	−.012	−.008	.028	.029	1.034	−.008	.028	.030	1.087
8. Recreation	−.002	.002	.021	.020	.950	.002	.021	.021	1.000
9. Education	−.002	−.002	.004	.004	.998	−.002	.004	.004	1.049
10. Miscellaneous	.150	.155	.035	.038	1.094	.155	.035	.040	1.149
Income flexibility ϕ^c									
11.	−.127	−.129	.064	.064	1.008	−.129	.064	.067	1.061
Constant terms α_i^c (×100)									
12. Food	−.008	−.008	.148	.153	1.034	−.008	.148	.161	1.087
13. Beverages	−.036	−.046	.098	.087	.887	−.046	.098	.092	.932
14. Clothing	−.073	−.061	.097	.100	1.027	−.061	.097	.105	1.080
15. Housing	.164	.169	.122	.115	.943	.169	.122	.121	.991
16. Durables	−.087	−.044	.150	.137	.915	−.044	.150	.145	.962
17. Medical care	.238	.230	.085	.083	.978	.230	.085	.088	1.028
18. Transport	.179	.166	.102	.104	1.026	.166	.102	.110	1.079
19. Recreation	.045	.031	.074	.070	.945	.031	.074	.074	.994
20. Education	.004	.003	.016	.016	1.024	.003	.016	.017	1.077
21. Miscellaneous	−.426	−.441	.139	.145	1.038	−.441	.139	.152	1.091
Proportionality constant λ^{c2} (×10⁴)									
22.	.671	.607	.094						
23. Mean					.984				1.035

TABLE A5.15

MONTE CARLO SIMULATION RESULTS WITH Σ^{*c} FOR 100 TRIALS, NORWAY

Commodity	True value	Σ^{*c} unknown				Σ^{*c} known			
		Mean	RMSE	RMSASE	(5)/(4)	Mean	RMSE	RMSASE	(9)/(8)
(1)	(2)	(3)	(4)	(5)	(6)	(7)	(8)	(9)	(10)
Income coefficients β_i^c									
1. Food	-.180	-.183	.029	.027	.919	-.183	.029	.028	.975
2. Beverages	.010	.011	.017	.014	.861	.011	.017	.015	.915
3. Clothing	.021	.020	.021	.020	.916	.020	.021	.021	.972
4. Housing	-.145	-.145	.024	.022	.927	-.145	.024	.024	.985
5. Durables	.026	.026	.019	.019	.955	.026	.019	.020	1.015
6. Medical care	-.009	-.010	.013	.013	1.007	-.010	.013	.014	1.070
7. Transport	.293	.291	.025	.023	.933	.291	.025	.024	.991
8. Recreation	.002	.005	.020	.020	1.015	.005	.020	.022	1.078
9. Education	-.003	-.002	.006	.006	.914	-.002	.006	.006	.970
10. Miscellaneous	-.016	-.013	.022	.020	.936	-.013	.022	.021	.994
Income flexibility ϕ^c									
11.	-.485	-.496	.083	.082	.989	-.496	.083	.087	1.050
Constant terms α_i^c ($\times 100$)									
12. Food	.160	.169	.102	.096	.945	.169	.102	.102	1.003
13. Beverages	-.073	-.076	.061	.055	.900	-.076	.061	.059	.956
14. Clothing	-.204	-.196	.080	.071	.888	-.196	.080	.075	.943
15. Housing	.502	.495	.084	.078	.935	.495	.084	.083	.992
16. Durables	-.026	-.027	.067	.066	.981	-.027	.067	.070	1.042
17. Medical care	.018	.021	.037	.041	1.094	.021	.037	.044	1.161
18. Transport	-.550	-.545	.081	.080	.997	-.545	.081	.085	1.059
19. Recreation	.148	.139	.086	.083	.964	.139	.086	.088	1.024
20. Education	.000	-.001	.018	.017	.934	-.001	.018	.018	.992
21. Miscellaneous	.024	.020	.069	.064	.931	.020	.069	.068	.989
Proportionality constant λ^{c2} ($\times 10^4$)									
22.	.413	.367	.070						
23. Mean					.950				1.008

TABLE A5.16

MONTE CARLO SIMULATION RESULTS WITH Σ^{*c} FOR 100 TRIALS, NETHERLANDS

Commodity	True value	Σ^{*c} unknown				Σ^{*c} known			
		Mean	RMSE	RMSASE	(5)/(4)	Mean	RMSE	RMSASE	(9)/(8)
(1)	(2)	(3)	(4)	(5)	(6)	(7)	(8)	(9)	(10)
Income coefficients β_i^c									
1. Food	−.132	−.137	.043	.038	.884	−.137	.043	.040	.924
2. Beverages	−.024	−.024	.014	.012	.877	−.024	.014	.013	.917
3. Clothing	.157	.161	.029	.028	.968	.161	.029	.029	1.012
4. Housing	−.046	−.048	.020	.018	.897	−.048	.020	.019	.938
5. Durables	.051	.052	.031	.028	.887	.052	.031	.029	.927
6. Medical care	−.027	−.026	.013	.014	1.064	−.026	.013	.014	1.113
7. Transport	.051	.052	.016	.015	.976	.052	.016	.016	1.020
8. Recreation	−.002	−.003	.016	.016	1.003	−.003	.016	.017	1.049
9. Education	−.006	−.008	.012	.012	1.004	−.008	.012	.012	1.050
10 Miscellaneous	−.023	−.018	.025	.024	.928	−.018	.025	.025	.970
Income flexibility ϕ^c									
11.	−.842	−.840	.104	.101	.907	−.840	.104	.106	1.011
Constant terms α_i^c (×100)									
12. Food	.049	.069	.198	.188	.952	.069	.198	.197	.995
13. Beverages	.085	.084	.085	.078	.926	.084	.085	.082	.968
14. Clothing	−.896	−.913	.141	.142	1.005	−.913	.141	.148	1.050
15. Housing	.228	.230	.095	.087	.916	.236	.095	.091	.958
16. Durables	−.129	−.128	.160	.165	1.033	−.129	.160	.173	1.079
17. Medical care	.316	.316	.052	.055	1.067	.316	.052	.058	1.116
18. Transport	−.045	−.044	.090	.085	.952	−.044	.090	.089	.995
19. Recreation	.046	.050	.064	.059	.924	.050	.064	.062	.967
20. Education	.095	.100	.046	.046	1.011	.100	.046	.048	1.057
21. Miscellaneous	.250	.229	.112	.101	.900	.229	.112	.106	.941
Proportionality constant λ^{c2} (×10⁴)									
22.	1.068	.977	.134						
23 Mean					.959				1.003

TABLE A5.17

MONTE CARLO SIMULATION RESULTS WITH Σ^{*c} FOR 100 TRIALS, ICELAND

Commodity	True value	Σ^{*c} unknown				Σ^{*c} known			
		Mean	RMSE	RMSASE	(5)/(4)	Mean	RMSE	RMSASE	(9)/(8)
(1)	(2)	(3)	(4)	(5)	(6)	(7)	(8)	(9)	(10)
Income coefficients β_i^c									
1. Food	−.129	−.128	.022	.022	1.017	−.128	.022	.024	1.106
2. Beverages	−.020	−.019	.018	.015	.838	−.019	.018	.016	.911
3. Clothing	.037	.036	.019	.016	.853	.036	.019	.018	.927
4. Housing	−.198	−.197	.027	.020	.736	−.197	.027	.022	.800
5. Durables	.089	.090	.018	.016	.880	.090	.018	.018	.957
6. Medical care	−.015	−.015	.018	.016	.884	−.015	.018	.017	.961
7. Transport	.181	.179	.022	.018	.846	.179	.022	.020	.919
8. Recreation	.023	.022	.019	.015	.815	.022	.019	.017	.886
9. Education	−.004	−.003	.006	.005	.796	−.003	.006	.005	.866
10. Miscellaneous	.036	.036	.014	.013	.964	.036	.014	.014	1.048
Income flexibility ϕ^c									
11.	−.695	−.711	.091	.080	.881	−.711	.091	.087	.958
Constant terms α_i^c (×100)									
12. Food	.033	.047	.176	.172	.973	.047	.176	.187	1.058
13. Beverages	.106	.095	.126	.122	.972	.095	.126	.133	1.057
14. Clothing	−.262	−.248	.192	.146	.764	−.248	.192	.159	.831
15. Housing	.536	.511	.197	.170	.861	.511	.197	.185	.936
16. Durables	−.272	−.273	.146	.140	.955	−.273	.146	.152	1.038
17. Medical care	.289	.290	.102	.099	.974	.290	.102	.108	1.059
18. Transport	−.472	−.465	.162	.147	.909	−.465	.162	.160	.988
19. Recreation	.015	.018	.115	.102	.885	.018	.115	.111	.963
20. Education	.020	.012	.035	.031	.894	.012	.035	.034	.971
21. Miscellaneous	.006	.013	.114	.101	.882	.013	.114	.110	.959
Proportionality constant λ^{c2} (×10⁴)									
22.	1.966	1.663	.372						
23. Mean					.885				.962

TABLE A5.18

MONTE CARLO SIMULATION RESULTS WITH Σ^{*c} FOR 100 TRIALS, FINLAND

Commodity	True value	Σ^{*c} unknown				Σ^{*c} known			
		Mean	RMSE	RMSASE	(5)/(4)	Mean	RMSE	RMSASE	(9)/(8)
(1)	(2)	(3)	(4)	(5)	(6)	(7)	(8)	(9)	(10)
Income coefficients β_i^c									
1. Food	−.126	−.124	.037	.035	.952	−.124	.037	.037	1.012
2. Beverages	.024	.022	.027	.023	.864	.022	.027	.025	.918
3. Clothing	.055	.058	.027	.025	.938	.058	.027	.027	.997
4. Housing	−.122	−.124	.034	.030	.896	−.124	.034	.032	.952
5. Durables	.042	.045	.024	.022	.904	.045	.024	.023	.960
6. Medical care	−.009	−.011	.016	.014	.880	−.011	.016	.015	.935
7. Transport	.109	.105	.027	.027	.996	.105	.027	.029	1.059
8. Recreation	.053	.056	.019	.020	1.040	.056	.019	.021	1.105
9. Education	.002	.002	.011	.010	.853	.002	.011	.010	.907
10. Miscellaneous	−.028	−.029	.024	.026	1.069	−.029	.024	.027	1.136
Income flexibility ϕ^c									
11.	−.378	−.391	.089	.075	.847	−.391	.089	.080	.901
Constant terms α_i^c (×100)									
12. Food	−.065	−.071	.171	.172	1.005	−.071	.171	.183	1.068
13. Beverages	−.008	−.001	.127	.117	.920	−.001	.127	.124	.978
14. Clothing	−.441	−.446	.142	.127	.891	−.446	.142	.135	.947
15. Housing	.419	.415	.164	.158	.963	.415	.164	.168	1.024
16. Durables	−.077	−.087	.124	.112	.902	−.087	.124	.119	.959
17. Medical care	.095	.101	.073	.073	.998	.101	.073	.077	1.060
18. Transport	−.075	−.057	.135	.138	1.021	−.057	.135	.147	1.085
19. Recreation	−.090	−.102	.098	.102	1.044	−.102	.098	.109	1.109
20. Education	−.058	−.059	.048	.042	.881	−.059	.048	.045	.936
21. Miscellaneous	.300	.307	.114	.116	1.021	.307	.114	.123	1.085
Proportionality constant λ^{c2} (×10⁴)									
22.	1.302	1.153	.221						
23. Mean					.947				1.006

TABLE A5.19

MONTE CARLO SIMULATION RESULTS WITH Σ^{*c} FOR 100 TRIALS, AUSTRIA

Commodity	True value	Σ^{*c} unknown				Σ^{*c} known			
		Mean	RMSE	RMSASE	(5)/(4)	Mean	RMSE	RMSASE	(9)/(8)
(1)	(2)	(3)	(4)	(5)	(6)	(7)	(8)	(9)	(10)
Income coefficients β_i^c									
1. Food	-.175	-.172	.039	.038	.979	-.172	.039	.041	1.040
2. Beverages	-.036	-.038	.025	.022	.870	-.038	.025	.023	.922
3. Clothing	.090	.086	.030	.029	.958	.086	.030	.031	1.017
4. Housing	-.099	-.095	.031	.028	.906	-.095	.031	.030	.962
5. Durables	.085	.077	.030	.027	.891	.077	.030	.028	.946
6. Medical care	-.060	-.057	.016	.017	1.103	-.057	.016	.018	1.171
7. Transport	.282	.278	.035	.032	.913	.278	.035	.034	.970
8. Recreation	-.011	-.009	.020	.020	1.001	-.009	.020	.021	1.063
9. Education	-.005	-.005	.005	.004	.861	-.005	.005	.005	.913
10. Miscellaneous	-.071	-.066	.036	.034	.929	-.066	.036	.036	.986
Income flexibility ϕ^c									
11.	-.154	-.146	.103	.083	.807	-.146	.103	.088	.857
Constant terms α_i^c ($\times100$)									
12. Food	.247	.238	.159	.145	.912	.238	.159	.154	.968
13. Beverages	.042	.048	.095	.088	.928	.048	.095	.093	.985
14. Clothing	-.222	-.200	.122	.117	.955	-.200	.122	.124	1.014
15. Housing	.458	.437	.119	.099	.837	.437	.119	.105	.888
16. Durables	-.270	-.243	.114	.107	.941	-.243	.114	.114	.999
17. Medical care	.158	.151	.052	.056	1.064	.151	.052	.059	1.129
18. Transport	-.569	-.562	.154	.135	.877	-.562	.154	.143	.931
19. Recreation	.092	.085	.080	.078	.965	.085	.080	.082	1.024
20. Education	.010	.009	.021	.018	.820	.009	.021	.019	.869
21. Miscellaneous	.053	.037	.127	.119	.936	.037	.127	.126	.993
Proportionality constant λ^{c2} ($\times10^4$)									
22.	.524	.465	.087						
23. Mean					.926				.983

TABLE A5.20

MONTE CARLO SIMULATION RESULTS WITH Σ^{*c} FOR 100 TRIALS, JAPAN

Commodity	True value	Σ^{*c} unknown				Σ^{*c} known			
		Mean	RMSE	RMSASE	(5)/(4)	Mean	RMSE	RMSASE	(9)/(8)
(1)	(2)	(3)	(4)	(5)	(6)	(7)	(8)	(9)	(10)
Income coefficients β_i^c									
1. Food	−.105	−.104	.043	.034	.803	−.104	.043	.038	.897
2. Beverages									
3. Clothing	.069	.066	.031	.027	.887	.066	.031	.031	.991
4. Housing	−.130	−.134	.036	.034	.930	−.134	.036	.038	1.039
5. Durables	.073	.071	.022	.019	.877	.071	.022	.022	.981
6. Medical care	−.020	−.015	.026	.021	.813	−.015	.026	.023	.909
7. Transport	.031	.032	.026	.023	.870	.032	.026	.026	.972
8. Recreation	.013	.009	.025	.023	.947	.009	.025	.026	1.058
9. Education									
10. Miscellaneous	.070	.074	.030	.031	1.029	.074	.030	.035	1.150
Income flexibility ϕ^c									
11.	−.370	−.389	.108	.099	.021	−.389	.108	.099	.916
Constant terms α_i^c (×100)									
12. Food	−.140	−.130	.191	.155	.812	−.130	.191	.173	.907
13. Beverages									
14. Clothing	−.335	−.331	.126	.107	.851	−.331	.126	.120	.951
15. Housing	.711	.725	.162	.142	.878	.725	.162	.159	.980
16. Durables	−.403	−.402	.099	.088	.898	−.402	.099	.099	1.003
17. Medical care	.309	.288	.110	.097	.883	.288	.110	.108	.986
18. Transport	.015	.013	.113	.096	.854	.013	.113	.108	.953
19. Recreation	−.052	−.047	.113	.104	.926	−.047	.113	.117	1.034
20. Education									
21. Miscellaneous	−.106	−.115	.140	.122	.874	−.115	.140	.136	.976
Proportionality constant λ^{c2} (×10^4)									
22.	.795	.637	.190						
23. Mean					.880				.983

TABLE A5.21

MONTE CARLO SIMULATION RESULTS WITH Σ^{*c} FOR 100 TRIALS, U.K.

Commodity	True value	Σ^{*c} unknown				Σ^{*c} known			
		Mean	RMSE	RMSASE	(5)/(4)	Mean	RMSE	RMSASE	(9)/(8)
(1)	(2)	(3)	(4)	(5)	(6)	(7)	(8)	(9)	(10)
Income coefficients β_i^c									
1. Food	−.127	−.125	.029	.025	.863	−.125	.029	.027	.916
2. Beverages	.002	.003	.011	.010	.971	.003	.011	.011	1.029
3. Clothing	.017	.013	.020	.019	.974	.013	.020	.020	1.034
4. Housing	−.118	−.113	.022	.022	.968	−.113	.022	.023	1.027
5. Durables	.088	.084	.019	.017	.937	.084	.019	.018	.995
6. Medical care	−.003	−.003	.005	.005	.913	−.003	.005	.005	.969
7. Transport	.087	.085	.023	.019	.840	.085	.023	.020	.892
8. Recreation	.027	.027	.017	.017	.987	.027	.017	.018	1.048
9. Education	.000	.002	.009	.009	1.001	.002	.009	.009	1.063
10. Miscellaneous	.027	.027	.021	.022	1.035	.027	.021	.023	1.099
Income flexibility ϕ^c									
11.	−.396	−.405	.075	.066	.890	−.405	.075	.071	.946
Constant terms α_i^c (×100)									
12. Food	−.090	−.093	.076	.069	.906	−.093	.076	.074	.962
13. Beverages	−.046	−.050	.032	.037	1.145	−.050	.032	.039	1.215
14. Clothing	−.066	−.055	.065	.064	.993	−.055	.065	.068	1.055
15. Housing	.280	.268	.061	.055	.899	.268	.061	.058	.954
16. Durables	−.216	−.208	.057	.050	.871	−.208	.057	.053	.925
17. Medical care	−.002	−.003	.017	.014	.870	−.003	.017	.015	.924
18. Transport	.055	.057	.062	.055	.885	.057	.062	.059	.940
19. Recreation	.080	.078	.052	.048	.911	.078	.052	.050	.968
20. Education	.015	.011	.020	.021	1.031	.011	.020	.022	1.095
21. Miscellaneous	−.010	−.008	.067	.059	.885	−.008	.067	.063	.940
Proportionality constant λ^{c2} (×10⁴)									
22.	.306	.271	.051						
23. Mean					.942				1.000

TABLE A2.22

MONTE CARLO SIMULATION RESULTS WITH Σ^{*c} FOR 100 TRIALS, SPAIN

Commodity	True value	Σ^{*c} unknown				Σ^{*c} known			
		Mean	RMSE	RMSASE	(5)/(4)	Mean	RMSE	RMSASE	(9)/(8)
(1)	(2)	(3)	(4)	(5)	(6)	(7)	(8)	(9)	(10)
Income coefficients β_i^c									
1. Food	-.049	-.048	.066	.055	.835	-.048	.066	.060	.908
2. Beverages	-.003	-.005	.027	.021	.778	-.005	.027	.023	.846
3. Clothing	.031	.027	.036	.033	.915	.027	.036	.036	.994
4. Housing	-.114	-.110	.048	.041	.868	-.110	.048	.045	.943
5. Durables	.039	.037	.032	.027	.860	.037	.032	.030	.935
6. Medical care	-.002	-.001	.030	.022	.748	-.001	.030	.024	.813
7. Transport	.130	.129	.033	.029	.891	.129	.033	.032	.969
8. Recreation	.015	.014	.022	.018	.808	.014	.022	.020	.878
9. Education	-.012	-.011	.012	.011	.917	-.011	.012	.012	.997
10. Miscellaneous	-.034	-.031	.024	.025	1.043	-.031	.024	.028	1.134
Income flexibility ϕ^c									
11.	-.291	-.298	.078	.066	.836	-.298	.078	.071	.907
Constant terms α_i^c ($\times 100$)									
12. Food	-.349	-.347	.307	.262	.856	-.347	.307	.285	.930
13. Beverages	-.016	-.007	.144	.113	.785	-.007	.144	.123	.853
14. Clothing	-.235	-.214	.153	.146	.949	-.214	.153	.158	1.032
15. Housing	.406	.378	.239	.209	.875	.378	.239	.227	.951
16. Durables	-.216	-.205	.149	.125	.839	-.205	.149	.136	.911
17. Medical care	.220	.213	.122	.096	.786	.213	.122	.104	.855
18. Transport	-.155	-.154	.149	.143	.959	-.154	.149	.155	1.043
19. Recreation	.009	.015	.092	.078	.851	.015	.092	.085	.925
20. Education	.054	.047	.052	.047	.903	.047	.052	.051	.982
21. Miscellaneous	.282	.275	.113	.118	1.038	.275	.113	.128	1.128
Proportionality constant λ^{c2} ($\times 10^4$)									
22.	.499	.423	.094						
23. Mean					.873				.949

TABLE A5.23

MONTE CARLO SIMULATION RESULTS WITH Σ^{*c} FOR 100 TRIALS, ITALY

Commodity	True value	Σ^{*c} unknown				Σ^{*c} known			
		Mean	RMSE	RMSASE	(5)/(4)	Mean	RMSE	RMSASE	(9)/(8)
(1)	(2)	(3)	(4)	(5)	(6)	(7)	(8)	(9)	(10)
Income coefficients β_i^c									
1. Food	−.044	−.042	.031	.028	.905	−.042	.031	.029	.961
2. Beverages	−.017	−.016	.019	.015	.815	−.016	.019	.016	.865
3. Clothing	.077	.073	.017	.017	1.014	.073	.017	.018	1.077
4. Housing	−.067	−.063	.027	.022	.810	−.063	.027	.023	.861
5. Durables	.036	.034	.015	.014	.958	.034	.015	.015	1.016
6. Medical care	.001	.001	.011	.011	.972	.001	.011	.012	1.032
7. Transport	.044	.044	.018	.018	.979	.044	.018	.019	1.039
8. Recreation	−.024	−.024	.014	.015	1.039	−.024	.014	.016	1.103
9. Education	−.002	−.002	.004	.004	.913	−.002	.004	.004	.969
10. Miscellaneous	−.006	−.005	.019	.019	1.016	−.005	.019	.021	1.079
Income flexibility ϕ^c									
11.	−.184	−.183	.069	.069	1.002	−.183	.069	.073	1.064
Constant terms α_i^c ($\times 100$)									
12. Food	−.225	−.230	.126	.114	.907	−.230	.126	.121	.963
13. Beverages	.023	.019	.081	.068	.845	.019	.081	.072	.897
14. Clothing	−.301	−.285	.068	.069	1.007	−.285	.068	.073	1.069
15. Housing	.161	.145	.102	.084	.818	.145	.102	.089	.869
16. Durables	−.083	−.076	.057	.058	1.011	−.076	.057	.062	1.073
17. Medical care	.114	.115	.047	.047	.994	.115	.047	.050	1.055
18. Transport	.109	.109	.070	.071	1.021	.109	.070	.076	1.085
19. Recreation	.114	.116	.063	.062	.995	.116	.063	.066	1.057
20. Education	−.002	−.002	.017	.016	.935	−.002	.017	.017	.993
21. Miscellaneous	.090	.089	.079	.076	.967	.089	.079	.081	1.027
Proportionality constant λ^{c2} ($\times 10^4$)									
22.	.344	.305	.057						
23. Mean					.949				1.007

REFERENCES

Barten, A.P. (1977). 'The Systems of Consumer Demand Functions Approach: A Review,' _Econometrica_ 45: 23-51.

Bera, A.K., R.P. Byron and C.M. Jarque (1981). 'Further Evidence on Asymptotic Tests for Homogeneity and Symmetry in Large Demand Systems,' _Economics Letters_ 8: 101-5.

Bewley, R.A. (1983). 'Tests of Restrictions in Large Demand Systems,' _European Economic Review_ 20: 257-69.

——————— (1986). _Allocation Models: Specification, Estimation and Applications_. Cambridge, Mass.: Ballinger Publishing Company.

Byron, R.P. (1970). 'The Restricted Aitken Estimation of Sets of Demand Equations,' _Econometrica_ 38: 816-30.

Deaton, A.S. (1972). 'The Estimation and Testing of Systems of Demand Equations: A Note,' _European Economic Review_ 3: 399-411.

Laitinen, K. (1978). 'Why is Demand Homogeneity So Often Rejected?' _Economics Letters_ 1: 187-91.

Meisner, J.F. (1979). 'The Sad Fate of the Asymptotic Slutsky Symmetry Test for Large Systems,' _Economics Letters_ 2: 231-33.

Selvanathan, E.A. (1987). _Explorations in Consumer Demand_. Ph.D. Thesis, Murdoch University, Western Australia.

Theil, H. (1987).   'The Econometrics of Demand Systems,' Chapter 3 in H. Theil and K.W. Clements, _Applied Demand Analysis: Results from System-wide Approaches_. Cambridge, Mass.: Ballinger Publishing Company, pp.101-62.

Working, H. (1943).   'Statistical Laws of Family Expenditure,' _Journal of the American Statistical Association_ 38: 43-56.

CHAPTER 6

FURTHER EVIDENCE ON THE FRISCH CONJECTURE

6.1 INTRODUCTION

Frisch's (1959) famous conjecture states that the income elasticity of the marginal utility of income decreases in absolute value as the consumer (or country) becomes more affluent. Frisch (1959, p.189) provides some numerical conjectures for the dependence of the elasticity (which he calls the 'money flexibility') on the level of real income, which we quote below:

"We may, perhaps, assume that in most cases the money flexibility
has values of the order of magnitude given below.

-10   for an extremely poor and apathetic part of the population.

-4   for the slightly better off but still poor part of the population with a fairly pronounced desire to become better off.

-2   for the middle income bracket, 'the median part' of the population.

-.7   for the better off part of the population.

-.1   for the rich part of the population with ambitions towards 'conspicuous consumption.'

It would be a very promising research project to determine the money flexibility for different countries and for different types of populations. A universal 'atlas' should be constructed. It would serve an extremely useful purpose in demand analysis."

In this chapter we verify whether or not Frisch's conjecture is supported by data from 18 OECD countries. In Chapters 3 and 4 we estimated demand equations which treated the money flexibility as a constant. As Frisch's argument is that this is not constant, the analysis in this chapter can be considered a type of diagnostic test of our previous demand equations.

6.2 ESTIMATING THE INCOME FLEXIBILITY

We estimate the money flexibility in reciprocal form which we call the 'income flexibility', denoted by ϕ. We start with the absolute price version of the Rotterdam model (see Section 1.8). In this model, the demand equation for commodity i in period t is

$$\overline{w}_{it}Dq_{it} \ = \ \theta_i DQ_t + \sum_{j=1}^{n} \pi_{ij}Dp_{jt} + \varepsilon_{it}, \qquad (2.1)$$

where ε_{it} is a disturbance term and all other notation is as before.

Under preference independence the Slutsky coefficients in (2.1) take the form (Clements, 1987)

$$\pi_{ij} \ = \ \phi\theta_i(\delta_{ij} - \theta_j), \qquad i,j=1,...,n, \qquad (2.2)$$

where δ_{ij} is the Kronecker delta. Substituting (2.2) in (2.1) we obtain

$$\bar{w}_{it} Dq_{it} = \theta_i DQ_t + \phi \theta_i [Dp_{it} - DP'_t] + \varepsilon_{it},\qquad (2.3)$$

where $DP'_t = \Sigma^n_{i=1}\ \theta_i Dp_{it}$ is the Frisch price index. This equation makes clear the importance of the value of ϕ in determining the price responses. We use (2.3) for i=1,...,n goods to obtain estimates of the income flexibility by treating the marginal shares as known.

The systematic part of the demand equations [the expression in the right-hand side of equation (2.1) for i=1,...,n, for example] comes from the utility-maximization theory of the consumer. Traditional theory has little, if anything, to say about the random components of the demand equations [the disturbances ε_{it} in (2.1)]. However, Theil (1975/76, Ch.2) has developed the theory of rational random behaviour which deals with the properties of the disturbances. He shows that under rational random behaviour, the variances and covariances of the ε_{it}'s of (2.3) take the following form

$$\text{cov}[\varepsilon_{it}, \varepsilon_{jt}] = \sigma^2_t \theta_i (\delta_{ij} - \theta_j),\qquad (2.4)$$

where σ^2_t is an unknown parameter independent of i and j. Going back to equation (2.2), it can be seen that $\text{cov}[\varepsilon_{it}, \varepsilon_{jt}]$ is proportional to the corresponding Slutsky coefficient π_{ij}.

Let $\Gamma_t = \Sigma_{i=1}^{n} \overline{w}_{it}(Dp_{it} - DP_t)(Dq_{it} - DQ_t)$ be the Divisia price-quantity covariance; and $\Pi'_t = \Sigma_{i=1}^{n} \theta_i(Dp_{it} - DP'_t)^2$ be the Frisch price variance. To let ϕ in (2.3) potentially vary over time, we replace it with ϕ_t. Theil (1975/76, Ch.15) also shows that under (2.4), the weighted-least-squares (WLS) estimator of ϕ_t is

$$\hat{\phi}_t = \frac{C_t}{\Pi'_t}, \tag{2.5}$$

where

$$C_t = \Gamma_t + DQ_t[DP_t - DP'_t]. \tag{2.6}$$

The sampling variance of $\hat{\phi}_t$ is

$$\mathrm{var}\,\hat{\phi}_t = \frac{\sigma_t^2}{\Pi'_t} \tag{2.7}$$

and an unbiased estimator of σ_t^2 is given by

$$\hat{\sigma}_t^2 = \frac{1}{n-2}\left[V_t - \hat{\phi}_t C_t\right], \tag{2.8}$$

where

$$V_t = \sum_{i=1}^{n} \frac{1}{\theta_i} \left[\overline{w}_{it} Dq_{it} - \theta_i DQ_t \right]^2. \tag{2.9}$$

In Appendix A6.1 we present an alternative derivation of expression (2.5) which does not require the assumption of rational random behaviour.

6.3   322 ESTIMATES OF THE INCOME FLEXIBILITY

Under Working's (1943) model, the marginal share θ_i and the budget share w_i differs by a constant, β_i. That is, with a country superscript c and a time subscript t added,

$$\theta_{it}^c = \overline{w}_{it}^c + \beta_i^c, \qquad\qquad i=1,...,n^c, \tag{3.1}$$

where β_i^c is the income coefficient satisfying $\Sigma_{i=1}^{n^c} \beta_i^c = 0$. Note that we use $\overline{w}_{it}^c$ in place of w_i in (3.1); this $\overline{w}_{it}^c$ is the arithmetic average of the budget shares in periods t and t-1.

In Chapter 3 we estimated by maximum likelihood model (2.3) with (3.1) for $i=1,...,n^c$ goods for each of the 18 OECD countries. To allow for trend-like changes in taste etc., we added a constant term to each equation, which we denote by α_i^c. We presented the estimates of this model in Tables 5.2 and 5.3. In Appendix A6.2 we present the marginal shares using in (3.1) the estimates of the income coefficients and the observed $\overline{w}_{it}^c$'s.

We use these estimates of the marginal shares to estimate the income flexibility. With constant terms added to the model, the estimator of ϕ_t and its variance are still given by (2.5) and (2.7) with the addition of a country superscript (c). However, the term C_t in (2.5) becomes C_t^c which is defined by (2.6) minus $\Sigma_{i=1}^{n} \alpha_i^c Dp_{it}^c$; and V_t in (2.8) becomes V_t^c defined by (2.9) with the negative of the constant $(-\alpha_i^c)$ added to the term in the square bracket. To implement adjustments involving the α_i^c's, we use their estimates presented in Table 5.3.

Table 6.1 presents the 322 estimates of the income flexibility for each year in the 18 countries. We shall come back to the last row in the next section. Figure 6.1 presents the histogram of the 322 income flexibilities. As can be seen, most of the estimates are clustered around -.5.

6.4 A CONSTANT INCOME FLEXIBILITY FOR EACH COUNTRY

Equation (2.5) defines a one-period estimator of the income flexibility. In this section we present a multi-period estimator.

TABLE 6 1

INCOME FLEXIBILITIES IN 18 COUNTRIES

(Standard errors are in parentheses)

| Year | U.S. | Canada | Sweden | Switzerland | Denmark | Australia | France | Germany | Belgium | Norway | Netherlands | Iceland | Finland | Austria | Japan | U.K. | Spain | Italy |
(1)	(2)	(3)	(4)	(5)	(6)	(7)	(8)	(9)	(10)	(11)	(12)	(13)	(14)	(15)	(16)	(17)	(18)	(19)
1953	–	–	–	–	–	–	–	–	–	–	-2.63	–	–	–	–	–	–	–
1954	–	–	–	–	–	–	–	–	–	–	-1.22	–	–	–	–	–	–	–
1955	–	–	–	–	–	–	–	–	–	–	.27	–	–	–	–	–	–	–
1956	–	–	–	–	–	–	–	–	–	–	-.83	–	–	–	–	–	–	–
1957	–	–	–	–	–	–	–	–	–	–	-.62	–	–	–	–	–	–	–
1958	–	–	–	–	–	–	–	–	–	–	-.72	–	–	–	–	–	–	–
1959	–	–	–	–	–	–	–	–	–	–	-1.95	–	–	–	–	–	–	–
1960	–	–	–	–	–	–	–	–	–	–	-1.21	–	–	–	–	–	–	–
1961	-1.42	-.24	–	-.55	–	-.47	–	-1.12	-.31	–	-1.99	-.29	-.66	–	–	–	–	–
1962	.43	-1.85	–	-.72	–	.07	–	-.76	-.01	–	.06	-.87	-.40	–	–	–	–	–
1963	.04	-1.53	–	-.69	–	-.37	–	4.23	.14	–	.33	-.84	.40	–	–	–	–	–
1964	-.17	-.97	–	-.71	–	-.70	–	-1.54	.61	–	-1.59	-.80	-.69	–	–	–	–	–
1965	.56	-.77	-.56	-.96	–	-.08	-.02	-.42	-.05	.26	-.89	-.89	-.64	-.76	–	-.54	-.06	.10
1966	.31	-.93	-.32	-.50	–	.42	-.33	-.54	-.23	-.56	-1.31	-.27	-.06	.95	–	-.26	-1.01	-.17
1967	-.76	-.19	-.79	-.58	-.56	-.35	.00	-.78	-.48	-.46	-.56	.48	.51	-.03	–	-.08	-.27	-.02
1968	-.26	-.90	-.01	.21	-.04	-.27	-.42	-.09	-.09	-1.24	-.73	-.83	-.15	.08	–	-.18	-.37	-.14
1969	-.29	-.28	-.69	.16	-.33	-1.20	-.28	-1.07	-.63	-.15	-.12	-.67	-1.67	-.25	–	-.21	.01	-.27
1970	1.13	-.87	-.67	-.90	-.06	-.32	.69	-.19	.02	-1.68	-1.24	-.93	-1.21	-.37	–	-.43	-.35	-.57
1971	.87	.86	-.80	.18	-.45	-.40	-1.24	-.79	-.17	-.43	-1.03	-.69	-.32	-1.33	-.10	.48	.30	.49
1972	-.52	-.91	-.69	-.51	-.69	-.51	-.51	-1.52	-.29	-.62	-.01	-.51	-.95	-1.10	-1.08	-.92	-.57	-.65
1973	-1.00	-.67	-.86	.45	-.79	-.89	-.43	-2.43	-.25	-1.00	-1.23	.06	-.82	-.17	-.28	-.64	-.14	-.61
1974	-.48	-1.02	-.66	-.54	-.79	-1.07	-.62	-.69	-.90	-.42	-.48	–	-.52	-.08	-.50	-1.09	-.72	-.43
1975	-.78	-.47	-.66	-1.58	-.54	-.66	.10	-1.20	.12	-.31	-1.06	–	-.87	.24	.13	-.09	.06	-.23
1976	-.56	-.59	-.30	-.07	-.35	-.37	-.34	1.50	.09	-2.07	-.13	–	-1.07	.27	-1.25	-.34	-.01	.04
1977	-.49	-.86	-.75	-1.23	-.47	.05	-.42	-1.09	.59	.35	-.83	–	-.62	-1.54	-.29	-.21	.00	-.09
1978	-.89	-.53	-.49	-.77	-.97	-.60	-.82	-1.24	-.83	-.55	–	–	–	-.35	-.67	-.79	–	-.03
1979	-.41	-.35	-.57	-1.09	-.29	-.28	-.48	-.94	-.51	-.48	–	–	–	-.31	-.73	-.36	–	-.08
1980	-.42	-.32	-.80	-.35	-.72	-1.14	-.56	-1.06	-.67	-.61	–	–	–	-.29	-1.10	-.39	–	-.09
1981	-.56	-.43	-.49	-.79	-.72	-.35	-.79	-.13	-.07	-.80	–	–	–	-.45	-.82	-.34	–	-.48
Weighted mean	-.49	-.64	-.63	-.50	-.51	-.53	-.46	-.65	-.15	-.59	-.84	-.64	-.40	-.30	-.46	-.40	-.26	-.22
	(.07)	(.14)	(.16)	(.14)	(.09)	(.07)	(.07)	(.14)	(.05)	(.17)	(.09)	(.11)	(.13)	(.16)	(.09)	(.06)	(.07)	(.06)

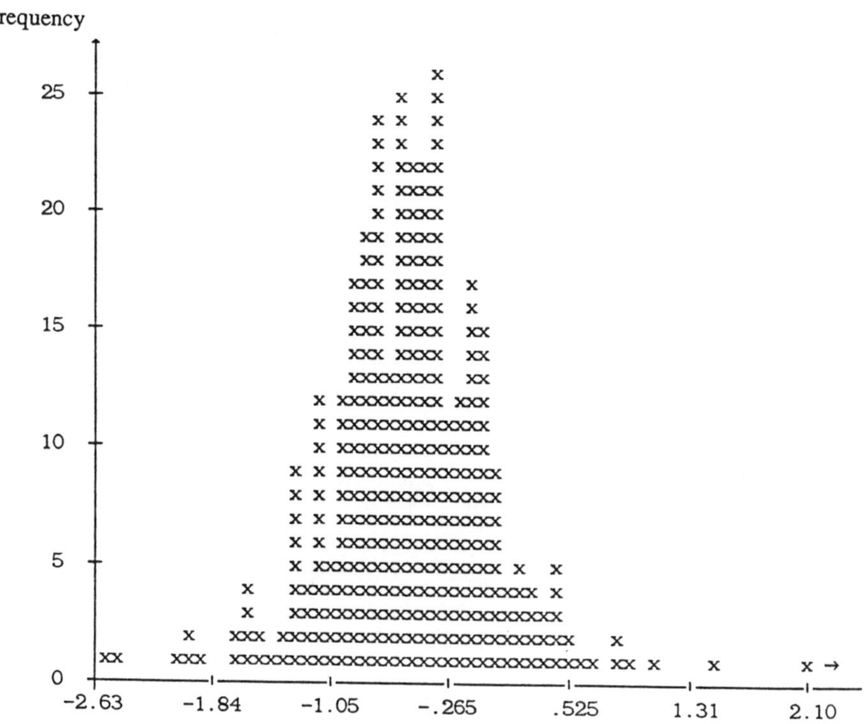

Figure 6.1

Assuming that the disturbances are uncorrelated over time, it can be easily shown that an estimator of the common value of ϕ^c for all T^c years in country c is given by a weighted average of $\hat{\phi}_t^c$, t=1,...,T^c, the optimal weights being inversely proportional to their variances (Theil, 1975/76, Ch.15). That is,

$$\hat{\phi}^c = \sum_{t=1}^{T^c} \omega_t^c \hat{\phi}_t^c , \qquad\qquad (4.1)$$

where $\omega_t^c = \Pi_t^{c\prime}/\Pi^{c\prime}$, with $\Pi^{c\prime} = \Sigma_{t=1}^{T^c} \Pi_t^{c\prime}$. Also we have

$$\text{var } \hat{\phi}^c = \frac{\sigma^{c2}}{\Pi^{c\prime}} . \qquad\qquad (4.2)$$

An unbiased estimator of σ^{c2} is given by

$$\hat{\sigma}^{c2} = \frac{1}{(n^c-1)T^c - 1} \sum_{t=1}^{T^c} [V_t^c - \hat{\phi}^c C_t^c].$$

The last row of Table 6.1 presents for each country the weighted mean of the income flexibilities and its standard error. These are obtained from (4.1) and (4.2). In Chapter 3, we estimated for each country model (2.3) with (3.1) under the assumption that the income flexibility is a constant over time. Now we shall compare these estimates with those obtained as weighted means of the time-varying estimates. Since the two estimates are derived from basically the

same model, one would expect them to be close. Rows 1-18 of Table 6.2 give
the two sets of estimates. As can be seen, they are quite close to each other.

Applying the same procedure as above to $\hat{\phi}^c$, c=1,...,18, we obtain a
cross-country weighted mean of the income flexibilities,

$$\hat{\phi} = \sum_{c=1}^{18} \omega^c \hat{\phi}^c, \qquad (4.3)$$

where $\omega^c = \Pi^{c\prime}/\Pi'$, with $\Pi' = \Sigma_{c=1}^{18} \Pi^{c\prime}$. The weights ω^c are inversely
proportional to the sampling variances. The variance of $\hat{\phi}$ is given by

$$\mathrm{var}\ \hat{\phi} = \frac{\sigma^2}{\Pi'}, \qquad (4.4)$$

with

$$\hat{\sigma}^2 = \frac{1}{\sum_{d=1}^{18}(n^d - 1)T^d - 1} \sum_{c=1}^{18} \sum_{t=1}^{T^c} [V_t^c - \hat{\phi}C_t^c]$$

an unbiased estimator of σ^2.

Using (4.3) and (4.4), we obtain the following estimate of ϕ for all
countries

$$\hat{\phi} = -.46\ (.03). \qquad (4.5)$$

TABLE 6.2

TWO SETS OF ESTIMATES OF THE INCOME FLEXIBILITY
IN 18 COUNTRIES

(Standard errors are in parentheses)

Country	Weighted means	Individual country model estimates
(1)	(2)	(3)
1. U.S.	-.487 (.064)	-.384 (.066)
2. Canada	-.642 (.132)	-.554 (.120)
3. Sweden	-.626 (.155)	-.580 (.088)
4. Switzerland	-.501 (.130)	-.551 (.075)
5. Denmark	-.513 (.083)	-.465 (.084)
6. Australia	-.527 (.064)	-.463 (.077)
7. France	-.462 (.068)	-.527 (.077)
8. Germany	-.646 (.133)	-.602 (.100)
9. Belgium	-.152 (.049)	-.127 (.069)
10. Norway	-.583 (.162)	-.484 (.088)
11. Netherlands	.838 (.087)	-.842 (.107)
12. Iceland	-.642 (.108)	-.695 (.089)
13. Finland	-.404 (.126)	-.378 (.081)
14. Austria	-.297 (.150)	-.154 (.093)
15. Japan	-.459 (.081)	-.370 (.101)
16. U.K.	-.396 (.057)	-.396 (.071)
17. Spain	-.255 (.067)	-.291 (.073)
18. Italy	-.218 (.059)	-.184 (.074)
19. All countries	-.462 (.023)	-.449 (.022)

The weighted means in rows 1-18 of column 2 are from the last row of Table 6.1; the entry in row 19 is from equation (4.5). The estimates in column 3 are from column 12 of Tables 5.2 and 5.4. The figures in parentheses in column 3 are the asymptotic standard errors.

As can be seen from the histogram of the one-period estimates presented in Figure 6.1, the value -.46 lies in the vicinity of the interval where the frequency attains its maximum.

In Section 4.4 we pooled the data for 15 of the OECD countries and estimated a common demand model. In this model, the income flexibility is a constant with respect to time and countries. The last entry in column 3 of Table 6.2 gives the estimate of ϕ from this model. Its value of -.45 is remarkably close to the previous cross-country estimate given in equation (4.5) of -.46. Note also that the two standard errors are very close (.022 vs .023).

6.5   TESTING FRISCH'S CONJECTURE

As indicated in Section 6.1, Frisch conjectures that the money flexibility should decrease in absolute value as the consumer (or country) becomes more affluent. As ϕ is the reciprocal of the money flexibility, the conjecture is that ϕ should increase in absolute value with increasing real income. In Section 4.8, we tested this hypothesis across countries. We found that the data for 15 OECD countries did not support Frisch. In this section we again test Frisch, this time within and across countries.

We use Theil's (1975/76, Ch.15) methodology to test whether the ϕ_t^c's presented in Table 6.1 vary in response to changes in income. To do this, we regress the ϕ_t^c-estimates for a given country on the logarithm of real income (y_t^c),

$$\phi_t^c = \eta_0^c + \eta_1^c y_t^c + \xi_t^c, \qquad t=1,...,T^c, \qquad (5.1)$$

where η_0^c and η_1^c are parameters to be estimated; and ξ_t^c is an independent disturbance term with mean zero. The logarithm of real income is given by the accumulated value of the Divisia volume index,

$$y_t^c = y_{t-1}^c + DQ_t^c,$$

with initial value $y_0^c = 0$ and where DQ_t^c is the Divisia volume index presented in Table 2.7. Frisch would expect η_1^c to be negative (as $\phi_t^c < 0$) and significant, indicating that ϕ^c declines algebraically with increasing income.

We use WLS to estimate (5.1), where the weights are inversely proportional to the standard errors of the $\hat{\phi}_t^c$'s. The first 18 rows of column 2 of Table 6.3 present the t-statistics for the null hypothesis that $\eta_1^c = 0$ against the alternative $\eta_1^c < 0$ for each country. As can be seen, for all countries except France and Finland, the t-values are not significant at the 5 percent level. For these two countries, the t-values are insignificant at the 1 percent level. Although the η_1-estimates for 12 of the 18 countries are negative (as expected by Frisch), 10 of them are insignificant at the 5 percent level and all

TABLE 6.3

t-STATISTICS FOR THE FRISCH CONJECTURE AND ESTIMATES OF THE INCOME FLEXIBILITY IN 18 COUNTRIES

(Standard errors are in parentheses)

| | | Estimates of the income flexibility | |
| Country | t-statistics | Restricted WLS-estimates | Weighted means |
(1)	(2)	(3)	(4)
1. U.S.	$t(19) = -.57$	-.556 (.071)	-.487 (.064)
2. Canada	$t(19) = 2.45$	-.681 (.077)	-.642 (.132)
3. Sweden	$t(15) = -1.15$	-.661 (.044)	-.626 (.155)
4. Switzerland	$t(19) = -1.01$	-.660 (.111)	-.501 (.130)
5. Denmark	$t(13) = -1.22$	-.592 (.062)	-.513 (.083)
6. Australia	$t(19) = -1.61$	-.426 (.082)	-.527 (.064)
7. France	$t(15) = -2.41*$	-.488 (.055)	-.462 (.068)
8. Germany	$t(19) = .25$	-.627 (.132)	-.646 (.133)
9. Belgium	$t(19) = -.40$	-.211 (.064)	-.152 (.049)
10. Norway	$t(15) = -1.45$	-.663 (.068)	-.583 (.162)
11. Netherlands	$t(23) = .68$	-.915 (.094)	-.838 (.087)
12. Iceland	$t(11) = .71$	-.620 (.094)	-.642 (.108)
13. Finland	$t(15) = -1.87*$	-.223 (.076)	-.404 (.126)
14. Austria	$t(15) = -.94$	-.361 (.083)	-.297 (.150)
15. Japan	$t(9) = -1.62$	-.581 (.132)	-.459 (.081)
16. U.K.	$t(15) = -.78$	-.378 (.078)	-.396 (.057)
17. Spain	$t(11) = .65$	-.206 (.076)	-.255 (.067)
18. Italy	$t(15) = .38$	-.137 (.056)	-.218 (.059)
19. All countries	$t(16) = -2.06*$	-.410 (.043)	-.462 (.023)

A '*' denotes significant at the 5 percent level (but insignificant at the
1 percent level) using a one-tailed test.

are insignificant at the 1 percent level. Thus we conclude that the income flexibility is unrelated to real income in most countries. In other words, there is little support for Frisch within countries.

The first 18 rows of column 3 of Table 6.3 present the WLS-estimates of η_0^c in (5.1) under the restriction $\eta_1^c = 0$. These are interpreted as ϕ^c-estimates also. For comparison, in column 4 we reproduce the weighted means of the ϕ_t^c's presented in the last row of Table 6.1. In most cases, the two sets of estimates agree fairly well.

Next, we analyse the effect of real income on the value of the income flexibility across countries by estimating

$$\phi^c = \eta_0 + \eta_1 y^c + \xi^c, \qquad\qquad c=1,...,18, \qquad (5.2)$$

where η_0 and η_1 are parameters to be estimated; y^c is the logarithm of the per capita GDP in 1975; and ξ^c is an independent disturbance term with mean zero. We use the income flexibilities presented in the last row of Table 6.1 and the per capita GDP's given in column 4 of Table 2.2 to estimate (5.2) by WLS. (Note that these per capita GDP's are in international dollars and are thus comparable across countries.) The last entry of column 2 of Table 6.3 presents the t-value for the null that $\eta_1 = 0$ against the alternative $\eta_1 < 0$. As the one-tailed critical values of $t(16)$ are -1.75 and -2.58 at the 5 percent and 1 percent levels, respectively, the observed t-value is significant at the 5 percent level, but insignificant at the 1 percent level.

The fact that η_1 is negative and significant at the 5 percent level gives some support for Frisch's conjecture across countries. To pursue this matter further, in Figure 6.2 we plot the absolute value of the weighted income flexibility against the weighted logarithm of GDP for the 18 countries. As can be seen, these data do not reveal any clear-cut visual evidence in support of Frisch. This is in agreement with our results in Section 4.8.

6.6 COMPARISON WITH OTHER STUDIES

The above findings are not strongly in agreement with the Frisch conjecture. Our conclusion is that the income flexibility seems to be more or less invariant in a wide variety of economic circumstances. How does this result agree with previous studies?

Brown and Deaton (1972) report estimates of the income flexibility from various studies obtained with different demand models (the linear expenditure system, the Rotterdam and constant elasticity models). They conclude that the results show no evidence of a relationship between the value of the income flexibility and real income.

Weighted Absolute Value of Income Flexibility vs
Weighted Logarithm of GDP in 18 Countries

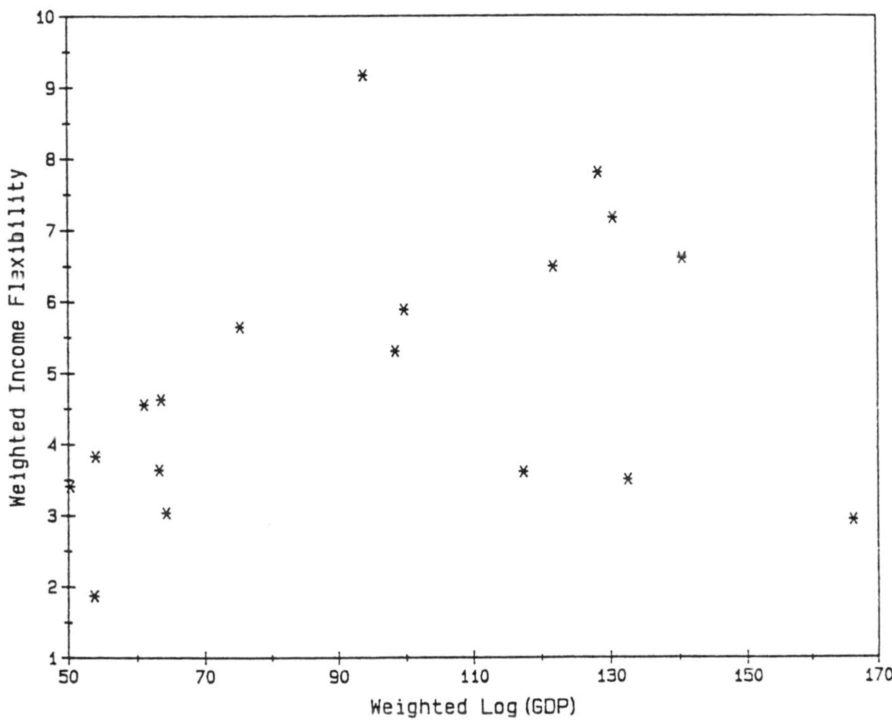

Figure 6.2

DeJanvry et al. (1972) collect estimates of ϕ from several studies and, in essence, estimate equation (5.2). They find a statistically significant relationship and hence confirm Frisch. As noted by Theil (1980), however, the validity of their conclusion is based on the uncritical acceptance of the previous estimates.

Lluch et al. (1977) use time-series data for 14 countries (developed and underdeveloped) at various levels of commodity aggregation to estimate a variant of the linear expenditure system. They find strong evidence in support of Frisch at the four-commodity level of aggregation, but less support at the two- and one-commodity levels.

Theil (1987) tests Frisch's conjecture for 30 countries using a method similar to that employed in Section 6.5. He compares the estimates for η_0 and η_1 in equation (5.2) for all 30 countries with those obtained with 29 countries, by leaving out one country at a time. None of the estimates of η_1 is significant and he concludes that the sample cannot support Frisch in spite of the large income variation. Theil and Brooks (1970/71) use a modified version of the Rotterdam model in which the income flexibility is a function of real income. They also obtain the result that ϕ is unrelated to income.

This brief review indicates a lack of unanimity in previous studies about the status of Frisch. It seems, however, that the broad thrust of the literature has not been too supportive of Frisch's conjecture. Our inability to find any strong evidence in favour of Frisch seems to be in agreement with that broad thrust. It should not be surprising that such strong evidence is not available given that ϕ is the reciprocal of the income elasticity of the marginal utility of income: The marginal utility of income relates to a first-order derivative of the (indirect) utility function, so that its income elasticity relates to a second derivative. Stating that ϕ changes systematically with real income thus amounts to a statement about the third-order derivative of the utility function. It is usually very difficult to measure such higher-order effects.

Moreover, our ϕ-value of about -.5 for all countries seems to be consistent with previous estimates (see, e.g., Brown and Deaton, 1972). This implies a money flexibility of $1/(-.5) = -2$. Going back to Frisch's passage quoted in Section 6.1, this value corresponds to Frisch's 'median' part of the population. One may protest that the average OECD consumer is richer than the median consumer for the world as a whole, but it would be difficult to make this case with great force.

6.7 CONCLUDING COMMENTS

In this chapter we presented 322 one-period estimates of the income flexibility (ϕ, the inverse of the income elasticity of the marginal utility of income) from time-series data for 18 OECD countries. We then obtained a multi-period estimate of ϕ for each country by taking a weighted average of the one-period estimates. Using a similar method we also obtained an estimate of ϕ for all 18 countries simultaneously. This value is -.46 with standard error .03.

An analysis of the income flexibilities showed that they seem to be more or less unrelated to systematic differences in income. This result means that the data do not give strong support Frisch's famous conjecture about the income dependence of ϕ. This finding should, however, be qualified by the fact that only countries with relatively high incomes are included in the sample. We then presented a brief review of previous studies which revealed that our results were in broad agreement with those obtained by most others.

APPENDICES TO CHAPTER 6

A6.1 ALTERNATIVE DERIVATION OF THE ϕ_t-ESTIMATOR

Expression (2.5) for the estimator of ϕ_t was obtained under the assumption of rational random behaviour. In this appendix we present an alternative derivation which does not require this assumption.

Consider the demand model (2.3),

$$\overline{w}_{it} Dq_{it} = \theta_i DQ_t + \phi\theta_i(Dp_{it} - DP'_t),$$

where we have suppressed the error term. Multiplying both sides of this equation by $(Dp_{it} - DP'_t)$ and summing over $i=1,...,n$, we get

$$\sum_{i=1}^{n} \overline{w}_{it} Dq_{it}(Dp_{it} - DP'_t) = DQ_t \sum_{i=1}^{n} \theta_i(Dp_{it} - DP'_t) + \phi \sum_{i=1}^{n} \theta_i(Dp_{it} - DP'_t)^2. \quad (A1.1)$$

The right-hand side of (A1.1) can be written as

$$DQ_t \sum_{i=1}^{n} \theta_i(Dp_{it} - DP'_t) + \phi \sum_{i-1}^{n} \theta_i(Dp_{it} - DP'_t)^2$$

$$= DQ_t \left[DP'_t - \sum_{i=1}^{n} \theta_i DP'_t \right] + \phi \sum_{i=1}^{n} \theta_i(Dp_{it} - DP'_t)^2$$

$$= \psi\Pi'_t,$$

where the first step uses $DP'_t = \Sigma_{i=1}^{n} \theta_i Dp_{it}$; and the last uses $\Sigma_{i=1}^{n} \theta_i = 1$ and $\Pi'_t = \Sigma_{i=1}^{n} \theta_i(Dp_{it} - DP'_t)^2$.

The left-hand side of (A1.1) can be written as

$$\sum_{i=1}^{n} \bar{w}_{it} Dq_{it}(Dp_{it} - DP'_t) = \sum_{i=1}^{n} \bar{w}_{it} Dq_{it}(Dp_{it} - DP_t) + \sum_{i=1}^{n} \bar{w}_{it} Dq_{it}(DP_t - DP'_t)$$

$$= \sum_{i=1}^{n} \bar{w}_{it} Dq_{it}(Dp_{it} - DP_t) + DQ_t(DP_t - DP'_t)$$

$$= \sum_{i=1}^{n} \bar{w}_{it}(Dq_{it} - DQ_t)(Dp_{it} - DP_t)$$

$$+ DQ_t \sum_{i=1}^{n} \bar{w}_{it}(Dp_{it} - DP_t) + DQ_t(DP_t - DP'_t)$$

$$= \Gamma_t + DQ_t(DP_t - DP'_t)$$

$$= C_t,$$

where the second step uses $DQ_t = \sum_{i=1}^{n} \bar{w}_{it} Dq_{it}$; the fourth uses $\Gamma_t = \sum_{i=1}^{n} \bar{w}_{it}(Dq_{it} - DQ_t)(Dp_{it} - DP_t)$ and $DP_t = \sum_{i=1}^{n} \bar{w}_{it} Dp_{it}$; and the last uses (2.6). Therefore, (A1.1) becomes $C_t = \phi\Pi'_t$, so that

$$\hat{\phi}_t = \frac{C_t}{\Pi'_t}.$$

This is (2.5) of the text.

A6.2 THE ESTIMATES OF THE MARGINAL SHARES

In this appendix we present the estimates of the marginal shares θ^c_{it}. We compute these θ^c_{it}'s according to equation (3.1). We use in (3.1) the estimates of the income coefficients presented in Table 5.2 and the observed $\bar{w}^c_{it}$'s. Table A6.1 gives the θ^c_{it}'s for the 18 countries.

As can be seen, all except 23 of the 3135 marginal shares are positive. However, it should be noted that on average all marginal shares are positive. Since preference independence rules out negative marginal shares, we replace the negative θ^c_{it}'s with the sample mean $\bar{\theta}^c_i = (1/T^c) \Sigma^{T^c}_{t-1} \theta^c_{it}$ and then re-normalize such that $\Sigma^{n^c}_{i=1} \theta^c_{it} = 1$. The resulting values of the marginal shares are used in the computations reported in the text.

TABLE A6.1

MARGINAL SHARES FOR 10 COMMODITIES IN 18 COUNTRIES

Year	Food	Beverages	Clothing	Housing	Durables	Medical care	Transport	Recreation	Education	Miscellaneous
	θ^c_{1t}	θ^c_{2t}	θ^c_{3t}	θ^c_{4t}	θ^c_{5t}	θ^c_{6t}	θ^c_{7t}	θ^c_{8t}	θ^c_{9t}	$\theta^c_{10,t}$
(1)	(2)	(3)	(4)	(5)	(6)	(7)	(8)	(9)	(10)	(11)
					U.S.					
1961	.120	.013	.117	.077	.134	.009	.356	.069	.010	.095
1962	.115	.012	.116	.080	.133	.011	.355	.070	.011	.097
1963	.108	.012	.114	.081	.133	.014	.360	.071	.011	.097
1964	.101	.013	.114	.080	.134	.016	.362	.072	.011	.096
1965	.097	.015	.114	.078	.134	.018	.364	.074	.012	.094
1966	.098	.014	.114	.075	.134	.018	.364	.076	.013	.094
1967	.096	.013	.113	.074	.135	.020	.362	.078	.014	.094
1968	.092	.013	.113	.072	.134	.023	.363	.079	.015	.095
1969	.089	.013	.113	.070	.132	.028	.367	.079	.015	.095
1970	.088	.014	.111	.071	.129	.033	.365	.079	.016	.094
1971	.085	.015	.109	.072	.126	.038	.368	.079	.017	.093
1972	.078	.014	.108	.073	.125	.041	.375	.078	.017	.091
1973	.077	.014	.107	.073	.125	.042	.376	.079	.017	.090
1974	.080	.013	.106	.076	.124	.045	.371	.079	.017	.090
1975	.082	.012	.103	.079	.122	.048	.367	.079	.017	.090
1976	.080	.011	.101	.080	.120	.051	.372	.078	.017	.090
1977	.075	.009	.099	.081	.119	.053	.380	.078	.016	.089
1978	.072	.008	.099	.083	.119	.055	.382	.077	.016	.089
1979	.072	.007	.097	.085	.119	.056	.381	.077	.016	.091
1980	.072	.006	.094	.069	.117	.059	.378	.076	.017	.091
1981	.072	.006	.092	.092	.115	.065	.376	.075	.017	.091
Mean	.088	.012	.107	.078	.127	.035	.369	.076	.015	.093
					Canada					
1961	.182	.042	.079	.007	.140	.109	.220	.097	.012	.113
1962	.179	.043	.079	.010	.140	.099	.223	.098	.013	.116
1963	.176	.042	.077	.010	.139	.099	.228	.098	.014	.116
1964	.173	.040	.076	.009	.139	.100	.231	.100	.015	.117
1965	.170	.040	.075	.005	.139	.100	.235	.101	.017	.118
1966	.166	.040	.074	.002	.140	.100	.237	.103	.019	.120
1967	.162	.040	.073	.002	.139	.100	.235	.106	.021	.122
1968	.156	.040	.073	.004	.138	.099	.235	.108	.021	.124
1969	.152	.039	.073	.007	.137	.097	.234	.108	.026	.126
1970	.152	.040	.072	.014	.136	.093	.229	.108	.028	.128
1971	.151	.041	.068	.017	.134	.087	.230	.110	.031	.132
1972	.148	.039	.064	.011	.136	.084	.234	.115	.031	.137
1973	.149	.037	.063	.003	.139	.084	.237	.119	.030	.138
1974	.150	.035	.065	-.002	.141	.085	.237	.121	.029	.140
1975	.151	.033	.066	-.005	.140	.085	.238	.122	.029	.140
1976	.149	.032	.065	-.004	.139	.086	.240	.122	.030	.142
1977	.144	.031	.064	.001	.137	.087	.240	.122	.030	.144
1978	.145	.030	.062	.005	.135	.087	.239	.121	.030	.145
1979	.146	.029	.061	.006	.134	.088	.240	.120	.030	.147
1980	.145	.029	.060	.007	.132	.088	.240	.120	.030	.150
1981	.145	.029	.058	.010	.129	.089	.240	.119	.029	.151
Mean	.157	.037	.069	.006	.137	.093	.234	.111	.025	.132
					Sweden					
1965	.145	.088	.137	.011	.144	.001	.269	.127	.000	.079
1966	.139	.091	.135	.015	.143	.001	.269	.128	.001	.079
1967	.136	.094	.132	.020	.142	.002	.264	.130	.001	.080
1968	.131	.095	.127	.023	.142	.002	.267	.133	.001	.080
1969	.123	.096	.124	.026	.142	.002	.273	.135	.001	.079
1970	.118	.095	.122	.030	.143	.001	.274	.138	.001	.078
1971	.118	.094	.119	.034	.142	.002	.273	.142	.001	.075
1972	.117	.092	.117	.036	.142	.003	.273	.146	.001	.073
1973	.112	.090	.115	.039	.144	.004	.273	.149	.001	.072
1974	.105	.088	.117	.040	.147	.002	.275	.153	.001	.071
1975	.098	.089	.119	.037	.149	-.001	.279	.157	.001	.072
1976	.097	.087	.119	.037	.149	.000	.282	.158	.001	.071
1977	.099	.085	.119	.041	.148	.000	.281	.158	.001	.070
1978	.099	.083	.118	.049	.146	.000	.278	.156	.001	.070
1979	.095	.080	.117	.059	.141	.000	.279	.156	.001	.070
1980	.093	.078	.116	.066	.142	.000	.278	.156	.001	.070
1981	.094	.075	.115	.074	.139	.001	.278	.156	.001	.068
Mean	.113	.088	.122	.037	.144	.001	.274	.146	.001	.074

(continued)

Table A6.1 (continued)

Switzerland

1961	.247	.132	.140	.013	.181	.002	.158	.091		.036
1962	.242	.134	.139	.011	.180	.000	.162	.093		.037
1963	.239	.134	.139	.012	.179	.000	.163	.094		.039
1964	.237	.135	.139	.009	.178	.001	.164	.096		.041
1965	.237	.135	.137	.006	.177	.003	.165	.097		.042
1966	.237	.135	.134	.008	.175	.006	.166	.096		.043
1967	.234	.135	.131	.011	.172	.009	.167	.095		.044
1968	.228	.136	.128	.018	.169	.012	.170	.095		.044
1969	.223	.134	.126	.022	.168	.015	.173	.094		.045
1970	.220	.132	.125	.023	.167	.018	.176	.094		.046
1971	.216	.131	.124	.025	.165	.020	.177	.094		.047
1972	.213	.129	.123	.023	.165	.023	.180	.093		.050
1973	.209	.127	.122	.027	.164	.024	.178	.094		.055
1974	.208	.126	.119	.034	.162	.027	.172	.094		.059
1975	.210	.123	.114	.038	.157	.030	.171	.094		.062
1976	.206	.120	.110	.047	.152	.034	.174	.094		.063
1977	.203	.117	.108	.051	.150	.036	.179	.094		.064
1978	.204	.115	.107	.048	.149	.036	.182	.094		.064
1979	.203	.114	.106	.050	.148	.037	.185	.094		.063
1980	.202	.112	.105	.052	.147	.037	.186	.095		.062
1981	.203	.112	.105	.049	.146	.038	.188	.097		.062
Mean	.220	.127	.123	.028	.164	.020	.173	.094		.051

Denmark

1967	.091	.078	.131	.017	.159	.009	.334	.090	.000	.090
1968	.087	.077	.125	.029	.155	.009	.335	.091	.000	.091
1969	.081	.075	.123	.038	.153	.009	.337	.092	.001	.090
1970	.079	.070	.122	.045	.151	.010	.338	.094	.001	.091
1971	.077	.067	.117	.057	.147	.011	.336	.095	.002	.090
1972	.072	.067	.113	.066	.146	.011	.337	.095	.003	.089
1973	.071	.065	.112	.070	.146	.011	.339	.096	.003	.086
1974	.070	.062	.111	.081	.143	.011	.334	.099	.004	.085
1975	.062	.060	.109	.092	.142	.010	.333	.103	.005	.084
1976	.057	.056	.108	.094	.141	.009	.343	.105	.005	.083
1977	.057	.055	.109	.095	.138	.008	.345	.105	.005	.084
1978	.057	.055	.106	.100	.135	.008	.343	.105	.006	.086
1979	.051	.053	.104	.113	.132	.008	.343	.102	.007	.086
1980	.047	.051	.103	.131	.129	.008	.338	.099	.008	.086
1981	.050	.049	.101	.143	.126	.008	.332	.098	.009	.085
Mean	.067	.063	.113	.078	.143	.009	.338	.098	.004	.087

Australia

1961	.095	.085	.139	.071	.181	.040	.206	.111	.020	.051
1962	.089	.083	.135	.077	.179	.038	.211	.111	.021	.057
1963	.081	.080	.133	.079	.179	.035	.219	.116	.021	.057
1964	.078	.079	.133	.080	.179	.036	.221	.121	.021	.053
1965	.077	.081	.130	.081	.178	.037	.220	.121	.021	.053
1966	.075	.082	.127	.084	.175	.038	.219	.125	.021	.054
1967	.069	.081	.125	.086	.173	.039	.222	.128	.021	.056
1968	.061	.080	.122	.087	.176	.039	.226	.128	.021	.058
1969	.053	.078	.120	.090	.179	.039	.230	.130	.021	.061
1970	.047	.077	.117	.094	.178	.040	.233	.130	.021	.061
1971	.042	.076	.115	.098	.179	.043	.231	.131	.021	.061
1972	.038	.074	.115	.101	.181	.045	.232	.132	.021	.061
1973	.037	.072	.116	.100	.187	.045	.229	.133	.020	.061
1974	.032	.070	.115	.100	.193	.045	.228	.136	.019	.061
1975	.025	.070	.111	.104	.197	.048	.229	.138	.018	.061
1976	.022	.069	.108	.111	.196	.048	.230	.138	.018	.060
1977	.025	.066	.107	.120	.191	.047	.229	.138	.018	.060
1978	.027	.065	.105	.126	.184	.047	.229	.137	.017	.060
1979	.029	.065	.102	.128	.180	.047	.233	.137	.017	.061
1980	.032	.063	.100	.120	.180	.045	.236	.137	.017	.062
1981	.031	.062	.100	.131	.180	.046	.235	.137	.017	.063
Mean	.051	.074	.118	.000	.102	.042	.226	.129	.020	.059

(continued)

Table A6.1 (continued)

France

1965	.137	.035	.124	.030	.167	.038	.248	.058	.002	.160
1966	.133	.033	.121	.036	.164	.041	.251	.058	.002	.161
1967	.128	.031	.118	.042	.162	.044	.253	.058	.002	.161
1968	.121	.030	.115	.049	.162	.045	.255	.059	.002	.161
1969	.114	.029	.113	.054	.162	.047	.259	.060	.002	.160
1970	.108	.027	.111	.060	.160	.051	.261	.060	.002	.161
1971	.101	.025	.109	.065	.160	.053	.263	.060	.002	.161
1972	.096	.023	.108	.065	.162	.055	.266	.061	.002	.161
1973	.092	.023	.106	.067	.162	.057	.267	.062	.002	.161
1974	.088	.021	.104	.070	.165	.058	.266	.063	.002	.162
1975	.086	.019	.103	.070	.165	.063	.266	.064	.002	.162
1976	.082	.017	.101	.071	.162	.068	.270	.063	.002	.163
1977	.081	.015	.098	.073	.160	.069	.274	.064	.002	.165
1978	.079	.014	.095	.074	.158	.072	.275	.065	.002	.166
1979	.073	.013	.093	.076	.156	.076	.279	.065	.002	.167
1980	.067	.012	.091	.082	.155	.078	.280	.064	.002	.168
1981	.063	.011	.090	.087	.153	.080	.281	.063	.002	.169
Mean	.097	.022	.106	.063	.161	.058	.266	.062	.002	.163

Germany

1961	.250		.164	-.004	.181	.023	.264	.071		.051
1962	.244		.163	-.001	.181	.023	.269	.070		.051
1963	.239		.161	.005	.179	.022	.274	.069		.051
1964	.234		.159	.008	.178	.022	.278	.069		.053
1965	.229		.160	.005	.178	.022	.282	.070		.055
1966	.223		.160	.007	.176	.022	.285	.070		.056
1967	.219		.158	.015	.174	.022	.284	.070		.057
1968	.211		.157	.024	.171	.022	.286	.071		.058
1969	.198		.156	.029	.170	.021	.295	.071		.059
1970	.187		.157	.027	.172	.021	.304	.072		.059
1971	.177		.158	.026	.174	.021	.310	.074		.060
1972	.172		.159	.025	.176	.021	.311	.075		.062
1973	.169		.157	.029	.176	.021	.309	.077		.062
1974	.164		.154	.036	.175	.022	.305	.079		.065
1975	.158		.154	.039	.172	.023	.308	.090		.067
1976	.154		.151	.040	.169	.023	.318	.079		.066
1977	.149		.149	.039	.170	.022	.326	.078		.066
1978	.144		.149	.038	.170	.022	.331	.079		.067
1979	.139		.147	.041	.169	.022	.333	.080		.069
1980	.137		.146	.045	.169	.023	.331	.080		.070
1981	.136		.144	.047	.168	.023	.330	.079		.072
Mean	.187		.155	.025	.174	.022	.302	.074		.061

Belgium

1961	.156	.073	.095	.101	.199	.020	.077	.035	.001	.243
1962	.156	.072	.095	.102	.200	.021	.077	.035	.001	.241
1963	.152	.070	.095	.103	.200	.021	.079	.035	.001	.244
1964	.143	.071	.095	.097	.204	.020	.082	.035	.000	.253
1965	.138	.072	.094	.092	.207	.025	.084	.035	.000	.253
1966	.137	.071	.093	.090	.206	.029	.086	.035	.000	.253
1967	.136	.071	.090	.090	.204	.030	.089	.035	.000	.255
1968	.130	.073	.088	.089	.204	.031	.091	.035	.000	.259
1969	.125	.072	.088	.087	.206	.032	.092	.034	.000	.265
1970	.123	.072	.086	.086	.209	.033	.092	.035	.000	.264
1971	.118	.073	.086	.085	.215	.035	.091	.036	.000	.262
1972	.110	.073	.087	.081	.219	.037	.094	.037	.000	.263
1973	.102	.073	.086	.077	.222	.041	.097	.038	.000	.264
1974	.096	.070	.085	.077	.230	.045	.096	.039	.000	.262
1975	.092	.067	.084	.084	.226	.049	.099	.039	.000	.259
1976	.090	.065	.081	.086	.222	.054	.105	.039	.000	.258
1977	.085	.063	.080	.084	.222	.057	.107	.040	.000	.262
1978	.078	.062	.077	.088	.217	.060	.108	.041	.000	.268
1979	.073	.060	.076	.095	.213	.061	.110	.042	.000	.270
1980	.067	.060	.075	.102	.212	.060	.112	.042	.000	.272
1981	.060	.059	.073	.109	.210	.060	.112	.042	.000	.275
Mean	.113	.069	.086	.091	.212	.039	.094	.037	.000	.259

(continued)

Table A6.1 (continued)

Norway

1965	.086	.087	.133	-.003	.108	.028	.409	.070	.003	.079
1966	.080	.089	.131	-.003	.107	.029	.411	.071	.003	.082
1967	.074	.089	.130	-.005	.108	.029	.414	.072	.004	.084
1968	.071	.090	.130	-.006	.109	.030	.415	.073	.003	.086
1969	.065	.089	.127	-.007	.110	.031	.420	.074	.003	.097
1970	.064	.089	.127	-.005	.111	.031	.418	.075	.003	.086
1971	.065	.090	.126	-.003	.111	.033	.416	.076	.003	.083
1972	.059	.091	.123	-.004	.112	.035	.421	.078	.002	.082
1973	.055	.091	.120	-.004	.115	.037	.423	.080	.002	.082
1974	.051	.089	.116	-.001	.118	.037	.424	.082	.002	.082
1975	.048	.088	.113	-.001	.120	.037	.425	.083	.003	.083
1976	.045	.086	.112	-.002	.121	.037	.430	.085	.003	.084
1977	.037	.083	.112	-.003	.121	.035	.411	.087	.003	.083
1978	.034	.080	.112	.003	.121	.036	.441	.087	.002	.083
1979	.032	.080	.111	.012	.119	.037	.439	.097	.002	.083
1980	.027	.080	.111	.016	.117	.035	.411	.086	.002	.082
1981	.029	.078	.109	.019	.117	.033	.417	.085	.002	.082
Mean	.054	.086	.120	.000	.114	.034	.426	.079	.003	.083

Netherlands

1953	.202	.043	.330	.060	.155	.009	.101	.029	.015	.056
1954	.196	.041	.335	.058	.160	.011	.102	.028	.015	.055
1955	.186	.040	.335	.057	.168	.012	.104	.028	.016	.056
1956	.177	.038	.336	.056	.171	.013	.104	.028	.017	.056
1957	.176	.041	.333	.057	.176	.017	.103	.027	.017	.055
1958	.178	.045	.318	.061	.173	.021	.104	.026	.017	.057
1959	.177	.045	.311	.063	.172	.023	.106	.026	.019	.058
1960	.167	.044	.314	.061	.178	.024	.107	.026	.020	.059
1961	.159	.042	.317	.062	.180	.023	.108	.027	.020	.061
1962	.156	.042	.316	.062	.180	.024	.108	.027	.022	.062
1963	.151	.043	.313	.063	.183	.026	.108	.027	.023	.062
1964	.143	.043	.315	.061	.185	.027	.112	.029	.024	.063
1965	.135	.045	.310	.056	.185	.029	.119	.030	.025	.066
1966	.132	.046	.306	.056	.181	.033	.119	.032	.026	.069
1967	.128	.046	.301	.058	.176	.039	.119	.034	.027	.073
1968	.120	.044	.295	.059	.175	.044	.123	.035	.028	.076
1969	.108	.040	.294	.060	.176	.049	.127	.037	.028	.081
1970	.095	.037	.292	.059	.180	.053	.130	.040	.028	.086
1971	.086	.034	.293	.060	.184	.056	.130	.042	.030	.086
1972	.080	.034	.290	.064	.179	.064	.130	.041	.032	.088
1973	.074	.035	.284	.066	.177	.072	.131	.038	.033	.091
1974	.066	.032	.280	.067	.182	.077	.132	.039	.033	.094
1975	.056	.030	.275	.071	.182	.082	.138	.038	.033	.093
1976	.052	.030	.271	.077	.175	.085	.143	.039	.035	.093
1977	.051	.029	.269	.079	.172	.085	.143	.039	.036	.096
Mean	.130	.040	.305	.062	.176	.040	.118	.032	.025	.072

Iceland

1961	.077	.050	.137	.080	.183	.035	.282	.077	.001	.078
1962	.073	.050	.138	.079	.180	.037	.288	.074	.001	.081
1963	.069	.061	.110	.060	.102	.039	.303	.071	.000	.086
1964	.077	.046	.142	.045	.186	.041	.306	.070	.000	.088
1965	.075	.041	.142	.045	.190	.044	.300	.073	.000	.089
1966	.065	.043	.136	.048	.192	.044	.305	.077	.000	.090
1967	.058	.044	.129	.052	.195	.046	.304	.081	.000	.093
1968	.061	.045	.123	.061	.190	.053	.293	.083	.000	.091
1969	.074	.045	.120	.060	.186	.060	.286	.082	.001	.087
1970	.072	.044	.124	.036	.190	.062	.299	.082	.001	.090
1971	.050	.040	.131	.007	.199	.065	.326	.085	.001	.096
1972	.033	.042	.132	.000	.204	.069	.330	.088	.001	.101
1973	.031	.045	.123	.007	.207	.069	.326	.091	.001	.100
Mean	.063	.045	.132	.045	.191	.051	.304	.079	.000	.090

(continued)

Table A6.1 (continued)

Finland

1961	.203	.099	.160	.033	.115	.013	.210	.106	.015	.047
1962	.190	.100	.159	.032	.115	.013	.216	.110	.015	.049
1963	.184	.102	.152	.035	.113	.013	.224	.110	.017	.050
1964	.182	.103	.147	.035	.109	.013	.234	.109	.017	.052
1965	.177	.102	.143	.031	.108	.014	.244	.108	.017	.056
1966	.172	.104	.138	.030	.109	.016	.243	.108	.018	.062
1967	.168	.108	.140	.033	.112	.017	.232	.108	.019	.065
1968	.166	.110	.136	.032	.113	.017	.232	.108	.020	.066
1969	.159	.114	.133	.026	.112	.017	.246	.108	.020	.066
1970	.146	.118	.136	.020	.114	.017	.254	.109	.020	.066
1971	.138	.120	.135	.020	.115	.017	.255	.110	.020	.071
1972	.133	.121	.132	.016	.118	.018	.258	.111	.019	.074
1973	.126	.119	.132	.008	.122	.018	.265	.115	.018	.076
1974	.119	.116	.131	.008	.129	.018	.265	.119	.016	.079
1975	.119	.114	.127	.005	.133	.019	.266	.120	.014	.083
1976	.126	.113	.122	.000	.128	.020	.268	.123	.013	.087
1977	.134	.112	.119	.001	.123	.020	.267	.123	.011	.090
Mean	.155	.110	.138	.022	.117	.016	.246	.112	.017	.067

Austria

1965	.083	.052	.206	−.007	.173	.000	.369	.042	.002	.080
1966	.077	.050	.206	−.007	.175	.001	.375	.041	.002	.080
1967	.071	.049	.203	−.005	.176	.002	.382	.041	.002	.079
1968	.067	.049	.200	−.001	.174	.004	.386	.042	.002	.077
1969	.060	.048	.200	.002	.175	.007	.385	.043	.002	.076
1970	.059	.042	.202	.005	.175	.008	.387	.043	.002	.077
1971	.053	.035	.205	.006	.176	.008	.397	.042	.001	.077
1972	.042	.031	.209	.006	.179	.008	.408	.042	.001	.076
1973	.035	.029	.210	.011	.179	.008	.411	.042	.000	.076
1974	.031	.026	.208	.019	.178	.010	.408	.043	.000	.077
1975	.025	.021	.205	.027	.177	.013	.410	.044	.000	.079
1976	.021	.019	.202	.034	.173	.013	.416	.043	.000	.078
1977	.015	.019	.198	.038	.171	.013	.426	.044	.000	.076
1978	.012	.018	.196	.043	.168	.015	.426	.046	.001	.077
1979	.012	.017	.195	.048	.162	.016	.426	.045	.001	.079
1980	.008	.014	.195	.052	.158	.016	.434	.043	.001	.079
1981	.005	.012	.194	.058	.155	.017	.436	.042	.001	.080
Mean	.040	.031	.202	.019	.172	.009	.405	.043	.001	.078

Japan

1971	.193		.147	.034	.148	.059	.110	.106		.203
1972	.182		.149	.036	.147	.059	.112	.108		.207
1973	.174		.153	.033	.150	.059	.114	.108		.210
1974	.174		.155	.027	.150	.061	.119	.104		.210
1975	.178		.151	.025	.143	.067	.124	.102		.211
1976	.179		.150	.029	.137	.070	.125	.102		.210
1977	.175		.148	.033	.136	.071	.124	.102		.210
1978	.164		.144	.039	.134	.075	.125	.102		.216
1979	.151		.142	.043	.135	.078	.126	.102		.223
1980	.145		.140	.048	.135	.079	.126	.103		.224
1981	.143		.136	.057	.132	.082	.126	.103		.222
Mean	.169		.147	.037	.141	.069	.121	.104		.213

(continued)

Table A6.1 (continued)

United Kingdom

1965	.094	.073	.112	.044	.173	.006	.199	.095	.017	.187
1966	.090	.073	.110	.049	.171	.006	.200	.095	.018	.188
1967	.087	.072	.107	.052	.170	.005	.203	.096	.019	.188
1968	.081	.070	.106	.056	.169	.006	.207	.099	.019	.189
1969	.076	.069	.105	.059	.168	.006	.208	.101	.020	.190
1970	.072	.068	.105	.060	.166	.006	.209	.103	.021	.191
1971	.067	.064	.104	.060	.165	.006	.216	.105	.021	.192
1972	.059	.061	.102	.061	.167	.006	.223	.108	.021	.192
1973	.054	.060	.102	.062	.169	.006	.223	.110	.021	.194
1974	.054	.060	.103	.066	.168	.005	.218	.112	.021	.194
1975	.053	.061	.101	.071	.166	.005	.220	.112	.021	.192
1976	.052	.063	.096	.073	.163	.004	.226	.111	.021	.191
1977	.052	.063	.094	.076	.161	.004	.226	.110	.021	.193
1978	.050	.062	.094	.075	.161	.004	.227	.111	.021	.196
1979	.044	.060	.095	.073	.163	.004	.233	.111	.021	.197
1980	.038	.058	.092	.077	.162	.005	·.236	.111	.020	.200
1981	.032	.058	.087	.090	.160	.005	.236	.111	.021	.200
Mean	.062	.064	.101	.065	.166	.005	.218	.106	.020	.192

Spain

1965	.340	.034	.138	.040	.124	.026	.199	.049	.005	.046
1966	.337	.033	.137	.036	.123	.030	.207	.049	.005	.043
1967	.323	.034	.137	.035	.122	.033	.215	.050	.006	.045
1968	.311	.034	.137	.037	.121	.036	.217	.052	.007	.048
1969	.299	.034	.136	.036	.122	.039	.221	.054	.007	.051
1970	.287	.034	.135	.032	.126	.043	.224	.057	.008	.054
1971	.279	.035	.135	.028	.126	.048	.225	.059	.009	.056
1972	.271	.035	.137	.022	.126	.052	.229	.061	.010	.058
1973	.269	.034	.139	.017	.127	.052	.233	.062	.009	.059
1974	.271	.032	.138	.017	.125	.052	.236	.063	.008	.057
1975	.271	.029	.135	.019	.124	.053	.236	.066	.009	.059
1976	.268	.026	.133	.016	.124	.055	.238	.066	.011	.064
1977	.259	.023	.134	.009	.126	.057	.245	.066	.011	.070
Mean	.291	.032	.136	.026	.124	.044	.225	.058	.008	.054

Italy

1965	.301	.055	.171	.060	.100	.032	.125	.050	.003	.103
1966	.301	.054	.169	.059	.097	.034	.128	.050	.004	.104
1967	.296	.052	.170	.060	.095	.035	.135	.048	.004	.105
1968	.289	.050	.171	.062	.096	.035	.139	.048	.004	.106
1969	.283	.050	.170	.064	.096	.036	.142	.047	.004	.109
1970	.277	.048	.170	.063	.098	.038	.145	.047	.003	.111
1971	.271	.046	.172	.064	.099	.038	.148	.047	.003	.113
1972	.265	.043	.171	.069	.099	.038	.151	.046	.003	.115
1973	.261	.042	.173	.068	.101	.040	.150	.045	.003	.116
1974	.258	.040	.174	.067	.106	.041	.147	.045	.002	.121
1975	.255	.037	.171	.066	.109	.042	.147	.045	.002	.125
1976	.254	.033	.168	.062	.110	.043	.154	.045	.002	.128
1977	.251	.029	.169	.059	.112	.042	.160	.046	.002	.129
1978	.248	.027	.171	.059	.113	.040	.159	.048	.002	.132
1979	.243	.026	.171	.060	.111	.040	.161	.047	.002	.138
1980	.231	.025	.173	.062	.112	.041	.169	.046	.002	.141
1981	.231	.034	.171	.064	.112	.042	.176	.046	.002	.142
Mean	.265	.040	.171	.063	.104	.039	.149	.047	.003	.120

REFERENCES

Brown, A. and A. Deaton (1972). 'Surveys in Applied Economics: Models of Consumer Behaviour,' <u>Economic Journal</u> 82: 1145-1236.

Clements, K.W. (1987). 'Alternative Approaches to Consumption Theory,' Chapter 1 in H. Theil and K.W. Clements, <u>Applied Demand Analysis: Results from System-Wide Approaches</u>. Cambridge, Mass.: Ballinger Publishing Company, pp.1-35.

DeJanvry, A., J. Bieri and A. Nunez (1972). 'Estimation of Demand Parameters Under Consumer Budgeting: An Application to Argentina,' <u>American Journal of Agricultural Economics</u> 54: 422-30.

Frisch, R. (1959). 'A Complete Scheme for Computing All Direct and Cross Demand Elasticities in a Model with Many Sectors,' <u>Econometrica</u> 27: 177-96.

Lluch, C., A.A. Powell and R.A. Williams (1977). <u>Patterns in Household Demand and Saving</u>. Oxford: Oxford University Press.

Theil, H. (1975/76). <u>Theory and Measurement of Consumer Demand</u>. Two volumes, Amsterdam: North-Holland Publishing Company.

————— (1980). <u>The System-Wide Approach to Microeconomics</u>. Chicago: The University of Chicago Press.

————— (1987). 'Evidence from International Consumption Comparisons,' Chapter 2 in H. Theil and K.W. Clements, <u>Applied Demand Analysis:</u>

Results from System-Wide Approaches. Cambridge, Mass.: Ballinger Publishing Company, pp.37-100.

———— and R.B. Brooks (1970/71). 'How Does the Marginal Utility of Income Change When Real Income Changes?' European Economic Review 2: 218-40.

Working, W. (1943). 'Statistical Laws of Family Expenditure,' Journal of the American Statistical Association 38: 43-56.

Rational random behaviour 307
Relative price 73
Relative price version 25
Roberts 125
Rodseth 29,49
Root-mean-squared 205,242
      asymptotic standard error 260,273
      error 260
Rotterdam demand model 5,8,24,25,26,31,131,141,183,304

Salvas-Bronsard 131,183
Schultz 3,54
Seal 55
Second peril 262,274
Selvanathan, E.A. 3,8,54,68,126,146,183,248,252,301
Selvanathan, S. 157
Separability 157
Shazam 90
Simulations 180
Slutsky
      coefficient 7,31
      symmetry 4,5,6,8,9,10,127,135,143,178,187
Stening 126,248
Stigler 13,54,185,214,248
Stone 3,6,54
Strobel 206,243,244,248
Substitutes 8
Suhm 13,20,56,68,126
Summers 52,54,126,182,247,248
Supernumeray income 6
System-wide approach 2,3,5

Theil 2,3,7,8,9,11,13,19,20,24,26,29,38,42,50,51,54,55,56,68,97,126,128,130,131,
      132,136,137,141,144,146,149,163,170,183,186,214,215,238,240,247,249,
      251,252,262,273,276,302,305,306,311,314,320,332
Thomas 3,56
Two perils 252,273,276

Utility maximizing 2
van Driel 31,52
Wald test 10
Wales 6,13,53,185,186,248
Ward 246,249
Weighted mean 190,191

Williams 13,52,53,332
WLS 212,306
Working 2,56,186,249,252,302,333
     model 25,26,28,30,31,32,33,35,36,129,147,149,307

Yoshihara 6,56

Advanced Studies in Theoretical and Applied Econometrics

1. J.H.P. Paelinck (ed.): *Qualitative and Quantitative Mathematical Economics.* 1982
   ISBN 90-247-2623-9

2. J.P. Ancot (ed.): *Analysing the Structure of Econometric Models.* 1984
   ISBN 90-247-2894-0

3. A.J. Hughes Hallet (ed.): *Applied Decision Analysis and Economic Behaviour.* 1984
   ISBN 90-247-2968-8

4. J.K. Sengupta: *Information and Efficiency in Economic Decision.* 1985
   ISBN 90-247-3072-4

5. P. Artus and O. Guvenen (eds.), in collaboration with F. Gagey: *International Macroeconomic Modelling for Policy Decisions.* 1986   ISBN 90-247-3201-8

6. M.J. Vilares: *Structural Change in Macroeconomic Models.* Theory and Estimation. 1986   ISBN 90-247-3277-8

7. C. Carraro and D. Sartore (eds.): *Development of Control Theory for Economic Analysis.* 1987   ISBN 90-247-3345-6

8. D.P. Broer: *Neoclassical Theory and Empirical Models of Aggregate Firm Behaviour.* 1987   ISBN 90-247-3412-6

9. A. Italianer: *Theory and Practice of International Trade Linkage Models.* 1986
   ISBN 90-247 3407-X

10. D.A. Kendrick: *Feedback.* A New Framework for Macroeconomic Policy. 1988
    ISBN 90-247-3593-9; Pb: 90-247-3650-1

11. J.K. Sengupta and G.K. Kadekodi (eds.): *Econometrics of Planning and Efficiency.* 1988   ISBN 90-247-3602-1

12. D.A. Griffith: *Advanced Spatial Statistics.* Special Topics in the Exploration of Quantitative Spatial Data Series. 1988   ISBN 90-247-3627-7

13. O. Guvenen (ed.): *International Commodity Market Models and Policy Analysis.* 1988   ISBN 90-247-3768-0

14. G. Arbia: *Spatial Data Configuration in Statistical Analysis of Regional Economic and Related Problems.* 1989   ISBN 0-7923-0284-2

15. B. Raj (ed.): *Advances in Econometrics and Modelling.* 1989   ISBN 0-7923-0299-0

16. A. Aznar Grasa: *Econometric Model Selection.* A New Approach. 1989
    ISBN 0-7923-0321-0

17. L.R. Klein and J. Marquez (eds.): *Economics in Theory and Practice.* An Eclectic Approach. Essays in Honor of F. G. Adams. 1989   ISBN 0-7923-0410-1

18. D.A. Kendrick: *Models for Analyzing Comparative Advantage.* 1990
    ISBN 0 7923-0528-0

19. P. Artus and Y. Barroux (eds.): *Monetary Policy.* A Theoretical and Econometric Approach. 1990   ISBN 0-7923-0626-0

Advanced Studies in Theoretical and Applied Econometrics

20. G. Duru and J.H.P. Paelinck (eds.): *Econometrics of Health Care.* 1990
ISBN 0-7923-0766-6

21. L. Phlips (ed.): *Commodity, Futures and Financial Markets.* 1991
ISBN 0-7923-1043-8

22. H.M. Amman, D.A. Belsley and L.F. Pau (eds.): *Computational Economics and Econometrics.* 1992
ISBN 0-7923-1287-2

23. B. Raj and J. Koerts (eds.): *Henri Theil's Contributions to Economics and Econometrics.* Vol. I: Econometric Theory and Methodology. 1992
ISBN 0-7923-1548-0

24. B. Raj and J. Koerts (eds.): *Henri Theil's Contributions to Economics and Econometrics.* Vol. II: Consumer Demand Analysis and Information Theory. 1992
ISBN 0-7923-1664-9

25. B. Raj and J. Koerts (eds.): *Henri Theil's Contributions to Economics and Econometrics.* Vol. III: Economic Policy and Forecasts, and Management Science. 1992
ISBN 0-7923-1665-7
Set (23-25) ISBN 0-7923-1666-5

26. P. Fisher: *Rational Expectations in Macroeconomic Models.* 1992
ISBN 0-7923-1903-6

27. L. Phlips and L.D. Taylor (eds.): *Aggregation, Consumption and Trade.* Essays in Honor of H.S. Houthakker. 1992.
ISBN 0-7923-2001-8

28. L. Mátyás and P. Sevestre (eds.): *The Econometrics of Panel Data.* Handbook of Theory and Applications. 1992
ISBN 0-7923-2043-3

29. S. Selvanathan: *A System-Wide Analysis of International Consumption Patterns.* 1993
ISBN 0-7923-2344-0

Kluwer Academic Publishers – Dordrecht / Boston / London